FOREVER BLUE

FOREVER BLUE

The True Story of Walter O'Malley, Baseball's Most Controversial Owner,
and the Dodgers of Brooklyn and Los Angeles

MICHAEL D'ANTONIO

RIVERHEAD BOOKS

a member of Penguin Group (USA) Inc.

New York | *2009*

RIVERHEAD BOOKS
Published by the Penguin Group

Penguin Group (USA) Inc., 375 Hudson Street, New York, New York 10014, USA • Penguin Group (Canada),
90 Eglinton Avenue East, Suite 700, Toronto, Ontario M4P 2Y3, Canada (a division of Pearson
Canada Inc.) • Penguin Books Ltd, 80 Strand, London WC2R 0RL, England • Penguin Ireland,
25 St Stephen's Green, Dublin 2, Ireland (a division of Penguin Books Ltd) • Penguin Group (Australia),
250 Camberwell Road, Camberwell, Victoria 3124, Australia (a division of Pearson Australia Group Pty Ltd) •
Penguin Books India Pvt Ltd, 11 Community Centre, Panchsheel Park, New Delhi–110 017, India •
Penguin Group (NZ), 67 Apollo Drive, Rosedale, North Shore 0632, New Zealand
(a division of Pearson New Zealand Ltd) • Penguin Books (South Africa) (Pty) Ltd,
24 Sturdee Avenue, Rosebank, Johannesburg 2196, South Africa

Penguin Books Ltd, Registered Offices: 80 Strand, London WC2R 0RL, England

Library of Congress Cataloging-in-Publication Data

D'Antonio, Michael.
Forever blue : the true story of Walter O'Malley, baseball's most controversial owner, and
the Dodgers of Brooklyn and Los Angeles / Michael D'Antonio.
p.   cm.
ISBN 978-1-59448-856-6
1. O'Malley, Walter F. (Walter Frank), 1903–1979.   2. Baseball team owners—United States—Biography.
3. Brooklyn Dodgers (Baseball team).   4. Los Angeles Dodgers (Baseball team).   I. Title.
GV865.O63D36   2009   2008046311
796.357'64092—dc22
[B]

Printed in the United States of America
1   3   5   7   9   10   8   6   4   2

BOOK DESIGN BY NICOLE LAROCHE

While the author has made every effort to provide accurate telephone numbers and Internet addresses at the time
of publication, neither the publisher nor the author assumes any responsibility for errors, or for changes that
occur after publication. Further, the publisher does not have any control over and does not assume any
responsibility for author or third-party websites or their content.

For Dodgers of every era,
and their fans, forever blue.

Contents

FOREVER BLUE

On the night when major-league baseball died in Brooklyn, fewer than seven thousand fans went to the old ballpark in Flatbush to pay their respects. Most sat in the lower level, behind home plate, and along the baselines. In the big empty sections of the grandstand a light autumn breeze blew paper cups and empty peanut bags down concrete aisles and against rows of old slatted chairs. On the field, players moved with the extra weight of knowing that this time there would be no "next year." After many seasons of joy—in the face of Jackie Robinson, in the bellowing voice of Hilda Chester, and in the roar of standing-room-only crowds—Ebbets Field had become a desolate and unhappy place.

The Dodgers beat the Pirates 2–0. Organist Gladys Goodding played "Auld Lang Syne" as the grounds crew raked the infield and, out of habit, spread a tarp over the pitcher's mound. Emmett Kelly, the sad-faced clown who had performed his act before Dodgers games throughout the season, would recall seeing many women—and a few men—crying as they left Ebbets Field for good.

Brooklyn had already entered an era of loss. The daily paper, the *Eagle*, had died in 1955, and the trolley cars had stopped running in 1956. Several big retail stores and theaters had closed, and young families were moving to the suburbs of Long Island. Now the great Dodgers baseball team was leaving and there was nothing anyone could do about it. For some the wound was so deep and ragged that the pain would never quite disappear. Almost fifty years later, in one of the last interviews he gave before his death, Dodger pitcher Clem Labine's voice trembled as he recalled the day and asked, "Why did he do it?"

"He" was Walter O'Malley, the team's owner, and what he did would go down in history as a betrayal equal, in some minds, to Benedict Arnold's treason at West Point. At a time when people in Brooklyn were fighting to hold on to their optimism and identity, O'Malley uprooted the most important symbol of their plucky spirit and moved it to Los Angeles.

In the years since they moved west, the old Brooklyn Dodgers became the subject of more intense worship and hagiography than any ball club in history. The Yankees of Ruth and Gehrig were more worthy of awe and the Cubs have certainly earned the underdog love they enjoy every season. But Frank Sinatra sang of a ballpark in Brooklyn, not Chicago, and only the Brooklyn Dodgers of the 1950s could inspire Roger Kahn's *The Boys of Summer*, which became one of the biggest-selling baseball books of all time.

Kahn's elegy, published in 1972 and maintained in print ever since, was followed by an entire genre of Brooklyn Dodgers literature in the form of books, articles, and even academic papers. In many of these works, and more casual remembrances, O'Malley is portrayed as a villain. New York writer Jack Newfield famously called O'Malley one of the three worst human beings who ever lived. His colleague Pete Hamill, who has published at least twenty books, is known as much for his hatred of O'Malley as for anything else. When, in 2007, O'Malley was finally voted into the Hall of Fame, Hamill wrote "Never forgive, never forget" and declared that with his election the hall took all morality out of the honor of getting a plaque at Cooperstown.

But as much as Hamill might disagree, O'Malley actually deserved a spot in the hall. With his fateful decision to leave Brooklyn, he did more than anyone to make baseball a truly national game. And during his reign, the Dodgers became one of the greatest franchises in all of sport. From the day he moved to Los Angeles until he died in 1979, O'Malley's team would be the best in the National League, winning three world championships and seven pennants and finishing second seven times. (In all of baseball, only the Yankees had a better record.) O'Malley also built the first truly modern stadium in America, a gracefully designed ballpark that remains, after nearly fifty years, one of the best places in the world to watch a game of any sort.

Although a few hard cases in Brooklyn would never forgive him, millions of fans in the Los Angeles area came to regard O'Malley, who didn't need padding to play the role, as some kind of Santa Claus. They felt this way because he had given them the gift of elite-level baseball and affirmed their city's status as "major league." O'Malley became so popular in Los Angeles that on the fiftieth anniversary of the team's arrival in the city, a five-foot-high bronze frieze of his image was installed at the Los Angeles Memorial Coliseum Court of Honor. There he joined other sports figures—including Knute Rockne, Jackie Robinson, and Jesse Owens—deemed to have contributed to the "growth and glory" of the city.

THE ANIMUS AND the affection heaped on O'Malley long after his death raises an obvious question: How could a sportsman be so hated in one place and so beloved in another? The Brooklyn/Los Angeles divide suggests part of the answer, but parochialism does not explain it all. It's important to recall, too, that O'Malley was an imposing figure who wielded power over a popular institution and supervised many ambitious and headstrong individuals. Few people ever enjoyed more direct authority than the owner of a ball team in the days before free agency and the players' union. This power allowed him to accomplish great things, but it also aroused suspicion, envy, and animosity.

Any attempt to explain O'Malley must also consider the gaps in the record of his life. He was not the type who would reflect aloud on his motivations or reveal his innermost thoughts. From the outside anyone could see that O'Malley was devoted to his family and that he thoroughly enjoyed his wealth, status, and the trappings of success. But while he lived, he avoided close analysis. This was especially true when it came to events surrounding his acquisition of the team and the move west. Once these struggles ended, he rarely spoke of them in public. He insisted on calling old rivals his friends and usually declined to defend himself against his critics.

Because he was so reticent, anyone depending on the public record would be challenged to understand O'Malley, or the moves he made, with any real certainty. Fortunately he left behind a vast archive of personal and business files that help fill in the picture. Made available by his surviving children, these papers became the documentary foundation for this book. They reveal the inside story of O'Malley's rise from the son of a Tammany Hall pol to the boss of baseball and place certain historic events in a new light.

The O'Malley archive offers a new and more realistic perspective on the game's great sage, Branch Rickey, and on the long, torturous political fight that preceded the team's flight from Brooklyn. Beyond these issues, the O'Malley papers show how much he risked in building Dodger Stadium and that delays and rising costs brought him close to bankruptcy.

Short of having access to the man himself, the thoughts O'Malley expresses in his notes and letters, the diaries that chart his travels and contacts, and all the rest of the material in the archive make it possible to see the man more clearly than he has even been seen before. Add interviews with those who knew him, countless contemporary articles, and dozens of relevant books, and the portrait becomes even more reliable and distinct.

In the end, it's up to anyone who would judge O'Malley to consider the evidence and to attempt to see the man in full. If, ultimately, you reach more than one conclusion, you'll have something in common with many who knew him back when. He was not a simple person who would fit easily into a single category or simple definition. But then, what man or woman worthy of history's consideration ever was?

One

TWO O'MALLEYS

On the last day of August 1921, a short and stocky man with wavy dark hair walked alone to a witness chair set behind a small wooden table in the ornate council chamber at New York City Hall. Despite the ninety-degree heat, thirty-nine-year-old Edwin O'Malley wore a formal suit and tie. To his right, Washington and Lafayette peered down from gilt-framed paintings. To his left, huge windows that flanked a plaster statue of Thomas Jefferson let bright cathedral light into the room. Behind him, the gallery was filled with a legion of friends and political allies.

O'Malley, who clenched a soggy unlit cigar between his teeth, paused for a moment to take some papers out of his briefcase and spread them on the table. He then sat down, and stared defiantly through pince-nez glasses—the kind that Teddy Roosevelt wore—at the latest in a long line of investigators and legislators who had tried to destroy the city's legendary Tammany Hall political machine. O'Malley had spent weeks dodging the so-called Meyer Committee and charges that he and his department were guilty of graft and corruption. In this moment he seemed outnumbered and besieged. But if history was a reliable guide, he had nothing to fear.

Do-gooders had been trying to reform New York City since before Edwin O'Malley was born. The previous campaign had been conducted by an insider, Mayor John Purroy Mitchel. Aided by an ambitious political newcomer named Robert Moses, Mitchel had crusaded for a merit-based civil service. But like all the others before them, they had failed. John F. "Red Mike" Hylan, whom Moses called "the Bozo of Bushwick," drove them out in the election of 1917 and Tammany roared back to life.

As Red Mike's commissioner of public markets, O'Malley had come under scrutiny when the Meyer Committee focused on a city-run network of food warehouses. Noisy, dangerous, and infested with rats, these public markets housed dealers who were licensed to receive and distribute virtually everything anyone in New York ate or drank. The space controlled by the department's men was precious, and according to a butcher who testified before the investigators, $450 paid to an inspector named George A. Winter was the going rate if you wanted to transfer permits when a business was sold. Another market man had said that O'Malley had pressured him to sell his building on Vesey Street to the New York Telephone Company, which planned a massive skyscraper for the spot. A fishmonger's widow testified that she was threatened with eviction from the market if she didn't pay $1,000.

For the butcher and the fishmonger's widow, the hearings brought a moment of fame, but only the naïve would be shocked by their testimony. Generations of rule by political operators like G. W. Plunkitt—most famous for saying, "I seen my opportunities and I took 'em"—had affirmed that the city ran on graft. Politicians retained power by doling out jobs to the working class and big favors to those with money or influence. Everyone knew how the game worked, and many admired the ingenuity of those who played it well.

During the Meyer investigation, O'Malley had maneuvered so well that the committee had agreed to let him appear on his own terms. This included allowing him to make an uninterrupted opening statement that would address every issue raised by his accusers. On the day he testified, O'Malley pressed for another advantage: immunity from prosecution for anything he might tell the committee. Here the men from Albany drew a line. O'Malley, who insisted that his accusers were backed by powerful men in the food industry, was duly outraged.

"Is that the last instruction from the governor," said O'Malley, slamming his fist on the table, "to get me by hook or crook, or break both my legs, because I have been fighting the food interests?"

The crowd at City Hall applauded and O'Malley, not waiting for an answer, then launched a free-form monologue intended to take full advantage of the committee's assurance that he could speak without interruption. After offering brief denials of the graft and extortion charges, he commenced a detailed, rambling address on the value of a public markets system that began with a description of their founding and continued to include character sketches of the men who made it work. One, August Silz, "made the guinea hen famous," said O'Malley. "Unfortunately poor August is dead. He was a splendid character."

In his second hour O'Malley attacked his accusers. One had stolen chickens, said the commissioner. Another was complaining, even though her permits had actually been granted. A third must have been confused about payments made for the fixtures in a market stall. Everyone *knew* that city permits could not be bought or sold, he said.

O'Malley's testimony was a spectacular display of bluster and filibuster, so energetic that at one point an irritated deputy attorney general asked, "Are you electrically wound up?"

"Well, I don't know what you mean," answered O'Malley.

"You don't seem to run down."

"I am telling you what happened, about this thing."

And so it went for more than two full hours. At several points those hearing the testimony grew impatient with this grand display of talking without communicating, a practice the British called "talking Irish." A committee lawyer named Leonard Wallenstein actually rose out of his chair to demand that O'Malley provide direct answers to specific questions. To the delight of the crowd, O'Malley said he wouldn't let the lawyer "pin me down."

Wallenstein rose to his feet and shook a fist. "Now, Mr. Witness, you remember —"

"Aw, sit down, don't get excited!"

Behind O'Malley, the crowd erupted with prizefight cheers.

"You don't want me to tell you what I think of you!" shouted Wallenstein.

"I don't care! I wouldn't believe what you say anyway. Sit down. Keep your hands to yourself too."

More cheers.

"Is this a beer garden?" asked Wallenstein, straining to be heard.

Suddenly, from somewhere in the crowd, a man called out, "Get off of the stand, O'Malley!" It was John J. Halpin, a politically connected lawyer, who had cried out. "I appear as his counsel," he said. "I advise him to leave the stand."

"Throw him out!" commanded one of the Republicans on the panel.

Having told his story of the public markets and created a drama to please the crowd, O'Malley rose and swept the papers on the table into his briefcase. When Wallenstein asked if he refused to answer more questions, O'Malley answered, "I do!"

The Tammany men in the hall applauded loudly as O'Malley picked up his hat. They stood and kept clapping as he turned to walk out of the hearing with Halpin at his side. A large contingent followed, continuing to cheer as the embattled commissioner and his lawyer passed Washington and Jefferson and Lafayette, left the hearing room, and descended the marble steps of City Hall. The only thing they failed to do, as they showed their support for their man O'Malley, was hoist him on their shoulders.

The next morning the lead headline in the *New York Times* read "O'Malley, in Rage, Quits as Witness" and the paper predicted that the commissioner would have to resign. However, weeks and then months passed and O'Malley remained. The Meyer Committee would issue a report describing the public markets as a "vehicle for the collection of graft." Further evidence of the department's problems emerged in a trial related to a racket that targeted pushcart vendors, who were also under the department's purview. As he ruled on the pushcart case, Justice James Cropsey described a level of "lawlessness" in the markets unequaled since the days of the breathtakingly corrupt Boss Tweed.

Ultimately, Inspector Winter and nearly a hundred other "market men" were fired. The pushcart scheme was ended. And a lavish peddler's ball, which was planned to honor Edwin O'Malley on his fortieth birthday, was cancelled when it appeared that city workers had threatened to revoke the licenses of those vendors who refused to buy tickets. Some of the peddlers, who mostly spoke Yiddish, Polish, and Italian, said they were relieved by the cancellation, since few of them appreciated modern music or knew how to dance.

But though he wouldn't get his testimonial, Commissioner O'Malley kept his job and would serve until the end of 1925, when his patron's term ended. In that time O'Malley never shrank from the spotlight. When the Port Authority moved to take over food distribution, he began construction of a new $10 million public market in the Bronx. When the New York Housewives Sugar Committee marched around City Hall to protest high prices, he joined the mayor to cheer their complaints against "big food." And when a delegation from Japan came to visit, O'Malley served as eager host, tour guide, and publicist. S. Honda, the Japanese secretary of agriculture, liked what he saw but said he'd prefer to cut out the middlemen who rented the stalls and let the government sell directly to the public.

Before O'Malley left office, the leaders of Tammany Hall, who occupied a clubhouse called The Wigwam, would mourn the death of G. W. Plunkitt, who expired in 1924 at the age of eighty-two. (A memorial in the *Times* noted that Plunkitt, who died a millionaire, had begun *his* career in the public market.) As he settled into his new precinct at Calvary Cemetery, Plunkitt would have been fascinated to know that Robert Moses, the eggheaded reformer once defeated by Hylan, had learned to play the rough game he once abhorred and was gathering old-fashioned power and influence in both New York and Albany.

WHILE EDWIN O'MALLEY spent much of 1921 and 1922 in conflict with state investigators, his son Walter waged his own struggles a thousand miles away, at the Culver Military Academy in rural Indiana. An isolated and expensive haven for the elite—his class included Procter & Gamble heir Louis Nippert—Culver might seem, at first, a strange place to find the son of a Tammany pol. It had once seemed like a strange choice to Walter Francis O'Malley. The very idea of an exclusive, all-male, private military academy nestled behind cornstalks in Indiana offended his sixteen-year-old's political sensibilities. He was a man of the people, like his father.

"Me for the democratic principles!" Walter wrote to his "Pa" in the summer of 1920. "Public school, grammar and high school; then a city college."

The letter was sent from a Boy Scout camp in upstate New York where Walter worked as a counselor. The Scouts were formed in 1910 in response to widespread concern that American boys were becoming effeminate and dissolute. Walter had joined after moving with his family from the Bronx to Hollis, Queens, which was on the almost-rural edge of the borough. He loved the outdoorsy, quasi-military organization and was a superior Scout. Since Culver was like an extreme, round-the-clock form of scouting, his father had reason to believe Walter would thrive there too. Culver could also be a shelter from New York politics and a step up the social ladder.

Edwin O'Malley had great expectations for Walter. Father and son looked alike, with the same pursed-lip smile and twinkling eyes. While he spoiled the boy, Edwin also taught his son to be tough. "Chin up," he said. "Keep slugging. Never let anyone walk over you."

Walter's future was so important to Edwin that even as his political enemies circled, he had gathered his son's records from Jamaica High School in Queens and solicited recommendations from military men in New York. On August 12, 1920, Walter was accepted by Culver. And while his son was already developing a stubborn streak—"I don't like being told where to go," he said— Edwin O'Malley overruled his objections. Soon enough he was on a train headed west.

In early September this skinny boy with pale skin, slicked-back hair, and big black-rimmed glasses was settled on a campus that looked more like an army fort than a school. The mess hall and riding center were built with watchtowers. Crenellated parapets topped the dormitories. When Walter O'Malley looked out the window from his room, all he could see, including cadets dressed in the academy's high-collared gray uniform, would remind him of West Point in miniature.

It was no accident that Culver's uniforms, program, and architecture echoed the U.S. Military Academy. Founded in 1894, the school had been built and staffed by West Point alumni. They promised to make good boys into great men and to prevent rascals from becoming real troublemakers. Wendell Willkie, for example, had spent the summer of 1906 at Culver to atone for his sins at public school, which had included stealing a skeleton from a science lab. The hazing at the academy made him miserable, but he returned to his family so thoroughly cured of rebellion and prepared for a sober life that he would win the Republican nomination for president in 1940.

When O'Malley attended, Culver was dominated by a charismatic officer named Leigh Gignilliat—he pronounced it "Jin-eh-let"—who was responsible for the school's fame. He had formed the Black Horse Troop, which performed at Woodrow Wilson's inauguration in 1913. He also led the cadets to rescue townspeople stranded by flooding in nearby Logansport. By 1916, Gignilliat was Culver superintendent and, through his book *Arms and the Boy*, had become a national advocate for "straight bodies, straight minds and straight morals." Indeed, his boys were so strong and disciplined that they endured tonsillectomies and other surgery with only local anesthetic.

Daily life at the academy was governed by the official Routine of Duty and the "Culver Way," which stressed efficiency and cohesion. This included mundane activities like bathing. No ordinary showers or tubs for the Culver men. Instead they marched through a maze of pipes and automatic sprayers that resembled a modern car wash. This contraption could clean a battalion in minutes.

Even the special events scheduled to break the routine tended to promote the Culver way of doing things and to prepare the cadets to play swashbuckling roles on important stages. During Walter O'Malley's first year at the academy, he heard from more than a dozen prominent men—adventurers, leaders, and achievers—who addressed world affairs, military matters, and, more than once, the qualities that make for a moral, upright American male.

Although the moral condition of the young is a perennial American obsession, in the years immediately following World War I this worry had intensified. As four million young men returned from that horrific war, many brought a more realistic if not cynical view of human nature, authority, politics, and even fate. Soon Sinclair Lewis issued an indictment of repressive American mores called *Main Street*. He was joined on the best-seller lists by Theodore Dreiser, Carl Sandburg, H. L. Mencken, and others who assaulted American convention.

In this period of questioning, certain events fueled doubts about public institutions and the basic fairness of American society. Race riots shook major cities and strikes idled steel mills and docks. Even the sports page carried bad news as eight White Sox players were charged with fixing the World Series. After the truth came out, once-innocent fans could no longer assume that the game—long promoted as a bastion of goodness and virtue—represented America at its best.

Together, scandal, crisis, and social criticism challenged the idea that the United States was an exceptional country. In response, guardians of the mainstream did what they could to honor and reinforce traditional sources of strength and stability. At the extreme the Ku Klux Klan, which young Walter noticed was particularly powerful in Indiana, used the so-called Red Menace to justify attacks on immigrants, Jews, and Catholics. Moderates were content with standing up for the virtues of faith, strength, ingenuity, and capitalism, often through fraternal organizations, schools, and the press. Baseball installed as "commissioner" a federal judge named Kenesaw Mountain Landis and gave him extraordinary powers. Landis immediately barred the Black Sox conspirators for life.

While Landis sought to restore the mythic virtue of the great game, social commentators who saw nothing wrong on Main Street rose to defend its inhabitants. In *The Return of the Middle Class*, John Corbis acknowledged that the faith and well-being of the average American had been shaken but would soon be restored. In its effort to promote models of sober superiority the *New York Times* asked twenty different experts to name the most important American men. Woodrow Wilson and Thomas Edison appeared on nearly every one of the lists, which were heavy with businessmen and military leaders such as John J. Pershing and Leonard Wood.

Appearing at Culver, Major General Wood issued an address called "A Warning Against the Red Immigrant." In Wood, Walter O'Malley's cadre saw a man so close to ideal that he was a young Douglas MacArthur's role model. An Indian fighter and Rough Rider, Wood was almost the Republican nominee for president in 1920. He had been a major force behind the Palmer raids that had swept thousands of supposedly dangerous radicals into jail on little or no reliable evidence. (At the height of the Red Scare, fears were so high that an Indiana jury acquitted a man who had killed a foreigner who had shouted, "To hell with the United States.")

What the boys at Culver knew about politics depended almost entirely on what they heard from the likes of General Wood and the academy staff. Even mainstream news was hard to come by at the academy. Big-city papers didn't circulate there, and commercial radio—the first broadcasts were in the fall of 1920—was not yet available in rural Indiana. Chicago, the nearest big city, wouldn't get its first major station until 1924.

Although they would surely be excited by radio, the cadets were kept so busy marching, learning, and training that no one had much time or energy for the music or news it beamed from distant cities. This was especially true of parochial matters like investigations of municipal affairs. As Walter explained in a letter home, even the faculty was unaware of the public markets and Edwin

O'Malley's struggles. Freed from the cloud that hovered over the family name back in New York, Walter would have been able to pass as an ordinary plebe. However, he was hardly ordinary.

Within months of his arrival at the academy Walter O'Malley was pegged as a leader by his teachers, who reported as much to his mother and father. Of course, Walter was hardly a perfect cadet. In one two-month period he committed twenty-three infractions—most involved tardiness or failing to report—that were serious enough to make it into his record. But he also earned promotion to corporal faster than most and became well known by writing for the academy paper. And a reader doesn't have to check between the lines of his letters to his father and mother to see that he brought a bit of Tammany style to the barracks.

In one letter Walter notes that he defeated a host of senior officers to win election to an artillery battalion post. "I didn't even attend the election, so perfect was MY political machine," he writes, and then adds, "That is some awful egotism, hey?" In another letter Walter playfully reports that his new roommate is the nephew of Eugene V. Debs, the great socialist, but "he is a mighty fine fellow and not very radical—in fact he will be a strong Wigwam man when I get thru with him."

Walter O'Malley was mastering the system at Culver, distinguishing himself among cadets who had been at the school much longer and winning the admiration of the faculty. He dabbled in baseball and soccer but excelled on the school paper. Even when he got into real trouble, Walter's character and personality served him well. During his second and last year at the academy he interviewed government inspectors before he wrote an article about their visit. The trouble arose when he discovered that his notes were not quite complete and "I had to use my imagination and fill in the vacant places." The result was a piece that included misquotes and misinformation that outraged General Gignilliat, who destroyed the press run and demanded, "Who in blazes wrote that asinine article?" O'Malley confessed, apologized, and was forgiven. Unshaken, he sent a copy of his formal apology note to his parents and playfully requested they preserve it for his scrapbook.

Aided by reports from school authorities, Edwin and Alma O'Malley followed their boy's progress at Culver closely. In 1922, as graduation approached, his grades fell and Culver administrators took his name off the list for exams that might have gotten him admitted to Princeton. Alma traveled to see him for Easter and to talk to academy officials about her boy attending West Point. Walter had already opposed this idea, in a long and well-considered letter that included an objection to medical school—"I'd never be a success with the iodine and the knife"—and raised the idea that he might follow his father into public service. When Alma arrived, three senior faculty members argued against a military career for young O'Malley and suggested, instead, journalism or politics. She and Edwin agreed, and two years after Walter was overruled and sent to Indiana, he took a bit more control of his own destiny.

With West Point set aside and his dream school, Princeton, out of reach academically, Walter visited Cornell and found it too big. And, like Princeton, Cornell required a better academic record than he could show. O'Malley was beginning to see how his spring slump hurt his chances, and he confessed this much in a letter to a colonel at Culver, writing, "I wish that I had all the languages and everything else in the academic curriculum so that I could go anywhere!!"

The letter, written just weeks after he left Culver, was the first of a long correspondence he would maintain with academy officials for years to come. This habit of keeping in touch with an ever-increasing number of friends, teachers, colleagues, and acquaintances became an O'Malley hallmark. It also reflected the values of a time when proper etiquette—from the French word for ticket—was considered essential for those who wanted to gain entry to the upper class. Emily Post's *Etiquette in Society, in Business, in Politics and at Home* debuted in 1922 and was one of five similar guides published that year for anxious strivers. Whether coached by his elders or one of these books, Walter O'Malley became a master of social grace. Eventually he would accumulate hundreds if not thousands of correspondents. In a time long before the term was used, he was "networking" his way to people who would help him throughout his life.

When he was accepted and enrolled at the University of Pennsylvania, O'Malley could count several Culver alumni as fellow classmen and more still among the older students. (Later in life he would say that nearly forty classmates went from Culver to Penn.) Few freshmen could have had more support, and fewer still would have been as well prepared for the idiosyncratic, ritualistic, and intensely male environment of the Ivy League in the Roaring

Twenties. It's hard to imagine a place or a time when camaraderie, revelry, and bonhomie would have been more important to success.

RopES AND STAKES MARKED a battleground inside the famous Penn Quadrangle, where brick dormitories formed the four sides of a sheltered patch of green crisscrossed by walkways. The space, which was secluded from the nearby city streets, resembled the inner ward of a castle. At about five p.m. on a Wednesday at the start of the fall semester, Walter O'Malley joined hundreds of his fellow freshmen—the class of 1926—who poured into the quad. At five fifteen about three hundred sophomores, many dressed in their worst clothes, entered amid taunts and jeering.

O'Malley, and all the others who would fight, climbed over the ropes and into the ring, leaving their less aggressive classmates to join a crowd of onlookers that included members of the faculty who had witnessed this ritual before. The sophomores massed in the middle, forming circles of protection around twenty classmates, each of whom carried a small sack of flour.

The gates to the quad were swung shut. Someone outside the ring fired a pistol. (Presumably the cartridge was blank.) With cheers filling the air, O'Malley and his brothers stripped off their shirts. Each one had the number 26 dabbed in iodine on his chest and his back. Shouting and growling, they charged at the sophomores, breaking into the rings of defense and attacking the men at the center.

While the sophomores fought to protect the flour sacks, the freshmen swarmed and tore at them. Following custom, the assault included yanking at the sophomores' clothes until many of them were naked or nearly so. Flour flew through the air, coating faces and bodies. Breathless, sweating, and dirty, the students struggled until three sophomores, stripped but still clutching their flour sacks, were able to wriggle out of the scrum and flee. Another shot was fired signaling the end of the fight and a win for the "sophs."

As Walter would write to his parents, the Flour Fight was "a sweet little scrap," which was really the point. The fight was the thing, not victory or defeat. The annual battle, which sometimes produced concussions and broken bones, was part of a freshman initiation process based on long-standing traditions that governed life at Penn and other colleges. It was a variation on Penn's original sophomore-freshman contest, which involved a fight over a symbolic bowl that was so ferocious it had to be banned in 1916 after a freshman named William Lifson died of suffocation under a pile of wrestlers.

After Lifson's death, faculty, administrators, and community leaders tried to end the ritual battles. A substitute called the Penniman Bowl, named for the school's provost, promised glory to the class that won a series of more civilized games. But the peace was short-lived. By 1922 the Flour Fight was embedded in UPenn's local culture and a second traditional fight had also been started—the Pants Fight, an end-of-the-year brawl that involved, as anyone might imagine, ferocious attacks and counterattacks that ended with the losers stripped.

Extreme as they may seem today, during the era of hip flasks, raccoon coats, and ukuleles, initiation rituals were, like fraternities and eating clubs, the true focus of life at many universities. As one study of UPenn traditions noted, students regarded their college years as the last boisterous hurrah of immaturity, and the faculty encouraged this view. In this way, rather than promote or extend youthful rebellion, the college let young men blow off steam while preparing them to lead conservative lives and preserve bedrock institutions, including political parties, businesses, investment houses, and white-shoe law firms.

The emphasis was on men because the few women at Penn and most other Ivy League schools were not fully part of the life of the school. And, to be more precise, one should note that these institutions generally promoted white Christian men. Penn was a bit of an exception, more open to Catholics and recent immigrants. Jews were admitted to study, even if they weren't welcomed at fraternities. This policy was in part responsible for the school's ranking, which, in the minds of the American elite, fell somewhere behind the more discriminating institutions such as Harvard, Yale, and Princeton.

As might be expected, some young men were better prepared than others to rise to the top at a place like Penn. Toughened by the physical and social training at Culver, Walter O'Malley reveled in college life, writing home excitedly when, for example, the provost cancelled classes so that a victory by the football team, which was coached by John Heisman, could be properly celebrated. Students did a snake dance down Broad Street in downtown Philadelphia, and the night brought a bonfire and a rampage called a Rowbottom (after

a student who helped start the tradition) that involved hurling almost everything that wasn't too big to be lifted out of residence hall windows.

Aside from an oblique reference to stomach problems and concerns about
his mother's health—he reminds Alma that she was "*very* sick" in 1923—Walter
was obviously happy at college. By his second year he was doing his best to take
newly arrived boys from Culver under his wing and reporting on their progress
to a colonel at the academy. (In that same year he paid $45 for lifetime member-
ship in the Culver Legion for alumni.) He was a fraternity man, a reserve Army
officer, a member of an honorary military group called Scabbard and Blade,
and part of the Vigilance Committee, which hazed freshmen who failed to comply with certain rules like keeping their hands out of their pockets. And in an
early sign of his future interest in sports, he served on the committee that put
on the Penniman Games.

In the classroom O'Malley did adequate if not superior work. Some of his
best grades came in courses in the new and burgeoning discipline of psychology, in which he earned top marks in abnormal psych, qualitative analysis, and
orthogenics. The last was a popular but eventually discredited "science" that
focused on perfecting humankind through selective breeding. Penn, which
opened the first psychological clinic in the United States, was a national leader
in the field. Officials at Harvard, in comparison, would not open a clinic until
1928 and waited until 1934 to create a separate department of psychology.

Ever outgoing, personable, and precocious, O'Malley quickly developed a
close relationship with one of his professors, Edwin Twitmyer, who wore glasses
just like Edwin O'Malley's and shared the market commissioner's gift for understanding human nature. But where the politician worked from gut instinct,
Twitmyer relied on science to support his theories on everything from child
rearing (they are "just machines" until puberty) to poker, which he found to be
the only game that rewarded superior intelligence and character. He established
his own "laws of learning" based on work with fish, turtles, cats, porcupines,
and a chimpanzee named Mimi. Twitmyer was so famous and fascinating that
when Culver's General Gignilliat visited Philadelphia, the socially attuned
O'Malley brought him to the professor's house.

O'Malley's good grades in psychology were a reflection of a student playing
to his own strengths. An heir to both the Wigwam political tradition and the
Irish-American practice of blarney and charm, young Walter O'Malley grew

into a truly big man on campus. As a sophomore he became the first under-classman ever made president of his fraternity. In the fall of 1924 he relied on dozens of fellow Culver alums as well as his fraternity brothers to win election as president of the junior class. In a letter to a major at Culver he noted that his old school might be "a hot bed of politicians." The following year O'Malley won election again. It was only the third time in history that a class president was returned to office.

This was a confident and capable young man. He took to carrying a cane, which was a fad among college men, and often wore a striped jacket in the Penn colors of red and blue. Gone were the black-rimmed glasses, replaced by stylish silver frames, which went perfectly with his silk ties. He still combed his thick brown hair, dressed with grooming oil, straight back off his high forehead. But traces of boyish softness in his face were replaced by a strong chin and a sly-looking smile with lips pressed together that rarely showed any teeth. Walter started smoking pipes and cigars and joined his classmates at a speakeasy called Pop McKenna's. When he had enough cash he went to a downtown joint called the French Club and to the more upscale Normandie Hotel. He arranged for an annual student ball to be held at the Rittenhouse Hotel, and when a stomach ailment kept him from the party, he set himself in style in a room upstairs.

The motto for O'Malley's class was "Hard as nails, full of tricks. Pennsylvania '26." O'Malley had plenty of playful school spirit. On a trip to Harvard with the football team he was assigned to the group who handled the yard-marking chains and discovered it could be shortened with a little twist of the pole. In one of his election campaigns he made a show of obeying administration orders to destroy 2,000 cards that violated some rule—he set them on fire—and then quietly distributed replacements already ordered because of a misprint in the first batch.

Members of the Penn class of '26 began their final year on a tragic note, with news that an editor of the school paper had died over the summer from injuries sustained during a pants fight the previous semester. (Five surgeries, including one performed by a specialist brought to Pennsylvania from Buffalo, couldn't save him.) But after it was announced, Edwin Smyth Hall's death didn't seem to cause much concern. Initiation rituals continued, and no follow-up story appeared in the *Daily Pennsylvanian*. Instead the paper offered blanket coverage of the university football team, which was a major power in a sport that was booming in popularity. In the 1920s, college football drew the largest crowds of any sport and its stars were famous across the country.

Penn football games were so popular that tickets were sometimes difficult to obtain. In October 1926, Walter wrote to Katharina "Kay" Hanson at the College of New Rochelle to say he would use his pull to get her tickets for the undefeated team's big game with the University of Illinois. Kay was a slender, pretty young woman with wavy auburn hair and a shy smile. An avid sports fan who often attended Brooklyn Dodgers games at Ebbets Field with her uncle, she had known Walter for years. Her family owned a cottage in Amityville, Long Island, next to a summer place owned by Edwin O'Malley. Walter was taken with Kay and her younger sister, Helen. He taught her to ride a bicycle, and together the sisters baked cookies that they sent him every month. But it was Kay who captured Walter's heart. In the note he referred to a recent illness by asking, "How's the throat?" He signed it, "Faithfully, Walter," and playfully wrote "Retlaw"—Walter spelled backwards—on the envelope.

As a judge's daughter, Kay Hanson was prominent enough that a local paper in Brooklyn reported on a bridge party she hosted during a break from college. Kay pasted this notice onto a wedding shower invitation. On the other side of the card she glued a two-column piece on Walter O'Malley's victory in the campaign for president of the junior class at Penn. The bright-looking young man who stared out from the photo that accompanied the article dominated student politics and became chairman of the university-wide council. In his senior year came admission to the exclusive Friars Senior Society and at graduation he was declared Spoon Man, an honor reserved for the most respected fellow in class. Given his standing, it is hard to imagine that anyone else was even considered.

Walter collected his award at an end-of-year celebration called Hey Day. Like all the other traditions at Penn, this day of ceremony connected the young men at the school to one another and linked them with generations who had gone before. For seniors, four years of classes, male bonding, and social challenges were ended and they anticipated the opportunities reserved for the 10 percent of Americans who got any education at all after high school. Of course, Ivy League graduates made up a tiny percentage of those who earned college degrees, making them an elite among the elite. Add these advantages to the economic, social, and cultural excitement that came to be called the Roaring Twenties and it was a wonderful time to be a Penn grad.

Going into the world with his Ivy League degree, Walter O'Malley was prepared to achieve at a level closed to men like his father, whose political connections could take them only so far. In one of his last letters from college, written
to Edwin, he mentions an impromptu chat with Provost Josiah Penniman, an
official few students would know casually, and a private dinner with the U.S.
attorney for the district of Philadelphia, who offered advice on law school. The
note was written on office stationery for the Undergraduate Council, Walter F.
O'Malley, Chairman.

Two

A MAN ABOUT NEW YORK

I n his six years away at school, Walter O'Malley had changed from an earnest Boy Scout into a tough, competent, and ambitious young man. In that time New York City had been transformed too. Mayor "Red Mike" Hylan had been defeated by the flamboyant Jimmy Walker, who named a new commissioner of public markets. Bernard Patten was Edwin J. O'Malley's opposite: a nearly invisible functionary. His low profile wasn't unusual for the new administration. Except for the dashing police commissioner George V. McLaughlin, who once dove into the sea near Coney Island to help in a rescue, few of Walker's men ever got a chance to share the spotlight with the flamboyant mayor.

An irregular at City Hall but a fixture at nightclubs and speakeasies, Walker was a married man whose affair with a Broadway starlet half his age was the worst-kept secret in America. He represented a hedonistic New York that dressed well, drank heavily, and was up all night. His popularity proved the predictable effects of Prohibition. Instead of drying up the nation, it drove millions of social drinkers to discover that they rather enjoyed breaking the law. As they found common cause with Walker and other sophisticates, ordinary Americans became a little less restrained, repressed, and conformist.

The change was most visible in fashion, where the nineteen yards of cotton and wool once required to cover an American woman were replaced by seven yards of silks and synthetics. Out went the rubber girdle. In came rouge and lipstick and a thousand new creams and potions. Men began wearing two-toned shoes, fedoras, and, thanks to gangsters, pin-striped suits.

Rebellion was made easier by the era's great economic growth. New consumer-driven industries and a bull market on Wall Street made many Americans feel rich and optimistic. (To get an idea of this prosperity, consider that the number of cars on the road nearly tripled during the decade, to twenty-three million.) The wealth, new technologies, and styles had the effect of turning everyday life in a city like New York from a silent black-and-white movie into a bright Technicolor (another invention of the time) production with full sound.

Much of the color of the mid-1920s was supplied by automobile manufacturers who, thanks to a new chemical called pyroxylin, could challenge Henry Ford's all-black offerings with models decorated in Florentine cream, Versailles violet, and other exotic hues. The sound of the twenties came from the radio, which allowed the entire country to share the same music, dramas, news, and sports. Graham McNamee's live reports from the 1924 Democratic Convention, where 103 separate ballots were required to nominate John W. Davis, marked the moment when party politics became a glamorous media attraction. McNamee also gave America major-league baseball over the air, helping to turn the game into a national narrative with characters, plotlines, and morals. The story that baseball told the public in this period featured a hero—Babe Ruth—and a team—the Yankees—who performed so well, they made people forget about the Black Sox.

At the peak of twenties prosperity, it seemed like everyone had enough money to visit the ballpark or buy a radio to hear the games. Workers whose productivity gains were rewarded with higher wages were prodded to join the rich in the stock market through mutual funds. Stories of the windfalls made by professional moneymen and eavesdropping chauffeurs stoked dreams of wealth in every class. At the peak, when Walter O'Malley came home to New York, an unprecedented 20 percent of American households belonged to the investing class and John J. Raskob of General Motors declared, "Everybody ought to be rich."

SUDDENLY PLANTED IN Greenwich Village, Walter O'Malley found himself at the center of a new bohemia. He sampled all that the brightly lit city had to offer, from prizefights, to Al Jolson, to avant-garde productions at the Province-town Playhouse. Kay Hanson, the girl-next-door in Amityville, accompanied him on some of his excursions to shows and restaurants, but he also went out on the town with male friends, including other Penn alumni who had flocked to the big city after graduation.

After considering his options, O'Malley decided to become a lawyer. At-torneys met the kinds of people—judges, politicians, business leaders—who could offer a young man opportunities. And the gossip that flows through law firms and courthouses could make a person rich. Backed by his father, who had gone from the public markets into real estate, O'Malley was accepted at Colum-bia University's law school and in his first year commuted from an apartment on Waverly Place to classes in Morningside Heights. The faculty at Columbia was pioneering an esoteric new branch of legal thought called "realism" that made the school a prestigious center for theoretical research. O'Malley did well enough, but for the first time the realities of life interrupted his progress along a carefully plotted course.

In 1927 Kay, who had complained of a sore throat the previous fall, was di-agnosed with cancer of the larynx. Specialists recommended a combination of surgery and X-ray therapy. They said that the radiation would likely leave Kay infertile, and the surgery would render her unable to speak above a faint whis-per. That was *if* she survived the operation and the cancer didn't recur.

When Kay began treatment, she and Walter were, in their own words, "en-gaged to be engaged" but had not told their parents that their steady relation-ship was so serious. Imagining Walter without children, easy conversation, and perhaps prematurely widowed, Kay tried to break it off. When he learned of it, Edwin O'Malley also raised objections to their romance. Walter wouldn't listen to either of them. Telling Kay "I'll love you forever," he saw her through the pain and exhaustion, and the devoted pair adopted Irving Berlin's new hit "Always" as their song. Berlin had composed it just prior to marrying heiress Ellin Mackay—a marriage opposed by her family—and taking her to Europe on a widely publicized honeymoon.

I'll be loving you always
With a love that's true always.

Romantic as their struggle was, the songwriter and the heiress had it easier than Kay Hanson and Walter O'Malley. Though cured, Kay would never recover her voice and for the rest of her life would rely on a faint whisper, notes, and gestures to communicate. It helped that she had very expressive eyes and an engaging smile. She went back to the College of New Rochelle to finish course work on the degree she had been granted in absentia. After graduation she worked as a transcriber for the Braille Institute in New York and then enrolled at St. John's University's law school, intent on becoming what was a rather rare creature at that time: a woman lawyer.

In the meantime Walter left Columbia and transferred to night classes at Fordham's law school, which was on the twenty-eighth floor of the famous Woolworth Building. Eventually the O'Malley legend would hold that he transferred because Edwin lost his fortune in the Crash of '29 and could no longer support him. But the big stock market plunge was still two years away and Edwin was doing well enough to maintain a home in the city and hold on to his summer place on Long Island. It's more likely that Walter, having chosen love over his father's objections, preferred night school because it allowed him time to work, and he could pay his own way. The switch to Fordham also brought him in contact with a more practical approach to the law and a more varied group of fellow students. Fordham left it to the Columbia scholars to develop new theories of law and prepare recruits for old, established firms. Instead it served many sons of immigrants and workingmen, who trained to do the gritty work of contracts, litigation, criminal cases, and politics.

While he was at night law school, O'Malley took a job as an assistant engineer and surveyor for the city Board of Transportation, which was in the midst of building the Eighth Avenue subway line. He worked at this job for about six months, then partnered with a contractor named Thomas F. Riley in a drilling and survey business. The job often required O'Malley to labor all night long on a barge in the East River. The work saw him through the terrible economic turmoil that followed the stock market disaster of 1929, but it was physically grueling. In a December 1930 letter to his sweetheart, Kay, he explained that this duty was especially hard when a cold rain was followed by freezing temperatures and he came down with a cold: "Now I must go out on the East River in a gov't boat & survey some broken casings—sneeze—sneeze—sneeze—and it *is* cold."

Ever ambitious, O'Malley soon left Riley and entered the same line of work on his own with a firm he called O'Malley Engineering. Although the economy was grinding toward the Great Depression, public works projects continued and O'Malley won contracts to perform test borings for the Midtown Tunnel. He made so much money that he was able to maintain his Greenwich Village apartment and use the Mayflower Hotel as an occasional crash pad. O'Malley also worked with a relative who published an annual construction trade directory called the *Contractor's Registry*. With all this, he did well enough in his studies that when he took the New York bar exam he ranked among the 30 percent who actually passed. (He also got some help preparing for the test from a Fordham law professor and future federal judge named Harold Medina.)

O'Malley's schedule, filled with study, work, and social escapades, was hectic even for a young man. In between ball games and boxing matches he saw coloratura soprano Lily Pons make her American debut and Walter Hampden in his defining performance as Cyrano. But he was always careful to assure Kay that he was faithful and true. In one letter he wrote that instead of joining a party at the Carlyle Hotel, where his friend caroused with the women of Norman Bel Geddes's production of *Lysistrata*, he chose to be a "good little boy" and went home "to snore."

Though immersed in the pursuit of wealth and fun in one of the world's most sophisticated cities, O'Malley cherished the old-fashioned romance he maintained with Kay, who by this time had decided to leave law school. In one letter he recalls that he saw her signal him with flashing car lights as she arrived at the family house in Amityville. "I couldn't break away as Dad was in heavy conference with me. Gosh but I was disappointed." In the same note he mentions Kay's sister Helen, whom he nicknamed "Champ," and how they resembled each other. "Such a complicated wooing—(I'm glad you are not twins!)"

A letter sent in April of 1931 allowed Walter to joke about his parents, presumably straitlaced and easily shocked, going to see a controversial and sensual movie called *Tabu*, which was a love story set in the South Pacific. But he devoted many more lines to sensitive descriptions of the setting moon and signs of spring in coastal Amityville, including birds' nests, tulips, lilacs, schooling fish, and lavender blooming near the back door at the Hanson house.

In their private language, Walter and Kay referred to "g.t.'s," which were "good thoughts." He reports that he collected them in great numbers to ease the loneliness when she was not near and his shoulder would be "neglected." He counted them before falling asleep, and reported that one night, when he gazed up at her bedroom window in Amityville, he "tossed a g.t., which stuck very tenaciously to the pane."

By mid-July 1931, Walter and Kay were obviously committed to marrying each other despite any objections that might be made by Edwin and Alma. Walter wrote of telling the big news to a friend, who was thrilled. Weeks later a brief message scrawled in pencil on a page from a memo pad said, "Kay— Meet me at marriage bureau, municipal building, Brklyn, as soon as possible . . . look around for me."

Finally, on Saturday, September 5, 1931, Walter and Kay were married at St. Malachy's Roman Catholic Church near Times Square. Known as the Actors' Chapel, the little church recently had been the site of Rudolph Valentino's funeral and wake, which attracted one hundred thousand visitors. The O'Malley wedding was small and private, with just a few people looking on. His parents did not attend.

WALTER'S DISAGREEMENT WITH EDWIN and Alma over his marriage to Kay didn't cause a permanent rift. But it certainly marked a turning point in his life. Having paid for Fordham himself, started his own business, and chosen the woman he loved over his father's objections—"She's the same girl I fell in love with," he told Edwin—he was a fully independent adult.

Stubborn and sure of his own heart, Walter was the product of all that Edwin and Alma O'Malley had given him, including the love lavished on an only child, a confidence-building education, and his father's example of a life lived with bravado and conviction. What else could they have expected of him when it came to the most important decision of his life?

After a honeymoon in Bermuda, Walter and Kay stayed at his Greenwich Village apartment for a few months while workers finished constructing the building they would move to in January. Despite the growing global financial crisis, certain Manhattan construction projects had continued apace. In midtown the Empire State Building opened in the fall of 1931, with John J. Raskob among the first tenants. Fifteen blocks to the north, the Rockefeller Center complex, the largest private building project in history, rose on a twenty-two-acre site. On the East Side a massive apartment building designed by Rosario Candela rose seventeen stories high on a quiet little street between First Avenue and the East River.

Though deplored by Frank Lloyd Wright as a graceless block of cement and brick, 2 Beekman Place, where the O'Malleys reserved an apartment on an upper floor, signified solid, upper-middle-class achievement. Their apartment was large enough to accommodate their first child—a surprise, given Kay's cancer treatment—who arrived in May 1933. Theresa "Terry" O'Malley would be the first in the family to gain national fame when a neighbor who happened to be a photographer used her as a model in a magazine ad for Ivory soap. Of course, it was her face and not her name that became known. In the ad copy she was called Jerry.

Terry kept her mother busy while Walter, with his fresh degree and admission to the bar, built a legal practice from scratch. He rented an office in a new skyscraper called the Lincoln Building on East Forty-second Street, which was almost directly across from Grand Central Terminal. His first work involved a will for an Irish priest who had been delighted to find a familiar name from county Mayo in the phone book. Another early client was a man named Tom Anderson who was accused of rape. The case brought O'Malley to the city's notorious central jail, called The Tombs, and required a substantial investigation of the sordid facts. After two months, during which O'Malley took depositions and dug into events, the charges were dismissed. Although this early case ended with success, criminal law would not consume much of O'Malley's time. Instead, he would focus on civil cases, contracts, and real estate transactions.

At first glance, 1932 would seem to be the wrong time to start a business of any kind. In the summer the Dow Industrial Average sank to its lowest point in history, taking many banks and investment firms under. Bankruptcies, factory closings, and layoffs combined to create 25 percent unemployment nationwide and even worse conditions in certain communities. Buffalo, New York, for example, saw nearly 50 percent of those eager to work unable to find jobs. But hard times can create big demand for a few types of professionals, including lawyers.

"Times were very rough indeed," recalled O'Malley decades later. "A good many professional men were actually selling apples on the street corners of New York." However, the disputes that arise in times of economic crises require lawyers who would sort them out. The best would find more than enough work.

"Two of my very early law clients were relatives . . . They had invested in guaranteed mortgage certificates," O'Malley said. "The companies that loaned the certificates were not able to keep up the payments to the bond and certificate holders. I got interested in seeing what could be done legally to protect the investment of the people who had these certificates. This resulted in a rather interesting law practice during those troublesome years . . . We wound up representing several of the leading banks and trust companies and a number of the larger industrial companies in the East."

Beginning with those relatives who held mortgage securities and had come to him when their investments soured, O'Malley focused on distressed corporations and their investors, particularly those involved with real estate development. During the precrash boom, investment companies had devised a way to make risky mortgages into notes—guaranteed mortgage certificates—that were sold with the promise of high-interest payments. (A similar scheme would begin a financial crisis in 2007.) The Depression pushed so many developers into default on these notes that the bond guarantee companies couldn't repay investors. Working with the bondholders as a class and major lenders as trustees, O'Malley would reorganize the development project, provide relief for investors, and revive the property.

Demand for this service grew as thousands of bankruptcies led to mortgage and bond defaults across the city. Moving from one case to another, Walter O'Malley and the growing number of associates in his firm developed a reputation for getting the best for clients facing very bad situations. In Brooklyn, O'Malley impressed a politically powerful judge and Fordham alumnus named Albert Conway, who once did some lawyering in the public markets. Conway rose steadily and would eventually sit as chief of the state's highest court. In the 1930s he included O'Malley in a group of young attorneys sometimes called "Conway's boys," to whom he assigned various cases from the bench.

Another of Conway's boys, attorney Charles Mylod, became one of O'Malley's closest friends. Charlie hit it big early, becoming the main attorney for a titan of real estate, banking, and New York society named Robert Goelet.

The Mylods and the O'Malleys joined with couples named McLaughlin and McCooey to form a little social group they called the Myomacs. These young couples, blessed with enough money to enjoy some of the better things life had to offer, attended the opera, organized dinner parties, and even vacationed together in the Pocono Mountains.

The most prominent member of the Myomacs was Everett McCooey, a locally famous tenor whose father, John McCooey, was the most powerful political figure in Brooklyn. After working in the infamously corrupt public markets, John McCooey had founded Brooklyn's Madison Club, which he modeled on Tammany Hall. He used it to become the party boss of the borough, controlling patronage and politics for twenty-five years and wielding influence all the way to Washington. In his later years he was chubby and balding, with red cheeks, bright blue eyes, and a flowing white mustache. He ruled from an office where the door was never closed and he saw as many as two hundred people a day. As McCooey spoke, in a soft, low voice, each one was made to feel as if he were being let in on an important but confidential bit of information.

Of McCooey's three sons, the musical Everett was least concerned with politics. But an association with anyone in the family, just like his friendship with Judge Conway, couldn't have hurt Walter O'Malley. Indeed, anyone hoping to do business with the city, the borough, or in the courts would benefit from relationships with both Fordham alumni and leading Irish-American politicians, who wielded great influence. These relationships were built on mutual favors and reinforced in a never-ending cycle of dinners, fund-raisers, and social events. Few were better adapted to the customs and demands of this life than Walter O'Malley.

Whether he was sipping Dewar's White Label at the exclusive Stork Club or tucking into a steak at the members-only Brooklyn Club, O'Malley was always ready with a smile, a story, or a joke. He could talk about current events, politics, sports, art, or the opera. With a constantly growing number of contacts in business, finance, and politics, he often possessed information that could help a friend or client. And, like the old political boss John McCooey, he had a certain twinkle in his eye and a reassuring way of making others feel as if they were being admitted into a kind of happy conspiracy. He liked to make introductions, pick up checks, and tell stories.

In certain circles where life remained gay despite the Depression, business relationships were built in the most pleasant surroundings. At Belmont Racetrack, Walter could watch the thoroughbred Deduce, owned by the wife of his friend Judge Henry Ughetta, race against horses owned by other prominent women. (Mrs. Damon Runyon had a filly named Angelic and Mrs. John Hay Whitney owned Singing Wood.) Walter played in golf tournaments put on by real estate men, joined the rich and powerful at the Waldorf-Astoria to watch the Anvil Chorus, a Brooklyn-based lampoon group, skewer the rich and powerful, and played poker in a regular floating game.

In the spring of 1935, Walter O'Malley attended a season-opening baseball game in New York. The first note of baseball in his collection of date books, O'Malley's entry for April 23, 1935, did not include the name of the home team. On that day the Philadelphia Phillies met the Dodgers at Ebbets Field in Brooklyn, where sportswriter John Drebinger predicted "some 30,000 of the nation's most virile baseball addicts" would hail the return from spring training of Casey Stengel and the hometown team. However, it's likely that Walter went instead to Washington Heights, where the Giants and Braves would play at the Polo Grounds.

As a Bronx-born Giants fan, O'Malley would have known that the Polo Grounds was the place to be. With Babe Ruth making his first appearance in New York wearing a Braves uniform, Mayor Fiorello La Guardia was rushing home from vacation to throw out the first pitch. A sellout crowd of 50,000, including boxer James J. Braddock, watched as the game went into extra innings. In the eleventh Mel Ott hit a walk-off homer that brought a shower of hats and programs onto the field.

With Ott, Carl Hubbell, and O'Malley's favorite player, Bill Terry, the Giants had a good team that would play well through the season but finish eight and a half games out of the pennant. Although loyal fans were disappointed to have missed the World Series, at least they could look down on the rival Brooklyn Dodgers, who at seventy wins and eighty-three losses were almost irrelevant to the rest of the National League.

If O'Malley shared the sense of disdain mixed with pity that Giants fans felt for the Dodgers, his heart was about to change. He did substantial business in Brooklyn and was forging a powerful relationship with the borough's most important banker, George V. McLaughlin of the Brooklyn Trust Company, who also happened to be deeply involved with the struggling team. Soon enough, Walter O'Malley was going to care very deeply about the health, welfare, and success of the Brooklyn baseball team.

THE SAME George V. McLaughlin who served as Mayor Jimmy Walker's swashbuckling police commissioner, the head of the Brooklyn Trust Company resembled the tough but sophisticated men of 1930s movies. He was six feet tall and weighed more than two hundred pounds. He brushed his dark hair straight back from his forehead and had a cleft chin so strong that one reporter called it a "fighting jaw." Rarely seen without a cigar, McLaughlin wore double-breasted suits and fancy vests cut with separate pockets for singles, fives, and tens. A gifted and aggressive negotiator, he was known for his ability to see every facet of a problem and then talk his way to a resolution that benefited his side. In the twenties, which was the age of nicknames, he came to be called "George the Fifth."

McLaughlin's tough image had been helpful when he took controversial stands as a police commissioner, naming the first black sergeant in city history, promoting gun control, and ordering raids on gamblers at Tammany-connected clubhouses. According to the *New York Times*, there was glee among the old hacks when McLaughlin resigned, because he had refused to make exceptions for politicians and built his own base of public support by joining detectives and uniform officers when they raided speakeasies, smugglers, and gambling dens.

In his decade-long tenure at the Brooklyn Trust Company, McLaughlin had doubled deposits and made the company strong. (In so doing, he joined the ranks of enemies counted by old mayor Hylan, who had remade himself as leader of the World Monetary Reform League and spent the mid-1930s railing against bankers.) During this time McLaughlin also headed the Brooklyn Chamber of Commerce, joined John H. McCooey on a committee to raise funds for the poor, and was nearly drafted by the anticorruption Fusion party to run for mayor. Instead the party chose La Guardia, who, after he won, named McLaughlin to the Triborough Bridge and Tunnel Authority. The authority, which controlled vast funds for public works projects, was headed by Robert Moses.

A former young crusader, Moses had remade himself as a political insider. A confidant and adviser to governors and mayors, he held a variety of posts that gave him control over public projects across the state. Often relying on designs by a brilliant young architect/engineer named Emil Praeger, Moses would use the Triborough Bridge and Tunnel Authority's steady income from tolls to construct bridges, tunnels, highways, and other public facilities. He traded favors, sought powerful allies, and played to the public, who could read about his achievements in thousands of newspaper articles. But even in this new persona, he still disdained many of the old pols he had opposed as a young man, including the McCooey clan, whom he attacked by name in speeches that boosted La Guardia.

Moses knew George the Fifth, because both had belonged to Governor Al Smith's inner circle in the 1920s. But while Moses had devoted himself to public work, McLaughlin had turned his ambition toward private business. The bridge authority would satisfy any desire he had for civic service, and as a side benefit he would acquire inside knowledge of projects that would affect business and property values throughout the city and in nearby counties. A bright young attorney like Walter O'Malley, who had been introduced to McLaughlin by his father, Edwin, years before, could have found no better mentor.

Between 1935 and the end of the decade, Walter O'Malley's date books were sprinkled with meetings and meals with McLaughlin. They met often at the Brooklyn Club or at the Hotel Bossert, which was just a short walk down Montague Street from the trust company office. The hotel, which was famous for a top-floor nightspot called the Marine Roof, was mired in financial problems. O'Malley worked on this case over several years as the Bossert family went through bankruptcy.

In between sessions with McLaughlin, O'Malley served a growing list of important clients as near as Manhattan and as far away as Montreal. Included were the Episcopal bishop of Brooklyn, the National Audubon Society, and the engineering firm that built Rockefeller Center. He joined his father-in-law, children's court judge Peter B. Hanson, on the board of directors of Swedish Hospital, and became so prominent that after settling one real estate case he got a note from a man claiming to be family asking "please remember your poor relatives and give me charge of this building."

Still in his midthirties, and just a few years into his profession, O'Malley had climbed high. In 1938 his gross income from his legal practice was more than $100,000, which would equal $1.3 million in 2009. More impressive, however, was the wealth of relationships he had built. Besides McLaughlin, O'Malley knew, worked, and played with prominent real estate men, politicians, investors, lawyers, bankers, and judges. True to the ethnic diversity of New York, plenty of Jews and Italians were included in O'Malley's circle, along with the Irish. And while he often represented the rich and powerful, he also did his share of work for the down-and-out. In 1940, for example, he handled a libel case for a formerly powerful assemblyman from Brooklyn named B. J. "Barney" Moran who had lost party support and been run out of office. A year later Moran died alone in a single furnished room near Flatbush Avenue.

Whether he was helping out-of-luck politicians or opportunistic real estate men, O'Malley made use of the great social skills that made him so popular at Culver and Penn. He had a big appetite for life. People liked him, and he was welcomed to become a member of the state's oldest men's group, the Brooklyn Club. He also became an avid deep-sea fisherman, joining the Freeport Tuna Club and competing in the annual East Coast tuna tournament with his friend Everett McCooey. In 1939 he would win the prize for biggest fish caught with light tackle, and in 1940 he and McCooey would take the overall title for Freeport.

The deep-sea fishing gave O'Malley stories to tell at the Brooklyn Club, where he often attended those rituals of male bonding called "smokers" and banquets called "beefsteaks," where it was customary for a man to let his hair, if not his guard, down. A New York phenomenon that began in unions, political organizations, and social clubs, beefsteaks were raucous affairs where men equipped only with their fingers and deprived of napkins or tablecloths devoured endless platters of sliced and buttered tenderloin. Bread, crackers, or french fries were offered, along with a tidal wave of beer. By the 1920s more elaborate meals for the upper class—like the members of the Brooklyn Club—might have also included crab and other cuts of meat, but the greasy basics and loosened belts remained.

O'Malley was a fine banquet companion, and after just a few years he was invited to join a club-within-the-club that met in a downstairs room called the Coal Hole. (It was named after a famous tavern in London.) Known as the "Coal Holers," this group had been created by Charles Hercules Ebbets, owner of both the Brooklyn Dodgers and the stadium that bore his name. When he died in 1925, at age sixty-six, Ebbets left them $5,000 to pay for an annual dinner on his birthday, October 29. O'Malley was asked to join upon the death of an original member, and thus came to attend an exclusive and lavish annual dinner to celebrate the life of a powerful man he most likely never met.

ALTHOUGH HE NEVER KNEW Charlie Ebbets, O'Malley surely understood that he had personified the scrappy Brooklyn spirit as fully as any public figure in the borough. Ebbets had served on the council when Brooklyn was an independent city, and he had long been an amateur sportsman. Present at the team's founding in 1884, when they were known as the Brooklyns, Ebbets had acquired stock gradually until he became president of the local major-league baseball team in 1898. In that year the city of Brooklyn became a borough of New York City and disappeared as an independent municipality. The Brooklyns disappeared, too, as a wave of marriages moved Ebbets to call them, if ever so briefly, the Bridegrooms. Although modern brand makers would cringe at the practice, name changing was common in early baseball. The Yankees were known, at different times, as the Highlanders, the Invaders, and the Porchclimbers. The Red Sox had been the Plymouth Rocks and the Beaneaters.

The Bridegrooms became the Superbas in time to bring the 1900 pennant home to the faithful at their stadium, Washington Park. After fires damaged or destroyed other wooden ballparks around the country, Ebbets looked for a place to build a modern concrete-and-steel stadium. He quietly focused on a sparsely populated neighborhood called Pigtown, where intermediaries who served a dummy corporation secretly bought parcel after parcel. Though dominated by an ash dump and home to wandering pigs, cows, and goats, the area was close to downtown, Grand Army Plaza, and the Brooklyn Navy Yard, where thousands of men and women worked. It could be reached by several trolley lines and would be served by a subway that was already under construction. In early 1912, Ebbets announced he was ready to build a stadium in Pigtown that would cost $750,000 and seat thirty-five thousand.

Although it was an entirely private enterprise, the design and construction of Ebbets Field was reported in the press as if it were a grand community project, like a new bridge or, to be more precise, a cathedral. In a country with no national church, baseball had become a secular religion. Scribes turned players into mythic heroes or villains, and outcomes of games were plumbed for life lessons. When prayers were ignored, heartbreaking losses became mysteries of the church. When sore-arm pitchers suddenly recovered, fastballs were seen as minor miracles. And as part of the greater national myth, in which America was always pastoral, manly, and fair, the game came to inspire florid and patriotic oratory.

The Ebbets Field groundbreaking ceremony was a showcase for this art. Borough president Alfred E. Steers talked about the great players of the past—in this case the 1870s—as if they were gods and elevated the team from its status as an athletic squad and business to make it an emblem of the community's identity and aspirations.

> I was born in this neighborhood and every bit of the ground is dear to me, and it gives me much pleasure to be here, fans and ladies and gentlemen and see the start of this proposed magnificent ballgrounds. I tell you what I want to see and I know you all want to see it too and that is for Brooklyn to proudly take her place at the top of the baseball world
>
>   —loud cheers—
>
> as she did in the days of old when I was a boy and used to peek through the holes in the fence.
>
>   —more cheers—
>
> And I think Mr. Ebbets will give us the best team in the country and it will play right here in this park.
>
>   —prolonged cheers—

Always a showman, Ebbets made sure to use a silver and ebony shovel to dig the first scoop of earth at the site. Someone in the crowd shouted, "Dig up a couple of new players, Charlie!"

IF ENTHUSIASM COULD HAVE set the pace, Ebbets would have opened his stadium before September. But construction problems slowed progress, raised expenses, and forced him to sell half of his stock to a pair of wealthy brothers named Edward and Stephen McKeever. By this time Ebbets was calling his team the Robins, in honor of manager Wilbert "Uncle Robbie" Robinson. The name of the team would remain in flux for years, but eventually the Trolley Dodgers and then the shorthand version—the Dodgers—would be adopted in honor of the many lines that crisscrossed the borough and forced its citizens to be ever nimble.

When his stadium was finished in April of 1913, thirty thousand came for the opening ceremonies and an exhibition game with the Yankees. Fans who arrived at the main entrance discovered an ornate rotunda with a soaring domed ceiling, gilded ticket booths, and a white Italian marble floor inlaid with red tiles in the pattern of the stitches on a baseball. Overhead, light came from a chandelier designed to look as if it were made of bats and balls. Valet parking service was offered to the swells who came by car, while businessmen were welcomed to use public phones equipped with desks and chairs.

Before play started, a band played "The Star-Spangled Banner" and Charlie Ebbets helped to raise the stars and stripes on a flagpole behind center field. He then marched toward the dugout and the band struck up a popular song, "Here Comes Your Daddy Now." Ebbets's face broke into a grin. He *was* the father of big-time baseball in Brooklyn and he reveled in the role.

The opening game went well, as a home run by Casey Stengel helped give the Brooklyns a victory. And though the facilities were strained by the crowd, the stadium was a hit. The new home saw the team win pennants in 1916 and 1920, but Ebbets would never capture a world championship. In the twenties, attendance at his park generally lagged behind the numbers reported by the Giants and the Yankees. In the struggle to keep up with his competition, Ebbets invented more than a dozen special "holidays" to promote the team and draw bigger crowds, especially women and families. These gimmicks helped, but they weren't a substitute for a winning team.

Often referred to as the Daffiness Boys by sportswriters, the Dodgers in this time were best known for bench riders who read magazines instead of watching the games, outfielders who went for their flying hats instead of the ball, and base runners who turned hits into outs. Fans thought they saw the worst when a batted ball hit outfielder Hack Wilson in the head as he argued with a heckler in the stands. Then Babe Herman set his own pants on fire by tucking a hot cigar in his pocket. By 1937 the team was so bedeviled by the basic elements of the game that manager Burleigh Grimes, declaring "It's all in the feet," brought in a track coach to show the boys how to run.

All of the errors and defeat earned the Dodgers another nickname, "Dem Bums," but also endeared them to the masses of the borough who could relate to finishing second, third, or worse in life's competitions. The Dodgers faithful heckled and berated the team, but they also loved them with a ferocity unmatched by fans anywhere. They were truly Brooklyn's own, and the feeling was reinforced by the fact that so many of the players lived in the borough. Their kids went to local schools and their wives shopped at the corner market. They commuted to work on the same trolleys that fans rode. When Harry "Cookie" Lavagetto was bitten by a wirehaired terrier—the bite was so severe that it sent him to the hospital—it happened at a homey Brooklyn restaurant called Whither's, not some fancy joint in Manhattan. As fixtures in the community, the players were like the town team in a midwestern village or a factory team in a New England mill town. People believed they knew them.

Brooklyn's love for the Dodgers was genuine and, whatever the score, the game was bound to be a good show. For this reason Ebbets Field was also popular with out-of-town visitors, including many movie stars, who delighted in grandstand eccentrics like the leather-lunged, cowbell-ringing lady named Hilda Chester and a ragged band of musicians who called themselves the "Dodgers Sym-phony." The park was also home to the immensely wealthy Mrs. Izaak Walton Killam, who was always accompanied by a uniformed servant bearing refreshments, and a champion heckler called Abie the Milkman. But while Abie had the right to criticize, because he obviously loved the team, cracks from outsiders were not tolerated.

On a summer evening in 1938, Frank Krug, a visitor from Albany, went to a bar called Pat Diamond's in the Park Slope neighborhood. Set on the corner of Ninth Street and Seventh Avenue, Diamond's was about a mile from Ebbets Field, where the reviled Giants had just defeated the Dodgers. The owner's son Bill, who was tending bar, said, "The Dodgers, whoever first called them bums was right. Don't you think so, Frank?"

As a son of Brooklyn, Bill Diamond had every right to criticize the old town team. Frank Krug did not. But he spoke anyway.

"It takes the Giants to show them up as bums too. Ha ha! What our guys did to them today! Why don't you get wise to yourself? Why don't you root for a real team?"

Hearing this, a local named Robert Joyce reacted.

"Shut up, shut up, you bastards! You lay off the Dodgers, you bastards."

"Don't be a jerk," answered Krug.

"A jerk! I'll show you who's a jerk!"

Laughter followed Joyce out of the bar. He went to the post office where he worked and retrieved a pistol. Returning to the bar, Joyce killed Frank Krug with a single shot to the head and then fired on Bill Diamond, wounding him in the belly. After he was arrested, Joyce said he had reached the point where he couldn't bear any longer the stress of rooting for the bumbling Dodgers.

FORTUNATELY FOR CHARLES H. EBBETS, the era when his team was so bad it drove loyal fans to violence came after he had died. Most would blame the disarray on the field on confusion and feuding among the owners. In a twist of fate that only the Dodgers could suffer, Ebbets's death had been followed two weeks later by the passing of the co-owner, who had just seized control of the business. Edward J. McKeever had caught a cold at Ebbets's funeral, taken to bed, and died of pneumonia. His brother Stephen would live to run the club for twelve years. A bit eccentric, McKeever appeared at the ballpark in a derby hat and always carried a gold-handled cane. He loved to dispense free tickets and to show off the colostomy bag that he wore after abdominal surgery. Charming as he was, McKeever couldn't exercise much leadership over the franchise: he held only a quarter of the voting stock. The rest was divided among heirs to the two deceased partners, leaving exactly 50 percent in the hands of the Ebbets family and 50 percent with the McKeevers.

Charles Ebbets's heirs resented the McKeevers and, in the words of one knowledgeable observer, "for a great many years it was almost impossible to do anything constructive." Contests over control were fierce, complex, and almost continual. At one point the National League threatened a takeover if the Dodgers refused to accept a fifth board member, George Barnewall of the Brooklyn Trust Company, who could break tie votes on key decisions. Barnewall was installed and with the aid of generous loans from his bank—made when no other lender would come forward—the business was kept afloat.

During this muddling time, as the team's performance eroded a Brooklyn fan's patience and the Great Depression chewed on his wallet, the stadium that Ebbets built suffered the same neglect as the roster. Although the grass in the outfield still dazzled in the sunlight, in the grandstand and the rotunda paint peeled and dust piled up. Beer spills, hot dogs, and dirty restrooms gave the place a circus smell, especially on hot, humid days. Eventually the stink, on the field and in the stands, got so bad that the splintered owners group couldn't ignore it. Leland Stanford MacPhail, a baseball executive as fiery and demanding as the Dodgers' fans, was hired to end the misery.

The son of a wealthy banker, MacPhail went to a military academy as a boy and attended the University of Michigan's law school, where he became friends with former major leaguer and future baseball legend Branch Rickey. They were an odd match. In those early years and, for that matter, throughout his life, MacPhail would be a profane, booze-guzzling, free-spending brawler with a powerful need to be the loudest man in any room. Rickey would cultivate the opposite image: thrifty, preachy, and extraordinarily verbose. In Rickey-ese, a man might study "a new tangent" for his life, a fellow who took his pension wasn't retired, he was "superannuated," and cheers from the grandstand were "ungovernable effusions."

Despite their great difference, MacPhail's determination and self-confidence impressed Branch Rickey. As an Army captain in World War I, MacPhail joined a group that tried to kidnap Kaiser Wilhelm from a Dutch prison so he could be prosecuted by American authorities. MacPhail and company got close enough to steal the Kaiser's ashtray before being stopped.

After the war, MacPhail got into baseball with the help of his father's money, which was invested in the Columbus Senators, a minor-league affiliate of the St. Louis Cardinals. Branch Rickey, who ran the St. Louis organization, became his baseball mentor. The Great Rotarian, as some called him, built a system for recruiting and training hundreds of youngsters to be ballplayers. Rickey pushed his program like an evangelist rounding up souls. Some of those who bought into it behaved like religious converts, even calling themselves "Rickey men." And like any determined shepherd, Rickey made a special effort with the most wayward prospects, including MacPhail.

In 1934, Rickey recommended MacPhail for a job in the big leagues, running the Cincinnati Reds. At Cincinnati his protégé used every promotional trick he could imagine to raise attendance, even installing lights for the first night games in major-league history. Some, like the writer who said the lights were so good the ball stood out like a bald head in a steam room, approved. Others, like

Washington Senators owner Clark Griffith, insisted the idea would never catch on. For MacPhail the experiment was a success because it drew fans and earned him a spot in history even if he probably borrowed the idea from the Kansas City Monarchs of the Negro League, who had often played under a portable light system that they took along on road trips.

When he made it to Brooklyn, MacPhail tried all the things that had worked in Cincinnati. Some, like the Dodgers Knothole Gang, were practically free of real cost. By joining this club, up to ten thousand youngsters, who might grow into paying customers, would get free admission to certain games when they could fill out an otherwise thin crowd.

Other moves required more effort. MacPhail got the Brooklyn Trust Company to extend the team more credit—roughly $500,000—so he could renovate the stadium, install lights, and buy better players. An over-capacity crowd that attended the first night game roared when the big lights, called mazdas, were switched on. Before play started, they got to see another MacPhail promotion. Jesse Owens, hero of the 1936 Berlin Olympics, gave a couple of Dodgers a head start and almost beat them both in a hundred-yard dash. (He was nosed out by Ernie Koy.) The game itself was one for the record books, as Cincinnati rookie John Vander Meer pitched his second consecutive no-hitter.

Watching it all from on high was a contingent of sports reporters, in coats and ties, who thoroughly enjoyed one of MacPhail's other innovations: an open bar for the press. Free drinks for thirsty reporters showed that MacPhail understood that the team needed the press to connect with paying fans. The press created and then fed the public craving for celebrities and pro sport had to compete with every other form of entertainment for attention. In New York, where three baseball teams competed for attention and ticket sales, MacPhail had to do whatever he could to keep reporters focused on the Dodgers until they could draw fans the old-fashioned way, by winning.

MacPhail's own antics, including the occasional punch thrown in anger, helped to keep the boys on the baseball beat hanging around just so they didn't miss anything. For the fans he created promotions like Music Appreciation Night—free tickets for anyone arriving at Ebbets with a musical instrument—and he installed one of baseball's first organs with a gifted musician named Gladys Goodding to play it. (Goodding, who began her musical career as a piano player for silent movies, played organ for hockey games at Madison

Square Garden, a job that made her available for the Ebbets gig.) To spice things up on the field, MacPhail obtained shortstop Leo "The Lip" Durocher from Branch Rickey in St. Louis.

A flashy, arrogant scoundrel with mobster friends, Durocher had been a moral rehabilitation project for Rickey. His early life in Springfield, Massachusetts, had been hard. He had practiced petty thievery, learned baseball, hustled pool, developed an appetite for finer things—money, clothes, cars—and generally avoided school. It was there that "Fuck you" and "You son of a bitch" became his catchphrases. He became so tough that as a young man he walked away from his one and only child, a daughter, and erased her so thoroughly from his life that she never appeared in his autobiography.

In Brooklyn, Durocher was reunited with his former Yankee teammate Babe Ruth, whom MacPhail had brought to Ebbets to work as a sideline coach. Once partners in debauchery, Ruth and Durocher had had a falling-out when it seemed The Lip had stolen the Babe's watch. Durocher would forever insist the charge was false, but people in baseball generally took Ruth's side. The Babe referred to the weak-hitting Durocher as "the all-American out." Durocher took every chance to humiliate the aging star, right down to slapping him and calling him a baboon during a clubhouse confrontation. He gradually destroyed the Babe's chance to become manager and got the job for himself.

Having recruited Durocher as the tough guy who was going to make the Dodgers winners, MacPhail then used Walter Lanier "Red" Barber and his silky southern voice to announce the transformation to the world. Defying an agreement among local big-league owners, who feared that putting a significant number of games on the radio would destroy attendance, MacPhail brought Barber from Cincinnati to broadcast every game, home and away. Play-by-play on the radio helped bring the entire borough into the Dodgers family.

Barber, who had once tried to become a blackface vaudeville performer, was a brilliant showman. His broadcasts became so popular that some Brooklynites would recall walking down the street on a summer day when windows were open and never missing a pitch because Barber's voice echoed from every apartment. Having proved that the broadcasts only increased interest and brought more paying customers to Ebbets, MacPhail took the next logical step, arranging for NBC's experimental television station W2XBS to show a Dodgers home game.

A division of the giant Radio Corporation of America, NBC was eager to make the picture technology developed by its parent company the industry standard, and had invested heavily in equipment to get lots of programs on the air. The company spent $125,000 on the world's first mobile broadcast unit (two converted buses), which brought two cameras to Ebbets Field. When the Dodgers played the Reds on August 26, 1939, cameras positioned in the stands at Ebbets captured the action and fed the pictures to the broadcast buses. The signal was sent via cable to the Empire State Building, where an aerial attached to the side of the building spit it into the atmosphere. Those who caught the program, which carried Barber's call for the radio, saw the first pro game ever televised. It was not, however, the first ball game ever put on the air. That honor had already gone to Princeton and Columbia universities, which had allowed broadcast of their game played at Baker Field in Philadelphia a few months earlier.

Nevertheless, the show broadcast from Ebbets, a Dodger victory over the Reds on August 26, was a success. New telephoto lenses allowed for close-ups of players in the dugouts and pitchers winding up. These views brought TV-watching fans closer to the game than those who bought tickets. There was no doubt about the quality of the view or the technical challenges of the setting. Television could do baseball. It could also sell products, as Barber demonstrated with a bowl and a box of Wheaties. The big question was whether baseball could find a way to make it pay. Otherwise it would be dispatched as a threat to attendance at the ballpark and the bottom line.

Profit was MacPhail's ultimate goal, but he was also a baseball romantic and preferred to enjoy himself and reward his friends along the way to the bank. In 1939 he returned his mentor's many favors by giving twenty-five-year-old Branch Rickey Jr.—some called him "Twig"—an office job. That same year Ford Frick, president of the National League, brought another young man to Brooklyn to get a job with the team. A year younger than Twig, Emil "Buzzie" Bavasi had been Frick's neighbor in the wealthy suburb of Scarsdale. After graduating from college he had accepted his mother's offer of an expenses-paid year off. Three months into this adventure he ran into Frick, who declared the vacation over. MacPhail hired him and within weeks he was an office boy who was welcomed to chime in on such heady matters as player trades. (He nixed the acquisition of a pitcher he had faced, and clobbered, during college.) Baseball, he quickly decided, was a great business.

BY THE END OF the 1939 season, as the Coal Holers gathered once again to honor Charles H. Ebbets, everyone could see that the old man's team was being revived by MacPhail and Durocher. Seventh in 1938, they finished third in 1939. More important, they no longer did those things that made them daffy bums. Nobody got hit by a fly ball when his head was turned. No one's pants caught on fire. Instead, they played as hard as their fans rooted, and for the first time outdrew both the Giants and the Yankees. Nearly one million tickets were sold to Brooklyn games in 1939, a year when the average big-league team drew about 550,000. The transformation could have warmed old Ebbets in his grave.

Walter O'Malley was the youngest of those who honored Ebbets that October. The others were the departed's contemporaries. They were not going to see much of what the future held for their community, baseball, and their friend's team. However, a bright, younger man with his eyes and ears open would recognize the changes at hand as America shook off the Depression and might feel, in his bones, the opportunity growing in Brooklyn.

More crowded every year, the eighty square miles that was Brooklyn in 1939 boasted the largest population of the city's boroughs. At 2.8 million, up from 1.2 million in 1890, it would have been the second-largest city in America, were it still independent. The borough was also economically strong, with two hundred miles of bustling waterfront dominated by the Brooklyn Navy Yard, where at its height seventy thousand workers built ships for the Defense Department. Near the waterfront rose factories, coal yards, warehouses, and rougher neighborhoods where the members of an organized-crime gang whom the press called Murder Incorporated did much of their business. Farther from the docks stretched stable middle-class communities built along avenues and boulevards that stretched for miles in every direction.

The streets of Brooklyn stitched together what once was a region of twenty-five villages, each with its churches and shops, and remained a collection of communities with strong identities. Within these communities young families sometimes lived in ethnic enclaves. Brooklyn had a Little Syria and a Little Sweden to go with communities of blacks, Hispanics, Europeans, and others. But the borough also contained mixed areas like Crown Heights, where all religions and nationalities came together.

Most of all, the borough was as thoroughly middle class and civic minded as a major metropolitan community could be. Along with Coney Island it offered a great art museum, an academy of music, a university, and a medical school. In Brooklyn it was easy to get a great cheap meal—franks and beans at Joe's—and one of best steaks in the world at Gage and Tollner or Peter Luger. At any of these places you might find yourself sitting next to a judge, a mobster, a factory worker, or a Dodger ballplayer and feel completely at ease.

O'Malley understood what Brooklyn was, because after the birth of his second child, a son named Peter who arrived in December 1937, he moved his family to a big apartment in a building called Albion Court on the corner of St. Marks and New York avenues in the heart of the borough. Peter's birth, which had been preceded by several miscarriages, was such a joyous occasion that Walter sent a letter to General Gignilliat at Culver, requesting that his son be registered in the class of 1950.

Albion Court was in a neighborhood called Crown Heights, which was a fashionable area of detached homes, brownstone row houses, and graceful apartment buildings occupied by families from a broad mix of ethnic backgrounds. Within easy walking distance were several schools, the Brooklyn Children's Museum, and Brower Park. Kay O'Malley's parents lived a block away and her sister and her family were almost as close. St. Gregory's, which became the family church, was a short walk away. With three bedrooms, the O'Malley apartment was comfortable but hardly grand. The one thing that made it different from the others in the building was a special window that jutted out from the brick face of the building, which Walter installed so that he could practice a new hobby: growing orchids.

Although his law office remained in Manhattan, Walter O'Malley's life, like his orchids, became well rooted in Brooklyn, where he found his home, his friends, and his most important allies in business. As a symbol of this commitment he bought season tickets to the Dodgers games.

"That was a great way for entertaining clients—active or potential—and I used my seats quite effectively for that purpose," O'Malley would recall in the 1960s. "It became generally known that you could find Walter O'Malley at a Dodger ball game in Ebbets Field almost each night." He spoke in a deep gravelly voice and a slight accent that combined two boroughs and might be called

Bronx-lyn. "Purpose" almost sounded like "poi-pus" and the word "potential" began with a strong "poh."

In 1939, George McLaughlin asked O'Malley to represent the trust company in the reorganization of the *Brooklyn Daily Eagle* newspaper—the bank was a creditor—and he began attending meetings related to the financial concerns of another major trust company client, the Brooklyn Dodgers. The trust was the team's major lender and guardian of the half interest controlled by Charles H. Ebbets's heirs.

"The ball club owed the trust company an awful lot of money," O'Malley would recall many years later. It was also behind in tax payments and under scrutiny from an insurance company that held a mortgage on Ebbets Field. McLaughlin called O'Malley into his office and said, "I'd like you to go over there and do a little troubleshooting and see what you can do."

Three

THE DODGER BUSINESS

On April 19, 1940, a cold and overcast day, New York baseball began a new season in an old familiar way. At Yankee Stadium, seventy-three-year-old baseball commissioner Kenesaw Mountain Landis—white-haired, craggy-faced, and rigid of mind—distributed rings to the team that had defeated the Cincinnati Reds to win the 1939 World Series. It was the American League Yankees' fourth championship in a row, their eighth in twenty years, and fans regarded the event as routine. After the ceremony the home team notched a matter-of-fact victory over Washington. The cheers for the final out echoed against empty seats, as paid attendance in the vast park was less than sixteen thousand.

In a distant borough and a world away in baseball terms, the Dodgers began their home season on the same chilly Friday. They played the Giants, who had been among the best in the National League during the recent Yankee run. The Giants' success stung Brooklyn fans, who felt almost worse about their rivals' wins than they did about Dodger defeats. But as any sportswriter worth his metaphors could explain, each spring brought new hope to the ballpark as well as the garden. And this year Brooklynites could base this feeling on something more substantial than fertilizer. In 1939, Leland Stanford MacPhail's efforts had lifted the team to its best record since 1930, and the squad promised to be even better in the coming season. This hope, which brought twenty-four thousand to cozy Ebbets Field, was affirmed as the Leo Durocher–led home team crushed the hated visitors 12–0.

Somewhere in the Ebbets crowd Walter O'Malley, dressed in a business suit and tie, cheered the brilliant pitching of Hugh "Apple Cheeks" Casey and applauded the three-for-four hitting of third baseman Cookie Lavagetto. Nobody could remember the last time the Dodgers had defeated the Giants so readily. Wise fans would protect their hearts by keeping their expectations low, and it would take another year before the team would actually win a pennant. But as this season progressed, it became obvious that the Bums were better.

The Dodgers would sell nearly one million tickets in 1940, and with the exception of two lean years during the Second World War, attendance would average a profitable 1.2 million in the decade to come. Previously the team had broken the million-fan mark just once in fifty-six years. The popularity of the Giants and Yankees would surge in a similar fashion. With no other pro sport drawing half as many fans, the forties began a golden age of baseball.

As he watched the Dodgers from his season ticket seats, Walter O'Malley enjoyed more than a little inside knowledge about the team. He liked baseball, but he wasn't besotted with the game, like so many romantics who see in it all of life and human nature in microcosm. O'Malley wasn't an expert on strategy or the fundamentals of pitching, hitting, and fielding. But he could have told the fellow in the next seat all about the team's financial prospects. Curious about ticket sales, concessions, or contract costs? If he didn't have the figures in his head, he could get them for you.

O'Malley knew all about the Dodgers because George V. McLaughlin had asked him to monitor the team's operations and the moves made by its divided board of directors. The Brooklyn Trust Company had a keen interest in the team as a lender—the Dodgers owed about $500,000—and as executor of the Ebbets estate. The team hadn't paid a dividend since 1932, but MacPhail's successful reconstruction project had boosted attendance, which promised improvements in the account books.

For three years MacPhail had done everything short of setting the infield on fire to keep the show in Flatbush exciting. More than any baseball man of his time, MacPhail directed a team as though he were putting on a Broadway show. Yes, there was an athletic competition involved, but the games would never be played if the Dodgers didn't make real money. Profit required lights (for night games), music (from Gladys Goodding), and constant ballyhoo in the press.

With each of the local papers devoting entire sections of their daily editions to sports, the press literally gave away publicity to teams and players. Sportswriters under pressure to produce scoops and entertain readers merrily colluded with any attempt to generate drama on or off the field. Everything about a team, including contract negotiations, executive changes, and the moods, opinions, and manipulations of team owners, was fair game. Coverage was so complete that, along with game stories, the sports pages delivered readers an education in business, law, psychology, and whatever branch of medicine covered a player's injury. Little of it would be considered investigative reporting in the modern sense, but columnists could be especially critical, playing to their readers while skewering a team, player, manager, or owner.

Few private enterprises permitted so many words, facts, and figures about its operations into the public realm. The only thing comparable was the movie industry, which also depended on publicity to sell tickets. But while Hollywood's story was well controlled by a handful of moguls, professional baseball was just too big and unruly to muzzle. Counting the minor leagues, thousands of players, office staffers, coaches, and others were involved in the game. Most were competitive types with needy egos who naturally tried to use the press to gain an advantage in battles on and off the field. A bit of undermining information leaked to the right writer could bring down a rival.

In the competition for attention, the fierce MacPhail was the most harddriving of the lot, and it was sometimes hard to tell the difference between his press stunts and his natural outbursts. In June 1940 he charged down from his box seats and onto the field when outfielder Joe "Ducky" Medwick was beaned—a fastball to the left temple—by Cardinals pitcher Bob Bowman.

Captured in a photo printed by the *New York Times*, the scene in the moment after Medwick fell to the ground looked like a crucifixion in the batter's box. Medwick lies faceup with his feet pointing down the third-base line and his arms straight out. The umpire, pitcher, and catcher stand in a circle around him, staring down. Medwick's soft cap—batting helmets were still years away— rests upside down in dirt near his right shoulder and his bat lies just a few feet away.

As the shocked crowd of 6,460 paying customers (and about 5,000 Knot-holers) looked on, players and coaches ran out of the dugouts and onto the field. Some gathered around Medwick. Others seemed ready to fight. A red-faced Lee MacPhail stormed out of the stands and onto the field. Medwick, who was recently acquired from St. Louis in a deal involving $125,000 cash, was an asset worth protecting. MacPhail raged around the infield looking for a fight but got no takers.

The next day the *Brooklyn Daily Eagle* called the beaning a case of attempted murder, and as reporters dug into the story they learned it might have been premeditated. Bowman and Medwick had exchanged words—something about the weak-hitting Durocher's limp bat—in an elevator at the Hotel New Yorker the night before the game. The district attorney, a rabid Dodgers fan named William O'Dwyer, opened an investigation.

No one could ever be sure whether MacPhail had purposefully inflamed the drama. Certainly the *Eagle* had an interest in using it to sell papers and O'Dwyer reaped some benefits from the publicity. And then there was the sheer pleasure a reporter or politician might derive from jumping into the controversy. These were the kinds of fellows who enjoyed a nice scrap.

But as usual, the team benefited the most from all the noise. Every seat for the next game was sold and thousands who would have purchased tickets to stand were turned away because police were afraid to let the Dodgers jam too many angry fans together. Those who expected bloodshed almost got it in the third inning after St. Louis catcher Arnold "Mickey" Owen slid hard into second baseman Pete Coscarart and player-manager Durocher muttered some fighting words at Owen, who had been called out by the umpire. Owen wheeled around to confront Durocher and before they could be separated, punches flew.

The brawling kept the Dodgers in the papers and Brooklyn's blood boiling for weeks, which meant bigger crowds at the ballpark. When tempers finally cooled—the DA dropped the case—MacPhail and Durocher brought "The Boy Wonder" Harold "Pete" Reiser up from minor-league Montreal and sent him out to play right field. (Medwick, by the way, would never again be his aggressive self at the plate.)

Incredibly passionate and athletic, Reiser was no ordinary prospect. St. Louis general manager Branch Rickey believed he had almost unlimited potential. But the wily Rickey had lost control of Reiser's contract when Commissioner Landis found him guilty of manipulating the minor-league system.

Reiser was among scores of players who had been emancipated by Landis, but Rickey secretly arranged for his protégé MacPhail to buy his contract for $100, hide him in the minor leagues for a while, and then return him to St. Louis. The scheme was spoiled when Durocher discovered Reiser's talents and showed him off to the New York sportswriters. Suddenly everyone knew about Pete Reiser's potential. Durocher felt compelled to double-cross his friend Rickey and delight the Dodger faithful by letting the boy play at Ebbets.

Reiser was the latest in a parade of new players whom MacPhail promoted as the Second Coming. Although each one came at a price, the benefits outweighed the cost and gate receipts rose to the point where August found George the Fifth trying to buy out the McKeever heirs on behalf of the Ebbets estate. Obviously impressed by what his monitor O'Malley was reporting, McLaughlin considered buying the stock and flipping it, like a piece of real estate, to someone who was willing to pay a good price for a team that had a devoted local community, a growing national following, and a shot at breaking the Yankees' hold on the world championship.

Who was interested in buying? The first to raise his hand was Mike Jacobs, a renowned boxing promoter. Jacobs had made a fortune and broken Madison Square Garden's control of New York boxing by arranging bouts for Joe Louis at a time when other promoters didn't want to book black fighters. Louis dominated the sport, and Jacobs used his profits to support the Twentieth Century Sporting Club, a firm he founded with partners that included writer-raconteur Damon Runyon. Jacobs generally got what he wanted by throwing lots of money around and negotiating rich radio contracts to recoup his investment. In this case he was offering $2 million for the team, its real estate, and its minor-league affiliates.

Although the trust company seemed willing to sell, the McKeever heirs were not. Stephen McKeever's daughter, Marie ("Dearie"), who had married James Mulvey, the president of the Samuel Goldwyn movie company, understood her investment's value. Sounding very much like an ordinary fan, but acting as a wise stockholder, she said: "I've stuck with the Dodgers all through the hard times. Why should I sell now when things are getting better?"

The sale was blocked and in a matter of days trust company officials were downplaying the idea that a serious negotiation was ever conducted. But the fact that Jacobs wanted the Dodgers signaled in the clearest way that the franchise was back. Ever since he hawked theater tickets as a teenager in the lobby of the Normandie Hotel, Jacobs had shown an uncanny ability to pick a winner, whether it was a Broadway production or a heavyweight fighter. If he wanted the Bums, then they were Bums no more.

EVEN THOUGH IT FELL through, the Jacobs deal would have caught Walter O'Malley's attention and provided a little distraction from the biggest event of his life that year: his mother's death. Just fifty-seven years old, Alma Feltner O'Malley died on June 1, 1940, at the family's summer house in Amityville, Long Island. She left behind the sentimental proof of her life's focus. Tucked into an envelope was a small white flower, pressed and dried. Her son had picked it in 1921, when he was at Culver Academy, and sent it to her for her thirty-eighth birthday. In the same keepsake collection she had preserved letters he had sent home from college, and even a note he had written to her when he was elementary-school age. At the bottom were dozens of *X*'s, each representing a kiss, written in an unsteady hand.

Walter O'Malley could take some solace in his mother's attachment to the tokens he had sent. But now he could count only his father as a connection to his childhood. For his part, Edwin J. O'Malley would stay close to his son, although Alma's passing made him grow quieter. He visited often at the summer house in Amityville, but it now was a place for Walter and his family. There young Terry and Peter swam, sailed, and went on beachcombing adventures with neighborhood kids. Walter and Kay would welcome friends and neighbors for parties and dinners and weekends in the sunshine. Kay even bought glassware and linens decorated with the word "Myomac," to honor her closest friends. Indeed, she was so fond of this group that she once bought space in the program for an event at the Brooklyn Academy of Music so they would see "Greetings from the Myomacs" when they went together to a performance.

The Myomacs were frequent visitors at the O'Malley apartment in Brooklyn too. World War II brought shortages and rationing, so the couples would pool their coupons to buy a roast, or some other special item, for a shared dinner. The apartment at the Albion was comfortable, though hardly showy. The O'Malleys' lifestyle was not extravagant. Walter often cooked, even if it meant rushing home from the office, and Spam sandwiches were a staple. On Saturday mornings it was pancakes, and Walter would whistle while at the stove. He never consulted a cookbook.

As a grown man Peter O'Malley would remember his father as generally easygoing, but he had firm expectations when it came to how the children behaved with their mother. Discipline was rarely required, and because she needed them to help her communicate, the two children were especially close to their mom.

On a typical afternoon kids played ball outside, where gas rationing kept traffic light. Inside, the radio in the kitchen was tuned to Dodgers games. (Kay was a devoted fan who often kept score at home.) Peter and Terry could play Ping-Pong on the dining room table or sprawl on the flower-pattern rug in the living room to play marbles near the strange, mirrored TV set. For a treat they might get a piece of chocolate "blackout" cake from Ebinger's Bakery or walk around the corner to get ice cream on Nostrand Avenue.

By the early 1940s, Kay was well adjusted to her disability. When notes and facial expressions weren't enough, she could make herself understood by producing sounds without her vocal cords, and would talk with Walter and the children this way. She also used a telephone click system, rapping her ring on the receiver, to give yes or no answers when her husband checked in. After the phone rang and Kay answered, she'd signal she was there with a *click click*. From there the call would go something like:

Want me to pick up anything on the way home?

Click click. (Yes.)

Bread?

Click. (No.)

Eggs?

Click.

Milk?

Click click.

The phone code was part of everyday life, and especially for the children, who never knew their mother's full voice, it was an unremarkable routine. The same goes for the teamwork they employed to get household errands accomplished. If the car was in the shop—Kay loved to drive—Terry would call to ask if the repair was finished. If a special order had to be placed with the butcher,

Peter might telephone. The same process would help Kay to connect with her friends for a visit or plan to see her extended family.

Kay's parents lived nearby, as did her sister Helen, who had married an attorney named Harry Walsh. When it came time to send the children to school they were enrolled at the Froebel Academy, which was across the street from a small city park. The academy was not the O'Malleys' first choice—the parish school was full—but it turned out well. Considered the founder of the modern kindergarten, Friedrich Froebel recognized a child's need for activity and blended academics with songs, dances, cooking, gardening, and play. Froebel schools were warm, open places. Parents came and went at any time. While the spirit of the place made the need for discipline rare, it was always applied gently. Not surprisingly, once his children were enrolled, Walter joined the academy board.

The breadth of O'Malley's commitments in the early 1940s might make one wonder why he didn't leave the Froebel Academy board work for someone else. Along with his busy law practice, he also owned a building supply company that operated in the city and on Long Island and served as a director for Brooklyn Borough Gas, the Trommer Brewery, and the Todd & Brown construction and engineering company. (A premier firm, Todd & Brown had built Rockefeller Center in Manhattan.)

Despite all these obligations, O'Malley put more and more time into the Dodgers. In the team offices he discovered some shoddy business practices and a leaky system for handling the bags of cash generated by the sales of tickets, hot dogs, and beer. (As the coins and bills passed through too many hands, a sizable amount went missing.) His attention helped to fix these problems, and the Brooklyn Trust Company gained some confidence in the team's ability to repay its debts.

O'Malley also became a regular at ball games, which he attended with business associates, friends, and family. The 1941 season, which saw Joe DiMaggio's fifty-six-game hitting streak and Ted Williams batting .406, brought the rebuilt Dodgers the National League pennant. The Brooklyns won by two and a half games over St. Louis, but more satisfying to many was the fact that the Giants ended the year twenty-five games out of first place.

One day the baseball historian Bill James would declare that the '41 edition of the Dodgers was one of the greatest teams ever fielded. With Reiser and

Wyatt, the Brooklyn team had the best hitting and pitching in the National League. Led by Kirby Hughes and Whit Wyatt, the Dodgers had the best pitching corps and the wily Durocher made sure they were managed properly. Considerable credit also went to the steadying influence of catcher Mickey Owen—the same Mickey Owen who tangled with Durocher the previous year—whom MacPhail had signed away from the Cardinals during spring training.

When the Dodgers clinched the '41 pennant in Boston, they began a celebration that continued as their train to New York barreled southward. By the time they reached the Bronx the players, coaches, manager, and hangers-on had soaked up enough alcohol—the bill was over $1,400—to preserve a dead whale. Loyal fans from Brooklyn headed to Grand Central Station to greet them. Eager to take part in the celebration, Rickey and MacPhail went to 125th Street Station, where they planned to join the team for its big arrival. However, Durocher persuaded the conductor to skip 125th Street so that his players wouldn't be tempted to escape dealing with the crowds of eager fans at Grand Central. In the blowup that ensued the next time he saw MacPhail, Durocher became the first manager ever fired on the day he won a pennant. The next day he was re-hired.

In this era some people thought it wasn't a genuine World Series unless the Yankees were in it. The Dodgers played in a genuine series, made all the more grueling by weather so hot that sportswriters worked in their undershirts and Mayor La Guardia rode to the games in a police motorcycle sidecar so he could catch the breeze. The first three games were low scoring, with one-run margins. The Yankees won the first and third. The Dodgers took the second.

The turning point of the series came in the ninth inning of the fourth game when Hugh Casey appeared to strike out Tommy Heinrich for a Dodger win. But the pitch, a big, sweeping curve, hit the side of catcher Mickey Owen's glove. As the ball skittered away, Heinrich ran safely to first. With two outs the Yanks then scored four runs and held off the Dodgers in the bottom of the inning to win. After the game MacPhail walked fully clothed into the showers to console Owen.

The Yankees finished the Dodgers off the next day. The loyalists at Ebbets, who knew how great their team was, were so lost in their grief that hardly any of them noticed that at the end of the game a fire broke out on the roof of the grandstand.

The defeat would haunt fans and players alike through the fall. (Owen returned to his farm in the Midwest and in a ritual of expiation sold his herd of goats—no use keeping these reminders of his World Series role—and replaced them with cattle.) In contrast, the team's executives and owners reveled in their ledger-book victories. In his 1941 report to his board of directors, MacPhail crowed about increased revenues and cash surpluses. Looking at the Dodgers' greatest financial asset, young players who could be developed or sold, he added, "Brooklyn is on a better basis today from a standpoint of player production than any club in the National League except St. Louis."

BRIGHT AS THE FUTURE seemed in the fall of 1941, even MacPhail would find his optimism challenged after the December 7 Japanese attack on Pearl Harbor finally pushed America into the Second World War. In February of 1942 the Dodgers went to spring training camp in Havana in a subdued mood. As fighting forces were mobilized, young men were drafted and resources were shifted to military purposes. Future Hall of Famers Hank Greenberg and Bob Feller joined the service over the winter. Dodger Don Padgett spent just a few days in spring camp before he left for the Army.

Ballplayers being ballplayers, those who remained on the team managed to enjoy themselves in their tropical training grounds. Havana's casinos, nightclubs, and recently opened Tropicana cabaret offered more distractions per square mile than any other spring training site. Games at La Tropical Stadium were casual affairs that attracted prominent vacationers and locals. Ernest Hemingway attended almost every day and befriended several players. He took them to a shooting club where they fired on both real and clay pigeons and then to dinner at his country house with his third wife, Martha Gellhorn, the famous war correspondent.

The after-dinner conversation at the Hemingway house focused on the war and battles in Burma, where the Japanese were sweeping aside Allied defenders on their way toward China. (Hemingway had once reported from Burma and predicted that China's last overland supply route would be severed.) Sometime after Gellhorn went to bed and he gave the players signed copies of *For Whom the Bell Tolls*, a thoroughly drunk Hemingway challenged the man nearest his size, Apple Cheeks Casey, to play his favorite game: fighting.

Casey was more like Hemingway than the writer could have imagined. He was plagued by self-doubt and dark moods and drank to great excess. When Hemingway challenged him, he demurred at first. He was fourteen years younger than Hemingway and had boxed competitively. He didn't want to show up the man in his own house. But the old writer kept pushing until Casey agreed.

Hemingway disappeared and returned with two sets of red boxing gloves. He laced on one pair and Casey put on the other. When all was ready, Hemingway attacked Casey with all his might, throwing kicks along with punches. Finally a bookcase came crashing onto the floor, making a sound like an explosion. Gellhorn came downstairs and, as one of the players remembered it, Hemingway said, "Oh, we are just playing. Go to bed, honey." The fight continued until Casey knocked Hemingway down for good. Soon afterward, the gathering broke up. If the two men ever met again, no record of the event was made, but they were joined, in a way, in death. Casey, distraught over a series of tragedies, would commit suicide by shotgun on July 2, 1951. Exactly ten years and one day later, Hemingway would do the same.

The '42 Dodgers missed capturing the pennant by two games as the Cardinals ended the season by winning twenty-one out of twenty-six games and grabbing first place. (The key to their success was the Rickey-built farm system, which supplied replacements for veterans who went off to war.) St. Louis upset the Yankees to win the World Series and prove Rickey's wisdom by winning three more pennants and two more series in the next four years.

With most of the Dodgers' star players serving military duty, the team would take a nosedive, becoming Bums again as they slumped to third in 1943 and then seventh in 1944, with a 63–91 record. But while the Dodgers watched the Cardinals grab pennants and rings, in this time they got something more important for the long term: the services of Branch Rickey.

THE DODGERS HAD an opening in their executive offices because at the end of the 1942 season Larry MacPhail opted out of a five-year contract to join the U.S. Army. He announced this decision at a press conference where he appeared in his usual double-breasted suit, joked with friendly reporters, and then sobbed as he reminisced about his Brooklyn experience. Days later he reported for duty in Washington, where he was commissioned a lieutenant colonel. Although he wanted to serve in the artillery, MacPhail was too old for combat. He was assigned to the supply service. Rumors about Rickey coming to Brooklyn spread immediately. The prospect of a Rickey man being replaced by the original himself thrilled local fans.

A gravel-voiced man with bushy eyebrows who generally appeared in a cloud of cigar smoke, Rickey was baseball's genius impresario. He spoke in such a flowery and philosophical way that reporters sometimes left him feeling completely confused and befuddled. But no one in the history of the game enjoyed a better reputation for hard work, sound judgment, and leadership. Indeed, his well-known public persona—learned, moral, sober, and loquacious—had long served as a kind of disinfectant for the sport, counteracting the effects of scandal and disreputable characters.

During Rickey's brief (1905–07) career as a no-hit, no-field major-league catcher, professional ballplayers were typically rough characters and the game was rife with gamblers and con men. When he stopped playing he went to the University of Michigan to earn a law degree, worked in and out of baseball as an executive, and then fought in World War I. He got back into baseball management in St. Louis at the time of the Black Sox scandal—eight White Sox players were indicted for throwing the World Series—when public trust for the sport was at its lowest point.

In Branch Rickey, the morally bankrupt game had a man who first gained notice beyond the sports page as a tireless campaigner for the temperance movement and the benefits of virtue and sobriety. Inside baseball, he developed a reputation for shrewd judgment and moral superiority that moved one St. Louis sportswriter to describe him as "a trifle too good, too religious, too strict, too Puritanical . . ." Rickey liked to get a player young so he could mold him, and preferred him to marry and have children as soon as possible. Family responsibilities made a man more reliable and more pliable during salary negotiations.

Player contract talks generally meant take-it-or-leave-it deals averaging $5,000 per year. "They were tough with money. You would go in and Mr. Rickey would say, 'We've decided to let you come back,'" recalled Carl Erskine, whom Rickey would sign in 1946. "He was a great psychologist. With me he took the father-figure approach and it worked. I never felt like I was really cheated, but those conversations were not like ordinary business negotiations."

But then, baseball was not an ordinary business. A 1922 Supreme Court decision allowed the sixteen owners in the National and American leagues to operate as a monopoly. They refused to allow new teams and cities into the game, which meant no major-league ball west of the Mississippi or south of Washington, D.C. In 1940 a group that offered $5 million to move the bedraggled St. Louis Browns to Los Angeles was rebuffed because the other owners didn't want their teams traveling that far to play games. A year later, after a season when attendance was an abysmal 165,000, Browns owner Donald Barnes pushed again for the move but was blocked.

While the owners limited distribution of their product, they controlled their main cost—player salaries—with a bit of boilerplate language found in every contract. Called the reserve clause, it required a player to renegotiate with his team every winter or sit out the upcoming season. Further control was exercised by the commissioner, who was appointed by the owners and could punish a player for defecting to an upstart league or otherwise challenging the monopoly. Other restraints on free trade, like the ban on black ballplayers, were practiced by silent agreement.

The owners, who were millionaires back when that meant something, found it easy to agree on policies and practices, because they were as much partners as competitors. Sure, each one wanted to win a pennant and reap the windfall of World Series ticket sales and greater fan interest the following season. But before they could compete for the big prize, they needed to protect their sixteen fiefdoms and their leagues. As the legendary baseball man Joe Cronin would say, "The players come and go, but the owners stay on forever."

Led by Rickey and the St. Louis organization, the owners and their managers had tightened their hold by acquiring minor-league teams that faltered during the Great Depression. The minor-league clubs became training sites where very young players would, as Rickey said, "ripen into money." When a man was ready for the big leagues, he could be brought up at nominal expense or his services could be sold at a windfall profit to another club.

In this way the minor-league teams operated like farms filled with racehorses in training to run or go to auction. Like racehorses, the players saw none of the cash that was exchanged for their performances and potential. But that doesn't mean that executives like Rickey didn't love them. He idealized the game and its players and practiced a form of psychological denial common among team owners and executives. Athletes didn't work at baseball, he reasoned, they *played* it. It was practically an art form, and talking about baseball as if it were any other crass business was so impolite that it might even break the spell of belief that bound people to the game.

Most fans felt the same way as they flocked to ballparks for a few hours of distracted bliss, investing their hearts and minds in performances that were divorced from their real world of war and struggle, gains, and losses. As Williams Carlos Williams wrote in his poem "The Crowd at the Ballgame," they came to see "the flash of genius—all to no end save beauty." It was this ephemeral beauty that was supposed to motivate the players, and it was this same beauty that was sold to those who bought tickets because watching a game made them feel something about their team, their community, and themselves.

As he sold players and fans on the aura of baseball, Rickey also used his charm and his persuasiveness to get the most cash possible for himself. In St. Louis his base pay rose to $50,000, which was ten times the amount paid the average player and twice the amount paid to the National League's top performer, Mel Ott. Rickey also got a commission on player sales and other incentives that boosted his income to $80,000, a bit more than the salary paid to the president of the United States.

Rickey was known to the public for a blend of piety, toughness, ambition, and achievement that represented the era's ideal white, Protestant, midwestern man. He sometimes used the phrase "ferocious gentleman" to describe the kind of person he admired, and the tag stuck to him. His thinking about baseball players became so influential that in September of 1942, when Red Barber published an essay called "Prescription for a Ball Player," it read as if it had been pulled out of Rickey's brain: "A player may have man power, a live body, the right disposition and yet fail because by his habits off the field he weakens himself. Many a career has been destroyed by bad moral habits."

The formula called for a fine fellow who would have appealed to America's mothers and fathers. If they could believe the heroes of the diamond were honest and true and went to bed early to protect their health, they might buy their sons tickets to see games and even take in a doubleheader themselves. This was how image became money. Of course, real fans knew that most ballplayers fell short of the ideal, and some of the very best performers—like the raucous Ruth and rough-edged Durocher—missed the mark by a mile. (Always ferocious,

Durocher often had trouble with the gentleman part of Rickey's equation.) Many fans admired those rascally players who could perform when hungover or under investigation. This was doubly true in spit-and-grit Brooklyn, where many considered a punch below the belt perfectly acceptable, as long as it was thrown by a member of the home team.

The Dodger team was loaded with scrappy players but lacked leadership. James Mulvey, who represented McKeever's heirs, and George Barnewall of the Brooklyn Trust Company, which stood for the Ebbets clan, handled the search for MacPhail's replacement. Mulvey, who was movie producer Samuel Goldwyn's tough right-hand man, tried to knock down the idea that the club was "on its knees to Mr. Rickey." From his perspective Rickey had reached the end of his contract with the Cardinals, and at age sixty-one he might not have had many moves left. In Brooklyn, a richer club than St. Louis, he might get the chance to install his system and buy the best players in the pursuit of a dynasty to rival the Yankees. As Mulvey told the press, "It's the best job in baseball."

Like Mulvey, Rickey used the press to make certain points. At first he refused to confirm or deny reports that he might leave his beloved St. Louis. Four days later, after a twenty-four-hour visit to New York, he flatly denied meeting with Dodgers officials—or talking about the team "with anyone"—even though he stayed with his son Branch Jr., who had worked in the Dodgers' front office since 1939.

It took about a week for the denials to turn into a deal. When it was done, the ferocious gentleman got a five-year contract and bonuses based on attendance and the team's performance. He also negotiated an extra no other executive could claim: a 15 percent commission on every player contract he sold. Theoretically this arrangement would motivate the old wheeler-dealer to get top value, which was good for the club. But just like a stockbroker, the only one certain to profit from every trade was the new general manager. Whatever the price another club might pay for one of his men, Rickey would get his cut.

In the moment he became Brooklyn's GM, Rickey talked in a way that suggested the team go back to the name Bridegrooms. He said that he envied the rival Cardinals, who had eleven young pitchers "all married with children" to bring to spring training. He also cracked down on gambling in the Dodger clubhouse, which under Durocher had become an informal casino where men played cards and dice and placed bets on horses with a resident bookie named

Memphis Engelberg. (Durocher was so confident in Engelberg's picks that he let the man fill out his betting card for the track.) Rickey banned Engelberg, stopped all the gambling, and fired Durocher's friend, a coach named Charlie Dressen, who wasn't allowed back until he showed he could control his betting habit.

The crackdown on a club that was notoriously wide open in a town that loved a rascal made some question whether Rickey was a good fit. His highfalutin way of speaking made one Giants executive cackle about his prospects in the gritty borough. "Rickey in Flatbush!" he said. "That's like *Alice in Wonderland.*" Sportswriters were both mesmerized and amused by Rickey's pronouncements. Tom Meany of the newspaper *PM* dubbed him "The Mahatma," after India's intellectual revolutionary Mohandas Gandhi. The nickname stuck.

Although Rickey worried about being accepted, Brooklyn turned out to have room for him. This was a place that had accommodated endless waves of immigration and supported, with equal fervor, a world-renowned art museum and the Coney Island amusement park. Besides, years of frustration had left Dodgers fans ready to embrace anyone who promised to lead them to victory, including a teetotaler from the Midwest. Rickey sealed their affection at a Rotary Club dinner he addressed soon after he was hired. Dodgers fans "say 'Pooh on the Giants,'" he noted, "and they are right."

ALTHOUGH HE DIDN'T SHOW up in any of the press reports, Walter O'Malley was present when the Dodgers brought the genius of St. Louis to Brooklyn. As George the Fifth's monitor and frequent legal adviser to the team, he would have been concerned about the contract the team offered Rickey and how its many incentives would affect the club's bottom line. However, he wasn't yet involved in the daily affairs of the baseball business. Most of his time still went into his law practice, and for a brief time in 1943 he considered leaving civilian life entirely to join in the war effort.

With his military schooling, reserve experience, and legal/business skills, O'Malley figured he was qualified for the rank of lieutenant colonel and he was interested in meaningful service overseas. In February 1943 the Army gave him a physical exam that included a race in shorts and T-shirt around 39 Whitehall

Street, a massive federal building in lower Manhattan, which he apparently passed.

Much as he wanted to serve, O'Malley was not willing to be mere fodder for some bureaucracy. In early March he wrote to an Army official explaining that he didn't want to abandon his legal practice "just to be assigned to some stupid task in this country." In another passage he said, "Frankly, I am not going to make what would be, to me, a tremendous sacrifice if, as a result, I am going to find myself behind a desk passing on five- and ten-cent requests." Although he had seen others take this route "just to have someone salute them," O'Malley was not so driven to see himself in khaki that he was willing to sacrifice his time and fortune—with a businessman's flourish he called it "capital"—for some inconsequential duty.

The match O'Malley wanted would never be made. By mid-March the Army declared him unfit for combat because of a recurrent hernia and did not offer him the kind of administrative job he hoped to win. But he would find a way to contribute to the war effort as managing director of the Kingsbury Ordnance Plant, which Todd & Brown had built in the Indiana countryside, near Culver Academy. It was hardly a full-time occupation, however, and O'Malley was able to devote increasing amounts of time to the Dodgers, where he would see Rickey at the top of his game and witness history.

Rickey often spoke of baseball in a self-conscious way, as if he understood it was not an essential thing, like science or medicine or law. But he also thought in historical terms and knew he was an actor on a stage that faced a very big audience. If he was going to do anything of consequence in his life, it would be in the game. For this reason, and the fact that it made business sense, Rickey met with both the Dodgers directors and George V. McLaughlin to discuss bringing a black player into the big leagues.

The setting was a lunch at a private dining room at the New York Athletic Club. Rickey began by offering a dismal assessment of the Dodgers' future without an influx of new, young players. Since the war effort claimed almost every able-bodied boy the moment he became a man, he proposed a plan to scout and sign players as young as fifteen. This group "might include a Negro player or two," said Rickey.

Across the table, George V. McLaughlin sat silent for a moment. As police commissioner, McLaughlin had named the first black sergeant in the city police department's history and saw that his decision was generally accepted. Considering similar integration in baseball, he said, "I don't see why not." Referring to the prevailing prejudice in baseball, he added, "If you find the right man, who is better than the others, you'll beat it."

McLaughlin could not have been shocked by Rickey's proposal. It was not an original idea. Politicians in New York, including Brooklyn's famous communist city councilman Peter Cacchione, had been calling for integration for years. College sports editors had jumped on the bandwagon in 1940 with a pro-integration petition and in 1942 both the Cleveland Indians and Pittsburgh Pirates said they were looking for black players and intended to conduct tryouts.

But while he wasn't the first to raise the idea, Rickey would pursue it in a more deliberate manner. Instead of a showy tryout where dozens of black players might demonstrate their talents, he would search quietly for a prospect, groom him in the minors, and bring him up at the right moment. And while he would agree that breaking the game's bigotry was important, Rickey would also describe this effort as a matter of good business.

He was right. In barring blacks, baseball had done what no reasonable industry would ever do: turned its back on a vast and available pool of customers. The sport's leaders might argue that fans would stay away from integrated games, but since no major-league team played south of the Mason-Dixon line, and black athletes drew huge crowds of whites to boxing matches and track meets, this fear was unwarranted. Fans liked winners, whatever their color, and the first team to tap this great pool of talent would win.

The early search for a player who would break segregation included a secret mission carried out by O'Malley the lawyer, who flew to Havana to see a Cuban infielder named Silvio Garcia. Although a bit old for a prospect—he was born in 1914—Garcia was a terrific fielder and good hitter who had batted better than .400 in spring training games against the Dodgers. In Havana, O'Malley discovered Garcia was serving in the Cuban military. He didn't think it would be wise to hire someone out of a foreign army to replace an American who had gone to war. Rickey took his advice.

Garcia lost his chance, but the process that would lead to the end of big-league segregation had begun. Rickey continued to search for his pioneer while he revamped the team's leadership. He invited Durocher to return as manager and kept his son in the position of farm team director. He retained Buzzie Bavasi as a junior executive and recruited a clutch of veterans—George Sisler, J. Rex Bowen, Clyde Sukeforth, and Wid Matthews—to coach and scout talent.

Fanned out across the country, Rickey and his men soon discovered and signed a corps of young players who would go to war and then return to Ebbets Field. Among them were future Hall of Famer Edwin "Duke" Snider and pitchers Carl Erskine and Ralph Branca. While he would have to wait out the war before he could use these young prospects, Rickey immediately grabbed a couple of aged free-agent outfielders—Paul Waner, thirty-nine, and Johnny Cooney, forty-two—to replace Pete Reiser, who had joined all the other major leaguers in the service. Facing wartime opponents, Cooney and Waner both played well.

Rickey knew talent, but his judgment wasn't perfect, and he sometimes went too far with his moralizing. In 1943 he traded a quality player named Babe Dahlgren to the Phillies for an outfielder who chose not to report and a utility player named Alban Glossop. Glossop proved a bust. Dahlgren had an all-star year in Philadelphia. Why did Rickey let him go? He believed false rumors that Dahlgren smoked marijuana and, rather than trust him, chose to get rid of him and then contributed to the gossip. The truth wouldn't come out until long after Dahlgren's death in 1996.

That Rickey was capable of such harsh judgment based on destructive gossip might surprise a casual fan who accepted the man's public persona. But as much as he cultivated a refined Christian image, Rickey could be cold and unfair (hence one of the many nicknames he received from New York writers: El Cheapo). Altogether he was a complex and egocentric man who was brilliant but also flawed. Soon enough Rickey would begin working with a younger man who could match his intelligence and his ambition, if not his baseball genius.

During the war years, Walter O'Malley had gradually taken on more of the Dodgers' legal work. The transition suited O'Malley, who enjoyed being around baseball. The ball club also needed the help. Onetime Culver boy Wendell Willkie, who long led the legal group that had served the Dodgers, had begun traveling the world to support the war effort. He joined rallies in support of European Jews, advocated the rights of American blacks, and authored *One World*, which called for peacekeeping by international forces and sold more than a million copies. He hardly ever had time for the Dodgers anymore.

O'Malley became the equivalent of house counsel for the team and gradually relinquished his role in the law practice he had started after leaving Fordham. He spent more and more time at the Dodgers' office, which was in the
ten-story Mechanics Bank Building on Montague Street, and at Ebbets Field,
where the daffiness days of strikeouts and errors seemed to return. The Dodgers finished 1943 with just eighty-one wins and twenty-three and a half games
out of first. But at least the team held on to its name. In a bid to rev up interest,
Robert Carpenter Jr., owner of the last-place Philadelphia club, tried to cheer
up fans by letting them select a new nickname—Blue Jays—and they played as
the Jays for the entire season.

In the game of business played off the field, which O'Malley played with the
same ferocity that Durocher and Rickey brought to the diamond, the Dodgers
proved to be much stronger. Early in 1944, a Brooklyn businessman named Max
Meyer, who was Casey Stengel's friend and once owned part of the Boston
Braves, approached the Dodgers about the stock held by the Ebbets and Edward
McKeever heirs. Although Steven McKeever's daughter, Marie "Dearie" Mulvey,
once again refused to sell, Meyer negotiated for the 75 percent of the team held
by the others. An agreement seemed close until Meyer suddenly withdrew his
$1 million offer. An argument would ensue, with George the Fifth insisting
that Meyer had offered no credible reason for backing out. But whatever his
excuse, Meyer had at least accomplished two important things: First he established the fact that a controlling interest in the Dodgers could be had. Second,
he had set a rough price for the stock.

Four

RICKEY, O'MALLEY, AND SMITH

I n the early 1940s, baseball thought so much of itself as a national emblem that owners, managers, and athletes suffered over whether play should continue during wartime. Was the country in such peril that the games would be unseemly? Or was baseball so much a part of the nation's identity that they were needed to boost morale? Commissioner Landis wrote the president for guidance. Keen politician that he was, Franklin Delano Roosevelt was not about to interfere with the sporting sacrament. He replied:

> I honestly feel that it would be best for the country to keep baseball going . . . Baseball provides a recreation which does not last over two hours or two hours and a half, and which can be got for very little cost. . . . As to the players themselves, I know you agree with me that the individual players who are active military or naval age should go, without question, into the services. Even if the actual quality to the teams is lowered . . .

The games continued, but as FDR predicted, the quality declined as hundreds of ballplayers traded one uniform for another. During the war years the Dodgers saw about three-quarters of their men under contract leave for the military. As a result, the Brooklyn roster, like those in other cities, was filled out with old-timers, promising teenagers, and many who wouldn't have made it out of the minors under normal conditions. Typical was John "Fats" Dantonio of the New Orleans Pelicans, who became a Dodger catcher in 1944, played a total of fifty games, hit zero home runs, and made fourteen errors. But still the games went on, because sport was a patriotic necessity. The British had carried on with cricket, even during the Blitz; and after the Nazis invaded the Soviet Union, 100,000 people went to a soccer game at Dynamo Stadium in Moscow. It wasn't the quality on the field that counted but the spirit.

Besides continuing to play, teams helped the war effort by conserving critical commodities. They took the rubber out of baseballs (making it less lively for hitters) and held spring training in the North to conserve fuel. (The Dodgers made camp at Bear Mountain resort fifty miles north of the city, and used indoor facilities at West Point.) Teams also conducted bond drives and charity games to support troops abroad. Brooklyn fans bought nearly forty-three thousand tickets—eight thousand were purchased by contributors who didn't ask for a seat—to an exhibition game that raised almost $59,000 for the Navy Relief Society.

In June of 1944, the three New York teams played one of the strangest baseball contests ever held, with every dollar collected at the gate going to war bonds. The fifty thousand who jammed the Polo Grounds first got to see a pregame circus of baseball talent announced by former mayor Jimmy Walker, still a dandy at age sixty-three. A Choctaw Indian teenager named Calvin Coolidge Julius Caesar Tuskahoma McLish, who was a Dodger pitcher, won a fungo-hitting contest with a blast that traveled 416 feet 5 inches. (Hitting this way involves tossing a ball in the air and smacking it with a special skinny bat.) Dodger catcher Bobby Bragan was best in the throwing competition, firing from home plate to a barrel at second, and George Stirnweiss of the Yankees finished first in the base-running race. Next the fans were treated to skits and tricks performed by a retired major leaguer who made his living by performing as a pregame clown. Al Schacht's bits included a pantomime of a pitcher getting shellacked by invisible hitters and pulling an extravagant meal out of a huge catcher's mitt and dining on home plate.

When they finally got to the game, the Yanks, Giants, and Dodgers followed a format devised by a math professor at Columbia. The setup gave each squad six innings in the field and six innings at bat. The Dodgers scored five runs, the

Yankees one, and the Giants none. Brooklyn showed the better pitching, including a good performance by eighteen-year-old Ralph Branca, who had been a major leaguer all of three weeks and was the best of a young lot, including McLish and Charlie Osgood, whom local writers dubbed the Kindergarten Boys. "The people got in free if they bought a bond, and it was our chance to do something for the war," recalled Branca many years later. "I also got the chance to pitch against hitters for the Yankees, who we wouldn't see otherwise."

Although it was dimmed a bit by the war, Branca was living a young ballplayer's dream. He had pitched for New York University on May 30, signed his pro contract on June 6, (the same date as the "D-Day" Allied invasion of Europe), and played in his first major-league game on June 11. In his first three appearances—all away games—he threw for six and one-third innings, giving up just two hits and one run. Reality finally struck in his first game at Ebbets Field, when the Giants hit Branca hard. In the season that followed the war bond exhibition, the kid from Mount Vernon, New York, struggled with an earned run average of over seven per game and walked twice as many hitters as he struck out. However, he was a bit better than McLish and Osgood, who appeared in one game that season and never again pitched in the majors.

At season's end the lowly St. Louis Browns won the American League title with the lowest winning percentage in history. The triumph of the Browns, who had lost 111 games as recently as 1939 and never before claimed a pennant, was a symbol of degraded major-league play. Sportswriters were so aghast they refused to name a member of the team the league's Most Valuable Player. For their part, the Dodgers finished forty-two games behind the Cardinals, who beat the Browns in a streetcar World Series that generated so little excitement that the games drew fewer fans than the minor-league championship played in Baltimore that same year.

In another first, Commissioner Landis missed the 1944 World Series. He had attended every one since he was elected by the owners, in 1920, and his absence signaled something serious. The seventy-eight-year-old Landis had gone to a Chicago hospital in late September, ostensibly for a checkup, but had been kept there by doctors. In November, with his specific illness still secret from the public, an owners committee recommended he be given a new seven-year term in office. Intended to boost the old man's morale, the vote was merely symbolic. Before the month was over, Landis died of heart disease.

Baseball's first and to this moment only commissioner, Landis was recalled as a man who was so firm that he banned the Black Sox players for life, and so fair that he suspended the great Babe Ruth for defying his rules on postseason exhibition tours. He was proud of the ways he had helped ballplayers individually and as a group: when Landis released more than a hundred players from onerous minor-league contracts, he even claimed, with unintentioned irony, that he had freed "slave" athletes. In the celebration of his life, little if any notice was made of the well-known fact that he had done nothing to help free the game itself from the shame of racial segregation. Instead he had maintained the silent agreement that kept black players out. Likewise, no one mentioned that with Landis gone and the war's end on the horizon, a game that had been preserved in amber when the old judge took control in 1921 was about to enter a great new era.

ANY OUTSIDER WHO EXAMINED baseball in the waning years of the war would have seen a low-grade product, miserable attendance figures, and withering press attention. In Brooklyn, Walter F. O'Malley could make a closer evaluation as he quietly performed his lawyer's work for the Dodgers and consulted every once in a while—in Room 40 of the Hotel Bossert and at the Brooklyn Trust Company—with his banker friend George V. McLaughlin.

Though hardly an expert on the game, O'Malley was falling in love with baseball as it was played on the field and in the front office. He threw himself into mundane legal chores—contracts, labor issues, tax matters—and made a thorough study of the more exciting parts of the business. Broadcasting rights, corporate sponsorships, and even stadium management fascinated O'Malley, as did the team's relations with the press and public.

There was something about a baseball team, unlike every other business, that made people open their hearts. Teams carried the hometown, written across their chests, onto the field. Sportswriters turned their performances into ongoing epics of victories and defeats, dreams achieved, and hopes dashed. And as the games, statistics, incidents, and images piled onto each other, fans first imagined and then accepted without much doubt or dissent that their team reflected something about the character of a certain place or person. Fans, cities, and entire regions would come together as a group to identify with a team.

(Thanks to its place as the center of the national media, New York teams also had followers scattered across the country.) And whether it made sense or not, thousands if not millions of people experienced personal highs and lows as if what happened on the field were actually happening to them in real life.

In the minds of New Yorkers, and for that matter all Americans, the Dodgers *were* Brooklyn in all its striving and insecurity, its hopes, and its fears. This close identification was a matter of interpretation, of course, a mass delusion born of the human desire to turn life itself into a story. But it happened nonetheless. Players got their roles as heroes, goats, underdogs, et cetera. Managers and executives were supposed to guide the team like the wise elders of the village. For the owners there was fun and profit—just as long as you won enough games to keep the hopes of the fans alive.

Unfortunately, the Dodgers weren't winning enough games in the mid-1940s, and so few people went to Ebbets that the mood in the stands could be downright gloomy. No one liked to lose, but the team's struggle during the war years was, if not planned, expected. In his May 1943 report to the board, president Branch Rickey abandoned the rah-rah spirit he demanded of others and announced, "It is now my judgment that this club cannot win the pennant." He predicted that the Dodgers would finish no higher than fifth (actually they came in third), openly resigned himself to short-term mediocrity, and focused on his long-term strategy.

The future would be built on youth. Always wary of "ten-year men" who had passed their prime, Rickey wanted to trade or sell popular, highly paid stars like Fred "Dixie" Walker and Dolph Camilli and replace them with cheaper, younger prospects. To find these prospects he wrote to thousands of high school coaches and recruited more than one hundred of them to act as "bird dogs" for his scouts. Following their leads and staging dozens of tryouts across the country, the Rickey men evaluated nearly five thousand young players and signed the best to low-cost contracts. Some of these would make the big club. Others would be sold at a profit to teams that didn't work so hard to find and develop players. In this way the investment in scouting/training could become a self-funding project that delivered perennial dividends on the field and at the bank.

With such a big supply of inexpensive talent, Brooklyn was poised to compete for both profits and championships as soon as the war ended and life returned to normal. If history was any indicator, all of baseball was going to enjoy a great lift once the troops came home. After World War I, gate receipts had bounced back smartly, but more important, except for the worst years of the Great Depression, attendance had grown more rapidly than the population. In 1920, 106 million Americans bought 96 million tickets. In 1940, 132 million people purchased 135 million tickets. It didn't take much foresight to imagine that when the GIs came home, married, and had children, the robust growth in population and baseball would resume. And since they weren't making any more major-league teams—the same sixteen had held a monopoly since the year O'Malley was born—fans would have no choice but to go to the same old ballparks and support the same old teams.

Sitting in "the catbird seat" (one of Brooklyn broadcaster Red Barber's favorite expressions), O'Malley saw that the team's operation was becoming more rational and its finances more stable. He also understood baseball's long-term potential. Still relatively young at age forty-one, he could anticipate being part of future glories. Others were not so sanguine. By early 1944, Edward McKeever's heirs had endured nearly twenty years of boardroom squabbles, financial perils, and uneven play on the field. The big-league team had finished the previous year with just a small profit and on the first road trip of this new season lost ten out of fourteen games. Soon the Dodgers' goal became avoiding a last-place finish. No longer interested in waiting for what *could* be, Edward McKeever's descendants notified team lawyer O'Malley that they wanted to sell their quarter interest in the team as soon as they could get a decent price.

The other owners had claims on stock as it became available, and so O'Malley first consulted James Mulvey, whose wife, Marie, was the other McKeever daughter and thus controlled 25 percent of the club. The Mulveys weren't interested in upping their stake. The fractious Ebbets heirs, who numbered more than twenty and owned half the club, were even less inclined toward buying. They wanted out of baseball entirely but were still too mired in their own conflicts to make a deal. The most prominent among them, Charlie Ebbets Jr., had recently changed the complex family dynamic by dying in a Brooklyn boardinghouse and leaving two-thirds of his estate to a former housekeeper and one-third to his actual wife.

With the way clear of other bidders, and all the inside information he needed, O'Malley began to work on the deal that would set the course for the rest of his life. At a price of about $250,000, the McKeever block was too expensive for him to handle alone. But if he broke it into smaller pieces, then he could keep one for himself and get a seat on the board of directors. From this position it would be possible to eventually buy out the Ebbets family, should they ever settle their differences.

Before he could carry out his big plan, O'Malley needed to find partners. He turned first to Andrew Schmitz, a longtime Dodgers fan who was Everett McCooey's partner in an insurance firm. Schmitz agreed to participate in buying the 25 percent of the stock owned by the McKeever estate. O'Malley then approached Branch Rickey with the offer he had waited a lifetime to hear.

With only sixteen teams, the fraternity of major-league owners was small, and despite his efforts to join, Rickey had been excluded for forty years. This time he was invited into an owners group eager for his baseball credentials. Rickey didn't have any money to put into the deal. In fact, he was $300,000 in debt and so short on assets that he had borrowed on his life insurance. No problem, said O'Malley: he could arrange financing. It would have to be nearly total, said Rickey. "We're prepared to carry you," answered O'Malley.

The "we" O'Malley mentioned included the Brooklyn Trust Company, which would supply much if not all of the actual cash paid to the McKeever group. McLaughlin's bank was having a record year and had recently raised its dividend by 15 percent. He could expect that the Dodger loans would be repaid through postwar revenues, and with the McKeevers out, McLaughlin would expect to see a friendlier face—Walter O'Malley's—on the board of directors.

The stock sale was completed six weeks after the end of the season. It was announced with just the slightest bit of fanfare—a brief press conference where O'Malley and Schmitz presented themselves as "Brooklyn boys" who were determined to keep ownership "in Brooklyn, where it belongs," said Schmitz. Though he and O'Malley had little baseball experience, fans were reassured by the news that the Mahatma of Montague Street had three years left on his contract as president of the team.

This assurance was genuine. Rickey enjoyed unqualified support from Schmitz and O'Malley. Rickey got further backing a few months later when Schmitz was replaced by a new owner, John L. Smith. The president of Pfizer Phamaceuticals, a Brooklyn company, Smith called Rickey "a fine operator, a moral man, a man with faith and principles, grand company even if he won't take a drink. . . . I know that the writers kid him a lot about his double talk, so called, but he is a very coherent man, believe me."

By the summer of 1945 those who followed the team closely understood that the O'Malley ownership group had their eyes on the Ebbets shares, too. Now on the board of directors, where he acted as secretary, O'Malley began negotiations to purchase them. The other side was represented by George V. McLaughlin and two of the Ebbets heirs, Joseph A. Gilleaudeau and Grace Slade Ebbets. Their goal was a price that would allow everyone with a claim to the original estate enough cash to end disputes that had raged in the courts since 1925.

Although George the Fifth had been O'Malley's mentor and ally, he didn't make it easy. He and the other negotiators turned down offers staked at the price paid for the McKeever shares, holding out for a premium. At one point, six months passed without much progress. The two men saw each other often, and even went to see some boxing matches in early March, but the negotiations remained deadlocked.

McLaughlin had no reason to rush. Charles Ebbets had been dead twenty years. What were a few months more? McLaughlin also had plenty of other work to occupy his time. The bank was growing, and as a commissioner of the Triborough Bridge and Tunnel Authority, which was headed by Robert Moses, he was deeply involved in a massive program of bridge, tunnel, and parkway construction. McLaughlin could wait for O'Malley and company to meet his terms for the Dodgers stock.

IN THIS TIME, the O'Malley group did business as if they already controlled the team. At Rickey's urging, the Dodgers bought a minor-league team in Fort Worth for roughly $50,000, even though the Texas League, where it competed, didn't plan to play until the war was over. Before spring training began, the team raised the number of players under contract to over five hundred. Once they returned from the war, these players—enough to stock the entire National League—could be scattered in the Dodgers' network of minor-league clubs, where they would be trained according to Rickey's principles, which emphasized basic athleticism and clean living.

These moves were made with confidence now that Commissioner Landis, the main opponent to Rickey's type of player-development scheme, had died.

No one else in the game seemed to mind if a big-league club wanted to scoop up minor-league teams and turn them into feedlots for the majors. And Landis's eventual replacement, a U.S. senator from Kentucky named Albert "Happy" Chandler, would not rise against this practice. Chandler would be more concerned with major-league baseball's relationship with the wider society. He would order ballplayers to stay away from gamblers, bookies, and racetracks and would be in favor of integrating the game.

As spring training began, the leagues faced restrictions on travel in order to save fuel, and a manpower crisis that affected every team. The most able-bodied ballplayers were at war, and many of those who were too old or otherwise unfit for combat had been assigned by the government to stateside jobs that they couldn't leave without permission. Nevertheless, baseball would soldier on. In Washington, the Senators' owner, Clark Griffith, said, "We're going to play even if we have to use nine old men."

Just eight lonely players showed up for the first day of the Dodgers' camp at Bear Mountain. Manager Leo Durocher, who later described many of them as "not really ballplayers, just guys wearing uniforms," was so discouraged he said he might play shortstop himself. The Lip had played fewer than thirty-five games as a fill-in since 1941, and he was almost forty years old. At this he was still younger than catcher Clyde Sukeforth, a forty-three-year-old scout who hadn't played since 1934 but trained at Bear Mountain and would catch eighteen games in the coming season.

Happy to stir up some publicity, Rickey told reporters he would give Durocher $1,000 if he played the first fifteen games of the regular season. Durocher, who lived the high life and always looked for ways to make money, cornered Rickey and got him to repeat the challenge. "I'll take it," he crowed. Durocher played second base on opening day, started there for the second game of the season, but took the bench in favor of a pinch hitter in the fifth inning. Having proved to himself that he wasn't up to the grind, he never played again.

Although he departed the field, Durocher still managed to be part of the show. On the day after he gave up second base, he drew a thousand laughs at the Polo Grounds when he swiped Mayor La Guardia's hat before the opening pitch of a game against the Giants. Throughout the season Durocher bellowed to reporters and harassed umpires with such fury and glee that he was often banished to the clubhouse.

Fans in Brooklyn enjoyed Durocher's street-tough act, and more than a few expressed themselves with equal passion, whether they were with him or against him. Sometimes fruits, vegetables, and even beer and pop bottles rained down on the field along with the booing and the catcalls, but for the most part the abuse fans delivered was verbal and not physical. Typical was one heckler, seated high above third base, who made sure half the people in the stadium heard him lace into Durocher after Lippy challenged an umpire's call in the second inning of a Saturday night game in early June. The Dodgers manager was "a crook and a bum" who was "trying to steal the ball game," shouted twenty-one-year-old John Christian, who had gone to Ebbets Field with a bunch of friends, including a local basketball star named Jacob "Dutch" Garfinkel.

The game went Brooklyn's way early and became a 9–1 laugher. (Even Fats Dantonio got two hits in four at bats.) But Durocher wasn't amused. He was still annoyed by the previous day's game, which the Dodgers lost by handing eight unearned runs to the hated Giants by committing eight errors. Their humiliation was captured in a magnificent compound sentence composed by John Drebinger of the *New York Times*:

After Ott opened with a single, Augie Galan dropped a fly ball in left, Infielders Bazinski and Luis Olmo gummed up a couple of double play grounders, and for a final stroke, Center Fielder Goody Rosen, who was playing almost in the shadow of second base, doubtless to see what was going on around there, saw Mungo clout the ball over his surprised noggin for a rousing triple.

Whatever the reason for Durocher's pique, he ordered a stadium security guard—a hulking fellow named Joseph Moore—to bring the heckler to an office under the stands. In Christian's version of events, once they were alone, Moore hit him in the head with a weapon. (A later account said it was brass knuckles.) The Lip then used the same weapon to break his jaw. A decorated veteran of the very same U.S. Army that had finally defeated the Nazis three days earlier, Christian filed a complaint with the police, who tracked down Durocher and Moore and brought them to the hospital, where he identified them as his attackers.

A grand jury thought enough of Christian's claim to charge Durocher and

Moore with assault, prompting the kind of crisis that could hurt the Dodgers. It was one thing for Durocher to bark at umpires or for a rhubarb to turn into a melee on the field. It would be quite another if fans thought that if they blew a stray raspberry, they risked getting into a brawl with a security officer and the team manager.

Eager to protect the club, Rickey the baseball man and O'Malley the lawyer responded artfully to guide both the legal response and public sentiment. O'Malley quietly kept in touch with the district attorney's office, consulted directly with the manager and even conferred with George the Fifth on the matter. Durocher and Moore got a dream team for his defense before such a term was ever used. It included a former prosecutor, a criminal-defense specialist, and an investigator who went to Christian's neighborhood, the rough-edged part of Brooklyn called East New York, to check out the complainant. The private eye watched Christian for a rather boring two days as he hung out at a corner drugstore, handled slips of paper, and took one trip to Manhattan. The report, filed with O'Malley, concluded that he was a bookie even though "there has been no definite proof of this."

With little evidence to challenge Christian's motives or character, Durocher was ordered to settle a civil suit or risk losing his job. The cash that did the trick, $6,750 (the equivalent of $75,000 in 2009), came from a liability insurer and donations made by Durocher's buddies, including the comic actor Danny Kaye, who was a devout Dodgers fan. Kaye was riding high on reviews for his performance in *Wonder Man* (only his second starring role), which opened on the night that Durocher met Christian under the grandstand.

While O'Malley worked the legal end, Rickey defended his man and all Dodger players in a long-scheduled address to the local Rotary Club, which, in the sometimes small town that was Brooklyn, was led by former Dodgers board member George Barnewall. Flanked by several players and Durocher himself, Rickey said his organization "stands as a unit against unfair abuse, against indecent or unfair remarks from fans in the stands." Durocher said nothing about the criminal charges but did a little cheerleading about how his players "have it in mind to bring the pennant here."

Judge Samuel Liebowitz, who presided over Durocher's criminal trial, had risen to fame as the lead defense lawyer for the nine Scottsboro Boys, blacks who were wrongly accused of raping two white women in Alabama. (Over many years all nine were either acquitted, pardoned, or paroled.) At the Durocher trial Brooklyn's loyalties became clear when the judge tried to empanel a jury. The pool of potential jurors was filled with so many rabid Dodgers fans that more than seventy-five were questioned before a dozen could be seated.

The trial was a matter of conflicting stories, with Christian holding to his original report and Durocher insisting the man had slipped on a wet floor. Prosecutors suffered a setback when Dutch Garfinkel, who never saw what happened to Christian behind the closed door of the office he entered with Durocher, testified that the young complainant was a tough fellow who could defend himself.

By the time the trial was over, the twin mystiques of baseball and Brooklyn had turned the story of an assault on an injured vet into a Frank Capra–esque fable of the tough little manager who had confronted a no-good loudmouth. A verdict was reached in half an hour and the crowd of two hundred spectators erupted in cheers when foreman Hyman Shapiro uttered the words "Not guilty."

A big grin came over Durocher's face as Judge Liebowitz declared the verdict a just one and added he was glad the manager had been vindicated and "no discredit has been placed on the great American game of baseball."

Elated onlookers breached the barrier separating them from the defense table and swarmed Durocher. He had to fight his way out to the sixth-floor hallway, and when the elevator arrived, so many people crowded in with him that it sank down a foot before the door was closed. After the operator stopped on the fourth floor to get rid of excess weight, Durocher reached the lobby and then the sidewalk, where he was cheered again as he got into a friend's car and departed.

It was left for Commissioner Chandler to offer an opinion different from the crowd at the courthouse. "If ever there was a miscarriage of justice . . ." he said, "this was it. They didn't fool me at all, of course, I knew how crazy they were in Brooklyn about their ball team."

DURING THE SEASON THAT took place while Durocher faced assault charges, he rewarded the loyalty shown by O'Malley, Rickey, and all of Brooklyn by leading the team to a much-improved record. Instead of eighth place and more than forty games behind the Cardinals—their fate the year before—the Dodgers took third and missed the pennant by just eleven. (Philip "P.K." Wrigley's Chicago Cubs finished first and lost the World Series to Detroit.)

The team also made progress institutionally, as the group O'Malley created in 1944—minus Andrew Schmitz, who dropped out—finally met the Ebbets family's price for its 50 percent block of stock. The serious negotiations had resumed in June with a bid of $650,000 and had been concluded in August at a price that was reported as both $750,000 and $800,000 (about $8 million in 2009). At either figure, this represented at least a 50 percent increase over the price paid McKeever's heirs less than a year earlier. Given the club's wartime cash flow, they could hardly expect to get more. It was a good deal for O'Malley's side as well. With roughly $1 million, much if not all of it borrowed from the Brooklyn Trust Company, they secured control of a franchise with a rabid following that was poised to dominate the National League.

The sale was announced on Tuesday, August 14, at a 12:30 p.m. press conference at the Hotel Bossert, a date O'Malley recorded in red in his appointment book. The deal brought to an end the decades-long McKeever-Ebbets feud, which had twice brought the Dodgers to the brink of bankruptcy. John Smith, who wanted the pleasure of being involved with a team he loved but not the headaches, left things in the hands of Rickey and O'Malley, who became an effective management duo. As president, Rickey tended to the development and management of the team that took the field. O'Malley became vice president of the board and focused on the Dodgers operation as a business—revenue, expenses, and so forth—and its financial health.

The three men formalized their power-sharing in a document that divided ownership in thirds but also expressed their joint interest in controlling the team's affairs. This agreement bound them tightly together. No one partner could sell his shares to an outsider without allowing the others to match the offer. In the case of tie offers, the advantage went to the partners over an outsider. If one of them died, his heirs could sell to the remaining partners at the price he paid originally, plus any interest payments made to a lender.

In the face of this firmly united group, James Mulvey was odd man out, and he became an isolated and sometimes hostile member of the board, refusing to join the others in voting to accept reports and standing against renewal of Rickey's contract. Mulvey was accustomed to fighting against the odds. As president of Samuel Goldwyn's independent film company, he had spent decades battling major studios to get access to theaters and audiences. In that struggle, however, he had allies among the other independents. On the board he had none. The conflict reached a high point at a meeting where Mulvey refused O'Malley's request that he explain himself. "No comment" was all he said. At the next board election Mulvey was removed and state judge Henry Ughetta joined the directors group along with Hector Racine, who was president of the Montreal Royals, a Dodger-owned franchise in the International League.

BY SUMMER 1945 the war in Europe was over and the tide in the Pacific was running the Allies' way. In June the Philippines were liberated and four days later American forces captured Okinawa. Although complete victory would wait until September, the dreadfully awesome atomic attacks on Hiroshima and Nagasaki proved the inevitable. The troops, just about all of them, were coming home soon. They would bring their hopes for happy and prosperous civilian lives and, to some degree, a broader perspective on the world and human nature based on what they experienced abroad.

War had brought together Americans of different ethnicities, cultures, religions, and race. This mixing would be exaggerated in the media. Nearly all black soldiers and sailors, for example, had been consigned to second-class status for most of the war. Nevertheless, some hearts and minds were changed by contacts in the ranks and certain official acts. In 1941, President Roosevelt had outlawed discrimination in defense industries. General Eisenhower had welcomed black combat volunteers in early 1945, and in September the secretary of war appointed a commission that would soon recommend an end to all forms of segregation in the military.

At home, Gunnar Myrdal, backed by the Carnegie Foundation, had recently published a landmark book called *An American Dilemma*, which would begin a national conversation on race and usher in the civil rights movement. (With great prescience Myrdal wrote in his introduction that "not since Reconstruction has there been more reason to anticipate fundamental changes in American race relations...") In July, New York officials led by Governor Dewey created the first state fair employment law, which banned racial discrimination in hiring. In August, New York City mayor La Guardia brought the issue directly to baseball by appointing a committee to investigate discrimination in the game. Given his statements about "sheer prejudice" in the major leagues, no one could doubt where the mayor was heading.

Having already committed themselves to integrating the sport, the time had come for the Dodgers to act. With the help of a black reporter from Pittsburgh named Wendell Smith, Rickey began to focus on a Negro American League star named Jack Roosevelt "Jackie" Robinson. Having served a few tumultuous years in the military—he won a court-martial case based on trumped-up charges—Robinson was discharged before the war ended, without ever going overseas. He was already twenty-four years old when he joined the Kansas City Monarchs and hit .387 while playing shortstop. In early 1945, Red Sox officials facing local political pressure brought him to Fenway Park for a pro forma tryout. Robinson performed brilliantly, hitting one ball after another against or over the famous big green wall in left field. But the Red Sox, who never intended to sign a black player, let him go. A discouraged Wendell, who had accompanied Robinson to Boston, stopped to see Rickey on his way home.

With support from his partners O'Malley and Smith, Rickey invested heavily in scouting Robinson and other black players while at the same time disguising his intentions. He sent three different men to watch him play on three different occasions. All three gave Robinson top marks. Rickey also spent roughly $30,000 to create the Brooklyn Brown Dodgers and a new six-team Negro League that he would later admit was never intended to last. The United States League would, however, provide cover for Brooklyn scouts and others to scour the country for black ballplayers without admitting they wanted them for the majors.

On August 29 it was Sukeforth who brought Robinson to the Dodgers' offices at 215 Montague Street, Brooklyn. In the course of two hours Branch Rickey questioned, challenged, and confronted Robinson with racist taunts and a pulled punch, to test his temperament and character. Robinson had already proven himself a great player. The team would need him to be a stable, mature, restrained man. He was, and he left with a contract and an emotional bond with Rickey and the Dodgers, all of which he had to keep secret.

Finally, on October 23, 1945, Robinson was presented to the press in Montreal, where he signed a contract with Brooklyn's top farm team, the Royals. Club officials acknowledged that a backlash might develop. Nevertheless, the

Dodgers went forward with Robinson steeling himself for the challenge and saying little apart from "I realize how much it means to me, to my race and to baseball. I can only say I'll do my very best." The team let it be known that this pioneer would not be alone for long. The scouts had identified more than two dozen black players with major-league potential and the Dodgers intended to sign them.

In the months after Robinson was signed to play in Montreal, he joined a barnstorming team in Venezuela that included some of the greatest players in the Negro leagues, including catcher Roy Campanella, who would soon sign with the Dodgers too. On February 10, Robinson married his longtime sweetheart Rachel Isum at the Independent Church of Christ in Los Angeles. According to Rickey's design, Rachel would play a critical role in Jackie Robinson's odyssey. She would be the only wife allowed at spring training in Florida, where just one other black man, a pitcher named John Wright, was among the more than two hundred players.

Rachel Robinson's special status at the training camp also reflected the way both Rickey and O'Malley sometimes blended the personal and the professional. Both men fancied themselves good judges of character, and both emphasized the value of marriage and family life for members of their team. Rickey favored young men who had strong attachments. O'Malley had an uncanny ability to recall the names of wives and children and made a point of asking about them. Players and employees were made to feel part of the Dodgers family, a status that brought both benefits and responsibilities.

In Jackie Robinson's case, Rachel was quickly recognized as the most influential and positive force in his life. She was a nurse by profession and came across as exceedingly kindhearted, but she was also a serious woman with high standards. This assessment was made by the young Dodgers executive Buzzie Bavasi, who had recently returned from fighting in Africa and Italy. Charged with investigating Jackie Robinson's character, Bavasi considered checking out Robinson's reputation in his home area, Southern California, but went to Montreal instead. A game was played that night; he sat behind the players' wives.

Like O'Malley and Rickey, the recently married Bavasi was devoted to his wife and believed that a man's marriage and family life were crucial to his character. He spent the entire game subtly eavesdropping on the wives. A bit older than the others, who were all white, Rachel Robinson was comfortable at the center of the conversation and spoke with a direct intelligence that impressed Bavasi.

The next morning Bavasi surprised the group on Montague Street when he arrived at the office. "That was a quick trip to California," said Rickey. Bavasi explained that after a few phone calls to sources in California he had gone to Montreal instead. He then reported that "if Jackie Roosevelt Robinson is good enough for Rachel Robinson he is good enough for the Dodgers."

ALTHOUGH THE DODGERS WERE free to sign Robinson and eventually move him up to the big leagues, the owners of the Brooklyn team faced resistance from every other member of their exclusive fraternity. In late August 1946, representatives of the sixteen major-league teams met secretly in Chicago at the Blackstone Hotel on Michigan Avenue. Their focus was a report completed by a committee that had been assigned to look at the most controversial issues facing the sport. (Larry MacPhail would eventually claim to be its main author.) Two passages that were excised noted that baseball was a monopoly and that the reserve clause binding players to teams would fail a test in court. However, the owners retained in the report a warning against integration, and then accepted it by a vote of fifteen to one. Rickey, the lone dissenter, would eventually reveal this vote as a rejection of his integration project, although others would say they merely accepted, but did not endorse, the report.

Whatever the other owners thought of integration, they would have trouble arguing with Robinson's performance. During a season in which he won the International League batting title he also led the Royals to a home field victory in the Little World Series. After the last out was made, the Montreal fans literally carried him off the field on their shoulders.

Robinson was just one of many Dodger success stories in 1946. In all, five of the Dodgers' minor-league affiliates won their league championships. One franchise, a new one established by Buzzie Bavasi in Nashua, New Hampshire, accomplished this feat by fielding the first integrated team to represent a U.S. city. Catcher Roy Campanella and pitcher Don Newcombe, two African-American players signed as part of the Dodgers' grand integration strategy, were rejected by a manager in Indiana who feared a racial backlash; they were popular stars in New Hampshire. The club's player-manager was Walter Alston, who would one day run the big-league club.

As successful as the farm teams were, hopes for the big club were held in check by a sense of realism. Rickey's long-term plan called for reconstructing the team with veterans like Pee Wee Reese and Pete Reiser, who should have plenty of years left on their bodies, and the best of the hundreds of youngsters in the farm system. Although fans were told that the team intended to win right away, the board of directors understood that this process would take time. They were aiming for a World Series in 1948, said Rickey. Of course, no one explained this to the players.

In April the Dodgers won eight and lost three. The month of May was marked by a couple of spectacular on-field fights—Dixie Walker lost a tooth—and equally scrappy play. By Memorial Day, Durocher had managed around spotty pitching to lead the Dodgers to the top of the standings. At the end of June the Dodgers led the second-place Cardinals by seven and a half games, but this margin wouldn't last. The two teams were evenly matched and Brooklynites suffered as the Dodgers staggered toward the season's end. In mid-September they needed the aid of huge swarms of flying insects to save them from being swept by the Cubs in a three-game series. The flies descended on Ebbets Field in a cloud, harassing first the fans in the stands and then the players. For the first and only time in major-league history, umpires called the game over, on account of bugs, as the Dodgers were winning. However, even with the aid of insects the Brooklyn team couldn't clinch the pennant and came to the last day of the regular season tied with the Cardinals for first place. Both lost, setting up the first pennant playoff ever conducted by the National League.

Starved of a championship for as long as there had been a World Series, Brooklyn fans were thrilled by the prospect of the Dodgers getting only their fourth crack ever at the big prize. More than a hundred of them camped overnight on Montague Street hoping to buy tickets for the playoff games. By eight a.m. on October 1, the crowd numbered three thousand. By noon there were ten thousand people standing in a cold rain. The crowd was all for the Dodgers, but New York bookmakers favored the Cardinals, who had dominated the Brooklyn team—fourteen wins against eight losses—in the regular season.

The teams played true to form in the best-of-three playoff. The St. Louis nine won the first game, which was played on their field, 4–2. Two days later they thumped the Dodgers 8–4 at Ebbets. With the last out, a fan ran onto the diamond and stole the cap off Cardinal outfielder Enos Slaughter's head. With the help of the police, Slaughter got his cap back and the Cardinals went on to beat the Red Sox and win the World Series.

EVEN WITH THE PLAYOFF defeat, the O'Malley-Rickey-Smith group had seen far more excitement and success than they could have expected in their first full year as owners of the Dodgers organization. The minor-league teams were winning and held more great prospects, black and white, than any other farm system. Attendance in Brooklyn had soared, contributing to a healthy profit. Players earned extra pay for the playoff games, and Rickey declared that the office staff would get bonuses drawn from the receipts for the postseason gate. In mid-September Rickey also announced that, win or lose, the Dodgers players would each receive a Studebaker car, thanks in part to his friend who headed the car company. In response, the players pitched in to give Rickey a boat big enough to use for deep-sea fishing.

All of this generosity was displayed at Ebbets Field, where the boat was presented before a game and sample cars were parked on the field so that players could inspect them prior to making their orders. Everyone was happy except, according to some, Walter O'Malley. He was reportedly concerned because the car giveaway left the team on the hook for taxes.

If O'Malley was uncomfortable with the car giveaway, taxes may have been one reason. There is also evidence in team records that the cars were not entirely a gift from Studebaker and that the Dodgers put up a substantial amount of cash to purchase them. But it was also quite possible that he didn't like the idea of promising big bonuses to players whether they won or lost. This act, which amounted to a reward for losing, did set an odd precedent. And O'Malley wouldn't have been unreasonable if he questioned why just one of the team's four owners got to play Santa Claus in autumn, personally distributing big gifts while the others were absent.

No one knew the team's books better than O'Malley, and the facts were not as rosy as one might expect. Attendance for 1946 was more than 50 percent higher than it had been in dismal 1945—when the Dodgers lost money—but that was true throughout the league, as thirteen million military men came home and many celebrated with a ball game, a beer, and a hot dog. Sports in general enjoyed an all-time peak in popularity. Interest in pro and college football soared. Horse racing, golf, and tennis all drew record crowds, and demand for boxing tickets was so great that promoters sold their first $100 seat.

What no one seemed to notice was that even with the pennant race and the sellout crowd for that extra playoff game, the Dodgers actually fell shy of the league average for increased attendance. The nearby Yankees, with a newly renovated stadium, drew almost half a million *more* fans with a team that was out of contention by July. Sport was a booming business, but winning was no guarantee that the Dodgers of Brooklyn would lead the competition for profit, which was O'Malley's game.

The Dodgers faced other problems that were invisible to the fans and press. James Mulvey was demanding compensation for past services to the board, plus expenses. Although he was negotiating the dispute with Mulvey's lawyer, O'Malley was worried about this conflict exploding into a serious stockholder conflict. At the same time, some of the Ebbets heirs were considering a lawsuit to resolve their dissatisfaction with the sale of the family interest in the team. O'Malley didn't expect them to get anywhere with their pursuit of a surcharge on the transaction, but if they did, they would deepen the team's already sizable debt.

Rickey's aggressive minor-league expansion also put pressure on the bottom line. It shifted money that could be used in Brooklyn to the purchase of land in Montreal and Cambridge, Maryland, and to run farm teams across America. The sale of players to other teams was supposed to defray these costs. But Rickey bought as well as sold, and at year's end the profit from this activity, minus the fee he took off the top of each check received, was just $25,000. This was not even enough to cover the added cost of scouting for black players. Given all these business problems, O'Malley may well have griped about Rickey.

And then there was the matter of old-fashioned competitiveness. In O'Malley and Rickey the ownership group had two fiercely intelligent, aggressive, disciplined, and ambitious men who were accustomed to having their way. Charm and the instinct for success seemed to be in O'Malley's blood. The same was true for Rickey. But they were very different in style. One was a Main Streeter from the Midwest who wore his moralizing Christianity on his sleeve and sometimes gawked at celebrities in Manhattan restaurants. The other moved comfortably in every circle of New York society, enjoying life's pleasures and using his wit to disarm bankers and bartenders alike.

But style was not substance, and when it came to competition and self-interest, both men used their gifts to gain whatever advantages could be had. Rickey was deeply self-interested and highly manipulative and indirect in dealing with others. Though outwardly paternalistic and pedantic, he could be coldly calculating when it came to bargaining over player salaries—thus earning the nickname El Cheapo—and dressing up trades to entice other clubs to pay top dollar. He also lowered his Christian (and intellectual) standards when necessary. A case in point was Durocher, a violent bully whose antics Rickey overlooked for many years. This kind of favoritism, and willingness to suspend his own moral code, led Commissioner Landis to call Rickey "a hypocritical Protestant bastard."

For his part, Walter O'Malley was a master of bonhomie—quick with a joke, a story, and an arm around the shoulder—who made friends easily and felt comfortable in private clubs and associations where relationships could help a man get things done. In the mid-1940s he belonged to no fewer than eighteen of these groups. Some, like the Metropolitan Club—founded by Vanderbilts, Whitneys, Morgans, et cetera—represented the height of social networking. Others brought together real estate men and lawyers. And a few of them, like the Civil Service Reform Association, sought merely to do good works. With these connections, O'Malley kept up with events in the city's courthouses, boardrooms, and banks.

Like Rickey, O'Malley inspired great loyalty in those whom he drew close. There would be O'Malley men as well as Rickey men, and these groups would eventually come into conflict. But this wouldn't happen for a few years. Indeed, in 1946, despite reports that O'Malley had begun to complain about Rickey, he gave the team's chief baseball man everything he wanted. When Rickey said he needed cash to keep Coach Charlie Dressen—"the one man I don't want to lose"—he got $12,500 for him. When he wanted a $65,000 aircraft that would be used for scouting, O'Malley voted to make the purchase and to set aside $7,200 for a pilot. He also voted to give Rickey, who already drew much more cash out of the club than any executive or player, $5,000 in expense money that he could spend with no accounting required.

These moves amounted to a strong vote of confidence for an impresario who was getting the leeway and the license to pursue his art in its highest form. In the meantime it would be up to O'Malley to confront the troubles looming over at Ebbets Field, the Dodgers, and the baseball business at large.

AS THOUSANDS OF REAL and would-be ballplayers returned from war, and the country and its national game were freed from the state of emergency, the play on the field was the only constant. For owners and team presidents it was no longer enough to hire the right men and wave to the fans from your box seat. Professional basketball and football were growing in popularity, and commercial television threatened to provide people with free entertainment that might keep them at home and away from the ballpark. Owners also faced new competition for the best players as a band of wealthy Mexican brothers named Pasquel launched a campaign to bring major leaguers south.

Led by brother Jorge, who was president of La Liga Mexicana and appeared in public dripping in diamonds, the Pasquels signed eighteen American major leaguers in the first few months of 1946. Among them were two Dodgers, young Luis Olmo and veteran Mickey Owen. The team's reaction was focused on Owen, the four-time all-star catcher who had dropped the ball in the 1941 World Series.

Owen had wavered in his decision but jumped after he heard that Branch Rickey intended to punish him for even considering a move. His hitting produced a victory in his first game as a member of the Veracruz Blues, and when Commissioner Chandler suspended every American who was playing in Mexico, Owen responded with the calm of a man who had received his year's pay, and bonus, in advance. He said that Chandler was trying to scare others who saw, in Mexico, a chance to break a system that kept young players underpaid and disposed of older ones while their talents were still intact. The threat to the status quo was even greater than Owen described.

The Pasquels were determined to break the monopoly of the American major leagues and create a wide-open market for players. Equal to their American counterparts when it came to showmanship, they invited Babe Ruth to tour their league. Though weakened by cancer, which would soon be discovered, Ruth put on batting exhibitions and bantered with reporters. In Mexico City he criticized the standard contract, which prevented players from seeking better pay, and declared the major leagues a monopoly. On the way home he made another headline when his plane stopped at Corpus Christi for refueling. Red-faced from a sunburn, Ruth argued for players like Owen. "A guy can't play baseball all his life," said Ruth. "He might as well make as much money as he can while he is able."

The American owners responded to the Pasquels in various courts around the country, suing to stop them from enticing players to break their contracts. Before jumping into the controversy, O'Malley met with an attorney for the Pasquel brothers. O'Malley, who tended to worry about preserving baseball's special legal status, came away with serious doubts about doing battle in the courts. "I have tried not to be prejudiced, but my persistent view, with which you are familiar, is that this situation should not be in the courts," he wrote to Rickey. He said he was worried about putting the reserve clause and "the question of monopoly up to the courts for determination."

As team president, Rickey didn't heed O'Malley's caution. Instead the Dodgers made a federal case out of the Owen issue, filing suit in the U.S. District Court in his home state of Missouri. A judge temporarily blocked the Mexican league's efforts to bargain with players, but the suit was soon dismissed. For a moment it seemed that a free market for baseball talent would bloom. But it turned out that the Pasquels lacked the cash to keep up the challenge. In less than two years several teams in their league failed and the dream of a major circuit faded away. Owen and others who jumped at offers from the Pasquels would return to play in America after Commissioner Chandler shortened suspensions issued to punish them.

Although the Pasquels failed to achieve parity with the leagues in the United States, the concerns they awakened—about baseball's monopoly and its labor practices—would never quite disappear. In Cleveland, players drafted demands for a minimum wage, expense money, and a pension fund. The Pittsburgh team went so far as to embrace a union organized by Robert Murphy, a Boston lawyer who had been prodded into action by some ballplayer friends who informed him that some major leaguers were paid as little as $3,500 per year, or roughly 5 percent of Branch Rickey's typical bonus. Their ultimate goal was an end to the "reserve clause" in every contract, which barred a player from negotiating with another team unless he was released outright or his old organization sold the contract to the new club.

Though rarely a fast-moving group, the owners did respond quickly to the unrest. Led by Chandler, they welcomed player representatives to join a committee for dealing with contract issues. Before the season ended they had agreed on a $5,000 minimum salary, increased expense money for travel and moving, limits on the amount a player's salary could be cut from year to year, and a commitment to create a pension system.

The agreement soothed the players. Robert Murphy ended his campaign and in the future would be recalled mainly for the extra cash players got for daily expenses, which they came to call "Murphy money." But even though he would leave the scene, Murphy had started something that wasn't going to end. The players had discovered their leverage, and a wise baseball executive would recognize that plantation-style economics of the past were not going to hold for the future.

THE FUTURE WAS ON O'Malley's mind as he tried to plot the Dodgers' fortunes. He negotiated higher payments from advertisers who wanted space on the walls at Ebbets Field and time on the Dodger radio broadcasts. O'Malley also got involved with the nuts and bolts of putting on the games, including contracts with vendors and maintenance at Ebbets Field. When he reviewed the condition of the ballpark, he discovered that many important repairs and renovation projects had been delayed as, from one year to the next, crews chose to get by with a little scrubbing and a coat of fresh paint.

Not that paint came cheap. It cost a minimum of $30,000 each year to pay for the labor and paint required to spruce up the interior of the park. Fixing public walkways, worn and cracked by millions of footsteps, would cost nearly as much. And these figures paled when compared with fixing the toilets. In 1946 the estimate for this job, which was a matter of public health as well as convenience, was $100,000.

Conditions at Ebbets had been bad for years. Periodically, visits by various city inspectors had required the team to make emergency fixes to avoid losing the occupancy permit for the stadium. The electrical system, taxed by the addition of lights for night games, was especially troublesome. Years later Buzzie Bavasi would admit that he used his influence with a distant relative—his sister's father-in-law, who ranked high in the fire department—to avoid citations and shutdowns. Many other parks built in the same period, including Tiger Stadium, Braves Field, and Wrigley Field, were kept alive in the same way. But nothing could be done about the biggest problem at Ebbets: the lack of space.

The stadium in Brooklyn was constrained by its small lot, which was wedged into a congested neighborhood. Other older parks had been expanded to seat as many as forty-six thousand (Comiskey Park in Chicago), but Ebbets remained stuck at thirty-two thousand, the smallest capacity in the National League. In both major leagues only Griffith Stadium in Washington, D.C., host of the American League Senators, was smaller. A full house in Washington was twenty-nine thousand, but with the Senators finishing no higher than sixth for eight straight seasons, demand for those seats was not great. Even in 1946, when they climbed to fourth, attendance fell below the league average.

In Brooklyn, where big games now drew more people than the stadium could hold, every fan who walked away represented lost revenue. This loss was made more evident by the fact that the Yankees could seat sixty-seven thousand and the Giants could get more than more than fifty-four thousand into the Polo Grounds. Often the Giants' biggest gates in a season came on the days when the Dodgers visited. The execs on Montague Street could only dream of welcoming so many paying fans and selling them beer and pop and hot dogs and peanuts along with a game.

Not one to abandon his dreams, in the summer of '46 Walter O'Malley brought the now-famous engineer Emil Praeger to look at the house that Ebbets and the McKeevers built. A favorite of the regional development czar Robert Moses, Praeger was an expert in structural engineering who had also worked on parks and highways. He was known to the general public for designing New York parks and wartime engineering exploits, including the rapid construction of a protected harbor at Normandy during the D-Day invasion. At Ebbets, Praeger found a problem that defied an easy long-term fix. A big investment in renovations might make all the toilets flush and the wiring safe, but given the structure and the location, a significant expansion to create more seating was out of the question.

Even if a way could be found to add thousands of seats, the Dodgers would still face a second big problem: no parking. Designed and built long before the car culture took hold, Ebbets was served by just a few small lots that could handle six or seven hundred cars. With the war just months in the past, it was already obvious that America's future was coming on four wheels. Auto production rose from about seventeen thousand cars in February 1946 to more than eighty-five thousand in September. And with William J. Levitt and others building thousands of new homes on Long Island, it was also clear that many of those cars would be kept in the suburbs by young war veterans—Dodgers fans—who were moving out to start families. If Ebbets was cramped and run-down, or it was impossible to park, why would they come to Brooklyn for a game?

The answer—they wouldn't—was obvious to Walter O'Malley, and so was the solution. On October 14, 1946, he wrote Emile Praeger to suggest he apply his "fertile imagination" to the matter of "enlarging or replacing our present stadium." A week later he made a report to the board of directors, raising for the first time the possibility of a modern new play space for the team and its fans. The issue was set aside, but O'Malley wasn't going to let go of it.

At age forty-three, O'Malley could be expected to look further into the future than Rickey, who was sixty-five, and Smith, who was fifty-seven. He could imagine being active in the game for decades more and would not accept second-class performance. However, a shabby ballpark with inadequate parking would hurt ticket sales and revenues. Without revenues, the team couldn't pay star players and risked succumbing to a cycle of losing on the field and at the box office.

As a younger man, O'Malley was also more sensitive to the change promised by the new mass medium of television. In 1945 the chief engineer at General Electric foresaw a billion-dollar industry. However, as of 1946 the pioneers of TV had not yet figured out how to make it pay. At the time, almost every broadcast minute was being produced as original content by individual stations. This made the cost of programming extremely high. At the same time, advertisers who couldn't be sure about the size of their audience were reluctant to pay much for commercials.

One obvious exception to this problem of high production costs and unreliable audiences was baseball. Every big-league team in America was already producing seventy-seven home games per year. Add cameras and a bit of narration and these games became television dramas, complete with heroes and villains and endlessly varying stories. Given the relatively low cost of production and baseball's great appeal, it seemed a perfect fit for the medium, the teams, and sponsors.

Although O'Malley saw the opportunity, the Yankees seized it first, selling the rights to broadcast every Bronx home game in 1947 for $75,000 to the Dumont Television Network. After meeting with the other networks in New York, O'Malley zeroed in on CBS, meeting frequently with executives and sportscaster Bob Edge.

For O'Malley, this duty was not a hardship. It brought him into the exciting world of a new medium at a time when it was controlled by a handful of people. (Thanks to a demonstration put on by CBS, O'Malley and his co-owner Smith were among the first in New York to see color television.) In the end, O'Malley came up with a three-year arrangement for somewhat less than the Yankees received but nevertheless got the Dodgers onto the airwaves in 1947. At the same time the Giants went with NBC.

No one knew the effect TV might have on pro teams. Despite the money they got for broadcasting rights, many owners had worried when radio arrived because they thought people who could hear the games for free would stop coming to the ballpark. But no loss of attendance was ever noted, and it was quite possible that broadcasts of the games, especially reports that were as vivid and warm as Red Barber's, actually expanded the team's audience and enticed more people to come to games from greater distances. Optimists believed that television might also lure more people to the ballpark. Pessimists feared that since it provided a live picture of events, it might actually make people feel as though they didn't have to see the game in person to experience it fully.

If television suppressed attendance, owners would have to find some way—advertising, higher rights fees, or special subscription-only broadcasts—to wring money out of this new machine. In the meantime they would go ahead with the experiment. The timing of baseball's arrival on TV was perfect for the fans in New York, because the game was about to begin the most exciting decade it would ever know.

Five

O'MALLEY'S DODGERS

After Walter O'Malley's friend Everett McCooey sang the national anthem, Jackie Robinson sprang from the shadows of the dugout and into the sunshine and cheers that made Ebbets Field glow. He wore a royal blue cap decorated with a white *B*, and a white jersey with the number 42 on the back and the word "Dodgers" embroidered in blue script on the front. The first pitch he ever saw in a real major-league game was thrown by Johnny Sain of the Boston Braves, who was beginning an all-star year. Sain baffled Robinson that day. But even though he didn't get a hit, he played well at his new position, first base.

In time, Robinson's Ebbets Field debut, which was on April 15, 1947, would be recognized for the historic moment it was. So many books and films would focus on his life that it would become one of the most documented events in the postwar era. But a bit of myth would arise too. For example, the overflow crowd that Robinson and others would recall wasn't present that day at Ebbets, as roughly six thousand seats were empty. (A much bigger crowd went to opening day for minor leaguers in Jersey City.) And considering its later resonance, the end of segregation in major-league baseball got surprisingly light treatment from the *New York Times*. It wasn't even mentioned in Roscoe McGowan's game report, and columnist Arthur Daley noted Robinson's arrival without a word about race and only after covering several other topics, including the absence of Leo Durocher, whom he called "the little man who wasn't there."

Durocher was absent because of a scandal that had been playing out for months in the tabloid press. The controversy followed such a twisted path that anyone trying to trace it would have been well advised to bring plenty of bread crumbs. It started in the fall of 1946 when the Yankees hired away Dodgers coaches Charlie Dressen and John Corriden. The man responsible was Larry MacPhail, who had returned from the war to become a stockholder and president of the team in the Bronx called the Yankees.

Like the Dodgers, who were controlled by a trio of owners—Smith, Rickey, and O'Malley—the Yankees were run by MacPhail and his partners Daniel Topping and Delbert Webb. Topping had become a millionaire in the steel business. Webb, who was even richer, was involved in real estate and construction. A schemer of the first order, Webb would become a fixture in Las Vegas, building the Flamingo Hotel for mobster Bugsy Siegel and developing a competing casino called the Sahara. Though in different leagues, both financially and on the field, the Yankees and Dodgers ownership groups were natural competitors for fans in New York. For this reason the roaring, combative MacPhail generally did what he could to disrupt the Dodgers.

In this case, MacPhail was rumored to be courting Durocher and making the move easier for him by hiring two of his coaching buddies. Fearing that The Lip would jump, the Dodgers quickly signed him to a contract that made him the best-paid manager in the game. At $70,000, his reported salary was set higher than any player's and was nearly triple the amount paid to the mayor of New York.

The next Durocher development had nothing to do with MacPhail. It was instigated by the powerful syndicated columnist Westbrook Pegler, who published a series of articles that criticized the Dodgers manager for alleged associations with gamblers and mobsters. In time the pugnacious Pegler would descend into libel and irrelevance, becoming a living cartoon of an angry, hard-drinking, and paranoid vigilante. But as of 1946 he was widely read and respected for columns that had revealed union corruption and won him a Pulitzer prize in 1941. If Pegler wanted Durocher out of baseball, which he did, the Dodgers had to respond. O'Malley and Rickey spent much of the late autumn trying to deal with his attacks on their man and their effect on the team's reputation.

Under orders from the owners, Durocher was sent to see Commissioner

Chandler, who demanded he stop spending his off-season days and nights at the Hollywood home of George Raft, an actor who played gangsters on the screen and hung around them in real life. (Raft had reportedly won $100,000 betting on baseball.) Durocher agreed, but his moment of grace was short. In January 1947 the press screamed about his romance with a beautiful actress named Laraine Day, who had just consented to star opposite John Wayne in *Tycoon*. At twenty-six, Day was fifteen years younger than Durocher. She was also married. While her angry husband complained to reporters, Day got a Mexican divorce and married Durocher in defiance of a California court. He was branded a "Love Thief" by the *Los Angeles Herald Examiner*.

The spectacle of immorality caught the attention of everyone from Commissioner Chandler to the head of the Catholic Youth Organization (CYO) in Brooklyn, who threatened to pull thousands of kids out of the Knothole Gang boosters club. The uproar was more than enough to irritate O'Malley, who had just previously dealt with Durocher's civil and criminal cases involving John Christian.

"Why didn't you talk some of these things over with me for a little friendly advice?" he asked in a letter to Durocher days after the marriage. "The trouble with you, is that you limit my ability to signal stealing." (By this he meant that Durocher made it hard for O'Malley to help him out of personal and legal difficulties.)

Years later the Dodgers' road secretary, Harold Parrott, who wrote a newspaper column under Durocher's name, would claim that O'Malley was actually happy to see Durocher in trouble. The Lip was a Rickey man and the two owners were frequently at odds, argued Parrott. But if O'Malley had it out for Durocher, he went to great lengths to cover his feelings. He met more than once with the irate priest who led the CYO, trying to no avail to cool his moral outrage. He also stood up for Durocher when Commissioner Chandler held a secret hearing at the end of March 1947 to determine the manager's fate. Durocher had precipitated Chandler's move when he as well as Rickey complained to sportswriters that a couple of gamblers—including the infamous Memphis Engelberg—had been Larry MacPhail's box-seat guests at an exhibition game in Havana. Their point? If Durocher was supposed to avoid such contacts, shouldn't MacPhail?

An outraged MacPhail claimed libel and demanded the commissioner act. He did, summoning Durocher, the owners of both clubs, and other witnesses to a meeting where he intended to get to the bottom of things.

THE SETTING WAS a onetime nightclub space on the top floor of a hotel in Sarasota, Florida. A single chair was set in front of the table where the commissioner sat flanked by an assistant and a stenographer. MacPhail was there, accompanied by another Yankees owner, Dan Topping, the perpetually tanned, sporting millionaire who had recently been divorced from the Olympic skating champion Sonja Henie. (As ambitious and volatile as she was glamorous, Henie married three times and was romantically linked with, among others, Tyrone Power, Van Johnson, and Joe Louis.) The Dodgers were represented by O'Malley and Arthur Mann, a former sportswriter who was Branch Rickey's assistant. A death in the family kept Rickey himself away.

Conducting the meeting as if it were a Senate committee hearing, the commissioner questioned a series of witnesses who testified under an oath of secrecy. An old scout and then a Yankee coach took the hot seat to serve as character witnesses for MacPhail and Rickey. Next, one of Durocher's former players, Augie Galan, confirmed that the Dodgers' clubhouse had been a gambling den in the early 1940s but insisted that Durocher hadn't taken advantage of anyone. A player who lost big invariably got his money back, even if it was presented as a bonus for a good performance.

By the time Durocher occupied the witness chair, the proceedings had been so agreeable that O'Malley had arisen just once to ask questions. When he did, he got Charlie Dressen to confess that Memphis Engelberg the bookie had been more *his* friend than Durocher's. Otherwise, O'Malley let every bit of testimony go unchallenged because none of it seemed to damage his man. When Durocher got his turn, he tried to direct Chandler's attention to MacPhail's association with undesirables, but the commissioner didn't seem interested.

Before concluding, the commissioner gave MacPhail a chance to speak. He said he wasn't satisfied because he wanted to hear from Rickey. Chandler agreed to give the old man of baseball a turn in the chair at a second meeting, in four days. As the hearing ended and the men went their separate ways, the one participant who later described it—Arthur Mann—had trouble imagining where Chandler was headed. However, Durocher had a bad feeling about his immediate future, which was based on the fact that just prior to the meeting Chandler had said, "Somebody may wind up getting kicked out of baseball."

At the follow-up meeting, sixty-six-year-old Rickey—all bushy eyebrows and gravelly voice—bristled with moral outrage as he defended everything that he and Durocher had said about MacPhail's associations in Havana. As one aging and esteemed son of Main Street addressing another, Rickey had reason to hope that the controversy could be settled. But then Chandler skirted the MacPhail issue and focused his questions on Durocher's colorful history. The more he asked about Durocher's behavior, the worse it looked for The Lip.

When the commissioner reached the end of his witness list he calmly asked his last one, Yankees ticket manager Arthur Patterson, to leave him alone with Rickey, O'Malley, and Mann. According to Mann, Chandler then got up and came over to the table where the three Dodgers executives sat. He paused and asked, "How much would it hurt you folks to have your man out of baseball?"

Boom! Rickey's fist hit the table. "Happy, what on earth is the matter with you?" he said. "Why, that boy has more character than that fellow you just sent out of the room."

Chandler took a letter out of his coat pocket, flashed it at the Dodgers group, and explained that it was from a "big man" in Washington who wanted Durocher disciplined. The Dodgers contingent left fearing the worst.

Besides the ominous warning from some mystery man—FBI director J. Edgar Hoover is a good guess—Chandler had to consider the integrity of the game and his own standing as commissioner. In his effort to live up to Kenesaw Mountain Landis, Chandler would be judged on his decisiveness and toughness. With Durocher he had a widely recognized renegade who enjoyed limited support outside of greater New York. Brooklyn loved Durocher's spit-in-your-eye impulses, but players, managers, executives, and fans of the teams on the receiving end did not. Who would make a better target for a commissioner eager to show his toughness?

Finally, Chandler had to consider recent scandals in baseball and other sports. A recent investigation of minor-league teams in Louisiana had uncovered a gambling ring so out of control that bookies dressed in uniforms worked in one team's clubhouse. Pro football had been shaken by a plot to fix its championship game, and the boxer Ray Robinson had reported an attempted bribe.

On April 3, the National Football League banned two Giants stars from the game, ending their careers. Neither had accepted a bribe, but NFL Commissioner Bert Bell acted because they had spoken with would-be fixers and failed to report it. Bell had made an example of the two players to guard football from the mere suggestion of impropriety. He had also set an example for Chandler, who decided to fine certain Yankees and Dodgers and banish Durocher for a year. He delivered the news in a call to Rickey. "All parties to this controversy," he added, "are silenced from the time this order is issued."

There were no tears when Chandler spoke this time, only Rickey shouting "You son of a bitch!" into the phone.

With no option for appeal, the only thing left to do was give Durocher a proper send-off. The opportunity arrived, ironically enough, when the same club that the CYO had deserted in protest, the Knothole Gang, held its annual season-opening banquet at the Hotel St. George, a massive Brooklyn landmark with more than two thousand rooms.

A seasoned performer—he often appeared on popular radio shows—Durocher attended the banquet with the beautiful Laraine at his side and played the down-but-not-out role to the hilt. He praised the Brooklyn fans, predicted great things for the team, and promised, "While I won't be here physically this season, I'll be dreaming of them and in my heart will be with them every day." Speaking for the Dodgers and 1,100 boosters jammed into the ballroom, Walter O'Malley stood and said, "To Leo and Laraine, we're not saying good-bye but 'We'll see you soon.'"

O'Malley tried to make the reunion happen sooner rather than later by traveling to Cincinnati to offer one last appeal to Commissioner Chandler. Rickey did the same, going all the way to the former senator's home in rural Versailles, Kentucky, to discuss the problem. Nothing came of this effort, but the memo Rickey sent to O'Malley about the meeting contained an odd artifact. In the first paragraph he wrote, "First we discussed the reasons for him furnishing to me a certain FBI agent, the cost of whose employment is to be borne by the Commissioner other than expenses incident to the agent's work."

What would Rickey need with an FBI agent? In those days baseball officials often used private investigators to determine whether players might be associating with gamblers, but for a team to use a federal agent would be unusual if not illegal. A hint appears in the second paragraph, which refers to Babe Dahlgren, whom Rickey accused of drug use, and to "hearings" involving Larry MacPhail. In their meeting Chandler predicted that MacPhail would "not be in baseball much longer."

When they finished their two-hour talk, Happy Chandler presented Rickey with a Kentucky smoked ham. He then drove his visitor to the airport in nearby Lexington and stood waving until the Dodgers plane was airborne.

AFTER CONSIDERING EIGHT NAMES offered by his office men, Branch Rickey decided to replace Leo Durocher with Dodgers scout Burt Shotton, who hadn't managed regularly in the big leagues since 1933. Shotton was summoned from Miami, where he was watching prospects, with a telegram that read, "Be in Brooklyn in the morning. See nobody. Say nothing. Rickey."

A longtime Rickey ally, Shotton was a sixty-two-year-old with gray hair and a soft voice who couldn't have been more different from Durocher. He wore street clothes in the dugout, which meant he couldn't walk onto the field, and in almost forty years he had been tossed out of a game only twice by umpires. As it turned out, this steady, philosophical demeanor would be just what the Dodgers required.

The season that Leo Durocher sat out would be one of the most important in the history of baseball. On the field the Dodgers played so well and so consistently that they grabbed first place just before the mid-season all-star game and never relinquished it. Robinson became Rookie of the Year by stealing 29 bases, scoring 125 runs and hitting .297. Young pitcher Ralph Branca started more games than anyone in the league and finished second in wins and strikeouts.

Branca was on the mound at Ebbets Field for the worst moment of the season, when Pittsburgh's Culley Rikard hit a wicked line drive toward the wall in center field. Pete Reiser chased the ball at full speed, nabbed it in the tip of his glove, and then crashed into the wall. The ball stayed in the glove, which meant Rickard was out, but so was Reiser, as the impact gave him a concussion. Blood poured from a V-shaped wound in his head as players from both teams ran to help him.

Reiser was carried off the field on a stretcher and Walter O'Malley accompanied him to Swedish Hospital, where he waited for doctors to examine his center fielder and admit him. Although X-rays revealed no bones were broken, Reiser's recovery would take weeks and require a trip to Johns Hopkins Hospital in Baltimore, where he saw a specialist in neurology. Although it was not revealed at the time, Reiser's injury left him with a case of vertigo that would severely limit his career. Before the crash he was a .300-plus hitter who appeared in well over a hundred games per season. After, he would average less than .250 and appear in about sixty-five games a year.

Remarkably, Reiser's injury and absence had little effect on the Dodgers of '47. After they claimed the pennant by an easy five games, roughly half a million people watched a victory parade—players in open cars, the Dodger Sym-phony playing from a flatbed truck—that wound from Grand Army Plaza to Borough Hall. Along the route, players were showered with confetti. The storm was particularly intense when they passed the towering Williamsburg Bank building and workers sent down a blizzard of shredded paper: pink, red, white, and green. Banners and handmade posters praised the team. Only one, at a warehouse, sounded a negative note. It read, "Wait Until the Yanks Get You."

No one in Brooklyn could recall a bigger, more exuberant celebration, and it only got more intense when the cars stopped in front of Borough Hall and roughly one hundred thousand people applauded, hollered, and whistled for the players, who climbed up onto a bandstand. The vast crowd cheered for the Long Island University Band and an Irish tenor who sang "The Star-Spangled Banner." They applauded borough president John Cashmore as he gave each of the players a gold watch, and hollered for Pee Wee Reese, who blew kisses at the young women and girls. A representative of the *Sporting News* gave Jackie Robinson his Rookie of the Year Award and he joined Dixie Walker to promise a World Series win. When the National League pennant was raised atop Borough Hall, the roar of the crowd echoed down nearby streets.

While the Dodgers and their fans indulged in a little delirium over their good fortune, it was business as usual over in the American League. The Yankees finished twelve games ahead of the Tigers. They were favored to beat the Dodgers in the series and were expected to rely on postseason experience and better hitting to do it.

The first two games of the series were played in the Bronx and the Yankees won both comfortably. The Dodgers recovered when the action shifted to Ebbets Field. In game three they jumped out to a big early lead and held off the enemy to win 9–8. In the fourth game, fans in Brooklyn began to worry as Yankee pitcher Bill Bevens threw a no-hitter for eight and two-third innings. No one had ever pitched a no-hitter in the series, and Bevens had struggled to get as close as he did. In the fifth inning he gave up two walks, which allowed a run to score. Then, with two out in the ninth and the Yanks ahead 2–1, he let both Carl Furillo and Pete Reiser reach on walks. Dodgers manager Burt Shotton sent pinch hitter Cookie Lavagetto to the plate. He won the game with a double that hit the right-field fence.

But even as the Dodgers tied the series at two games per team, certain fans recalled 1941, when Brooklyn got close to the championship and lost to the same opponent. This was still Brooklyn, they thought, and these were still the Dodgers. As it turned out, the teams split the fifth and sixth games. In the finale, at Yankee Stadium, the Dodgers jumped out to a two-run lead in the second inning. They couldn't hold the advantage, however, and by the fourth inning the Yankees led 4–2. They added another run in the seventh, kept the Dodgers off the board, and captured the championship by a final score of 5–2.

Defeat brought a familiar sting, but fans who read the sports pages found relief from an outrageous but completely in-character postscript to the game. Straining to be heard above the celebration at Yankee Stadium, a red-faced Leland MacPhail had shouted to get the attention of nearby sportswriters and team officials and then blustered, "That's it! That does it! That's my retirement!"

The executive who had so zealously set out to win the series and defeat the Dodgers then came completely apart emotionally. In tear-soaked interviews with reporters he deliberately drew attention away from the team triumph and made the moment about himself. "I can't stand any more of this," he said. "My health won't take it." Before the evening was over, MacPhail made a sobbing address to the players in the clubhouse, got into a fistfight with an old friend, fired farm team director George Weiss, and had a closed-door shouting match with fellow owner Dan Topping. The next day Topping and Del Webb announced they had bought him out. MacPhail never again worked in baseball.

MacPhail's travails aside, the World Series was good for the two ownership groups that controlled the Yankees and the Dodgers. The boys in the Bronx benefited most. Their stadium could seat more than twice as many fans as Ebbets Field, which meant, on average, more than seventy thousand tickets sold—along with all the refreshments, programs, etc.—for each of the four Yankees home games. More income came from special World Series broadcasting rights payments, which brought each club more than $100,000. With just eleven stations operating nationwide, the first series on TV reached a very limited number of viewers. But the radio audience was vast, as almost one thousand stations carried the calls made by the Yankees' regular voice, Mel Allen, and the Dodgers' lead broadcaster, Red Barber.

The 1947 World Series marked Barber's ascent to the top of the broadcasting profession. The key moment came in the fourth game. An old baseball superstition holds that after the fifth inning no one should mention that a pitcher has a no-hitter going, for fear of jinxing the fellow. Mel Allen upheld the tradition, but Barber, who considered himself a reporter and not a rooter, did not. When he took the microphone, he let the world know that Bevens was onto something big. He also solidified his place as a favorite among the baseball cognoscenti, who valued a straight account over a homer's pleadings for the town team.

The same professionalism guided Barber's treatment of Jackie Robinson. As a son of the South, Barber had at first impulsively rejected integration of the major leagues and even thought he should quit in protest. But with the help of his wife, Lylah, and personal experience with Robinson, he quickly changed his attitude. Barber wasn't the only one who needed to adjust to the new racial reality. Before Robinson played an inning in the major leagues, Dixie Walker, Carl Furillo, and Bobby Bragan had campaigned to keep him from joining the team. The insurrection had happened at spring training and was put down by Durocher in a curse-filled middle-of-the-night tirade about using the best players of any color, "even if he has stripes like a fuckin' zebra."

The Dodgers had cohered as a unit early in the season, but Robinson still faced bigotry from fans and players around the league. One of the worst incidents came in Philadelphia, where taunts from the Phillies' dugout nearly drove him to break a turn-the-other-cheek promise he had made to Branch Rickey. In St. Louis the Cardinals threatened to strike over Robinson but were dissuaded when National League president Ford Frick threatened them with suspension.

As Robinson excelled on the field, his performance conquered prejudice and more black players joined the big leagues. On July 5, Negro League star Larry Doby took the field for the Cleveland Indians. On July 17, Hank Thompson played second base for the St. Louis Browns. In August the Dodgers also added a black pitcher, Dan Bankhead, to their roster. He hit a home run in his first at-bat.

In the coming decade, all but two major-league clubs would be integrated and the great experiment would prove an enormous moral and sporting success. In New York the Giants would get into the act rather quickly, bringing Monte Irvin and Hank Thompson to the Polo Grounds in 1949. The Yankees, however, remained stubbornly all-white as general manager George Weiss avoided integration until 1955. He told writer Roger Kahn that he kept blacks off his team because he thought they would draw minority fans to the park and his "box seat customers from Westchester County don't want to sit with a lot of colored fans from Harlem."

The Dodgers' mystique would be enhanced as the Bums-turned-winners also became symbols of progress and equality. The notion that the Dodgers got along well as a team became part of Brooklyn lore and was mostly true. But as Kahn and others would occasionally report, some white players resented the arrival of black competitors and expressed their feelings in racist language. Years later Kahn would recall that Preacher Roe complained about "them taking over" and Billy Cox asked, "How would you like a nigger to take your job?"

Overall, baseball had a great year in 1947, with average attendance in the National League reaching nearly 1.3 million. (This was a record that would stand for more than a decade.) The Dodgers helped create this boom when they took to the road, as an additional 325,000 people paid to see the visitors from Brooklyn, including Jackie Robinson. At home, however, the Dodgers with Robinson didn't draw nearly as well. At Ebbets Field they sold about twenty thousand more tickets than in the previous season. This was a little more than 10 percent of the league's average increase. Given that the team had Robinson, won the pennant, and increased its number of home dates by playing fewer doubleheaders, this was an extremely disappointing result. Decades later, one academic study would blame the Dodgers' poor performance at the gate on a decline in white attendance, which might suggest that the borough was not as open-minded as the team.

For generations white males had formed the fan base for the Dodgers. But after these fellows returned from the war and caught a game at Ebbets Field, they didn't take long to marry, have children, and leave the old neighborhoods. Enticed by low prices and cheap mortgages, thousands bought houses on Long Island, where the pursuit of happiness meant an evening cocktail instead of a beer at the corner tavern and a weekend barbecue rather than a ball game. Their places in the old borough were taken by poorer newcomers who tended to be black or Hispanic and not so interested in the previously all-white game of major-league baseball.

Eventually the middle-class march to the suburbs that began after World War II would be recognized as a major factor in the transformation of urban neighborhoods across the country. But this dynamic wasn't named, quantified, or even recognized in the beginning. All that the Dodgers management knew was that while they put the best team in the league on the field, they weren't keeping up with the competition at the gate.

The team's financial challenge was compounded by rising costs. Thanks to the new minimum salary, the pension plan, and the realities of the postwar economy, players were much more expensive across the board. The owners also faced increased wages for union stadium workers, and those with old facilities faced higher prices on repairs. The Dodgers were further taxed when they learned that the lights installed to permit night games in 1938 were not permanent fixtures and would require major improvement to meet city codes. These costs helped to explain why shareholders received no dividend in 1947, a problem that was raised at the annual stockholders meeting by James Mulvey.

Although he was odd man out in the Dodgers' ownership group, as president of Samuel Goldwyn's film company Mulvey was a powerful person with sharp business instincts. In the days after the World Series he had more than a passing interest in the other great spectator event of the season: public hearings on alleged communists in Hollywood conducted by the House Un-American Activities Committee (HUAC). While witnesses were hardly consistent or authoritative, the proceedings moved the American Legion to threaten to boycott all movies. An audience at a theater in North Carolina actually stoned the screen. Several foreign governments considered banning Hollywood's products. In November, Mulvey joined the worried leaders of the industry who gathered for a closed-door summit at the Waldorf-Astoria in New York. Despite Sam Goldwyn's opposition, the group blacklisted ten writers alleged to have communist leanings, agreeing not to hire them. Mulvey was named to a committee that would oversee the pact.

Somehow, despite the crisis in his own business, Mulvey kept a close eye on the Dodgers and persisted with questions about contracts and bank accounts, and was very interested in auditing the books. In response, O'Malley noted that along with paying these fixed expenses, money was being used to pay down mortgages and develop the farm system. More than $200,000 was going toward a new stadium Rickey wanted in St. Paul, and the team had to plan for an investment of $1 million or more to obtain land for a new major-league park in Brooklyn.

Mulvey wasn't satisfied by these explanations and would continue to press for information. He was especially concerned about the lack of documentation for Rickey's executive reports, which were made verbally from handwritten notes.

More complaints came from John L. Smith, who wasn't looking to make much money in baseball but certainly didn't want to lose any. For two years Smith had supported Rickey without much reservation, except for the time when he talked Rickey out of publishing a screed called *The Case Against Jimmy Powers*. (Powers was a sportswriter who branded Rickey "El Cheapo" and tried to hound him out of Brooklyn.) Around the start of spring training in March 1948, Smith invited another local sportswriter to don a white coat and take a tour of the Pfizer penicillin factory in the Bushwick neighborhood of Brooklyn. As they inspected the sterile production line where ten thousand gallons of chemical solution were required to make five pounds of the miracle drug, the Dodgers' supposedly silent partner gave him an earful about the club. He said that Branch Rickey acted as if he owned "the whole works" rather than just a piece of the team and made "financial gambles you wouldn't make in any other business." Rickey demonstrated these tendencies when he paid Durocher his full salary when he was banned and made him manager again when Chandler ended his suspension.

————

WHAT CONCERNED SMITH WAS the fierce game being played behind the scenes in the Dodgers organization. Since baseball executives rivaled politicians when it came to insincere backslapping, their struggles with each other were generally obscured from the press and public by constant pronouncements of mutual admiration and teamwork. (Even their most contentious letters would begin "My dear . . .") But men such as Rickey, O'Malley, and Smith were no less competitive than the players they put on the field. The main difference was that the executives played for different stakes. For them baseball wasn't mere entertainment or an ephemeral story told over the course of a season that becomes just a memory. It was, instead, a serious matter of money and power and lasting legacies.

The trick for an ambitious owner in the postwar era was to control expenses while fielding a team with enough stars, and potential, for fans to believe that a championship was always within reach. Under these conditions, teams sold more tickets to fans, who then spent extra on food and drink and programs. The Yankees proved this simple formula as they consistently made money by winning games. But as perennial winners the Yankees owners enjoyed the advantage of wealth, which allowed them simply to buy the best players. Others had to spend more judiciously and hope either to develop talent in the minor leagues or find undervalued men at a moment when they were ready to perform at a higher level.

The Dodgers owners had bet that Branch Rickey's eye for talent and his minor-league development program would help them match the Yankees' success. But by 1948, O'Malley and Smith seemed to have second thoughts about Rickey's performance. Although the other owners never discussed it publicly, Rickey's own salary and bonus of more than $200,000 per year represented one of the single biggest expenses in the team budget. This sum was roughly half the total paid to the entire team and was equal to the salary of the president of the world's largest company, AT&T. Most of it came from commissions on trades, and to his credit the crafty Rickey had saved the team big sums by routing the deals through the Montreal farm club, where no capital gains tax would be levied. Nevertheless, any stockholder who wondered about dividends would naturally focus on the fact that one of his fellow owners was paid so handsomely out of the team's revenues.

Rickey was also responsible for the organization's purchase of a football team—also called the Dodgers—that lost money at an alarming rate. The football Dodgers played in the upstart All-America Football Conference, which was founded in 1944. The league was dominated by extremely wealthy owners, who had engaged the more established National Football League in a bidding war for players. Salaries had gone up so fast and so far that profits in both leagues disappeared. This record had made John L. Smith and Walter O'Malley skeptical about joining the fray, but they had gone along when Rickey proposed it. The decision fulfilled an ambition that Rickey first expressed when he worked in St. Louis, where he tried but failed to pair a football franchise with a baseball team. In Brooklyn the idea would cost the ownership group more than $500,000 in the coming three years, as the football team lost, on average, $175,000 per season.

In this time Rickey also racked up new expenses related to spring training, as he signed contracts to create a camp for minor leaguers at a vacant naval air station next to the airport in Vero Beach, Florida. The location, which was owned by the city, had been offered by a local booster/businessman named Bud Holman. Rickey had toured it in 1947 and then sent Buzzie Bavasi to follow up with Holman and scout a few other spots.

Young Bavasi, who went to Vero Beach first, discovered in Holman a big, gregarious man with striking dark eyes, big bushy brows, and boundless enthusiasm. Holman's daylong sales pitch ended with a lavish party at his family's Blue Cypress Ranch. Set on 1,200 acres adjacent to a lake, the sprawling ranch house was built out of broad unfinished cypress planks and sported a veranda perfect for sunset parties. Isolated and fully stocked with food and drink, it was the kind of place that encouraged men to relax and feel at ease. Bavasi wound up spending the night and never went to the other cities. Instead he accepted Holman's proposal, which he made on behalf of the city, that the club lease a big tract of land suitable for ball fields and adjacent abandoned military buildings, including barracks and a dining hall.

When team officials inspected the Vero Beach property, they got a shock: roofs leaked, wind whistled through walls, and many of the sinks, toilets, and water pipes had been stolen along with the entire heating plant. With time and money the site would evolve into an efficient operation big enough to accommodate all the Dodgers' farm teams. But at the moment it represented another huge investment driven mainly by Rickey's desire to create the sports empire of his dreams. In the meantime, other issues that affected the team's long-term interests were set aside.

WITH RICKEY FOCUSING the team's money and manpower on projects like the Vero camp and the football operation, Walter O'Malley found himself alone as he tried to solve the team's stadium problems, which were made all the more urgent by the rise of television. As television delivered games to the public for free, it seemed to threaten attendance more than radio ever had because it gave the audience a better view of the game than the best box seats. For this reason Branch Rickey generally opposed televising games, arguing that while radio whetted a fan's appetite, TV satisfied it.

Just about everyone in the entertainment field faced a similar challenge. The free programming that TV delivered would make it harder to get people to leave their homes and pay for a play, movie, or concert. Since society was rapidly organizing itself around the self-contained nuclear family—husband, wife, and children who did things together—this would be especially true if the setting for live entertainment was not welcoming. No one wanted to bring a spouse and children to an inconvenient locale and sit in a shabby or uncomfortable theater or grandstand, just to see a performance.

But where there was danger, TV also offered an opportunity. The more viewers, the more a team could charge for licensing fees and advertising. (In 1949 the Dodgers would earn more than any team in the league on this basis.) And, like radio, TV might entice more distant fans to make a pilgrimage to the ballpark, where they could take in the whole experience—*feel* the game as well as see it—for themselves. If the ballpark was easy to get to and safe and pleasant inside, and if the food was good and the bathrooms were clean, they might even return.

In the case of the Dodgers and Ebbets Field, the ifs posed a problem. People with cars—and there were more and more of them—didn't want to drag their families around on trains and subways. They wanted to drive to the games, but since parking spots numbered in the hundreds, not thousands, this was a difficult and often frustrating prospect. Even if they did find their way to Flatbush and located a safe legal parking spot, these same fans found the ballpark to be cramped and shabby.

Although he was denied the funding to address these problems directly, O'Malley didn't stop working on them. On January 16 he discussed stadium concepts over lunch at '21' with Norman Bel Geddes, the famous designer responsible for Futurama, the General Motors pavilion at the 1939 New York World's Fair. A month later he explored buying land in downtown Brooklyn, near Borough Hall. In March he received a report from Emil Praeger on the possibility of building on a site near Fort Greene Park. He found that the property, worth about $1.3 million, was suitable for a stadium seating fifty-eight thousand. With a large public garage and open land nearby, parking would be less difficult than at Ebbets.

Besides working on the stadium issue, O'Malley kept looking for new ways to generate revenue and attention and push the club into the future. He made an agreement with Sears, Roebuck to sell Dodgers merchandise and licensed a clothing company called Pacific Mills to market shirts and scarves. (At this time few clubs offered official apparel to fans.) In mid-May O'Malley got together with executives from IBM to discuss putting a more modern electronic scoreboard up at Ebbets. A few days later he brought Rickey to see William Paley of CBS, who was rapidly building a nationwide TV network that might carry ball games.

Of course, TV viewers, sportswriters, and even fans leafing through the Sears catalog wouldn't be much interested in the Dodgers if they didn't win, and in 1948 they didn't win. Despite one of the best lineups in the game, the squad that took the pennant going away the year before struggled to finish third. Attendance fell by nearly half a million. Most galling of all for the owners was the fact that the Giants, who played worse, sold more tickets.

The problem had been obvious early in the season. On the first of June, Smith sent a long letter to Rickey that began with a note about how "Walter and I" hadn't been able to consult with him on "the adverse trend" on the field and at the gate. He wrote: "The feeling prevails that the team has changed in one fell swoop from a wholesomely belligerent ball club to a discouraged, ineffective and bewildered one."

Some of the trouble could be traced directly to Rickey's favorite bad boy, Durocher, who had returned as manager only to alienate Robinson at spring training by publicly humiliating him for being overweight. By mid-season even Rickey had had enough. He negotiated with Giants owner Horace Stoneham, who was looking to shake up his team, to take Durocher as manager so that he could give the Dodgers back to easygoing Burt Shotton. The man Durocher replaced over at the Polo Grounds was the legendary player Mel Ott.

Durocher's jump to the Giants was a coup for Stoneham, who now had an exciting and talented manager who could draw fans to the Polo Grounds. But it disoriented loyal fans of both teams. Brooklynites considered Durocher a traitor. Giants fans wondered whether he could be truly faithful to their team. And the fans weren't the only ones who had to make an adjustment: players and coaches were challenged too. "It was really serious," recalled Carl Erskine, who was a twenty-two-year-old Dodger rookie at the time. "As soon as Leo went to the Giants he was the enemy and some guys rode him hard. Jackie [Robinson] and [Don] Newcombe would say, 'Hey, Leo, check Babe Ruth's watch and tell me the time.' That got to him. You could tell."

The manager switch scrambled loyalties but didn't change the results on the field for the Dodgers, who finished third. They could take some comfort, however, in the fact that neither the Giants nor the Yankees made it to the postseason, either. Instead the Indians of Feller and Boudreau beat the Braves of Spahn and Sain four games to two. An all-time record for attendance was set in game five when 86,288 packed Municipal Stadium.

The crowds in Cleveland, as well as the growth in press coverage, proved that Americans still loved sports. A new national magazine called *Sport* gave the major leagues greater exposure, while newspapers expanded both the space devoted to the games and widened their range to include issues off the field. Front-office moves and the business competition among teams became fair game, especially for writers like Dick Young of the *Daily News* and Tom Meany of the upstart newspaper *PM*. Their more aggressive attitude marked the beginning of the end of a cozy era when many writers asked questions and wrote stories as if they were part of the clubs they covered.

People wondered why major-league baseball was confined to just ten cities east of the Mississippi and north of the Mason-Dixon line. Other regions, especially the West, had grown substantially since the major leagues were founded, and by all signs the trend was only going to accelerate. Los Angeles was already the fifth-largest city in the country and San Francisco ranked eleventh.

For years officials of the Pacific Coast League (PCL) had pressed to be recognized as a third major circuit. Their teams were among the best in the minors and could have held their own against many in the majors. If the American and National Leagues weren't going to come west themselves, why not elevate the PCL? Civic leaders played the baseball card during campaigns, telling voters that they deserved big-time ball. One, a county supervisor in Los Angeles named Leonard Roach, lobbied Chandler about getting a single major-league franchise to play in the massive Memorial Coliseum, which could accommodate more fans than the Cleveland stadium.

For fifty years the major leagues had resisted expansion, in part because teams were reluctant to travel great distances. But by the late 1940s, coast-to-coast air travel was becoming less expensive and, thanks to pressurized cabins, more comfortable. American, United, and TWA competed on these routes, steadily reducing flight times and improving service. It was easy to imagine that if a franchise or two were planted on the coast, visiting teams could jump west from St. Louis or Chicago without much trouble.

The appeal of a truly national pastime was obvious for the have-nots, but the haves faced uncertainty. Fans around the country were already listening to major-league games on the radio, which meant better licensing payments for the existing clubs. Every year thousands also made pilgrimages to the North and East just to see the stars and stadiums they had pictured in their minds. Others, who couldn't make such a trip, flocked to the exhibition games that teams played as they traveled home from spring training and bought tickets to see minor-league affiliates. In these ways and more, the current setup equaled cash for the sixteen existing clubs and meant change would come slowly. The oligarchs of the major leagues would only study the possibility of expansion while allowing television to deliver the game to an ever wider and more valuable audience. Broadcasts improved quickly in the late 1940s as almost every crew began using three cameras and, in New York at least, permanent control rooms were built in the stadiums. Network telecasts, especially those of the all-star games and World Series, drew huge audiences nationwide.

As always, whether they read the sports pages or caught games from broadcasts, fans looked for compelling characters and stories to follow, and in 1949 the Dodgers provided them. The team that took the field—which included players named Abrams, Furillo, Hermanski, McCormick, and Olmo—looked like the cast of one of those movies about World War II where every ethnic group got at least a walk-on role. The only difference was that the Dodgers also included two black starters, Robinson and Roy Campanella, and an African-American pitcher named Don Newcombe.

By his third season Robinson had established himself as a dominant player in the league and had moved to second base, where he joined with shortstop Pee Wee Reese to form a brilliant team within the team. A future Hall of Famer, Reese was sparkling in the field and swift on the base paths. The press made much of his being paired with Robinson because he was from Kentucky, a former bastion of the Confederacy. However, he handled the role so well that he and Robinson became symbols of happy racial progress. In a long profile John Lardner, writer son of the famous Ring, cited their "brilliance and harmony." Reese and Robinson even made a recording of a story for children, *Slugger at the Bat*, for Columbia Records.

With his fame, Robinson was expected to serve as a representative of the values of the game and all of black America. It being the era of loyalty investigations, Robinson was inevitably summoned by the House Un-American Activities Committee—the same body that had put Hollywood on trial the previous autumn—to comment on pro-communist statements made by Paul Robeson, the great actor, singer, and political activist. Robeson, who in 1943 had pleaded with the owners to integrate baseball, had apparently said that he loved the Soviet Union more than the United States and that black Americans should refuse to fight in a future war with the Soviets.

When Congress called, Robinson's mentor and benefactor, Branch Rickey, demanded that he comply. Rickey had recently begun adding strident anti-communist rhetoric to his public talks. In early 1949 he accused a lawyer representing ballplayer Danny Gardella, who had gone to the Mexican league, of "communistic tendencies." Gardella had challenged the reserve clause in the standard baseball contract, which seemingly bound players to a club even after their deals expired. Commissioner Chandler was desperate to keep the issue out of court and settled the case by paying him $60,000 and letting him back into the game. Rickey, meanwhile, had to turn to Walter O'Malley to get him out of a threatened slander suit, but this trouble didn't dim his politics. He pushed hard until Robinson agreed.

Appearing before the committee in July, Robinson offered a careful statement that revealed to the nation, for the first time, his sharp observations on racism in America. "Negro Americans," as he put it, didn't need a communist critique to see the injustice in segregation throughout society. "Negroes were stirred up long before there was a Communist party and they'll stay stirred up long after the party has disappeared, unless Jim Crow has disappeared by then as well."

Robinson made it clear that he agreed with those who had criticized Robeson's comments on the superiority of the Soviet system and how people ought to respond if called to war. He punctuated the point by saying he had "too much invested" in America to be persuaded by "a siren song sung in bass."

As he spoke in a high, tense voice, Robinson seemed somewhat pained to be in the position of representing fifteen million black Americans. And eventually he would admit that he had been exploited by the committee. But at the time he won praise from many whites, including editorial writers and leaders of veterans groups, for testimony that made him and his team even more popular across the country.

One in seven Americans could trace a relative back to Brooklyn, a demographic fact that created a Dodgers fan base even in places where you needed to make an overnight trip to see a big-league game. Throw in a terrific pennant race and the 1949 Dodgers became America's team before there was such a term, pulling more than 1.8 million fans to their road games. (This was two hundred thousand more than they attracted at home.) They won the pennant by a single game over St. Louis and, because the universe was in proper order, faced the Yankees in the World Series.

In the postseason the Brooklyns would lean heavily on Newcombe, who was one of the hardest-throwing pitchers in the league, rookie of the year, and an all-star. His power enthralled fans nationwide, including the one who lived in the White House. According to writer Roger Kahn, Truman had Newcombe on his mind when he met with a new Supreme Court justice on the first day of the World Series. "This big colored guy for Brooklyn is throwing hard," he said. "I wonder if DiMaggio will get to him."

Newcombe pitched so well that DiMaggio didn't get to him at all. Neither did anyone else until the ninth inning, when Tommy Heinrich hit a home run that gave the Yanks a 1–0 win. The Dodger spitballer Preacher Roe managed to win by the same score the next day, but that was the only game of the series they would win. The Yankees pitchers stymied most of the Dodgers hitters— including the new star Duke Snider—and with Casey Stengel's cagey managing won three in a row. Once again, as they had in 1941 and 1947, Brooklyn's boys had fallen to a pin-striped powerhouse that represented everything—wealth, elitism, segregation—that the Dodgers seemed to stand against. The hurt would last all winter long.

TO THE RELIEF OF everyone connected, the Brooklyn Dodgers football team didn't add to the disappointment on Montague Street because, by the autumn of 1949, the franchise had been merged with the Yankee football team, which was owned by Dan Topping. The demise of the Dodgers football franchise came early in the year as the entire league was threatened with collapse and Rickey went to Chicago to meet Cleveland Browns owner Arthur McBride and Benjamin Lindheimer, a racetrack owner who also held an interest in the AAFC's Los Angeles franchise. Together with league counsel Lou Carroll, they weighed whether they should continue to compete with the NFL, seek a merger, or dissolve. No decision was made and Rickey returned to New York late on January 19 with all three men in tow. They went straight to the Metropolitan Club, where they met Walter O'Malley and John Smith in the private Governor's Room. (Smith had already gone on record saying "I don't believe football has a place in Brooklyn.")

Like several other owners in the league, McBride and the Lindheimer group had enough money to continue the war with the NFL, even though it was costing both leagues millions of dollar a year. With Rickey, they asked O'Malley and Smith to carry on for one more year with the hope that the NFL would sue for peace and agree to create one big profitable league.

Here O'Malley showed his ability to set aside sentiment and get to the

Edwin J. O'Malley, who was appointed commissioner of public markets for New York City by Mayor John F. Hylan, with his wife, Alma Feltner O'Malley, and their son, Walter (circa 1907).
© walteromalley.com

Honeymooners Walter and Kay O'Malley enjoy a carriage ride in Bermuda. They were married at St. Malachy's, known as the Actors' Chapel, in New York City on September 5, 1931, with Father Patrick Gallagher officiating.
© walteromalley.com

Walter, Kay, and their two children, Terry and Peter, at their residence on St. Marks Avenue in Brooklyn in 1940.
© walteromalley.com

Walter O'Malley and Judge Henry L. Ughetta (LEFT) listen to Dodgers president Branch Rickey (CENTER). Judge Ughetta served as a member of the Brooklyn Dodgers' board of directors for more than a decade beginning in the late 1940s. © *walteromalley.com*

Ebbets Field, opened in 1913, occupied a crowded corner of Brooklyn with little parking space.
© *Brian Merlis collection, Brooklynpic.com*

Dodgers broadcaster Vin Scully interviews Dodgers president Walter O'Malley in front of the WWOR-TV camera in New York. Scully joined the Dodgers in 1950 as a sidekick to Dodgers broadcasters Red Barber and Connie Desmond. He was inducted into the broadcasters' wing of the National Baseball Hall of Fame in 1982. Lucky Strike and Schaefer Brewing were the Dodgers' main sponsors. © walteromalley.com

In 1954, O'Malley took a chance on a manager with no previous major-league experience when he named Walter Alston to lead the Dodgers. In just his second season at the helm, Alston guided the Dodgers to their first and only World Championship in Brooklyn. Under O'Malley and Alston in Los Angeles, the team would win championships again in 1959, 1963, and 1965.

© walteromalley.com

President Dwight D. Eisenhower visited Ebbets Field in Brooklyn to attend game one of the 1956 World Series. To the right of President Eisenhower are his son John Eisenhower (in uniform) and Secretary of State John Foster Dulles.

© walteromalley.com

After the Dodgers' goodwill tour to Japan in the fall of 1956, Kay and Walter O'Malley continued on a round-the-world trip. In Italy, they paused at the Roman Colosseum. © *walteromalley.com*

Under Walter O'Malley, the Dodgers were the first baseball team to purchase aircraft for team travel. The Dodgers made many road trips in the sixty-six-passenger Electra II shown here. The plane was named the *Kay O* after O'Malley's wife.
© *walteromalley.com*

When Walter O'Malley visited Los Angeles in May 1957, he took a fifty-minute helicopter ride to view possible downtown sites for a new stadium. The two-seat L.A. County sheriff's helicopter was piloted by Captain Sewell Griggers. © *Ralph Crane// Time Life Pictures/Getty Images*

In his first visit to Los Angeles since making the historic decision to head westward with the Dodgers, Walter O'Malley steps off the Dodgers' Convair 440 airplane at Los Angeles International Airport and is greeted by Los Angeles city councilwoman Rosalind Wyman and L.A. county supervisor Kenneth Hahn.

© Courtesy University of Southern California, on behalf of the USC Special Collections

Retired pitcher Carl Erskine attended the brief ceremony that preceded the start of demolition at Ebbets Field. Although he posed playfully with a wrecking ball painted to look like a baseball, he was saddened by the demise of the old park.

© Brian Merlis collection, Brooklynpix.com.

The construction of Dodger Stadium began in 1960. Walter O'Malley was at the site almost every day, from beginning to end.

© walteromalley.com

Opened April 10, 1962, the 56,000-seat Dodger Stadium cost $23 million to build. O'Malley invested an additional $1.5 million in landscaping in and around the stadium. Designed to be "family friendly," the stadium featured convenient parking and concessions, unobstructed sightlines, and numerous spotless restrooms. © Los Angeles Dodgers

Walter O'Malley at field level on Opening Day at Dodger Stadium, April 10, 1962. © walteromalley.com

"Favorite team?" said O'Malley. "I guess the year we beat our old enemies the Yankees in four straight in the World Series." World Series MVP Sandy Koufax, O'Malley, Don Drysdale, and Johnny Podres (LEFT TO RIGHT) enjoy the Dodgers' victory party at the Stadium Club on October 7, 1963. © Bettmann/Corbis

Dedication ceremonies of Dodger stadium on April 12, 1962. (LEFT TO RIGHT) Terry O'Malley Seidler holding her son Peter, Captain Emil Praeger, Walter O'Malley holding Terry's son John, and Kay O'Malley. A dedication plaque is located on the Top Deck level. © *walteromalley.com*

Peter O'Malley (LEFT) and his father, Walter, share a moment atop the visitors' dugout at Candlestick Park in San Francisco in June 1966. © *walteromalley.com*

Walter O'Malley was a part owner and vice president of the team when Branch Rickey signed the first African-American player to a major-league contract. Jackie Robinson made his debut with the Brooklyn Dodgers on April 15, 1947. The O'Malley family retired his uniform number, 42, in 1972. O'Malley is shown with Robinson and his wife, Rachel, circa 1960. © *Los Angeles Dodgers*

Walter O'Malley's rings from each of the Dodgers' World Championships, 1955, 1959, 1963, and 1965. © *walteromalley.com*

WALTER O'MALLEY
BROOKLYN, N.L., 1943-1957
LOS ANGELES, N.L., 1958-1979

AN INFLUENTIAL AND VISIONARY OWNER WHO INSPIRED BASEBALL'S MOVE WEST IN 1957. RELOCATED DODGERS FROM BROOKLYN TO LOS ANGELES AND OPENED NEW MARKETS FOR THE MAJOR LEAGUE GAME. SERVED AS PRESIDENT AND PRINCIPAL OWNER WHEN HIS CLUBS WON FOUR WORLD SERIES CHAMPIONSHIPS (1955, 1959, 1963 AND 1965) AND 11 PENNANTS. MAINTAINED AFFORDABLE TICKET PRICES WHILE GENERATING RECORD ATTENDANCE. DRIVING FORCE BEHIND DESIGN, CONSTRUCTION AND FINANCING OF DODGER STADIUM, A BENCHMARK FOR A NEW GENERATION OF MODERN BALLPARKS.

Walter O'Malley was posthumously inducted into the National Baseball Hall of Fame in 2008. © *National Baseball Hall of Fame* nub of a business problem. He asked how another year and a loss of as much as $300,000 would help one of the worst teams in the game. Even if peace were declared and the NFL owners invited some of the upstarts into their league, the lowly Dodgers were not going to be included. How could Rickey, McBride, and Lindheimer ask him to finance the conference when his team would inevitably die?

O'Malley had another idea. Besides Cleveland, which was perhaps the best football team ever built, he saw promise for the conference in Chicago, Baltimore, and New York. However, the AAFC's New York Yankees needed to be bolstered if they were to compete with the NFL Giants. If the owners wanted to continue their war with the older league, why not merge Brooklyn and the Yankees to create a better team?

No one at the meeting could give O'Malley a good reason to keep Dodgers football going. A day later Rickey announced the merger with Topping. The other owners in the American conference declared that the football war would go on with seven teams instead of eight. Rickey, who had made a mess of the franchise he had pushed so hard to acquire, confessed that the fans in Brooklyn hadn't supported his team because it wasn't very good, and that the problem would have taken years to fix.

The deal with Topping reduced the Dodgers' financial risk and was a victory for O'Malley, who had begun to assert himself more with Rickey. A few months before, he had opposed Rickey on a request by the broadcaster Red Barber, who asked the club for a loan so he could buy a house. O'Malley didn't like the idea of the club issuing home loans—he said that's what banks and mortgage companies were for—but the request was granted over his objection. He also stood firm against Rickey's proposal to build a fifteen-thousand-seat stadium for the minor-league team in St. Paul. "At this point," noted the minutes of a board meeting, "Mr. O'Malley renewed his usual speech against rebuilding or building in minor-league cities before the over-age stadium in Brooklyn was replaced."

In general, O'Malley seemed to have the support of the third partner in the controlling group, John L. Smith, but he didn't press the advantage; and while they tussled over issues, the O'Malley-Rickey relationship was complex. They worked well together on many projects, and O'Malley had been generous whenever Rickey asked for legal help. When Rickey bought his gentleman's farm, O'Malley traveled all the way to Chestertown, Maryland, to handle the closing. Later, O'Malley ran interference for Rickey while an attorney chased him for nearly a year over an unpaid fertilizer bill.

The two men also tried to get along socially. They often shared meals and Rickey even accepted O'Malley's invitation to go on a deep-sea fishing expedition. The families liked each other, and the O'Malley children sometimes sat with Rickey's wife, Jane, at the ballpark. But all along, these two strong-minded competitors held to very different ideas about baseball, Brooklyn, and business. These differences would come to a head when they lost the moderating influence of the third partner in the ownership group.

IN EARLY 1950, as the Dodgers prepared for spring training, John L. Smith felt tired and weak, but he tried to carry on as usual. He went to business meetings and tried to keep in touch with friends. He asked O'Malley to get a couple of tickets for his daughter and son-in-law to see a filming of the conductor Fred Waring's television show. The program was aired by NBC, but O'Malley was able to get the favor done by writing to a friend at CBS to say, "If Mr. Gimbel can talk to Mr. Macy, maybe you can use your good influence with NBC."

It was a little favor, the type of thing that friends with connections enjoyed doing. It also reflected the kind of relationship that O'Malley and Smith shared. They trusted each other and enjoyed their time together. When Smith wound up in the hospital and then learned he had terminal cancer, he naturally trusted O'Malley to help him with his affairs as he lived out his final months at home.

Although he would continue to read and sign key documents for the team, Smith was soon bedridden and unable to attend meetings. Many important decisions, including the renewal of Rickey's contract as club president, were put off and the two other members of the ruling trio stuck to their routines. Rickey oversaw the team and its farm clubs. O'Malley focused on business affairs, but had to take a break from his normal duties to fight a proposed state law that would have made it illegal to play two games in a single day and charge separate admissions. The proposed ban on so-called split doubleheaders was popular with fans but the law was unconstitutional, said O'Malley, and in the end Governor Thomas Dewey agreed. He vetoed the legislation that would have made it law.

When he wasn't defending the constitution and his box office, O'Malley worked on expanding radio exposure for the Dodgers, building a network that was bigger than any other in the league. Regionally, the live accounts by Red Barber and Connie Desmond already attracted a vast audience in the industrial Northeast. Radio was at its peak, and to improve the broadcast and ensure against Desmond's alcohol-related problems, a new young announcer named Vin Scully was added to the team.

Scully came from a struggling background many Brooklyn fans would admire. He had been two years old at the start of the Great Depression and was just five when his father died. His mother supported him and his sister by operating a small boardinghouse. She eventually married an English immigrant named Alan Reeve, whom Scully accepted as a father figure.

As a student at Fordham Prep, a Jesuit school, Scully had acquired a work ethic to go with his natural talent for public speaking. He also began to see how a kindness offered at just the right moment could change a person's life. One big example arose when he was about to attend a city-wide elocution contest but didn't have the right color shoes to go with his coat and slacks. The headmaster collected black shoes from a hundred donors, laid them out on the floor of his office, and brought Scully in to find exactly the right pair to borrow for the day. Scully came in third in the contest and went on to Fordham University and a job in radio sports. One of his most memorable early assignments involved a football game in Boston where no booth was available and he broadcast from the roof of Fenway Park in near-freezing temperatures without a coat or gloves. No one listening had any idea he was suffering.

Impressed when he heard Scully's work, Red Barber became his mentor and helped him get the Dodgers job. He also trained him to be straightforward and self-effacing. "Once I said that I had never seen a better ballplayer than Willie Mays," recalled Scully years later. "Red came to me and said, 'Son, you don't have any right to talk about the greatness of players you've seen. You've only been here two years.'"

With Scully completing the three-man team, the live Dodger broadcasts were more popular than ever in New York, but it's possible that even more people got their regular dose of Dodger drama from a different source. Beginning in 1950, more than one hundred stations across the country participated in the new national Dodger Network, which aired games as they were re-created from coded wire service accounts—"B1" meant ball one, "CS" stood for "called strike"—in a Washington, D.C., studio by Nat Allbright.

Imaginative announcers had been turning ticker reports into ball games for years. In the 1930s a young Ronald Reagan had performed this trick for a station in Iowa. Allbright, whose nasal voice became part of the background noise in barbershops, cafés, and homes across America, took this art to a high level. He used recordings of the music played by Ebbets Field organist Gladys Goodding and calibrated artificial crowd noise to reflect the actual attendance at each stadium. "Most people never knew our games were not live," he would recall. "In the Polo Grounds we had crowd noise amplified, fights in the stands, people going wild against the Dodgers—in other words, just like it was."

The Dodger Network was an instant hit, often getting higher ratings than broadcasts of the games played by local major-league teams. In the South, many African-Americans who became Dodger fans the minute Jackie Robinson was signed listened to the games religiously, always rooting for Brooklyn. (More than a few whites listened just as avidly, desperately pulling for Brooklyn to lose.) These same fans would turn out for exhibition games that the Dodgers staged in southern cities on their way home from spring training.

In 1950 the Dodgers were everyone's pick to win the National League pennant. In the annual preseason Associated Press poll, a huge majority of the reporters surveyed picked the Dodgers to win the National League pennant. The team had a strong spring training at Dodgertown—Robinson arrived only twelve pounds overweight—and swept through a series of exhibition games on its journey north.

On April 18, Rickey and O'Malley boarded a train at Pennsylvania Station for Philadelphia, where the Dodgers would play their first game of the regular season against the Phillies, whom the nation's sportswriters had picked to finish no better than fourth. Both men had been thinking about the future without John L. Smith, and at some point they sat together and tried to talk about it.

Despite his substantial income and bonuses, Rickey told O'Malley that he was in bad shape financially. He had borrowed so much on his life insurance policy that the premium came to more than $14,000 a year. This payment, added to the expense of keeping a hobby farm in Maryland and the cost of the loan he took to buy his Dodgers stock, put him under significant pressure at a time in life when most men consider slowing down. He was sixty-nine years old and concerned about leaving an estate for his family.

Somewhere between the Hudson and Delaware rivers, Rickey raised the possibility of cashing in his shares. Baseball teams being a kind of toy, rich men were always inquiring about buying in. In 1948 and '49, different men had talked about spending $1 million or more for Rickey's piece of the Dodgers. Under the Smith-Rickey-O'Malley agreement, partners had a right to match a bona fide offer, and while none was on the table at the moment, Rickey tested O'Malley to see what he thought about breaking up the owners group.

As he listened, O'Malley knew that while he was still alive, his friend John L. Smith would have to approve any sale; but, having watched the man decline, he couldn't imagine trying to get him to talk about it at this moment. "Desperately ill" was how he would recall Smith's condition. Unless Rickey had a definite offer from someone who couldn't wait, O'Malley wasn't going to bother Smith or his wife, Mary Louise.

Later Rickey would say that he had confessed his financial problems in the hope that O'Malley might make an offer to buy him out then and there. This didn't happen, and by the time the train pulled into Philadelphia the subject was dropped. The two owners went on to Shibe Park, where Don Newcombe was tagged for four runs in the second inning and the visitors fell by 9–1.

For the rest of the season the Dodgers would play well enough to run an exciting pennant race with these same Phillies. Duke Snider would emerge as a batting star, posting a .329 average and hitting thirty-one homers. Roy Campanella and Jackie Robinson would repeat as starters on the all-star team, and five other Brooklyn players would be picked as reserves. The Dodgers would stay in it to the end, finishing a close second. (Even so, they suffered a baffling 25 percent decline in attendance.) But as exciting as the play was on the field, the drama that would affect the team most profoundly took place out of public view and featured just two people, Walter O'Malley and Branch Rickey.

With John Smith dying, Rickey faced the possibility of losing the free hand he enjoyed running the team. At his age, he couldn't bear the thought of working for someone else. He also needed to secure his finances. The answer could be a friendly outside investor who might buy his stock for a good price. Rickey began looking for a buyer, discreetly trying to connect with wealthy men who had idle cash and an interest in the game.

In the meantime O'Malley visited Smith almost weekly and kept to a busy business schedule. Like so many Brooklynites, he had moved to Long Island, making his family summer place a year-round home, and this change added a significant commute to his schedule. He rode the Long Island Rail Road on most days, but if he ever found himself in a car when the team was playing, he could hear a broadcaster, Vincent Scully, developing solid partnerships with Red Barber and Connie Desmond.

In mid-May O'Malley attended a preview of a film, *The Jackie Robinson Story*, in which the Dodger star played himself. (Written in part by Rickey's assistant Arthur Mann, the movie was as much about the team president as it was about Robinson.) At the end of the month O'Malley joined Robert Moses and George V. McLaughlin of the Triborough Bridge and Tunnel Authority at the opening of the Brooklyn-Battery Tunnel, which joined Brooklyn and Lower Manhattan. The longest and, at $80 million, the most expensive ever built in the United States, the tunnel was another herald of the automotive era. An editorial writer at the *Times* noted that it would make it easier for the Dodgers and Giants "to get at each other's throats," but it also linked drivers to highways that would allow them to bypass Brooklyn on their way to Long Island.

As summer approached, John L. Smith sank closer to death. Just how much he suffered is impossible to tell, but his decline was rapid. Board minutes noted on June 21 that his condition was serious. On Monday, July 10, when O'Malley and Rickey were in Chicago for the all-star game, Smith died. He was sixty-one years old. Walter O'Malley recorded the event in a heavy hand, writing "John L. Smith died" in his date book in thick black pencil.

Days later Walter O'Malley paid his respects at Smith's home, attended his funeral, and rode to Connecticut in the funeral procession for the interment. Branch Rickey had business in New York but caught up with the funeral party by taking the team's Beechcraft airplane, which then brought both of the men back to New York.

On the flight home, Rickey told O'Malley that he had stayed behind to have breakfast with Ambassador Joseph Kennedy, the wealthy investor, movie man, and liquor distributor whose sons would make politics a family calling. Speaking over the noise of the plane's engines and propellers, Rickey said Kennedy had been working on a bid for his Dodger shares. A price of $1.3 million had been mentioned. Kennedy had even talked about his son Jack becoming president of the team if Rickey remained as general manager. But this morning Kennedy had backed out. Rickey wanted O'Malley to know that the deal had fallen through.

The conversation confirmed for O'Malley something he had suspected for more than a year: that Rickey was serious about wanting to sell. This suspicion had been one of many reasons he had for objecting to a multiyear contract for the Dodgers president, and now he knew for certain that the future of the Dodgers was in play. Three weeks later, on the afternoon of August 3, O'Malley went to see Mary Louise Smith at her home. She granted him her proxy as a stockholder, giving him 50 percent of the votes on the Dodgers board.

In the struggle for control of the team, O'Malley had the advantage. Rickey's contract would expire in October. If he wanted to stay, it would surely be under new conditions. If he wanted to sell, O'Malley would consider buying. He began the negotiations by offering just $350,000, roughly what Rickey's shares were worth when the owner's group was formed in 1945. Both Rickey and O'Malley knew that an independent analysis of the team's worth would peg the price of Rickey's shares at around $1 million. With the low offer Rickey would have a right to be offended. He also had motivation to find an alternative.

Still the best-connected man in baseball, Rickey found help in Pittsburgh. Real estate magnate John W. Galbreath, chairman of the board of the Pittsburgh Pirates, wanted to hire Rickey to bring a pennant to a city that hadn't seen one in more than twenty years. However, the rules of baseball prohibited anyone who owned shares in one team from working for another. To get Rickey away from Brooklyn, Galbreath put him together with an even bigger real estate man, William Zeckendorf, who was willing to offer $1 million for his slice of Dodgers stock. The sale would make it possible for the old genius to become both rich and a Pirate.

While all this maneuvering took place, O'Malley kept his ears open. Near the end of August he learned that the attorney, Lou Carroll, was suddenly representing Rickey in sensitive talks with the minority owner James Mulvey. Since Carroll had once worked for the Dodger partners, O'Malley confronted him. Citing the privacy of his client, Carroll refused to talk about what he was doing.

O'Malley fired off a telegram to Rickey requesting that he free Carroll to speak and to disclose whether he was working on a deal to sell.

In the future, Rickey would be cast as a victim of sorts, squeezed out of a job he deserved and forced to sell his interest in the team. In fact he was playing an active role in a contest with O'Malley, doing everything he could to drive up the price of his shares and also get one more shot at running a big-league team. Rickey set and cancelled several meetings with O'Malley. Finally, on the morning of September 19, a Tuesday, he met with Rickey at the team office on Montague Street. There, for the first time, Rickey revealed he had another offer. However, he refused to say who was behind the bid, which naturally raised O'Malley's ire. O'Malley pushed hard, noting that it was "the least a partner could expect" unless "they were North Koreans."

When Rickey wouldn't budge, O'Malley hit him with a surprise.

"Is it Bill Zeckendorf?"

A startled Rickey first asked where he had gotten the information. O'Malley didn't tell him, but on a legal pad where he made notes for the meeting O'Malley had jotted the name "McGrath" next to a line about a $50,000 "commitment fee" Zeckendorf wanted. Rickey then denied that Zeckendorf was the bidder. The two men parted with the issue unresolved.

It wasn't going to stay that way. Rickey was playing in O'Malley's backyard and of course the information was correct: Zeckendorf was the bidder. He quickly approved a contract for the sale to Zeckendorf at a price of $1 million, with a $50,000 fee to be paid should a competitor match the price. When presented with the paperwork, O'Malley had no choice. He wanted the team. He wanted to be rid of Rickey. He agreed to match Zeckendorf. Rickey would get a threefold profit on a six-year-old investment that had been handed to him with the convenience of instant financing. (Rickey would also get the $50,000 fee as a gift from Zeckendorf.) O'Malley would seize absolute control of the Brooklyn Dodgers.

The exact date when Rickey and O'Malley came to terms is difficult to pin down. During this time both men were busy with issues related to the Dodgers' race for the pennant against the surprising Phillies, who, led by pitcher Robin Roberts, prevailed by two games. However, a clue can be found in O'Malley's 1950 appointment book. On Wednesday, October 11, four days after the Yankees finished off the Phillies to win the World Series, he noted in red pencil a three p.m. meeting with Commissioner Happy Chandler at a Manhattan hotel.

(Chandler would have to be informed of any ownership change.) That night the Myomacs gathered to celebrate something at the Ritz-Carlton. It's a safe bet that they were cheering O'Malley's purchase.

On October 23 the Dodgers board met at the team office. James Mulvey, who had previously opposed Rickey's contract renewal, now suggested he be retained for another year as president. O'Malley said he was surprised by Mulvey's sudden support for Rickey, whose contract amounted to "a landlord's lease," meaning it favored him alone and was "unfavorable to the corporation." He added that he was "strongly opposed to the retention of Mr. Rickey under all circumstances" and the contract was not renewed.

On October 25 the stock deal was announced at a press conference where O'Malley insisted that Rickey's fate was not yet certain. Technically this was true, but no one who had been around the team would have believed it. Walter O'Malley became president of the Dodgers, and Rickey resigned the next day. On October 27 both men met with reporters at the Hotel Bossert; O'Malley and Rickey smiled, shook hands, and posed for the cameras like two politicians who had just savaged each other in a debate but had to prove there were no hard feelings.

"I have developed the warmest possible feelings of affection for Mr. Rickey as a man," said O'Malley. "I am terribly sorry and hurt personally that we now have to face this resignation."

Rickey congratulated O'Malley with tears in his eyes, and a photo from the event showed him looking downcast. Brooklyn had given him the best chance anyone ever had to make the perfect ball club, and yet he had fallen short. In baseball, everyone hopes for one more season, but at nearly seventy years of age, he couldn't count on it. At such a moment, feelings of nostalgia, loss, and frustration would have been natural. Rickey showed a little impatience, made a quip about a "prize bull" being shipped to his farm, and departed.

Outside the hotel he was followed to his car by reporters who wanted him to confirm that he no longer owned any stock. This was a key question, since the rules would prevent him from taking a job with another club if he still owned any bit of the Brooklyn team. Rickey offered an irritated reply. "I have no ownership in the Dodgers now!" he snapped. "N—O—W. Now!"

League officials would accept that Rickey was fully divested and within weeks he was general manager of the Pirates. However, the details in the sales contract executed by Rickey and O'Malley explain why pesky reporters had pressed him on his ownership status. As the terms showed, O'Malley had not paid in full for Rickey's shares. Instead he had made only the first of a series of payments that would continue over several years until the full $1 million was paid. This arrangement made it easier for O'Malley to finance the deal, but it also meant that a picky accountant could argue that Rickey remained a de facto Dodgers owner. No one ever used this issue to challenge Rickey's position with the Pirates, but the idea that it might occur would explain why Rickey had been so adamant—"N—O—W. Now!"—out in front of the Hotel Bossert.

Rickey wasn't the only one with reason to worry about reverberations from the stock deal. Two days earlier Walter O'Malley had suggested that living up to the Rickey legend would be an impossible and thankless task. But he did it in classic O'Malley fashion, speaking an important truth in such a calm, wry way that the deeper meaning would be noticed only on reflection. Responding to a reporter who had asked about the club's future, he said, "You may be sure that for the next seven or eight years Mr. Rickey will be credited with the victories of the Brooklyn ball club and that its losses will be charged to somebody else."

There, in a single sentence, was the essence of the challenge faced by Walter O'Malley as he assumed one of the most coveted positions in all of sport: president and controlling owner of a major-league baseball team. Since Rickey was practically a certified baseball genius, many would assume that his successor inherited a perfect machine. If it came apart, O'Malley would be blamed for operating it poorly. If it hummed smoothly, he would get no more credit than a maintenance man with an oilcan. The trick, if he could pull it off, would be in tweaking the controls a bit to achieve the goal that had eluded Rickey. Only a World Series win would make them O'Malley's Dodgers.

Six

O'MALLEY RULES

ll dark wood and heavy paneling, the Dodgers president's office was furnished with brass lamps, a black Bakelite telephone, and the kind of heavy wooden desk and chair that could make the man who used them feel solid. When Larry MacPhail occupied this space, a mounted moose head stared down from the wall. Branch Rickey replaced the moose with a portrait of Lincoln. Walter O'Malley favored Audubon prints—among them a bufflehead duck and a redwing blackbird—and the artist John Groth's stylish baseball illustrations. Only the ashy scent of burned cigars that Rickey left behind remained part of the decor. Walter O'Malley had the habit too.

Besides, he wasn't against keeping other reminders of his predecessor around if they had clear value to the team. For example, as soon as he took over the team he announced that the color-blind policy that brought Jackie Robinson to Brooklyn would continue. "Prejudices have no place in our society—and certainly not in sports," he said in an interview where he recalled that the Ku Klux Klan had been a "vicious force" in Indiana when he was a Culver cadet.

As he announced that he would continue in the direction Rickey set, O'Malley showed that he understood that change was inevitable when it came to race, baseball, and his team's relationship with its fans. For years the new Dodgers president had given serious thought to the special nature of the baseball business, especially the way communities identified with the players and the people who ran the organization. "It's so close to the public," he said, recognizing the almost civic nature of the enterprise. Too much change would disorient fans, but at the same time they wanted a winner and could be excited by a new ballplayer or manager who promised victory.

That was the reliable formula. Create excitement. Win games. Sell more tickets. But oddly, it wasn't working the way it was supposed to work. Victory had done a strange thing to the Dodgers and Brooklyn. O'Malley sensed it in the stands and saw it at the admissions gate. In 1950 the team had almost won the pennant for the second time in a row, but home attendance plummeted by almost 350,000. And it wasn't just the numbers that were down. Some of the love seemed to be missing too. "Now they're 'on' us when we lose," said O'Malley. "There isn't that same deep affection." Winning had taken away a bit of the mystique that made the players beloved when they were Bums.

O'Malley had never liked the way Branch Rickey called the team "ferocious gentlemen." It was a "pompous attempt at affectation that was utterly unsuccessful," he would say. He much preferred that people sometimes thought of the team as the Bums, as represented by the sad-faced hobo drawn by a sports cartoonist named Willard Mullin.

" 'C'mon, you Bums!' is not an opprobrium," said O'Malley. "Rather, it is an endearment" that connected fans with the team. To restore the bond, he brought back single-admission doubleheaders and set up an autograph area where players appeared at special windows to meet the fans. With enough visits to the ballpark a kid who wanted signatures from the entire team could get them.

With these little changes O'Malley could reinforce the sense of attachment that made people cry for joy when their team won and throw the odd tomato when they lost. But major-league baseball in general, and the Dodgers in particular, also faced bigger problems that would be more difficult to solve.

The first was the continuing rise of television. Between 1950 and 1951—a single year—the number of households with TVs would triple to ten million. With nearly one quarter of all homes claiming a set, vast numbers of people could see baseball in their living rooms. No one could say exactly how many times a fan chose to stay home and watch a game on the tube instead of going to the ballpark, or whether rights fees compensated for the lost revenue. But it did happen.

The second problem was the evolving American lifestyle. The most power-ful marriage wave in history, begun in 1943, was still going strong. New couples continued to flee cities for the suburbs, where the baby boom was under way. (The 1950 census showed a 40 percent increase over the previous decade in the number of children under the age of ten.) The comfort of family and home, which sometimes included a bomb shelter, seemed the ultimate protection from life's ordinary problems and even Cold War anxiety. It also exerted a strong pull on commuter husbands and fathers who were duty-bound to make home repairs, mow the lawn, and play catch with the kids. If they did go to see a ball game, they were likely to bring the family, and that meant they expected a safe, clean, wholesome environment.

The family man's needs were different from those of the traditional Brook-lyn fan, who brought a tougher attitude to Ebbets Field. The old fan wanted to shout at the Bums and curse out the umpires. To him, Ebbets was still the place where Leo Durocher punched out John Christian, and with beer always avail-able it could turn from Sunday picnic grounds to rowdy saloon in the time it took an umpire to shout, "Strike three!"

Sensitive to his changing audience, O'Malley tried to improve the mood at the ballpark with better security and maintenance. He also thought that he might get people to come to games if he presented a superior product on the field. To do this he intended to follow the model of the Yankee organization, which was run with businesslike efficiency. The owners in the Bronx set high standards, sought the best executives, and empowered them to pursue star play-ers and build winning teams that kept fans happy and the ballpark full. O'Malley adopted these rules for running his team and added some of his own. Under him, the Dodgers would answer every call, letter, complaint, or request as soon as possible. Players would get the support they needed to win, and fans would be encouraged to have fun.

Acknowledging his own limitations—he wasn't an expert on the game—O'Malley named two men who had worked for Rickey to run the baseball side of things, giving each of them the title of vice president. One, a forty-eight-year-old Rickey protégé named Lafayette Fresco Thompson, would handle the vast minor-league and player development program. The other, Emil "Buzzie" Bavasi, would oversee the major-league club.

At age thirty-four Bavasi was young for a job that amounted to general manager for one of baseball's best teams, but executive experience in the Dodgers' minor-league system had prepared him. Under MacPhail and then Rickey, Bavasi had gotten a graduate degree in running a baseball team, from the ticket window at Nashua to the boardroom at Montreal. He had even played four games in Class D in Americus, Georgia, when the team ran out of suitable players. He hit .333 and pitched the last inning of the season. (He was gleefully mobbed by the opposing team when he allowed the one and only home run ever hit by one of their men.)

O'Malley would trust Thompson and Bavasi and rarely interfere. He also turned to them for advice when hiring a manager. In the fall of 1950 Bavasi recommended that the fiery Charlie Dressen replace manager Burt Shotton. Although O'Malley would later confess some regret about the decision, which ended Shotton's long career in baseball, he went with the recommendation. Dressen was in.

The former Dodgers coach who had been mixed up in the old Durocher-MacPhail controversy, Dressen had spent 1950 managing the Oakland team to the Pacific Coast League championship. Street tough and wily—he excelled at stealing an opposing catcher's signs and signaling his batters—Dressen was an old-fashioned Brooklyn kind of guy. He was expected to motivate the team in ways that kindly old Shotton had not and get them back to the World Series.

With three men he trusted in charge of putting a team on the field, O'Malley could tend to big-picture issues. In his first weeks as president he met with Giants owner Horace Stoneham, National League commissioner Ford Frick, and the commissioner of all of baseball, Happy Chandler. O'Malley was concerned about TV rights, and at the time Chandler had just made a terrible deal for the broadcast of the World Series. He had allowed Gillette to buy the series for the next three years for $1 million. The razor company promptly sold the contract to NBC for $4 million, proving the true value of the broadcasts. With this blunder Chandler had lost any chance he had of being reelected commissioner. But O'Malley learned from Chandler's mistake and got $600,000 per year from his TV sponsor Schaefer Brewing.

At the end of November, just before heading for baseball's winter meetings, O'Malley entertained Victor Ford Collins, who, with Bob Cobb of salad fame, owned the Hollywood Stars of the PCL. Financed in part by the flamboyant film director Cecil B. DeMille, Collins and Cobb had bought the team in 1938 and had sold shares of stock to movie stars to get the money to build Gilmore Field, a neat new park at the corner of Beverly Boulevard and Fairfax Avenue. Stars games were a celebrity-watching venue where a fan might sit across the aisle from Spencer Tracy or behind Rosemary Clooney. By the end of the 1940s the Stars were a Dodgers affiliate and a dominant team in the PCL, drawing six hundred thousand a year to a stadium that seated fewer than thirteen thousand, which was all the more impressive considering Los Angeles had another PCL team, the Angels.

Like others, Cobb and Collins had been making the big push for major-league baseball in California. Whether Collins discussed the idea with O'Malley isn't clear, but O'Malley would soon hear a direct pitch from columnist Vincent X. Flaherty of the *Los Angeles Examiner*, the Hearst paper. Flaherty was an old-school, fedora-wearing newspaperman who would have copped (his language) to lots of shoulder-rubbing with powerful people in politics and business. Not content to merely report the news, he wanted to make it by helping to bring the big leagues to Los Angeles. In 1948 he accompanied former county supervisor Leonard Roach to the American League's annual meeting at Chicago's Palmer House Hotel, where they promoted the city. In 1950 he contacted every single club in the big leagues, including the Dodgers, attempting to sell them on moving west. He was focused most intently on faltering clubs in cities with two big-league teams, especially the Braves of Boston and the St. Louis Browns. The oldest franchise in the major leagues, the Braves were in decline but in far better shape than the Browns, who drew fewer than 250,000 in 1950. Browns owner Bill Veeck would explore Los Angeles and Milwaukee in hopes of making a move.

The Dodgers weren't in the same desperate straits. They planned to prosper with a competitive team and began by re-signing Roy Campanella, Gil Hodges, and Duke Snider to contracts in the $18,000 to $22,000 range. Jackie Robinson came back for $36,000. These sums were far below the six figures paid to stars like Ted Williams and Joe DiMaggio in the American League. But since they were bound by the reserve clause to make a deal or sit out the season, players generally took what they could get. For a National League team the Dodgers seemed to pay about average.

For some veterans, 1951 would mark their first spring training without Branch Rickey, and for Jackie Robinson in particular this change required some adjustment. The two had bonded as they broke the color line and their relationship was much deeper than player-executive. "Jack was very perturbed about it," recalled Don Newcombe. Rachel Robinson said, "Jackie played hard for the Dodgers after Mr. Rickey left, but he didn't have the same affection for the management." Others, like pitcher Ralph Branca, who thought Rickey's old-fashioned training methods ruined arms, were not troubled at all by his departure. Either way, the isolation and camaraderie at the Vero Beach training site would help meld players into a team whether Rickey was present or not.

The first year of the O'Malley regime at Vero Beach brought a fancy new dining room with tablecloths, waiters, and prime steaks cooked to order. The change shocked players who arrived on February 20 expecting the old cafeteria. Of course, the barracks were still so buggy and drafty that occupants coveted the bath mats as extra blankets. And certain parts of the property were so full of snakes that a stray ball was likely to stay lost. But with much better food and other improvements, Dodgertown became an ideal setting. Duke Snider would remember it as a place where he learned the strike zone and how to check his swing. Carl Erskine, a young pitcher in 1951, would recall it as a place of "snakes, bugs, spiders; and I loved it."

As owner, O'Malley would use the spring training base to promote team camaraderie and reinforce his relationships with executives, friends, and reporters. Many of these people were flown to Florida free of charge, on the team plane, and according to the O'Malley rules no one was allowed to pay for anything once they arrived at Dodgertown. In addition to the free Florida vacation, more than a few members of the press left camp with winnings from The O'Malley's nightly poker games. (The new nickname, The O'Malley, started appearing in the press when O'Malley became sole owner of the team. It recalled an old Tammany Hall politician whom George Washington Plunkitt called The McManus as a matter of deference and Irish custom and to distinguish him from lesser men with the same name.)

"He loved those poker games with the press," recalled Dick Walsh, who began working on the Dodgers staff in 1948. The games, which generally involved stud poker or five-card draw, "were a way for him to evaluate people and pass out a little money to certain people." Among the "certain people" were reporters who might be favorably influenced by a fifty-dollar pot, especially if O'Malley folded with what might be a winning hand. One poker player who never got this generous treatment was Roscoe McGowan of the *Times*, who was beyond influence and played so poorly that no one would have believed it if he won.

The poker game, which came with an open bar, was off-limits for ballplayers, who were expected to spend their time in camp getting in shape and developing their skills. The team discouraged players from carousing at night, but these rules weren't really necessary. The nearest city of any size, Orlando, was about a hundred miles away, and Vero Beach itself had just a few bars and restaurants. This isolation made it easy for coaches to keep tabs on their men. However, it also seemed to make local racial attitudes more resistant to change.

Even as late as 1951, Vero Beach was a starkly segregated and potentially dangerous place for black ballplayers to visit. They were banned from local golf courses and barbershops and couldn't get a meal at most restaurants. They could find a real welcome or haircut only in nearby Gifford, a black community that whites called "Niggertown." But this place could be reached only via an old bus that worked on an unpredictable schedule.

Worse than the segregation were the dangers that might arise unexpectedly in a place like Vero Beach. At the 1949 spring camp, pitcher Don Newcombe got into an argument with Fermin Guerra, a Cuban-born catcher (and sometime bullfighter) who played for the Athletics. The ill feeling was left over from a dispute they had had months before during a winter league game in Havana. This time Guerra crossed some verbal line and Newcombe responded by ripping a slat off a fence and using it to hit him. As a black sportswriter named Sam Lacy intervened, a white spectator began screaming about how a "nigger can't go after a white man that way," recalled Newcombe. The next morning the camp was alarmed by a rumor that a mob was coming to lynch Newcombe. While an airplane was readied to take him away, the local sheriff arrived with the word that no one had to worry because tempers had cooled when locals realized Guerra was Cuban. Just to be safe, however, black players would be confined to the camp until training ended.

Training at Vero ended early for the members of the big-league team because Dodgertown lacked a proper stadium for exhibition games. On March 9 they left the farm teams behind and went to Miami, where the brand-new Miami Stadium would be their preseason home. They traveled aboard a DC-3 prop plane the team had just acquired from Eastern Airlines. As with so many things in baseball, the DC-3 came with a story. This one featured Bud L.

Holman, the local businessman who had been instrumental in bringing the Dodgers to Vero Beach.

Holman was manager of the Vero Beach Airport, which Eastern Airlines served, and he was friendly with the airline's president, Eddie Rickenbacker, the World War I flying ace. Holman knew that the Dodgers were looking for a bigger plane when he attended an Eastern company picnic. He played a game of dice with Rickenbacker, who wagered a surplus DC-3 in a double-or-nothing bet. Rickenbacker lost and Holman got his pick of a fleet of planes that were being replaced by new Lockheed Super Constellations, the peculiar-looking airliners with four engines and triple tails. (According to Holman's son, who eventually flew the DC-3, Rickenbacker made up some of the loss by charging a premium for a pair of extra engines.) One side benefit of acquiring the plane from Eastern was that whenever it arrived at an airport where the airline had operations, crews recognized the plane and often cleaned it and restocked the galley free of charge.

In March of 1951 it took three trips for the DC-3 to get the entire Dodgers big-league show—players, coaches, executives, equipment—from Vero to Miami. Once there, they won four in a row and found a certain comfort level with the new manager, Dressen. Unlike Durocher, who had once made a public example of Jackie Robinson when he arrived at camp overweight, Dressen said he had no "doghouse" for players who fell out of favor and guaranteed that "everybody will get his chance."

From the very start Dressen was a bit obsessed with Durocher. He was determined to be different from him and to prove himself by beating the Giants. This mild obsession could be a distraction, but as Newcombe would recall, "Dressen had a great baseball mind," and the Dodgers were generally happy to play for him.

They weren't so happy playing at night in Miami, where temperatures turned chilly after sunset. Players grumbled about how they would have preferred to stay longer at the Vero Beach camp, where there were no lights and all the games were played in warm sunshine. O'Malley seemed to hear them and soon announced an agreement with the city of Vero Beach that would keep the team there for twenty-one years. He promised better housing and longer stays for the big-league team. Since per-player costs there were much lower than they were in Miami—a few dollars a day compared with around fifty dollars—this decision made good business sense even as it pleased cranky players.

O'Malley seemed determined to make his players happy. The airplane and the steaks at Vero Beach were two examples of this approach. A third could be found in his response to a surprise proposal from a Detroit pitcher who represented American League players in talks with the owners. Near the end of spring training, Fred Hutchinson announced that the players wanted a role in the selection of the next commissioner. (After losing a straw vote with the owners, Chandler had said his first term would be his last.) If the owners resisted, said Hutchinson, the players might go hire their own man—Chandler was mentioned—and authorize him to police the game.

When they heard this idea, the owners generally recoiled: "It's a bad situation," said Phillies owner Robert M. Carpenter. Only O'Malley seemed open to the idea. "The players are a fine, responsible group," he said, "and anything they say will merit attention."

This was O'Malley's style. He came from a political family. He had studied psychology and had dealt with unions at Ebbets Field. He understood what people wanted and how they might organize and pursue a shared goal. Although he surely coveted control just like every other owner, he wasn't going to overreact or dismiss the players' aspirations. Their desire to have a say was natural and would one day change the way the game worked. But this process would take a long time. The owners weren't facing a real player uprising, just a shift in their interest. O'Malley, who needed his men to win games, wasn't going to overreact.

The Dodgers got themselves into a winning rhythm on their way home to Brooklyn as the team made stops in Georgia, North Carolina, Washington, D.C., and Baltimore to win seven out of nine exhibition games. Before they got to New York, baseball writers polled by the Associated Press named them the favorites to win the pennant. With a lineup that included Roy Campanella, Jackie Robinson, Gil Hodges, and Duke Snider, the Dodgers were expected to hit, and they had pitching too. Ralph Branca and Carl Erskine had both matured and seemed ready to perform at a higher level. Preacher Roe (spitballs) and Newcombe (fireballs) had each won nineteen the previous year. There was no reason to think they couldn't do it again.

The borough that the Dodgers found when they arrived was still a proud and friendly place. Many players with families returned to homes in middle-class neighborhoods where they had put down roots and found acceptance and a minimum of annoying hero worship when they went to the corner grocery or the dry cleaners. Carl Erskine's experience was typical. Born and raised in the farming community of Anderson, Indiana, Erskine made his rookie debut in the summer of 1948. He had left a wife and baby behind and stayed in the Brooklyn YMCA. After his first game he went back to the Y and used the pay phone to call home and report that he had won. The next year he brought his family to Bay Ridge, a neighborhood that resembled a village within the borough, and it became their hometown. His neighbors included Duke Snider and Pee Wee Reese and their wives. The couples shared babysitters, went out to dinner together, and sent their kids to the same pediatrician.

Bay Ridge seemed like the same old place when the Dodgers returned in 1951, but Brooklyn was a little different. The Flatbush Avenue trolley, the last one that could bring fans near to Ebbets Field, had stopped running in March, after sixty years. (The borough that once had seventy different trolley lines was down to nine, and their days were numbered.) The trolleys weren't the only thing missing. Thousands of white middle-class Brooklynites had left for the suburbs. Some would be replaced by less-wealthy newcomers, mainly black and Puerto Rican, but the borough was headed for a slight loss in overall population and a steeper decline in high-wage jobs.

After employing seventy thousand (including Vin Scully's stepfather) during World War II, the New York Naval Shipyard—known locally as the Brooklyn Navy Yard—was down to fewer than fifteen thousand and headed toward closure. In 1950 Spalding sporting goods had moved its manufacturing operation from Brooklyn to a small town in Massachusetts. In February of 1951, while the Dodgers were in Vero Beach, the John F. Trommer brewery, a Brooklyn mainstay since 1897, was sold to another beer company. The label would continue for a while, but the brewery's jobs disappeared.

With the decline of Spalding, Trommer's, and the navy yard, Brooklyn was losing bits of its economic identity, and more good jobs would leave the borough as, across the country, factories were located outside major cities, where land was cheaper and labor was becoming more abundant. But none of these losses was as troubling for local businessmen as the sudden disappearance of Brooklyn's largest independent lender, George V. McLaughlin's Brooklyn Trust Company. In mid-1950, McLaughlin negotiated a merger with Manufacturers Trust of Manhattan. The deal brought a huge payoff for Brooklyn Trust stockholders, whose shares rose by one-third during the deal making. It also meant that borrowers who once had easy access to bank officials who knew their community lost their best source of financing.

For the Dodgers, the demise of an independent Brooklyn Trust Company marked the end of a special relationship that had seen the team through several financial crises. And as George McLaughlin moved into his new job as chairman of the Manufacturers executive committee, Walter O'Malley lost ready access to an old friend and mentor who had offered wisdom and advice during so many meetings in Room 40 at the Bossert. George the Fifth would still appear on O'Malley's calendar from time to time. They had lunch in late January 1951. But at age sixty-three, McLaughlin was getting out of the daily grind of banking. In two years he would retire from the business entirely, move his residence from Brooklyn to Park Avenue, and focus on civic duties such as his work with Robert Moses on the Triborough Bridge and Tunnel Authority.

Of course, O'Malley was doing well on his own and didn't need much counsel or financial support. He had become much richer in the late 1940s, mostly through the acquisition of the New York Subways Advertising Company from the Wrigley family. The company, which had a valuable city franchise to plaster the subway system with posters, had revenue of almost $4 million in 1949. This firm, combined with other holdings, gave O'Malley a portfolio that could backstop his Dodgers if help were ever needed. If a crisis arose, he could also sell a bit of stock to an investor, and there always seemed to be plenty of them around.

Baseball's charm, a commodity the Dodgers kept in great supply, was a reliable magnet for idle money. From the moment he got control of the team, O'Malley was visited by a long line of rich people who wanted part of the team. One of the first was the eccentric Mrs. Izaak Walton Killam, who, along with her butler, attended almost every game at Ebbets Field. Early in O'Malley's reign she invited him to her winter home in the Bahamas, where she offered $5 million for the team. He was so stunned that he dropped his drink on her. As servants rushed with towels, he declined the offer. Mrs. Killam took the rejection well and her loyalty to the team grew. A couple of years later she proved it during a visit to the Polo Grounds. After watching a young Giants pitcher, she gave an usher an enormous tip to bring Horace Stoneham to her box. When he arrived she offered him $100,000 for the young man's contract. Flabbergasted, Stoneham said an individual couldn't buy a ballplayer to use as an escort or dancing partner. Mrs. Killam said she was hoping to give the man's contract to Walter O'Malley because the Dodgers needed pitching, but in light of Stoneham's insult she withdrew the offer.

As a fan Mrs. Killam, eager to spend money to help her favorite team, may have been unique. More typically, Dodger maniacs called, wrote, and stopped O'Malley on the street to complain about Ebbets Field or give him advice about the team. Friends who wanted jobs for their relations wrote directly to him, and business propositions came, unbidden, from every direction. Even O'Malley's father, who was sixty-seven years old in 1951, began coming around to discuss real estate investment ideas.

In the years since his wife Alma's death, Edwin O'Malley had married a woman named Constance Heath, with whom he lived on East Seventy-second Street in Manhattan. The sketchy details left behind in letters suggest that Walter was wary of Connie and, in a reversal of roles, had expressed some discomfort about the marriage.

Despite all the new demands brought on by his fame, O'Malley clearly enjoyed the baseball team more than any other business and poured most of his time into playing his position as owner and executive. With Rickey and Smith gone he was free to focus on his stadium problem, and in May 1951 he made his first known contact with a government official on this issue, meeting with Commissioner Sidney Bingham of the city's board of transportation. (O'Malley had his eye on a part of Brooklyn where several transit lines connected with the Long Island Rail Road.) The discussion revolved around Emil Praeger's ideas for a new Dodgers home. Bingham was a retired Army colonel and veteran of the Normandy invasion. Since Praeger had designed the famous floating docks used to create an instant harbor at Normandy, he would have been more than familiar with the engineer and his reputation.

The contact with Bingham was true to O'Malley's style. He pursued a remarkable variety of issues and whenever possible went directly to the person who might have the right idea or the power to solve a problem. Days after seeing Bingham, he sat down with local congressman Emanuel Celler, a fourteen-term Democrat who was chairman of the House Judiciary Subcommittee on

Monopoly. Although he sometimes posed as a watchdog for the public, Celler also protected certain institutions. For example, he had warned of a "dangerous trend" in consolidation when Manufacturers swallowed the Brooklyn Trust Company, but also declared that the merger had been accomplished within the rule of law.

Now, with major-league baseball facing lawsuits over the restrictions of the reserve clause, Celler was organizing hearings on the game's business practices. Celler said he was going to focus on the ways owners granted themselves exclusive territories, restricted competition, controlled the minor leagues, and used the reserve clause to prevent players from moving from team to team in search of better pay. "If baseball is illegal," he said, "we must prosecute the owners or change the law."

Superficially, Celler seemed to be a critic, but he didn't want to mess with the American game. He was mainly interested in protecting baseball, as it was structured, with new legislation that would exempt the owners from antitrust regulations. Just what transpired when he met with O'Malley remained private, but after he saw the Dodgers owner, Celler put off the start of his hearings until July 30.

If Celler granted the delay as a favor to O'Malley, he wasn't the only powerful man subjected to the Brooklyn owner's charms. In May of '51, O'Malley also got together with Mayor Vincent Impellitteri, who became an occasional lunch partner and visitor at the owner's box at Ebbets. (Impy, as he was called, was a Fordham law grad and former Tammany Hall man who had managed to get elected without the hall's support.) O'Malley also made a specific effort to establish good relationships with his fellow team owners, especially Dan Topping of the Yankees and Horace Stoneham of the Giants.

Born just a year after O'Malley, Stoneham was a stout man with fair hair that he combed back from his head. His black-rimmed glasses and chubby pink cheeks gave him the look of a pampered prep-school boy. He had become the youngest owner in major-league history when he inherited the Giants from his father in 1936. Having been raised at the Polo Grounds, he had worked in almost every job—ticket taker, groundskeeper, administration—that didn't involve throwing, fielding, or hitting. Stoneham was notorious for his consumption of alcohol, and those who knew him said he often started the day with a drink. He was also known as a consistently good-natured fellow who loved the baseball business and adored his team. He often let people assume they were taking advantage of him when trading players when, in fact, he knew as much as anyone about how to operate a club.

But even with all his expertise, Stoneham was having no more luck than O'Malley when it came to their similar problems: an old crumbling stadium, too little parking, and unpredictable attendance. The Giants' home stadium in Harlem, which opened in 1911, was older than Ebbets Field. And although he never said much about it publicly, Stoneham was concerned about conditions in the neighborhood around the park, which was home mainly to lower-income African-Americans. He was worried that white fans were staying home, and attendance at the Polo Grounds—which was declining faster than at Ebbets— seemed to support his fear.

Stoneham might have done better if his team had won more games. Thirteen years had passed since the Giants last won the pennant. In 1951, fans could invest some hope in pitchers Sal Maglie and Larry Jansen, who were both headed toward twenty-three-win seasons, and a spunky lineup that included a new outfielder named Willie Mays, who was just nineteen years old when the season began. Jackie Robinson had seen Mays coming. "Sign him up," he had told Branch Rickey when Mays was still playing for the Barons, a Negro League team in Birmingham, Alabama. However, as Robinson would recall, "some scout said he couldn't hit a curve ball" and Mays became a Giant.

After hitting .447 with the team's top minor-league team in Minneapolis, Mays was called up to the big club on May 25. He immediately took control of center field, sending Bobby Thomson back to his usual position in left. He hit his first home run on May 29, which began a ten-day hitting streak. But there was more to Mays than his individual achievements. As Mays roamed the outfield making spectacular plays, manager Durocher saw that he gave the entire team an emotional lift.

According to the baseball experts the season was supposed to belong to the Dodgers, and for much of the summer it did. On August 9, Roy Campanella hit two homers as the Dodgers beat the Giants and found themselves leading the pennant race by twelve and a half games. No Dodgers team had ever enjoyed such a big lead. Walter O'Malley had watched Campanella and the Dodgers beat the Giants with General Douglas MacArthur at his side. When the game was over he introduced the general to the reporters covering the game. MacArthur was a finalist in the owners' search for a commissioner to replace Happy Chandler. In a brief item buried on page eighteen, the *New York Times* reported that O'Malley had been picked to sound him out, but the general said, "I was just attending another ball game."

Only four months earlier, President Truman had fired MacArthur as commander of American and United Nations forces in Korea. The move came after the general had threatened to invade China despite U.S. policy forbidding such an action. His dismissal set off a political uproar, with many Republicans and groups like the American Legion siding with the much-decorated MacArthur. Two thousand dockworkers in Manhattan and Brooklyn walked off their jobs in protest, and his return to the States had been a coast-to-coast victory lap as huge crowds met him in Hawaii, San Francisco, and Washington. When he arrived home in New York, Mayor Impellitteri gave him a ticker-tape parade. Two million people lined the sidewalk, skywriters wrote out messages above the parade route, and fireboats in the East River shot geysers into the air.

That baseball would turn to such a powerful historic figure—and he might actually consider the commissioner's job—said something about the game's special status in the American heart. Attendance was declining. Some franchises were flirting with bankruptcy. Yet, this mere sport could reach out to the most prominent leader of the greatest military power in the world. No one seemed to think it odd that he might consider a move from warfare to sport. And his presence in Walter O'Malley's box at Ebbets Field was almost unremarkable. Of course the laureled old general would go to a Dodgers game. In fact, he went to so many games in 1951 that the papers stopped publishing pictures of him in O'Malley's box.

Indeed, O'Malley and the Dodgers got much more attention four days later when he turned from mogul to maestro to host Music Appreciation Night at Ebbets. The event, which became a front-page sensation, grew out of a complaint from Local 802 of the American Federation of Musicians, which had spent much of the previous year in grueling but successful negotiations with TV and radio broadcasters. (Salaries were raised to as much as $220 per week.) Union leaders complained that the informal Sym-phony band that had produced thirteen years' worth of sour notes at Ebbets deserved to be paid something. A hundred dollars a week for the whole crew seemed reasonable, said the local's secretary, Charles Iuggi, and he asked that Judge Samuel Liebowitz, who had presided over the Durocher criminal trial, intervene.

Iuggi might have prevailed if the players in the Sym-phony actually wanted to be paid. Instead they protested when it seemed the union might try to stop them from performing when the team returned from a road trip. Bandleader Pat Palma was especially worried about team morale, should the so-called music end in the midst of a pennant run.

Delighted to take a role in this loopy drama, O'Malley negotiated a deal that required that two union musicians drop out of the band, making way for amateurs. The team owner, who said that part of the trouble was that the union chiefs "are Giant fans," celebrated the settlement by announcing that any fan who brought a musical instrument to the game on August 13 would be admitted free.

They came, 2,426 strong, toting saxophones, flutes, clarinets, and, in one case, a piano. Each one got a seat in a reserved section of the grandstand. With the mayor and borough president John Cashmore on hand, the men of the Sym-phony appeared wearing top hats and tuxedoes to lead the multitude in a piece that may have been "Hail, Hail, the Gang's All Here" but could have been *La Traviata*. By the end of the night, as the Dodgers notched a win against the Boston Braves, the event had been spontaneously renamed Music Depreciation Night, and it was installed in Brooklyn's collective memory as a moment when "ya shoulda been dere."

The only important thing—or, to be precise, important person—missing from the celebration that August night was Robert Moses, who O'Malley had hoped would join him, Impy, and Cashmore in the owner's box. No one was more important when it came to O'Malley's plans for a future stadium, and for the future of the Dodgers. Moses, who was hardly the type to enjoy cheering with thousands of working-class Brooklynites, had agreed to come to the game but then cancelled.

New York had never seen a political creature quite like Moses. For decades he had promoted himself as uniquely competent, visionary, moral, and wise. Thanks to bonding authority and the coins that were collected at bridges and tunnels, Moses came to control the largest pool of government money—hundreds of millions of dollars—available outside the federal treasury. He had secretly used this money to enrich politically connected attorneys, developers, banks, and others who, in exchange, lent him their loyalty. By all evidence, he never lined his own pockets, but this didn't mean he wasn't corrupt. He was Plunkitt in reverse, using millions of public dollars to gain power in order to express his personal vision of the future. By the time O'Malley came along, Moses was more powerful than any elected official in the state, including the mayor and the governor. He operated beyond oversight and was immune to the will of the voters. Anyone who thought to build anything with government help in New York only needed Moses to make it happen. Of course, the opposite was true too: if Moses didn't want your project, it died.

O'Malley was smart enough to know that he would need Moses's help to find enough land to build a new ballpark in Brooklyn. In canceling his appearance, Moses employed his usual muscle-flexing methods—he did this to mayors as well—to demonstrate both his status and his attitude. O'Malley, who was a minor player in the local political game, would have to bide his time. In the meantime, of course, he had a team to run and a role to play in the selection of baseball's new commissioner.

Although he flirted with the idea for about a month, General MacArthur eventually decided against becoming commissioner. (He had his eye on a somewhat more important executive position in Washington.) The baseball owners quickly narrowed the list of candidates to five, including the head of Coca-Cola, Cincinnati Reds president Warren Giles, and Ford Frick, chief of the National League. Frick would get the job on September 20, with Giles replacing him as league president. The outcome couldn't have been better for the Dodgers and O'Malley, who could count both men as friends.

IF ONLY THE '51 season could have ended for O'Malley and the Dodgers on the day of Frick's election. The Dodgers had awakened that morning in St. Louis after beating the Cardinals and climbing to four and a half games in front of Horace Stoneham's Giants, who had lost in Cincinnati. As they flew back to New York, the Dodgers hoped their victory and their rivals' defeat would mark the end of a worrisome trend.

The Giants were making a furious, emotion-fueled run at the pennant, inspired by an incident that occurred on August 9, the day Douglas MacArthur came to Ebbets Field. As Carl Erskine would recall it, the Dodgers won the game and afterward Charlie Dressen organized a group of players to taunt the Giants with a postgame ditty. Sung to the tune of "Roll Out the Barrel," it included the words "we've got the Giants on the run."

The incident was relatively tame, considering how things normally went with these two teams. "It was professional hatred," said Erskine, "and you could hear almost anything—and I mean anything—on that field." Even so, the Giants, especially shortstop Alvin Dark, were angered by what they heard and used it for motivation.

Beginning on August 12, the team from the Polo Grounds went on a tear, winning thirty-eight games and losing just seven. With solid pitching and clutch hitting they steadily closed in on the pennant, and no matter how many hopes and prayers rose over Flatbush, the final two weeks of the season went the same way. With the Dodgers questioning themselves and each other—"We were all afraid of making a mistake," said Pee Wee Reese—inexplicable fate brought them to the last games of the regular season in a dead tie with the surging Giants. They would finish up on the road, with a series in Boston and another in Philadelphia.

Eager to spoil the Dodgers' season, the Braves played as if they could grab the pennant for themselves, winning both games of a doubleheader on September 25. The Dodgers bounced back to rout them the next day but fell to the Braves again on September 27 on a disputed call at home plate. (In the argument that ensued, Campanella was ejected.) The loss left them half a game ahead of the Giants with two to play. It also made some players so angry that they kicked at the umpires' dressing-room door, eventually breaking it. Robinson was blamed, but in time this version of events would be refuted and it became clear that Preacher Roe had done the damage.

Walter O'Malley had attended the series in Boston hoping his team would seize the pennant, but when they faltered, he didn't seem to take it very hard. After the game the rookie Dodgers president invited Vin Scully to leave with him in a waiting car. Scully, still a bit awestruck by the major-league experience, happily accepted and didn't say a word when O'Malley told the driver to head for Logan Airport. For a moment he thought that O'Malley needed someone to haul his suitcase.

Instead of delivering baggage, Scully was invited to fly to Montreal, where the Dodgers' Triple-A affiliate was playing in the minor-league, or "little," World Series. At the game he saw two future Dodgers, Jim "Junior" Gilliam and Tommy Lasorda, help the team to a victory. Afterward, O'Malley took Scully to dinner, where he surprised him by showing him that the gladiolas in the vase on the table were edible. (The petals taste like peas.) Scully retired for the night at a posh hotel, marveling at O'Malley's capacity for surprise and good humor.

O'Malley and Scully rejoined the Dodgers in time for their last three regular-season games in Philadelphia. They lost the first, while the Giants were idle, and fell into a tie for the pennant. The next day Don Newcombe pitched a complete-game shutout. He would appear again the very next day, throwing hard in long relief and shutting down the Phillies again. But Jackie Robinson would be remembered as the hero of the day.

The game did not begin well for the Dodgers. With Walter and Kay O'Malley watching from box seats with Buzzie and Evit Bavasi, starter Preacher Roe and reliever Ralph Branca gave up six runs in the first three innings. Brooklyn scored just one. When the scorekeeper posted a Giants victory over Boston that put them ahead in the standings for the moment, despair swept over the crowd of Brooklyn fans who had traveled to the game. In his mind O'Malley began composing the telegram he might send Horace Stoneham to congratulate him on the Giants' improbable rush to the pennant. Then he thought, "You're being a traitor," and put the idea out of his mind.

By the end of the fifth inning, the score was 8–5. In the top of the eighth the Dodgers tied the score and Newcombe came out to replace Carl Erskine on the mound. With support from the small number of Brooklyn rooters in the park, he held the home team scoreless as the game went into extra innings. He was matched, inning for inning, by the young Phillies ace and future Hall of Famer Robin Roberts.

In the bottom of the twelfth, Philly first baseman Eddie Waitkus, famous for being shot by a deranged female fan in 1949, came to bat with two men out and the bases full. He seemed to win the game as he hit Newcombe's second pitch, a fastball, on a low line toward the right-field side of second. Reacting reflexively, Robinson threw himself at the ball, caught it just before it hit the turf, and kept it in his mitt as he fell hard enough to knock the wind out of himself. Teammates rushed to him, and as he lay still, some fans thought he had suffered a heart attack.

Two innings later, a still-groggy Robinson hit a solo home run that made the score 9–8 and brought the O'Malleys and Bavasis to their feet. In the words of *Times* reporter Roscoe McGowan, they "became as nearly hysterical as such normally composed people can be." The Dodgers held the lead through Philadelphia's turn at bat and gave themselves a spot in a two-out-of-three-game playoff with the Giants, who also won.

Back in New York, the O'Malleys' daughter Terry had spent the day in Amityville with her grandparents and then traveled by train back to college in New Rochelle. The Long Island Rail Road required her to change trains at Jamaica, Queens, where she heard the Dodgers were down 6–1. At Penn Station she learned the score was 8–7, but she missed hearing the play-by-play because she had to catch another train to New Rochelle. When she finally reached her dormitory, she was called to the phone for an "emergency" call. It was her father on the line, telling her, "Your mother and I have just seen the most exciting game of our lives." Terry asked for tickets for the next day's playoff game with the Giants. Her parents thought it would be better for her to go to class.

WITH THE YANKEES CLINCHING the American League and their two National League clubs beginning a three-game playoff, New Yorkers found themselves in a state of baseball grace that no city had ever experienced before. The local teams were stocked with eleven players and two managers—Durocher and Casey Stengel of the Yankees—who would make the Hall of Fame. Each team could also claim an icon who, as a matter of style, belonged in the super-elite category. Robinson of the Dodgers defined a turning point in race relations. Mays of the Giants made plays on the field that had rarely if ever been seen before, and the Yankee superstar DiMaggio was the most admired sports celebrity of his time.

On the morning of the first playoff game commuters toted radios on the subway so they could tune in to the game at work. As the game started at Ebbets Field, activity in schools, offices, and factories ground to a halt and crowds in taverns and bars grew hushed so the broadcast could be heard. People collected on the sidewalk to hear radios perched in open windows and fans who had to be out-and-about stopped at pay phones to dial a special number—ME7-1212—to hear the score courtesy of AT&T.

Although loyalists would insist they were nothing alike, the tension was just as high in Brooklyn as it was in Manhattan, where one woman appeared at the Automat on Forty-second Street wearing a housecoat and carrying a transistor radio tuned to the play-by-play broadcast. Too nervous to listen to the game alone in her apartment, she bought a cup of coffee, took a seat at one of the tables, and turned the volume down low. In Brooklyn seventy-five blood donors saw the game on a television set at a Red Cross Center. All but one left feeling drained of a little bit more than blood: he was the lone Giants fan in the group who saw his team win 3–1.

The game, which was the first ever broadcast on national television, was far from scintillating and, astoundingly, not a sellout. Some fans stayed home because they assumed there were no tickets available. Others were discouraged by cloudy skies. But given the intensity of the rivalry and the stakes, the 2,000 empty seats at Ebbets were a surprising sight. Things were worse the next day at the Polo Grounds, where there were just 38,609 people in a space built for 55,000. The Giants played as if they felt let down by their fans. They committed five errors and the Dodgers pounded them 10–0.

With disappointing ticket sales, Stoneham and O'Malley were denied the gate receipts they expected. But across the country millions of fans enjoyed the games delivered free over the radio. As the two most integrated teams in the game, the Giants and Dodgers attracted legions of African-Americans fans, who adopted the teams as their own, and whites who were curious about how the racial experiment was working out. The playoffs and the subsequent World Series would mark the high point of radio's role in bringing the country together for baseball. The games also came at a moment when the old medium's big new competitor, television, first demonstrated its true power.

Already planning to broadcast the World Series to the nation across a network of cables completed a week earlier, TV executives scrambled to give the nation the final Giants-Dodgers playoff game. The promise of actually viewing high-caliber baseball was especially alluring to Californians, who swamped dealers in San Francisco, Los Angeles, and San Diego. There and across the country sets tuned to the games were installed in hotel lobbies, store windows, and restaurants.

With the nation tuning in, the season came down to a final contest in Harlem. Tall, tough, and powerful Don Newcombe was called on to pitch for the

Dodgers. The intimidating Sal Maglie was named to take the mound for the Giants. This great matchup and the drama of a Brooklyn-Manhattan show-down should have drawn a standing-room-only crowd. Instead, fewer than thirty-five thousand showed up at the Polo Grounds. This relatively small num-ber would witness a game that would assume such a lofty place in baseball history that many more would claim they had been there.

Newcombe kept the Giants off the scoreboard for six straight innings. Maglie was fierce but not perfect as the Dodgers scratched out a run in the first inning on two walks and a Robinson single. The Giants managed to score the tying run in the bottom of the seventh when Bobby Thomson's sacrifice fly to center brought home Monte Irvin. It was the first run Newcombe had allowed in twenty-one innings. Though tiring, Newcombe then shut the Giants down.

Also exhausted and feeling the pressure, Maglie came out for the eighth and gave up four hits and a walk and threw a wild pitch to allow three more Dodg-ers to come home. Suddenly the Dodgers led by 4–1 and Maglie was done. This score held until the bottom of the ninth, when three quick outs would give Brooklyn the pennant.

The best of the Giants hitters—collectively averaging well over .300—were slated to bat in the ninth. In the dugout Newcombe said, "I can't make it" but Robinson convinced him to try and Dressen sent him out to the mound. Some of the fans, more confident of the end than any of the players, left the stadium. An announcer, using the public address system, told those who remained that when the game was over no one would be allowed on the field until the players were in their clubhouses.

The first Giant batter was Alvin Dark. Of all the Giants, he had been most offended by the Dodgers' clubhouse serenade back in August and had played the postseason games in a fury.

"We've gone this far," shouted Durocher. "Let's give them a finish."

Dark watched two pitches miss the plate and then hit a single to right. Next up was outfielder Don Mueller, who didn't have much power but was so good at scratching out hits, he was called Mandrake the Magician.

As Mueller took his stance, Dressen ordered first baseman Gil Hodges to hold Dark near the base. With just thirty steals in more than five hundred games, Dark was not a big threat to run, but Dressen feared that Durocher would try it anyway. Noting Hodges standing almost on first base, Newcombe worried about the big gap between his first and second basemen. "Charlie was trying to beat Leo instead of the Giants," he would say years later. "He was obsessed with it."

Like everyone else, Mueller saw the big gap and rapped Newcombe's first pitch through it for another single. Suddenly there were Giants on first and third. Out came the manager. In came the fielders. At the conference they conducted on the mound, Newcombe said he thought he could go on.

He was able to go on, but not very far. After forcing Monte Irvin into a pop-fly out, Newcombe was clobbered for a double by Whitey Lockman. Dark scored but Mueller sprained his ankle coming into third base. Durocher, who had been taunting Newcombe from his spot on the third-base sideline, sent in six-foot-five Clint Hartung to run for Mueller. Later he would joke that he wanted to be protected from Newcombe should matters get out of hand.

In the Dodgers bullpen, Coach Clyde Sukeforth had watched Ralph Branca and Carl Erskine warm up. When Dressen called for a pitcher to relieve Newcombe, Erskine had just thrown a ball into the dirt in front of the catcher. The coach reported the miscue and Dressen picked Branca.

A native New Yorker who first threw against big leaguers during the strange war bond round-robin held at the Polo Grounds, Branca understood what he was being asked to do. Years later he would confess that he felt as much nervousness as determination as he walked to the mound.

The batter, Bobby Thomson, was hitting well in the series and had already smacked a double and a single. In twelve regular-season at-bats against Branca, Thomson had gotten four hits—including a triple and a homer—and two walks. Dressen had the option of ordering an intentional walk to bring up the rookie Mays, who was struggling at the plate. (Over on the sideline Mays was praying against this prospect.) But Dressen let Branca pitch, and with the first throw the right-hander stymied Thomson with an inside fastball that was called for a strike.

Branca's second pitch, high and inside, was "the kind they've been getting me out on all season," said Thomson after the game. But this time the right-handed Thomson managed to turn enough to make solid contact and pull the ball to left field, where a curving wall stood roughly 315 feet from home plate. Branca stood on the mound silently urging the ball to "sink, sink, sink" so that it would stay in play.

In left field, the stands were double-decked and many hard-hit balls struck the face of the upper deck and remained in play when they bounced back onto the field. Low line drives hit toward the lower tier of seats tended to sink before they reached the wall and find their way into a left fielder's glove. This is what Dodger outfielder Andy Pafko remembered as he went back to make a play on Thomson's hit.

But this was no ordinary low line drive. It was hit so hard that it was still rising when it reached Pafko. Instead of sinking it flew over his head, dipped below the overhanging second tier, and landed in the lower stands for a home run.

Because it was the Dodgers and Giants, because it came at the end of the greatest pennant scramble in history, and because the score was 4–2 in the bottom of the ninth, Thomson's shot stunned the crowd at the ballpark. Across the country, millions who watched only the third game ever broadcast on national television saw something that a fan might never witness in a lifetime of visits to a ballpark. Around the world, radio listeners, including American soldiers stationed abroad, shared a moment that knitted a generation together.

"The Giants win the pennant! The Giants win the pennant!" shouted the radio announcer, Russ Hodges, and history was made.

As he rounded the bases, Thomson felt as if he were in a dream. He heard people screaming from the stands and saw paper being thrown in the air, but it was all hazy. He floated into home and was mobbed by teammates and coaches. Some Dodgers felt similarly strange. Pee Wee Reese was so shaken that he couldn't accept that the game was over. Even after he reached the clubhouse, he felt that play had merely been suspended and the teams would soon be called back onto the field and the Dodgers would get another turn at bat.

Everyone in the Dodgers organization took the loss hard, especially Branca. O'Malley, Bavasi, and Fresco Thompson went to the clubhouse to console their men. According to accounts from that time, O'Malley put a hand on Branca's shoulder and said, "It *is* only a game." But Branca, so filled with disappointment, apparently didn't even hear the words. Years later he couldn't be sure they had been said.

After consoling his men, O'Malley headed for the Giants' locker room. The defeat had deprived him of the satisfaction and profit that come with a pennant and World Series play. (O'Malley estimated he lost $500,000 in Series money. This was on top of the $25,000 he had already spent preparing to meet the

Yankees at Ebbets Field.) But he truly admired what his friend Stoneham, the manager Durocher, and all the Giants had accomplished. When he got inside he told them that they had played "the greatest baseball" he had ever seen.

In their postmortems, knowledgeable fans quickly recalled that Thomson had batted well against Branca in the regular season and they blamed Dressen. The most cynical fans suspected their team was somehow robbed of their rightful victory, and in time they would be proved at least partially correct. As the writer Joshua Prager would confirm in his authoritative book *The Echoing Green*, the Giants had used an elaborate sign-stealing system during their great rush toward the pennant and in the playoff series. The system involved a telescope, electric buzzers, and a carefully hidden spy who saw the fingers that opposing catchers flashed at their pitchers. The inside information was relayed to Giants hitters, who then knew which pitch to expect.

Sign stealing had always been a part of baseball, but using tools like a telescope and buzzer system violated the rules. Did it make much of a difference in the game? Giants fans would say that the advantage was negligible and repeat the oft-said baseball cliché that holds "if you ain't cheatin', you ain't trying hard enough."

After they found out about the spyglass and the buzzer, many Dodgers fans declared that they would never accept the Giants' win. More than fifty years later Ralph Branca continued to express a bit of anger about the incident. But one of the Dodgers' most ardent fans, someone who had a direct and lifelong personal connection with the team, chose to focus instead on the lessons learned from losing.

On the day the Giants won the pennant, Terry O'Malley had decided to defy her parents and skip classes to go to the game. Crossing the campus at the College of New Rochelle, she bumped into Joseph Scully, a gruff old philosophy professor, whose class she would miss. He smiled as he said, "Good luck to the Brooks."

The game was already in the second inning when Terry reached the Polo Grounds, but to her surprise she found general-admission tickets available. She paid, pushed through the turnstile, and then went looking for her mother and father. The Dodgers were leading 1–0 and her happy parents welcomed her to join them in their box. They sat together, their spirits soaring as the team took their three-run lead into the bottom of the ninth. With three outs, the Brooklyn

Dodgers would be headed for the World Series and another crack at the glory of beating the all-powerful Yanks. But then the Giants rallied and Thomson made his swing.

"Tragedy! Tears!" wrote Terry many years later.

In the bedlam that took place in the stands, Terry's mother said she would drive her back to New Rochelle while Walter and his vice presidents fulfilled their clubhouse duties. For much of the drive neither mother nor daughter could speak. Finally, Terry grumbled something about God and unanswered prayers.

If it had been anyone else, Kay O'Malley might have had trouble responding. But Terry was one of the very few who could watch her lips, listen to the sounds she made, and understand what she was saying.

"Do you think God wears a Dodgers hat one day and a Giants hat another time?" she asked. "Better to pray that the players do their best and no one gets hurt—that we will learn from baseball to be gracious winners and good losers."

Kay had more to say about how losing a game prepared a person to take responsibility in life and carry on after a setback. "Before you know it," she said, "spring training will start and life will begin again."

When they got to New Rochelle, the O'Malleys ran into Professor Scully in front of Terry's dormitory. He hugged them both and said, "I was afraid all the O'Malleys had jumped in the Harlem River."

Seven

CALIFORNIA CALLS

I n the early 1950s the people who played and watched could still rely on baseball to renew itself every spring when the previous year was forgotten and, in theory, everyone had a shot at a championship. The owners couldn't be so certain. Their game, in which the score was kept in dollars and cents, was threatened by grumbling about two issues: the reserve clause and the absence of teams in the West. During the summer of 1951, Congressman Emanuel Celler convened his monopoly subcommittee and heard a series of witnesses—led by Ty Cobb—insist that ballplayers were not "peons" and assure the public that the old game was essentially okay. The panel then fled the capital's August heat, promising to resume its examination of the national pastime when the season ended.

A few days after the almighty Yankees dispatched the Giants in the 1951 World Series, the subcommittee did go back to work. Chairman Celler's agenda was complex. Although he didn't say so publicly, he seemed intent on protecting the reserve clause and three bills already circulating in Congress would accomplish this task by exempting the game from the normal labor and business regulations. But anyone who listened carefully would recognize that the major leagues would have to offer something in trade. Congressmen from districts where voters and business leaders had long sought their own teams wanted to be heard and taken seriously.

One of the key representatives from the West was a first-term California

Republican named Patrick J. Hillings, who sat on Celler's committee. Hillings had won his mentor Richard Nixon's house district in the same 1950 election that saw Nixon use a red-baiting campaign to become a United States senator. Young and energetic, the twenty-seven-year-old congressman had already complained about major-league baseball's neglect of his home state. During the summer he rejected Commissioner Frick's musings about the PCL evolving into a big league when all of its clubs "are ready" and suggested instead immediate expansion or the transfer of an existing franchise or two.

The second round of hearings brought outspoken old Larry MacPhail, four years into retirement, an invitation to testify, and he rose to the occasion with an outlandish proposal for four new major-league circuits. Other witnesses talked about banning any system that might require fans to pay for games on TV and argued about the reserve clause. But the most consistently voiced complaint was about baseball's abuse and neglect of the West. Civic leaders, politicians, and minor-league officials all said something must be done. Columnist Vincent X. Flaherty (of Representative Hilling's hometown *Los Angeles Examiner*) made his case via telegram. Flaherty revealed that Chicago Cubs owner Philip K. Wrigley was ready to sell the territorial right held by his minor-league Los Angeles Angels to any big-league operator who wanted to move to the coast. (These rights prohibited other teams from locating in the city and surrounding region.)

In the end, Representative Celler made clear his allegiance to the major-league game and allowed that while it may well be a monopoly in violation of antitrust laws, it would be a mistake to "swoop down and enforce them." Instead, Congress would consider writing an exemption for the sport while watching to see how it responded to public concerns. No quid quo pro was spelled out, of course, but it was clear that after fifty-plus years the commissioner and the owners were expected to share baseball beyond its current boundaries.

Walter O'Malley didn't testify in Washington, but his absence said nothing about his status inside the game. As one owner quipped to a reporter, O'Malley was "no Rickey, but he's no fathead, either." He had a close relationship with Ford Frick and was already a member of the commissioner's executive council, which dealt with crucial policies. (After the Celler hearings the council set conditions that would allow only Los Angeles and San Francisco to join the major leagues, and then only if they adopted existing franchises.)

In New York, O'Malley was more visible than the Yankees owners or Horace Stoneham. In early November he appeared as a "defense witness" on a New York television show called *On Trial*. With Brooklyn federal court judge Harold Kennedy "presiding," O'Malley addressed the question of the night: "Should professional baseball be subject to antitrust laws?"

There was nothing remarkable in O'Malley's answer. He wanted to keep the reserve clause and said that those who complained about the farm-team system didn't understand that big-league clubs were keeping minor-league teams alive. O'Malley did take a risk, however, by offering actual numbers, drawn from his company's books, to support his arguments. He said that the string of Dodgers affiliates, which stretched from Nashua to Santa Barbara, lost $284,000 in 1950. This deficit was partly responsible for the organization as a whole losing more than $129,000 for the year.

During his half-hour performance, O'Malley was able to speak directly to his customers and reassure them that he wanted to preserve baseball "as the fans like it." The very next day Emanuel Celler made public the profit-and-loss figures that the Dodgers had given his subcommittee and argued that O'Malley had been too selective with his data. He said that if not for the losses of the Dodgers football team, the organization would have made a nice profit in 1950, just as it had every other year going back to 1945.

Without context, it was hard for anyone to make a judgment about the team's finances. What did it mean if, as Celler said, the Dodgers made roughly $2.3 million over five years? Did other clubs make more, or less? How about businesses with similar annual revenues? Did they enjoy the same profit margins? None of this information was offered to the public, and so it seemed that Celler's only purpose was to make sure no one felt sorry about the Dodgers' losses in 1950.

The congressman would make public a far more revealing set of numbers in the coming spring. Pulling together figures submitted by every club, the monopoly subcommittee published charts showing annual payrolls—for players, coaches, and managers—going back to 1927. According to the data, Branch Rickey had not deserved his El Cheapo nickname in Brooklyn. In his time there, the Dodgers' payroll fell roughly in the middle of the pack, year after year. In one of those years, 1943, it was actually the highest in the league.

Overall, baseball payrolls had nearly doubled in the period between 1927 and 1950. However, in the same period median family income in America tripled and—thanks to higher attendance, prices, and new types of revenues—clubs were receiving much more than twice the revenue they saw in the early 1930s. These facts suggested that the players were falling behind other workers and receiving a smaller portion of the money their work generated. But without more data, players couldn't do more than guess about these facts, and as individuals debating contract terms with team executives, they held little power.

As clubs signed, sold, traded, or simply released players, they gave sports reporters something to write about and fans something to talk about. Buzzie Bavasi handled the negotiations for the Dodgers' front office, wielding the reserve clause so cleverly that most players just took what they were offered. Essentially the same team would return in 1952, with the exception of pitcher Don Newcombe, who was drafted into military service. The decision on the manager belonged to O'Malley, who had told players in confidence that Dressen would return (this despite enormous pressure from fans who wanted him replaced). He had wanted to delay the announcement, but Jackie Robinson, who considered Dressen the best manager he had ever served, forced O'Malley's hand when he revealed what the Dodgers president had said.

As a matter of policy, O'Malley avoided getting involved with players, but he would sometimes intervene to solve specific problems. During the '51 season, for example, manager Dressen publicly berated a struggling young pitcher named Erv Palica. Dressen's outburst went beyond the normal complaining about performance to include an attack on Palica's character. Buzzie Bavasi made things worse when he added to the attack, needling Palica in the press.

The young pitcher, who was injured and worried about his pregnant wife, was not the type of player who would respond well to humiliation. Instead of getting angry and fired up, he became distracted and discouraged. He finished with just two wins and six losses. An article in the *Daily Eagle* noted that with just one more win Palica could have kept the Dodgers out of the playoff with the Giants and Bobby Thomson wouldn't have ever hit that home run. But this sentiment was not shared widely. Instead of blaming him, Brooklynites generally took Palica's side and many wrote letters to the club protesting the way he had been treated.

Faced with a public relations problem and an unhappy player who represented a seven-year investment in training and development, O'Malley suspended his hands-off policy. In the off-season he met with the pitcher and his wife. He apparently smoothed things over, because after a stint in the Army, Palica returned to the team. However, he never again had a winning season. Decades later, historian Carl E. Prince of New York University would say he had been shamed by Dodgers management and couldn't fit into the team's hypermasculine culture.

The notion that an executive would consult an employee's wife does seem paternalistic. But in baseball in the 1950s, people spoke of a team as a family, and the familiarity that developed during spring training and on road trips could blur the normal boundaries between employees and employers. O'Malley certainly felt it was natural to talk with Mrs. Palica and her husband. Similarly, when he believed he had problems to discuss with Jackie Robinson, he asked him to bring his wife, Rachel, to the office on Montague Street to help sort things out. This meeting happened during the first week of 1952 and would be seen as a low moment in their struggle to get along.

The relationship between O'Malley and Robinson was sometimes strained and always complex, in part because the spirit of Branch Rickey hovered over it. Aside from members of his family, no one had been more important to Robinson than Rickey, and he believed, erroneously, that Rickey had been coerced into selling his piece of the Dodgers and leaving Brooklyn. In his autobiography, Robinson would also report that O'Malley had complained to others about him, calling him a prima donna. He also speculated that O'Malley considered him to be "one of those 'uppity' niggers . . ."

Racism was a constant in Robinson's life and he was acutely aware of the many forms it could take. Early in his Dodgers career he had let certain slights and insults pass, but as the years went by he became more outspoken. By the early 1950s he was comfortable confronting even those who claimed to be friends. The influential sportswriter Dick Young warned Robinson that he was alienating people and should act more like Roy Campanella, who was more easygoing. "Any time I talk to you," he complained, "I'm acutely aware that you're a Negro."

As far as Robinson was concerned, Young was one of many who were just not comfortable with an assertive black man. But when Robinson put O'Malley into this group, he cited no evidence and he ignored the club's record of continuing to sign and promote both African-American and Hispanic players. Many years later Rachel Robinson would say that rather than racism, her husband may have been picking up on insensitivity and a bit of gamesmanship in the way O'Malley dealt with him at the January 1952 meeting.

The only record of what occurred when Jack and Rachel Robinson went to O'Malley's office is in Robinson's book. In it he recalls that the Dodgers president was upset about his player missing exhibition games, possibly exaggerating injuries, and complaining about segregated accommodations on the road. The one word he quotes O'Malley using is "crybaby."

According to the book, and in her own recollections decades later, Rachel Robinson did not appreciate being summoned to Montague Street to hear complaints about her husband. When she got the chance, she defended him completely, insisting, "Jack's heart and soul is with the baseball club, and it pains me deeply to have you say what you just said." She would recall that O'Malley quickly changed his tone and the meeting ended on a somewhat conciliatory note.

In time the relationship between O'Malley and the Robinsons would improve, but it would never be easy. However, O'Malley publicly praised Robinson, calling him "big-league in every aspect," and supported him through stormy conflicts with umpires and opponents.

O'Malley's statements and commitment to black ballplayers suggest he was not deliberately or consciously bigoted. But as a white man who was considerably older than Jackie Robinson, O'Malley probably didn't recognize how he would respond to certain words or actions. Summoning his wife to a meeting was a perfect example. For a proud and courageous man like Robinson, this would be felt as an insult. "It made us defensive from the start," recalled Rachel. And in suggesting that Robinson wasn't trying hard enough, O'Malley came dangerously close to certain stereotypes—was he saying that Robinson was lazy and shiftless?—and left both Rachel and Jackie feeling angry and suspicious.

Eventually Rachel Robinson would conclude that the early problem between her husband and Walter O'Malley was not so much about race or disrespect as it was about Branch Rickey. "Jack was what they called a Rickey man," recalled Rachel, "and after the struggle for control [of the Dodgers] Jack missed Mr. Rickey very much." Rickey had coached Robinson in life as well as baseball. "Be daring, be daring" is what she heard Rickey tell her husband. He missed that kind of encouragement.

"But following Branch Rickey was not easy" for O'Malley, added Rachel Robinson. He had asserted himself in response to Rickey, not as a matter of racial dominance. "Walter was interested in power," she said. So, too, was Jackie Robinson interested in power, and in the years to come both men would be challenged as they acquired it and used it to express their passions, ambitions, and dreams.

THE PURSUIT OF POWER was not something Walter O'Malley discussed openly, and it's hard to imagine he even reflected on it privately. Who, aside from the occasional megalomaniac, consciously craves raw power? Instead, high achievers tend to set extreme standards for themselves and chase their goals as an expression of their personalities. From his days at Culver and Penn, Walter O'Malley had poured himself into the pursuit of success, fortune, and public acclaim. He had sought his version of the good life—friendships, family, fun— with similar gusto.

By the early 1950s, O'Malley and baseball itself had reached a pinnacle. The Giants, Yankees, and Dodgers were all playing exceedingly well. The Yankees practically owned the American League pennant, and New York's National League clubs were regular contenders. Team owners became celebrities, and Walter O'Malley took great pleasure in the role. A night at the ballpark with Iraq's King Faisal? No problem. Dinner at Toots Shor's with the commissioner? Of course. A testimonial for John F. Kennedy at the Hotel St. George in Brooklyn? O'Malley was there too. A press conference in the morning, lunch with the mayor, and a Broadway show at night made for a perfect day in the life of Walter O'Malley.

Beginning a tradition that would continue for the rest of his life, the Dodgers owner-president spent long stretches of time at the spring training camp in Vero Beach where he entertained writers, friends, and baseball men with poker games, St. Patrick's Day parties, and other diversions. At Dodgertown, as it was called, he traded his business suits for casual clothes—one loud shirt sported pictures of American game fish—and wore a ball cap instead of a fedora.

The man didn't have to try hard to have fun, and soon stories of The O'Malley at spring training became part of Dodgers lore. Many involved impromptu contests that gave the owner a chance to impress as well as amuse his guests. One spring, idle talk about who could handle more manual labor led O'Malley, Bud Holman, and a couple of other wealthy men to a nearby tomato farm where a harvest was ready. Dressed in suits and ties, they persuaded the farmer, Clarence Hersey, to let them work, and they threw themselves into the task. They picked and hauled and washed tomatoes until the farmer himself was ready to quit. The loser of the contest was supposed to pay $2,000, but since no one conceded exhaustion, the outcome was a tie.

Another O'Malley legend was born when *New York Times* writer Roscoe McGowan casually asked about the fish in the heart-shaped Dodgertown pond. "Are there fish in it?" said O'Malley. "Are there fish in it? . . . There are a thousand fish in it and at least one of them is a foot and a half long. I'll take you over there this evening and catch him for you."

Never one to leave things to chance, O'Malley had anticipated this question and made sure the pond was stocked, because pictures of ballplayers hauling fish from the water "could have great publicity value."

At sunset McGowan was surprised when O'Malley, decked out in his fish-of-America shirt, tracked him down and practically dragged him over to the pond. The two men pretty much circled the shore of the muddy little pool while O'Malley cast both a baited hook and a lure. Undeterred by darkness and falling temperatures, O'Malley persisted until he caught something. It wasn't an eighteen-inch bass but a goldfish-size member of a species that locals called a "brim." O'Malley hadn't caught the big one but he had proved there was life in the lake. The two men retired to the comfort of the Dodgertown press bar with the most valuable catch of all: a good story to tell. McGowan published his version in the *Sporting News* under the title "O'Malley Not Izaak Walton, but Compleat Mangler as an Angler."

Good stories were invaluable for a business that depended on publicity, and O'Malley's relationships with reporters allowed him to keep the team in the public eye year-round. They appreciated that he answered the phone when they called and spoke candidly. Roger Kahn, who covered the team for the *Herald Tribune* for a few years in the 1950s, found him good company and generally reliable.

"Walter had a sense of style," recalled Kahn. "He could tell a joke." He could also pressure reporters to treat the team kindly and avoid controversy. With Kahn he did this by playing to the fact that the young writer was a graduate of the same Froebel Academy where he served on the board of trustees. "O'Malley would say that he gave me my diploma, but I know he didn't," recalled Kahn decades later. "Still, he liked to say it. And when I wrote something he didn't like he would say, 'I'm surprised that a Froebel boy could write something so negative.' Of course, after he had his say, we could have a drink later on. He understood how things went."

Kahn would recall only one instance when he felt misled by O'Malley, and this may have been the result of a joke gone awry. The trouble arose when O'Malley told him he had been an "admiralty lawyer" and Kahn reported it in a feature article. In fact, O'Malley had never practiced maritime law and the claim was probably a joke. When Kahn told O'Malley the trouble he caused he responded with a bit of doublespeak that became his trademark—"Only half the lies they tell about the Irish are true."

O'Malley's humor reflected a certain kind of Brooklyn charm based on winks, nods, and stories so outrageous, the listener was supposed to know they weren't true. O'Malley aligned himself and his team with the wisecracking character of the borough because it was fun, and because it was good for business. To strengthen the bond, he read most of the fan letters he received and answered many. This only increased the flow of mail, which brought good-luck charms—rabbits' feet came stuffed in envelopes—and advice on everything from the pitching rotation to ticket-selling schemes. One suggested a special day for the blind, to honor umpires. Another offered the idea of a "Dog Day" since every dog . . .

Though not quite Bill Veeck, whose taste ran toward midget batters and fireworks displays, O'Malley rejected Rickey-style conformity and excessive discipline. He wanted a team that showed some spunk and personality, and in this vein tried to lure the firebrand (and bipolar) Jimmy Piersall away from the Red Sox. "Hell, this is Brooklyn," he said. "We want characters. That's what our fans come to see." The *Sporting News* called him "The Mayor of Flatbush" and his name and face were in the New York papers as many days as not. Even casual fans recognized O'Malley on the street, and people who knew him well could impress their friends by claiming a connection with the Dodgers boss.

On a warm summer day, young Brian Mylod could send a buzz up and down Fourth Street in Brooklyn if he told his buddies, "Uncle Walter is coming."

Brian was five years old in the summer of 1952 and one of nine children belonging to the Myomac couple Katherine and Charles Mylod. But he was also O'Malley's godson, and when the Dodgers president tooled down the block in his big black car, Brian knew his standing with the neighborhood gang was going to rise. O'Malley would make a point of watching Brian play stickball or invite him to go for an ice cream. Sometimes he would let Brian pretend to steer the big car, leaving the other stickball players to gape in envy as they made their way to Lindy's or Lindroth's for a scoop of chocolate.

Brooklyn kids were accustomed to seeing Dodgers players, coaches, and executives in their neighborhoods, and they considered the team so much theirs that it seemed like part of their environment. Like the shift whistles at the navy yard and the *Brooklyn Eagle* landing on the stoop with a thud, the Dodgers were familiar and permanent. Brian Mylod almost took it for granted that he knew the owner of the team. Sometimes he got to visit O'Malley's box seats at Ebbets Field, and once he sat on Vin Scully's knee as he broadcast a game. These moments were exciting but not unnerving, because Uncle Walter made him feel happy and welcome.

In this little boy's eyes, O'Malley was a big man whose slicked-back hair and formal suits made him seem sophisticated and serious. He always had a cigar, which he plugged into a white holder, and sometimes the ash would collect on his necktie. He also had a way of connecting with people, even a kid, that made them feel as though they were being singled out for something special. "How's Brian doing?" he'd ask, and the youngest Mylod felt as if he were on top of the world.

THE DODGERS MADE ALL of Brooklyn feel on top of the world, except at World Series time. In 1952 the team was one of the most balanced ever put on a field. They hit well as a group, finishing first in homers, runs produced, and on-base percentage. And although Don Newcombe was lost to the Army, the Dodgers pitchers finished with the second-best earned run average in the league. The team won sixty of its first eighty-two games and reached September nine ahead of the Giants. Leo Durocher rallied his Polo Grounds crew for another late-season run, but this time Charlie Dressen lived up to Walter O'Malley's vote of confidence and held the Dodgers together. They won the pennant by four and a half games. The margin was supplied, in large measure, through the efforts of a new pitcher named Joe Black who starred as both a reliever and occasional starter.

A two-hundred-pound, hard-throwing right-hander, Black was yet another African-American star who helped the Dodgers prove the success of desegregation. With his Rookie-of-the-Year performance, he helped the Dodgers prove the wisdom of their early and deliberate integration policy. As later statistical studies would show, the team clearly got top play from its black pioneers, who, as a group, achieved at a much higher level than whites who came into the major leagues at the same time.

Unfortunately for Brooklyn, the bold signings that brought so many black stars to the Dodgers—and made them better than just about every other team in the game—did not make them better than the Yankees. Despite four home runs by Duke Snider and Joe Black's first-ever World Series win for an African-American pitcher, the Dodgers went down in seven games. For the fourth time in five years the team from the Bronx won the championship, and they did it with an all-white team built around stars—Mickey Mantle, Phil Rizzuto, Yogi Berra—brought up in the organization.

O'Malley wasn't disappointed in his team and during the season he had defended players from their critics. And though Branch Rickey said that Jackie Robinson and Pee Wee Reese were both in decline and should be traded, both would return in 1953, along with manager Dressen. O'Malley also promised that his front office was looking for another Joe Black to join the roster. But in an unguarded moment, when he was asked about the Dodgers' most pressing need, he responded, "Fans."

The Brooklyn team that won the pennant and nearly captured the 1952 World Series suffered a big decline in admissions. The ballpark saw roughly two hundred thousand fewer fans compared with the previous season. Baseball attendance was down in general, but the situation was worse than average in Flatbush. The most glaring illustration of the problem came during game six of the series, when the Dodgers had a chance to clinch the world championship. Five thousand Ebbets Field seats were empty that day. It was hard to explain such a thing.

In the short term, O'Malley could handle the drop in fan support and take some consolation in the fact that his friendly competitor Horace Stoneham and the hated Giants were drawing even fewer fans. The Giants had actually lost money—an average of $125,000—in each of the last four years, while the Dodgers profited due to healthy revenues from broadcasting and other sources. Although the high earnings seen in the late 1940s had faded, between 1952 and 1956 no other baseball team would make more money than the Dodgers.

But while there was no financial emergency, the organization could be undermined by the steady erosion of attendance. If the borough failed to support a pennant-winning team, what would happen when, inevitably, the Dodgers lost their edge? Die-hard Brooklynites might continue to buy tickets, but the casual baseball fan could easily get what he wanted at the Polo Grounds or Yankee Stadium. And for those who just wanted something to do on a Friday night or Sunday afternoon, New York offered more entertainment options than any other city in the world. Under these circumstances, it wasn't ever going to be *easier* to fill Ebbets Field. If nothing changed, the task would only grow more difficult.

What would be O'Malley's strategy? Ebbets Field was still old and costly to maintain. A new stadium, clean, efficient, and suited to suburban families, might entice fans. In the summer of 1952, O'Malley helped a writer at *Collier's* magazine put together an article about his concepts, developed with the help of Emil Praeger and Norman Bel Geddes, for just such a ballpark. Hyping "the future" was a staple for this magazine, which had recently devoted dozens of pages to space travel as conceived by Wernher Von Braun and others.

When published, O'Malley's futuristic vision called for a column-free, weatherproof dome—possibly movable or translucent—seating fifty-five thousand for baseball and ninety thousand for events like prizefights. The field, which could be made of artificial turf, would be placed below ground level, and parking would be arranged so customers could walk from their cars to their comfortably cushioned seats without much of a climb. Plans for traffic would allow thirty thousand people to leave the park within fifteen minutes, but if they chose to linger they could shop in an arcade of stores or have their oil changed by attendants in the parking garage. (These services, along with office space and the garage, would be available for neighborhood use every day of the year.) Everywhere machines would replace workers by taking tickets, opening gates, and dispensing food.

Pressed for his most realistic view, O'Malley told *Collier's* he believed that a stadium very much like the domed wonderland he described would be built eventually. Where and when were a different matter, he said, adding, "We've already had too much of that wait-'til-next-year stuff in Brooklyn."

It was an honest answer from an owner who couldn't be sure that Brooklyn and the Dodgers would merit such an enormous investment. Still, a new park seemed essential if the club were to remain in the borough and thrive. And O'Malley was the type to keep every option open for as long as possible. In late 1952 he used a chance meeting with George Spargo, who worked on slum clearance under Robert Moses, to remind him of the possible public benefits of a new Brooklyn ballpark. After many years with Moses, George Spargo had become one of the most powerful bureaucratic functionaries in New York. He did the gritty work of arranging rich contracts for politically important men who became Moses's dependents. Spargo and Moses would have to be involved if the government was going to help the Dodgers, but in a politically contentious place like New York City this wouldn't happen quickly.

While he waited, O'Malley embarked on a bit of a practice run, building a little ballpark for Dodgertown so his team wouldn't have to decamp for Miami for its spring-training games. Impressed by the design of the new stadium in Miami, where no seats were blocked by pillars or posts, he had Emil Praeger work on a similar plan for Dodgertown. O'Malley was involved in every aspect of construction, right down to the specifications for the cypress planks that would be used for seating. He also chose to name the park for Bud Holman.

As might be expected, the stadium project met some opposition. The entire campsite was owned by a local government agency and leased for the ceremonial sum of $1 per year and the promise of increased tourism. Local critics often questioned the trade-off, alleging that the Dodgers got a sweetheart deal. O'Malley did respond at times. When he came under fire in 1952, he wrote to a banker in Vero to warn, "I do not know how to run away from a fight." The critics backed off and the project went forward.

Emil Praeger needed less than a year to design and build the stadium, which became one of the most idyllic spots for baseball in the country. Gentle sloping walkways brought fans to the gate, and when they passed through they discovered a beautiful green diamond. Earth removed for construction was used to create berms that marked the limits of the outfield. Towering, graceful palm trees lined the perimeter of the entire property. Altogether the little park was a marvel of simplicity where spectators were almost as close to the action as parents at a Little League game.

When Holman Stadium opened on March 11, 1953, the visiting dignitaries included the governor of Florida and the president of U.S. Steel. They saw the Dodgers beat the Athletics, but O'Malley missed the game. After the opening ceremonies he disappeared for a meeting with Commissioner Frick, other members of the major-league executive council, and the owner of the Boston Braves, Lou Perini. At this private conference Perini discussed moving his team to Milwaukee. The Braves had suffered a shocking decline in attendance, going from one million in 1949 to less than three hundred thousand in 1952. Milwaukee beckoned with a new county stadium that would eventually hold more than fifty thousand.

No one outside of Perini's circle, which included the Milwaukee-based brewer Frederick Miller, knew he was working on a move. He had reassured people in Boston that he was staying put, at least for a year. And in Milwaukee they feared that Perini was actually trying to deny their dream of major-league baseball. They had good reason to consider him an obstacle. He owned the local minor-league team, the Brewers, and under the rules of the game he could prevent another team from making the city its home. Just days earlier Perini had used this power to block Bill Veeck's attempt to move his St. Louis Browns into the new stadium in Wisconsin. Veeck's team was in desperate financial condition and, to no one's surprise, he vowed to continue looking for a new home. (In a year's time the Browns would be the Baltimore Orioles and play under new owners.) But Perini's plan, which he had kept secret for months, would shock fans from Maine to Connecticut.

Within days of the Vero Beach meeting, baseball's owners gathered in St. Petersburg, Florida, for their spring conference. Perini's secret intentions were soon reported by the press. He hadn't blocked Veeck to protect the minor-league Brewers. He wanted the city, and the new municipal stadium, for the Braves. When the news hit Boston the mayor, governor, and state legislature first complained and then pleaded for the owner to reconsider. But he was in Florida, safe from the storm, and moving quickly.

In a conference room closed to the press, Perini spent more than three hours making his case before the National League owners. (He would have to receive their unanimous consent.) A dapper little man with a gap-toothed smile, Perini was a well-liked member of the owners club, where money and charm counted. He had taken control of a small family company at age twenty-one and with two equally determined brothers—they were called the Three Little Steam Shovels, after a children's book—built it into one of the country's biggest construction outfits, with projects all over North America. Perini had proven himself a business big-leaguer, but he had baseball troubles. Fans had abandoned the team: only 261,000 came to the park in all of 1952. He had lost $700,000 in the previous season. It seemed that Boston was no longer able to support more than one baseball team.

The National League owners listened and were sympathetic to Perini. Even though their peers in the American League had just told Bill Veeck he would have to wait to move his team—the season was too close—when Perini asked to change cities immediately, no one objected. When it came time to vote, O'Malley proposed approval for the immediate transfer. Horace Stoneham seconded the motion. Perini won.

And so it was that the oldest franchise in major-league baseball was suddenly uprooted. In Boston, Catholic Archbishop Richard Cushing comforted mourners with the suggestion that the loss should inspire them to contribute more to their city and to remember that they should not "take too much for granted." Some heeded the archbishop's call, but when the Braves came to play the Red Sox in a preseason exhibition, those who couldn't practice Christian charity shouted, "Hey, Perini, you bum, you!"

In Milwaukee the bum was a hero. Welcomed with a parade witnessed by more than sixty thousand baseball-mad locals, Perini rode in a convertible with Frederick Miller by his side and a caravan of players behind him. At the reception held in their honor, the team that had yet to play a game in its new hometown was showered with gifts, cheers, and praise. The celebration would continue for a week and end on opening day with just about every important person in the state, including the entire Wisconsin legislature, on hand.

"There was never anything like this in Boston," said Perini, even when the team won the pennant in 1948. He wished the other major-league owners could see him now.

The other owners may have been pleased and even amused to see that Perini was welcomed like a Caesar, but as the season wore on, they didn't have to witness events in Milwaukee firsthand to appreciate what the Little Steam Shovels had accomplished. They knew his deal for the stadium—low rent and profits on concessions—was so good that he volunteered to pay extra. They also saw his team make huge strides on the field. In 1952 the Braves had won just sixty-four games and lost eighty-nine. In 1953 the same core group of players started out like champs. In mid-June the team claimed first place and got a parade when they returned from a road trip. In early July the *New York Times* took the measure of the city and its team and declared that Milwaukee—long suffering its own inferiority complex—was "more Brooklyn than Brooklyn." Railroads ran special trains for fans. Hotels offered special rates on game days. Couples planned weddings around the home schedule.

Of course, fan frenzy can carry a team only so far. The Braves faded and the Dodgers asserted themselves, and by the end of July the real Brooklyn was in charge. In early September, Walter O'Malley flew to Milwaukee, where his team clinched the pennant. Based on their record of 105–49, the 1953 Dodgers were the best team since the 1944 Cardinals and one of the best ever. (No Dodger team would ever post a better record.) First in fielding and batting, the Dodgers got peak performances from a cadre of maturing players, including Campanella (MVP), Snider, Furillo, and Hodges. Although Don Newcombe was still in the Army, the pitching staff was strong, with Carl Erskine having his best year ever with twenty victories. And a pair of rookies, outfielder Jim "Junior" Gilliam and pitcher Johnny Podres, made unexpected contributions.

Podres, who won nine and lost four, was a lefthander from the tiny hamlet of Witherbee, in upstate New York, where his father worked in a mine and played for the town team. Podres would remember his dad, Joseph, as a pitcher worthy of the major leagues who stopped playing ball only when he broke both of his legs in a mining accident. Other than one trip to Ebbets Field when he was a sophomore in high school, all he knew about the big leagues he had learned from Red Barber's broadcasts. In 1953 he would become the second-youngest pitcher ever to start in the World Series, an honor he would have gladly exchanged for a victory.

As it turned out, Podres lost his first postseason start, and the Dodgers lost the series to the Yankees for the second time in as many seasons. It was the Yanks' fifth championship in a row and sixth in seven years. In about eighteen months Broadway would give America a musical called *Damn Yankees*, but the sentiment was already felt in every major-league city. It likely came into Walter O'Malley's mind as he walked to the visitors' clubhouse at Yankee stadium and told his players, "Once more, we'll have to wait till next year."

O'MALLEY WAS COMMITTED TO "next year," and with attendance up slightly—one thousand fans per game—he could pay what was required to retain the core of his team, including Snider, Hodges, Robinson, and Campanella. These stars were aging, however. Robinson, nearly thirty-five years old, was starting to lose some of his power. Anyone schooled in the Branch Rickey style of player management would have considered selling his services to another team, and so much speculation arose that Robinson felt compelled to announce that he would retire before moving to any team other than the Giants. No deal was hatched, however, and like the other Dodgers mainstays, Robinson signed for another season.

Fans who followed the issue in the press might have believed that O'Malley was less generous than his predecessors. At one point Robinson said as much, complaining that he had received not "a cent more" than he had in 1950. As he later confessed, this wasn't true. During O'Malley's short tenure Robinson had received raises totaling more than 30 percent and earned considerably more than Duke Snider, who was far more productive at the plate. After the 1953 series many returning players got raises, worked out by Bavasi under O'Malley's authority. Jim "Junior" Gilliam's salary was doubled. Campanella got a 25 percent hike.

But as generous as he was in some cases, O'Malley was not willing to stand with his wallet open for everyone. Always a sharp judge of talent, he was becoming a tougher negotiator. This evolution was a matter of experience—and maturity. O'Malley turned fifty just four days after the end of the World Series and his age had begun to show. His hair was thinning and his expanding belly pressed a bit against the closed buttons on his sport coats. A double chin had begun to soften the strong jawline visible in pictures from earlier days.

With time and success, O'Malley's confidence in his own style seemed to grow. Bavasi and Thompson were proving they could operate the major-league team and farm clubs. This allowed O'Malley to focus on developing the business and managing only the highest-level employees. Although they received market rates—and sometimes better—for their work, one-year contracts were O'Malley's standard.

This policy, one of O'Malley's bargaining hallmarks, kept people on their toes and protected him from ever having to pay for two managers—one on the job, another ousted but still under contract—as the Dodgers had in the past. He expected that anyone who was nervous about the future would accept his promise that a good performance would usually assure a renewed contract. O'Malley's other negotiating standard evolved slowly and was more a matter of temperament than stated policy. As those who challenged him would discover, he didn't like to be pressured. He would call a bluff every time.

Even before the end of the 1953 series, O'Malley had heard hints that his manager Charlie Dressen felt he held a strong hand. When the Giants signed Leo Durocher to a multiyear contract, Dodger shortstop Pee Wee Reese brought the issue to a reporter's attention. For the last two years Durocher had finished second to Dressen, and he wasn't the only manager getting a multiyear deal. The Braves, Red Sox, and Cardinals had all given their managers this security. "What about Charlie Dressen?" he asked Dave Anderson of the *Brooklyn Eagle.* "He's only on top." (Privately Dressen was hearing similar things from friends who said he should demand more from the Dodgers.)

Players, especially Jackie Robinson, liked Dressen so much that they didn't mind that the manager exaggerated his own powers. And even though the Dodgers had lost the series again, Dressen had guided them to an easy victory in the pennant race. And, as everyone knew, luck and chance were such big factors in World Series that it was not the best measure of a team or manager. O'Malley certainly understood this and seemed ready to give Dressen another one-year commitment. Then, on the day the Dodgers won the pennant, Dressen and his wife talked about his future and composed a letter arguing for a three-year agreement.

Childless and devoted to each other, Charlie and Ruth Dressen were as much a team as any couple might be. (Some would add their ever-present poodle to the mix.) Together they worked out the case that Charlie would present to O'Malley. She typed up their points, including the demand for $50,000 per year for three seasons. He tucked the pages into a pocket and the letter stayed there until the series ended. When the time came, Dressen made his case with

O'Malley and Bavasi during meetings on Montague Street. Little progress was made and as he left for the day Charlie remembered the letter.

"My wife and I have put our feelings in the matter of a contract into this letter," he said. "You might as well have it."

Ruth was in the hospital for tests and when Charlie saw her that night he described an unbreakable stalemate and seemed resigned to leaving Brooklyn. When the issue made it into the newspapers, the press and public alike were shocked. Some believed that O'Malley, encouraged by Bavasi, had long hoped to find a way to replace Dressen. Whether this was or wasn't the case, Dressen had boxed himself into a terrible position. He had also offended O'Malley, who had gone against the fans to hire him in the first place and to retain him after the Giants overtook the Dodgers in 1951.

O'Malley offered Dressen an out—a one-year contract—but he declined it. Before he left for the West Coast, where he would manage for minor-league Oakland, Dressen went to see O'Malley at his office. The owner, who believed that Ruth Dressen had wanted her husband to move to the West all along, returned the letter—"It was a pip," he said—to spare him any embarrassment. Magazines offered the Dressens as much as $2,000 for the few typed pages, but they never made it public.

With Dressen's departure, he and the Brooklyn Dodgers scored a first. Never before (or since) has a major-league manager followed a trip to the World Series with a jump back to the minor leagues. Speculation about Dressen's replacement focused first on the possibility that shortstop Pee Wee Reese might become a player-manager. Buzzie Bavasi would recall that O'Malley favored Reese, in part because he was respected by the team and adored by the fans. Bavasi agreed to offer Reese the job on the condition that if he turned it down, he could offer it to Walter Alston, who had been the manager at Nashua when Roy Campanella and Don Newcombe integrated the American minor leagues. In 1953, Alston had just won his second International League championship in four years managing the Dodgers' top farm team in Montreal.

When Bavasi went to Louisville to meet Reese, he discovered that the Dodger shortstop didn't think a thirty-five year-old without a day of managing experience was the right man to lead the Brooklyns to their final goal, a World Series. He took himself out of consideration. Bavasi next approached Alston, who accepted the job. When the decision was announced, the *Daily News* headline read, "Alston (Who He?) to Manage Dodgers."

IN PROMOTING HIS TOP minor-league manager, even though he had never run a big-league club, O'Malley showed confidence in his organization, including Bavasi, and in his own ability to judge people. He could have lured a big name from another team or drawn some famous ex-player or manager out of retirement. But with Alston he got someone who knew the Dodgers system and should be loyal and grateful for the opportunity to prove the talent he had shown in the minors.

The choice was, nevertheless, a surprise to many in baseball and a shock to many Brooklyn fans. It was not the only one they got in the wake of the World Series loss. After he was done negotiating with Dressen, O'Malley had turned to deal with the only other nonathlete who was considered essential to the team's identity, broadcaster Red Barber.

The voice of the Dodgers, and for many the voice of baseball, Barber had taught a generation of big-city fans that winning teams were "tearin' up the pea patch" and batters who were ahead on the count were "sittin' in the catbird seat." His cornpone expressions and silky voice had made him a wealthy radio star, but something in his attitude, or personality, rubbed O'Malley the wrong way. The feeling was mutual, according to Buzzie Bavasi. It could have been related to the loan O'Malley had arranged for Barber's home. It might have had something to do with Branch Rickey. Whatever the reason, said Bavasi, "Red hated Walter."

O'Malley had gotten Barber when he bought the team, and given his popularity he had stuck with him. But Barber would admit that the relationship was strained from the start and didn't get any better. Tom Villante, who worked as the Dodgers' broadcast producer in that time, would recall that O'Malley was irritated by Barber's growing tendency toward on-air digressions—he talked about books, sailing, steeples in the distance—and comments about bad weather that hurt ticket sales. Barber would write that O'Malley wanted him to direct cameramen to show the empty seats at Ebbets Field, so viewers might see the meager support the team was getting. Barber refused. No big conflict arose, but he could sense trouble.

"I had dug in," he said, "and he was digging in."

As so often happens, it was a trivial thing that seemed to tip the scale. "Red would wear this hat, a beret kind of thing called a *boina*, that we thought was sissified and not appropriate for a baseball broadcast on TV," recalled Villante. Barber had acquired the hat on a vacation in Spain and wore it when he was photographed for the 1953 Dodgers yearbook. The caption published with the picture made a lame joke about the cap, so he decided to wear it every day. Sponsor Schaefer Brewing complained. (Perhaps they thought the hat suggested wine, not beer.) Whatever their reasons, the sponsor controlled the set and O'Malley passed along their request that the *boina* disappear. Barber stopped wearing it on the air but seemed to have it on whenever he saw O'Malley. "Every time I ran into O'Malley," wrote Barber much later, "his eyes went straight to the *boina*."

Stubborn in his own way, Barber was also confident in his status at the top of his profession. When the 1953 World Series matchup was set, the sponsor asked him to broadcast the games for a fee of $200 apiece. This was the single biggest sporting event of the year, broadcast on television coast-to-coast, and the sponsor proposed to pay him less than what he received to announce a regular game for Brooklyn. He turned them down. The next day, Barber would report, he told O'Malley what had happened and the Dodgers owner said, "That is your problem. I'll nominate [Vin] Scully to take your place." Scully took the spot with Barber's blessing, and with his stomach churning performed well. Barber, who had been expecting something more supportive from O'Malley, decided at that moment that he was finished with the Dodgers.

As with every baseball story, this one had many sides. Buzzie Bavasi would recall that Barber had been looking for a new job before the World Series and that O'Malley, who had been committed to keeping him, changed his mind when he heard about it. The indisputable truth is that before November 1, 1953, Barber announced he was switching to the Yankees' TV booth and taking his pea patch and catbirds and "suck-egg mules" with him. He would be replaced by his protégé, Vin Scully.

In the future Red Barber would express both admiration and resentment for O'Malley. And his interpretation of certain events would vary widely. In 1970 he would write that O'Malley respected his allegiance to Branch Rickey. Many years later he would say, "My continuing friendship and regard for Rickey bothered him."

There would never be any ambivalence in Vin Scully's relationship with O'Malley. He was grateful for the opportunity O'Malley gave him at such a young age—he was not quite twenty-six—and would consider him a father figure for the rest of his life. Thoroughly trained by Barber, Scully joined Connie Desmond to give the play-by-play. Over time, Desmond's drinking problem would mean more responsibility for Scully, but he never wavered. Gifted with a beautiful voice and always thoroughly prepared, Scully was so good that fans didn't miss Barber for very long.

BY THE END OF 1953, Walter O'Malley had dismissed two popular, successful, and reliable Dodgers veterans—Dressen and Barber—and replaced them with eager newcomers who he could only hope would succeed. He had won another pennant but lost another World Series. It was enough activity and turmoil to keep anyone busy, but it wasn't half of what he had been required to manage.

The biggest crisis of the year had been a personal one, little noticed by the outside world. On a Friday night in early April his father had died of a heart attack while at home in his apartment on the Upper East Side of Manhattan. The death was sudden and unexpected. Just a month before, Edwin had visited Dodgertown for the opening of Holman Stadium and the St. Patrick's Day party. A photo from that day shows him looking strong and healthy and wearing a green shirt and a tie decorated with a shamrock.

More than twenty-five years had passed since Edwin O'Malley had been a public figure, and his death merited only brief notice on page eighty-eight of the *New York Times*. In the spirit of honoring the dead, the notice did not delve into the details of Edwin's problems at the public markets.

Difficult as it was to lose his father, O'Malley then had to resolve things with Edwin's second wife, Connie. In letters written soon after Edwin's death, Connie recalled Walter's objections to his father's second marriage and concerns about Edwin's business schemes. She said she didn't want anything from Edwin's estate, including social security benefits. O'Malley made an effort to soothe her feelings, and weeks later she wrote, "Although I may appear ungrateful to you, I am deeply touched by your thoughtfulness." By June the letters from Connie stopped, but O'Malley, an only child, was still left to grieve the loss of his father, the last connection to his mother, Alma, and to his earliest days in Hollis, Queens.

Aside from family concerns in 1953, O'Malley faced the big issue of his team's long-term future as a business enterprise. He was keenly ware of how the Braves, in moving west, had found a geographical cure for all their ills. O'Malley also knew that the Browns were seeking a similar solution and that the Athletics were not long for Philadelphia. After more than fifty years of frozen stability, major-league baseball was ready for big changes. Some cities, especially those with more than one team, were destined to lose, and others were going to gain as the game opened its arms to include more of the nation.

In New York the Yankees were secure, but it was hard to imagine that the city could support three big-league clubs for many more years. O'Malley loved Brooklyn, the Dodgers tradition, and the New York region. It was the only real home he had ever known and he wanted his team to be the one that survived to represent the National League. But years of engineering studies, real estate surveys, and financial analysis had only reinforced his belief that a new stadium was essential to this goal. It had also taught him that the one government official who could help him assemble the land and build a new stadium was Robert Moses.

In June of 1953 O'Malley wrote to the chairman of the all-powerful Triborough Bridge and Tunnel Authority seeking an audience. He told Moses he wanted to discuss "a new ballpark—one well-located with ample parking accommodations. This is a must," he stressed, "if we are to keep our franchise in Brooklyn." The note was brief and almost overly respectful. O'Malley didn't freight it with facts and arguments. He only requested a meeting.

On the same day O'Malley sent a more detailed letter to his old friend and mentor George V. McLaughlin, who served on the Triborough Bridge and Tunnel Authority board. Here he made a fuller argument, explaining that his ballpark would be privately funded and that the only help he needed from the government would involve finding the right area, relocating tenants and property owners, and then selling the land to the team. O'Malley believed that a 1949 federal housing law that was intended to promote urban renewal would authorize and pay for the authority to help in this way if parking facilities were included to give the project a public purpose. Moses was already engaged in a similar project in the Columbus Circle area of Manhattan, where dilapidated buildings would be leveled to make way for an indoor arena/convention center.

Title I of the Federal Housing Act of 1949 could be read to allow the kind of private/public project O'Malley wanted, and it would be used this way in other developments across the country. And Moses had already targeted parts of Brooklyn for slum clearance and rebuilding. Intent on making New York the world's premier urban center, the master builder would eventually level sixteen city sites and displace one hundred thousand tenants in the pursuit of a more perfect city. But his grand design did not include a new stadium for the Dodgers and in his response to O'Malley's June letter he rejected it outright, adding, "I'm sorry to have to write this letter but I know you want it straight from the shoulder."

The blow was not enough to stop the Dodgers owner. He continued to press for a meeting and in September sat with Moses in the Coal Hole Room of the Brooklyn Club. As O'Malley made the argument for a new stadium, he laced it with references to the old ball game, the traditions of the borough, and even the dreams of orphan boys. In the face of all this sentimentality, Moses may have melted a bit. The great builder had long considered a huge redevelopment program for downtown Brooklyn. Conceding the borough's devotion to the Dodgers, he briefly entertained the addition of a new stadium to his vision.

For a moment Moses and O'Malley were close to agreement. But it was only a moment. On October 20, Moses wrote again to say that he could not help O'Malley acquire a site and that a Dodgers stadium could not be included in a slum-clearance project. "I can see no way in which this can be done," he said.

This was the beginning of a long debate, during which the two sides often seemed to talk past each other. O'Malley sought help gathering together parcels of land for a stadium in Brooklyn but insisted he would pay for both the property and the building. Moses and others responded as if O'Malley were asking for public cash, which he wasn't. The one area of genuine disagreement involved a question of law and public policy. O'Malley thought a stadium with public parking facilities qualified as a public improvement under the federal law and would serve the people of Brooklyn and New York well. Moses did not agree.

One rejection could not stop O'Malley. The 1953 Dodgers were the best team the borough had ever seen, and he had to believe that with time he could get the public behind his proposal. But as he watched Lou Perini rack up profits and both the Browns and the Athletics planned moves to new cities, O'Malley needed options. For this reason he allowed himself to be courted by wealthy and influential men who wanted the National League's best club, Brooklyn's beloved bums, for the baseball-hungry citizens of Southern California.

IN THE SUMMER OF 1953, Vincent X. Flaherty, newspaperman, civic booster, and raconteur, contacted O'Malley on behalf of two rich and famous Texans who wanted to plant a major-league team in Los Angeles. Oilman Sid Richardson and buccaneer industrialist Clint Murchison, who owned as many as a hundred companies, had enough spare cash to buy every team in the big leagues. But according to Flaherty, columnist for the Hearst Company's *Los Angeles Examiner*, they only wanted the Dodgers and were inquiring about the price.

Already five years into his pursuit, Flaherty had poured enormous amounts of time and energy into the cause of bringing the major leagues to Los Angeles. Born and raised in Washington, D.C., he was the kind of sports-mad, hyperactive promoter who could always be found around baseball. His older brother Edmund "Pat" Flaherty had been, for a brief time, a major leaguer. After leaving the game he became a Hollywood actor, often playing minor roles in movies about sports. (He taught Gary Cooper to throw.) Vincent Flaherty followed his big brother to the West in 1945, leaving behind a newspaper job in Washington and a long-standing relationship with Senators owner Clark Griffith. After getting a job with the *Examiner* he quickly found his way into the circles of power, becoming a volunteer staff man for the self-appointed Los Angeles Citizens Committee for Major League Baseball. The leaders of this group included Howard Hughes, Conrad Hilton, Louis B. Mayer, and Reese Taylor, the president of Union Oil. In Flaherty they had a man who was convinced he was working for "the greatest thing in the history of baseball."

Between the Texas titans and the Los Angeles power brokers, Flaherty worked himself past the point of exhaustion in August of 1953 and wound up collapsing. Writing from a bed at St. John's Hospital in Santa Monica, he apologized for a break in his correspondence and then pressed O'Malley for an answer on the Murchison-Richardson bid. Promising absolute discretion—"not a word will ever be printed"—he asked, "Would you like to remain president if the property were moved here? Would you wish to retain any stock?"

In this note, Flaherty suggested that O'Malley had already responded to an earlier inquiry. "I received your very informative answer," he wrote, "and sent it immediately to Murchison." Just what O'Malley told him was never made public and no record of this communication has ever surfaced. But by the time Flaherty made his way east for the 1953 World Series, he had suspended his interest in the Dodgers and stopped talking about Texas moneymen. Los Angeles still wanted baseball, however, and Bill Veeck's St. Louis franchise seemed within grasp.

Veeck had devoted enough time to the Los Angeles option to learn that Union Oil was ready to pay him an all-time record fee for the TV broadcast rights to home games. Locals, whose hopes were raised by Lou Perini's success in Milwaukee, showed him plans for converting the massive Los Angeles Memorial Coliseum to host baseball. And Veeck believed he had worked out a schedule that would make it possible for opposing teams to fly in for several games in a row and return home without suffering too much strain.

Had Veeck been free to simply shift his team west, he would have done it. But he needed the consent of his fellow owners in the American League, and in the final weeks of the season they leaned toward Baltimore as the better option for the Browns. A few days before the Dodgers and Yankees began the 1953 series, Veeck spent ten hours at the Commodore Hotel in New York arguing the case before a league meeting. The owners also listened to delegations from various cities. Baltimore's presentation was the most complete. The LA group, headed by newly elected mayor Norris Poulson, said they could not put forward a specific ownership group but could raise the money to buy the club within a week.

For two more days the owners, Veeck, and the delegations from Baltimore and Los Angeles struggled over a franchise that had become the laughingstock of the major leagues. Veeck's mood went from despair to delight as the competition guaranteed he would get more than $2 million for the team. At one point Howard Hughes sent a $1 million check to back up the Los Angeles bid. However, in the end Baltimore won the vote, and the Browns became the Orioles. Norris Poulson hung around for the World Series. (Veeck would spend the next year and a half trying to figure out how to bring the majors to Los Angeles, but never quite putting the pieces together. He would not return to the game until 1959, when he would form a group to buy the White Sox.)

Watching all these events and listening to his sources, Vincent X. Flaherty left New York believing that the owners had actually approved the Los Angeles plan but reversed themselves under the threat of a lawsuit. "You will find that this is the true story," he wrote to Walter O'Malley. ". . . [T]he league had voted 8 to 0 to move the Browns to this city [Los Angeles] until the Browns attorney started tossing around threats and demands for immediate action."

Although the Browns were lost, Flaherty knew that America's third-largest city still deserved a team. During the series he had cornered then Brooklyn manager Dressen and got him to agree that the Dodgers could draw three times as many fans in Los Angeles. Flaherty invited O'Malley to secret meetings with Hughes, Hilton, Mayer, and the others, and promised they "would make a deal with you within 24 hours, to your complete liking."

To hear Flaherty tell it in this letter, which he sent after the World Series, Los Angeles promised huge attendance, perfect temperatures, and sunshine for every ball game. He even offered relief from the Dodgers' biggest on-field problem, the team in the Bronx. "Bring the Dodgers here," he said, "and you won't hear about the all-powerful Yankees again."

It must have been tempting: all that sunshine, all those eager fans, and all those dollars just waiting to be delivered. And given his team's defeat at the hands of the Yankees just days before, Walter O'Malley might have been tempted. But even after Flaherty called him on the phone and spoke as one Irish charmer to another, O'Malley resisted. He turned down the request for secret meetings and declined to consider offers to buy his franchise. For O'Malley, who loved a good scrap, the Dodgers were still a work in progress. He wasn't eager to run away from the Yankees; he was committed to staying in Brooklyn, facing the damn Yankees directly, and beating them.

Eight

═══════════

WOW! WOW! WOW!

On February 17, 1954, a breeze from the south blew a preview of spring into New York City, sending crowds to Central Park and Walter O'Malley to the streets of Brooklyn looking for a place to build a stadium. While a sea lion at the park zoo barked for visitors basking in sixty-degree sunshine, O'Malley found trucks parked three abreast, making it impossible for him to drive through the neighborhood called Fort Greene. He left his car on Atlantic Avenue and walked south to where a dilapidated meat market occupied a space bigger than a city block and retail butchers worked from shops along the street.

The Fort Greene Public Market, once under the supervision of Edwin J. O'Malley, was a giant warehouse, slaughterhouse, and butcher store that had served the city for decades. The chairman of the association that represented the market's dealers had recently written to Borough President Cashmore to complain about conditions, which he said were fast deteriorating and needed to be addressed in a sweeping way. Cashmore had passed the letter to O'Malley, who was naturally curious about a site that might be vacated if the city ever built a new market in a different spot.

On a typical day a visitor to the Fort Greene market could watch men in bloodied white aprons unload sides of beef, pork, and lamb from boxcars and deliver them to the wholesale stalls where butchers hacked and sliced to prepare shipments for local stores and restaurants. At loading docks trucks were packed with meat and poultry for delivery around the city. At retail shops that were also housed in the market, salamis and legs of lamb hung from hooks over counters where sellers and buyers—mostly local women—debated the price of roasts, fillets, and ground meat. The dealers and the customers spoke many different languages and their haggling mingled with the rumble of idling trucks to create the sound of street-level commerce.

Operated in the same location since World War I, the market was a grimy place that bustled with life early in the day. But after workers closed the shops, cleaned up the scraps, and hosed the blood into the sewer, it became shadowy and dangerous. In 1951 one of the city's most notorious crimes occurred in a building in the center of this district: a housepainter strangled and dismembered the daughter of an upstate postmaster. Her body was found in suitcases stored in lockers at a nearby Long Island Rail Road station. The papers called it the Torso Murder.

Given the rough conditions, including the odor that emanated from the market in summertime, few families actually lived in the neighborhood around the market. As he walked the streets, O'Malley saw just a handful of small apartment buildings and, aside from butcher shops, few significant businesses. Between the market and the old Long Island Rail Road terminal a couple of blocks to the west, he saw exactly what Robert Moses had already decided was a slum that should be cleared and redeveloped under the federal Title I program.

As city construction cocoordinator and chairman of the slum-clearance committee, Moses had already picked a private developer to reap the benefit from Title I funds and build in Fort Greene. The designee, Fred Trump, owned an empire of apartments in Brooklyn and Queens that made him far richer than Walter O'Malley. With Moses's help he stood to gain access to an unusually large city tract, accessible to both subways and the railroad, and ready for construction. It was the kind of arrangement Trump's son Donald would one day trumpet as a demonstration of his great power. In his father's day such deals were made quietly, lest someone other than the few developers already chosen by Moses try to get in on the Title I bonanza.

Walking through Fort Greene, Walter O'Malley looked for an answer to the objections Moses had raised about his proposal to build a ballpark in Brooklyn (the main one being the demand that any government-aided development serve a vital public purpose). The railroad was planning for new trains that couldn't be accommodated at its cramped old terminal. As O'Malley surveyed the site and then went to his office to write about his findings, he wondered if the Long Island Rail Road's need for more space would constitute proper use to get the government to condemn the property and move the occupants.

"Out of this could come a new ballpark, a parking garage, a new railroad depot and the elimination of a bad traffic bottleneck," wrote O'Malley in a letter he would send to publisher Frank Schroth of the *Brooklyn Daily Eagle*. "I have hopes that a study of the railroad's power to condemn land for *railroad purposes* will give us a peg on which to hang the hat." He also wrote that he would send Emil Praeger to make a study of the site, which was different from ones he had suggested before, and hinted that Schroth might help get it before the almighty Moses.

In the eight months since Moses had first rejected O'Malley's request for help, Schroth had become his sounding board in his campaign to change the man's mind. Schroth knew Moses well, but New York's master builder was difficult if not impossible to move. In October, Moses had sent a letter that practically sneered as he charged that O'Malley wrongly assumed "we can some how go out and condemn property for a new Dodgers field just where you want it . . ." In November he had struck an imperious note, correcting a typo in an O'Malley letter and then charging that the Dodgers wanted public funding for the entire project. (This was never the case. O'Malley wanted from the start to acquire land and build a stadium with his own money.)

Considering Moses's tone, another man might have retreated, but O'Malley wanted the Dodgers to thrive in Brooklyn and was convinced this couldn't happen without a new ballpark and thousands of parking spaces. The spaces were vital for fans who were moving to the suburbs—or already lived there—but would return to a modern stadium in a safe neighborhood where parking was easy.

Looking at the letters that flew between the three men, the persistence shown by O'Malley and Schroth seems almost comical. In April of 1954, Moses directed the general manager of the Triborough Bridge and Tunnel Authority to give O'Malley the brush-off. In this case, as always, George Spargo did as he was told, advising O'Malley to take his concerns to Brooklyn borough president

John Cashmore "before wasting any more time on it." Of course, Spargo knew that in a unified New York run out of City Hall in Manhattan, Cashmore lacked the power to take any action.

Undaunted, Schroth and O'Malley continued to lobby by mail and in person until Moses sent what he termed "positively my last Dodger spasm." In it he accused O'Malley of "beefing, threatening, foxing and conniving" and urged him to pursue the unworkable option of improving Ebbets Field, where there was no land available for parking.

Thirty-five years earlier, a young Moses had been part of a reformist mayor's attempt to break New York's system of power politics. With the rise of Red Mike Hylan and his cronies—including Edwin O'Malley—Moses had been defeated by Tammany Hall. Now he controlled vast sums of public money that made him more powerful than any Tammany man in history. Certain of his own virtue, Moses believed that he always acted in the best interests of the city. But this belief didn't erase the fact that Moses often gave valuable contracts and properties to key allies and in some cases these favors were the same as gifts courtesy of the taxpayer.

For his part, Walter O'Malley sought help but not a handout. He wanted to invest millions of dollars in a borough that others had begun to abandon. Of course, he might increase his profit, which is, after all, the whole point of business. But he would also invigorate a slum, raise the tax base, and maintain the team in Brooklyn as a source of community pride and economic activity for local shops, bars, restaurants, and hotels.

Certain his view of the future was clear, O'Malley wouldn't be pushed aside. Over lunches with Schroth and Moses and in visits to the Triborough Bridge and Tunnel Authority offices on Randalls Island, he continued the argument. He commissioned engineer Praeger to develop plans, which he then submitted to Moses, and sought support for a new stadium from community leaders. At one point he even tried to get Moses excited about Praeger's vision of a modern stadium—with no columns to obstruct views—that would be "a terrific improvement over anything that has ever been done." All Moses had to do was use his power to condemn and purchase the many properties where the project would be built. A private person or business could never assemble the land this way because owners would demand astronomical prices.

Taken altogether, O'Malley's efforts to persuade Moses show that he was determined and good-natured, even if Moses did try to intimidate him with the trappings of power. In every visit to one of Moses's offices, O'Malley would see that the great man was served by more aides, assistants, and attendants than a king. No one made a bigger show of power than Moses, and no doubt O'Malley noticed that, just like Branch Rickey, Moses reserved a spot for Abraham Lincoln in his office. Although Rickey hung a painting and Moses kept a bust of the Great Emancipator at Randalls Island, both men seemed to see something of themselves in the great president.

Given the effort he devoted to the stadium issue, O'Malley clearly wanted to stay in Brooklyn. But he wasn't hanging his future on a single strategy. Confronted with the challenge and opportunity of television, he began meeting with network executives and leaders of a new firm called Skiatron to consider schemes for commercial-free pay TV. (Paramount, Zenith, and RCA were also exploring this technology.) As one of the few teams with a truly national following, the Dodgers might find millions of fans across the country willing to pay a modest price—say, fifty cents—to see a televised game. Some of the revenue, described by Skiatron as "box-office receipts," could be reinvested in players who might give Brooklyn a Yankees-style dynasty.

Because no one would pay to see a flop, a future dynasty would depend on the team continuing its current run of success on the field. The club had played so well in recent years that fans had come to expect not just victories but pennants and, someday soon, a championship. This goal was on every Dodger's mind when they gathered at Vero Beach for another spring training in 1954. But they also knew that every season brought surprises; otherwise why play the games?

WHEN THEY ARRIVED at spring training in 1954, players discovered that O'Malley had built a pitch-and-putt golf course for them to use during breaks in their schedules. Black players were especially grateful because they were banned from local courses and this little layout had been created with them in mind. Don Newcombe would recall playing a friendly round with the owner and watching him move the ball to improve his lie, announcing it was his course and therefore governed by O'Malley rules. "He could make you laugh," said Newcombe, "and almost make you forget he was such a strong businessman."

Buzzie Bavasi would recall 1954 as the year that Walter Alston rose to the major leagues and a mysterious fan gave him a shock.

The fan began showing up as soon as camp opened. He was there every morning, an older fellow soaking up the Florida sun and gorging on free, all-you-can-see baseball. In different corners of Dodgertown he could watch pitchers train by throwing through strike zones outlined with strings or study base runners perfecting their slides in the sand. By ten o'clock he claimed his regular seat on a rock behind home plate at field number one to catch an intramural game.

Although players sometimes stopped to speak to him, the loyal fan was quiet and unobtrusive. He never hounded stars for autographs or wandered where he wasn't welcome. Amid the organized chaos of a camp that trained six hundred players, general manager Bavasi and road secretary Lee Scott considered the old man part of the scenery, until the morning when they were gazing across the training complex and happened to see the man slump over and then slide off his stony perch onto the ground. When he didn't get up, Bavasi and Scott ran to him.

As they reached him, the fallen fan was breathing his last. While an ambulance was summoned, Bavasi and Scott searched him for identification. They found wads of cash and a fistful of little scraps of paper. These were betting slips. The man wasn't just a fan of Dodgers players, he was their bookie.

IF YOU BELIEVED IN such things, you might have considered the death of a bookie at Dodgertown a bad omen for the 1954 season. In January the team was judged to be even better than the previous year's club and ready to win the World Series. But as players fell into their roles and Alston tried to adapt to his, a certain discomfort hung in the air. Duke Snider would recall that Alston struggled with his job and even "admitted to us that he was in over his head." Jackie Robinson "hated Alston," added Snider, "though I never knew exactly why."

Alston had helped every other black player on the Dodgers make it to the major leagues, but this record didn't make things easy for him with Robinson, who had loved playing for Charlie Dressen and had lobbied for Pee Wee Reese to be named manager. Robinson, who was still not adjusted to Branch Rickey's absence, also saw Alston as Walter O'Malley's man and this bothered him too.

(At one point the tension between the two men surfaced and Alston publicly challenged Robinson to fight it out, either in front of the team or in private. Tempers cooled before fists flew, but the relationship never got better than civil.) Under these conditions, and no doubt troubled by the way age was affecting his own performance, Robinson was irritable in the spring of 1954. He would stay that way for much of the season.

With an uncertain manager and an unhappy Robinson, the Dodgers were not a resilient team. Early in the regular season it became clear that a hand injury had made Roy Campanella a much less effective hitter. Next, pitcher Johnny Podres had an emergency appendectomy, which kept him sidelined for more than a month. By July 4 the Giants and not the Dodgers occupied first place. They won the pennant by five games over the second-place Brooklyns and then swept the Indians in the series.

The end of the season brought no manager drama. Even though the team finished short of the ultimate goal, a world championship, "we feel that he did all right," said O'Malley as he authorized Bavasi to renew Alston's contract. The manager accepted Bavasi's invitation without even asking how much he would be paid. Although no one could have guessed it would happen, the nonnegotiation set a precedent that would be followed until Alston retired in 1976. Every year he did his best. Every year O'Malley and his management group decided to bring him back for another season. In this way he quietly received the security that his noisy predecessor had been denied.

With Alston on the field and Bavasi handling trades, operations, and other daily tasks, O'Malley could focus intently on his specialty: baseball as business. Always sensitive to the problem of idle assets, in 1954 he created a summer camp at Dodgertown and hired a former track-and-field star named Les MacMitch-ell to run it. He sent as counselors his sixteen-year-old son Peter, an athlete at La Salle Military Academy on Long Island, and his daughter Terry, who had just graduated from the College of New Rochelle.

The boys' camp was a high-end affair, costing $500 (more than $4,000 in 2009) per child, but the experience would have made any baseball-mad kid delirious with big-league fantasies. After a flight to Vero Beach on the team plane, he would get a uniform and two weeks to learn fundamentals from old stars like Dazzy Vance and swat both baseballs and mosquitoes like a big leaguer. Two hundred attended each year, their tuition generating more than enough revenue to cover expenses. Beyond profit, the camp created an intense bond between camper and team. Much like retail politicking, this was retail fan building, and it promised a ripple effect that would surge through families and neighborhoods and into the future.

As much as anyone in the organization, O'Malley was attuned to the team's public image and the fans' interests. Unlike the owners at the Polo Grounds and Yankee Stadium, he wasn't shy about playing directly to the crowd. In February he let a reporter visit him at home for a story about his new greenhouse—a gift from wife Kay—and the orchid hobby he indulged every morning before work and every evening before bed.

In April, O'Malley hosted both Douglas MacArthur and Governor Thomas E. Dewey in his box for opening day. In July he playfully inserted himself into a Brooklyn neighborhood dispute that arose when a boy's Easter chicks grew into crowing roosters. Thirteen-year-old Daniel Gawronski appeared in court to report that his brood had been turned into meat and to pay a fine with the money he had saved to buy a baseball glove. The judge earned frightened Daniel's tears of gratitude when he dismissed the case and told him to keep his money, but O'Malley got the boy to smile when he sent word that he'd receive a new glove if he appeared at Ebbets Field the next morning.

Daniel got the mitt and O'Malley got the kind of publicity that reinforced Brooklyn's relationship with the ball club. But alone, goodwill gestures would not secure the future of O'Malley's team, especially if he had to compete with owners with bigger stadiums and fans more willing to pay to see a game. In 1954, Lou Perini again won first place in the attendance contest. His transplanted Braves drew three hundred thousand fans more than they had in the previous year. The Braves did this in little Milwaukee, a city one-tenth the size of New York, where they were obligated to pay just $25,000 rent to occupy a brand-new publicly owned stadium.

The Dodgers had almost the opposite experience. Although they won the pennant the year before, and gave the Giants a good fight before finishing second, the Brooklyn team sold 140,000 fewer tickets than in 1953. Among the sixteen major-league clubs, they were ninth in attendance, trailing four that hadn't played as well. Two, the Braves and Orioles, were new to their cities, and the excitement of the game's arrival could account for some of their extra financial success. But the others, the sixth-place Cardinals and the fifth-place

Tigers, were old-line franchises. They beat the Dodgers at the turnstiles primarily because they were the only choices available for anyone who wanted to see a game.

Every owner learned from what happened around the league, especially in Milwaukee. In midsummer 1954 the editors of *Sports Illustrated* made the Braves and their success the subject of the cover story of the first issue they ever published. Walter O'Malley concluded that Perini's experience "could be duplicated in almost any part of the country where an urban population is surrounded by solid suburban communities and where people travel mostly by automobile." The quintessential example of such a place was Los Angeles, which had opted for freeways over mass transit and become the capital of the modern car culture. But O'Malley also saw the future of baseball in Montreal, Minneapolis–St. Paul, Kansas City, and even Havana.

Kansas City got its opportunity first, as Connie Mack and his sons finally accepted that the city of Philadelphia could no longer support two teams. Ten days after the World Series they proposed selling to an owner who would move them to Missouri. Two months of wrangling would ensue. Among the many competing proposals came one from the same Texas oilman who had wanted to move the Dodgers in 1953: Clint Murchison. According to the press, Bill Veeck was involved with this bid—he had been seen wandering the Chicago hotel where owners gathered to consider it—but the decision went to Kansas City. Baseball's frontier would be pushed to the west, but only by 250 miles.

Economic realities, including a one-third decline in attendance since 1947, were forcing these changes on the major leagues. In twenty months, three cities had been reduced to single-team status and three new locales had gained franchises. Only Chicago and New York were left with representatives in both leagues. But nervous fans in those cities could comfort themselves with the thought that only the weakest franchises had moved and theirs were still strong. The Cubs, White Sox, Yankees, Giants, and Dodgers were so tightly bound to their communities, it seemed impossible that they would move. Let new teams be created for the West, where the sheer novelty of the major-league game would keep stadiums filled while the franchises were built up.

The expansion idea made sense until you considered that baseball teams were businesses and new city territories, especially ones as big as Los Angeles and San Francisco, represented great opportunities. The way the leagues operated, franchises were granted to owners who then had the exclusive right to put on major-league games in that territory. Winners of these rights get to extract the value without competition and without paying much at all for the privilege. Under these circumstances, why would the sixteen owners in the two leagues hand over such rich territory to newcomers? Anyone who studied the situation would presume that insiders were far more likely to get these prizes. This is why, all through 1954, rumors swirled around both the Dodgers and the Giants. In Brooklyn, where O'Malley was getting nowhere on his bid for help with a stadium, the Junior Chamber of Commerce had started a "Keep the Dodgers in Brooklyn" campaign. In Manhattan, Horace Stoneham felt he had to state publicly that the Giants were staying in New York.

"I'm not too well informed about prospects of major-league baseball in California, but why should the Giants be interested in moving there? How could we possibly build up such a strong rivalry as the one we enjoy here with the Dodgers?" he asked. The excitement generated by this mutual grudge was responsible for one out of every three tickets the Giants sold every year, he added.

IF HORACE STONEHAM WAS not well informed about the prospect of baseball in California, he was either willfully ignorant or the least-engaged owner in the major leagues. Two weeks before, his own manager, Leo Durocher, had told a crowd in California that he'd "sure like to see" the Giants move to San Francisco. Stoneham was also in receipt of a detailed report on baseball's prospects in Los Angeles by Philip K. Wrigley's Pacific Coast League club.

Written mainly by Bill Veeck, the study used reams of data on baseball's declining attendance and the opportunity in California to make an exceedingly persuasive argument for shifting one or two struggling teams to the West or creating new franchises to make up a ten-team league. In the fall of 1954, Veeck updated his report and sent carefully numbered copies to National League owners. It presented the inevitability of expansion. Among its major points were:

- Demand for baseball was great in both Los Angeles and San Francisco.
- Voters in San Francisco had approved bonds to build a big-league stadium, and Los Angeles was prepared to finance one too.

- With two teams in the West, transportation costs and scheduling for visiting clubs would be reasonable.
- The American League was secretly planning its own invasion of California.
- The game needed to be truly national to retain its financial power and popularity.

To hear Veeck tell it, the two California cities were paradises where people were wealthier than average and near-constant sunshine made conditions perfect for baseball. This was true, and so was his claim that with just these two cities added, baseball's market would grow by 25 percent.

Veeck's report amounted to a business plan for anyone who might want to put a major-league club in either city. It covered political issues, the cost of compensating local minor-league teams, and even summer rainfall figures (roughly zero inches per month in Los Angeles and .15 to .29 per month in San Francisco). He gave extra ink to the costs associated with setting up a franchise in Los Angeles, where no stadium bond issue had been prepared.

The emphasis showed exactly why Wrigley had backed this research. He wanted to sell his minor-league stadium and secure compensation for his Pacific Coast League franchise. By Veeck's figuring, Wrigley would get $2 million for his park and the land it occupied and $1 million for the franchise territory. Given public interest in bringing baseball to the city, he figured the stadium could be resold immediately to some public entity and then leased; altogether an owner would need to invest about $1.5 million in cash to establish a club in Los Angeles and $1.2 million to set up one in San Francisco.

Perhaps to avoid the suggestion that he was trying to lure a city's ball team into a move, Veeck's report imagined two new owners who would make the national circuit a ten-team league. But however the task was accomplished, Veeck and Wrigley urged the National Leaguers to act quickly: "The plain fact is that the league that gets to the Pacific Coast first will obviously maintain the edge of having a coast-to-coast set-up for a long time to come," because no other cities in the region would be ready soon for the big leagues, they maintained.

In San Francisco, the mayor was behind the baseball effort and the civic committee formed to promote it was chaired by a county supervisor. In Los Angeles, as Vincent X. Flaherty wrote to O'Malley, department stores offered customers pro-baseball petitions to sign and cars speeding along the freeways sported bumper stickers calling for a franchise.

Baseball was becoming such a big issue in Los Angeles that even the most unlikely political candidate could use it to great advantage. Rosalind Wiener (soon to marry and take the name Wyman) had been raised by parents who displayed FDR posters in their drugstore. At eighteen she was Helen Douglas's driver during the Senate race she lost as Richard Nixon smeared her with the charge that she aided communists. Undiscouraged, she threw herself into the 1952 Stevenson campaign for president—another loss—and then put herself up for city council. (Besides baseball, her issues included bringing museums to the city and a proposed ban on the sale of horror comics in places where young children could see them.) She was all of twenty-two years old.

The Wyman council campaign of 1953 was a months-long display of earnest door-to-door effort headquartered on the dining room table at her parents' house. Weekends brought young Democrats from all over the state to work as volunteers. They stuffed envelopes and made phone calls, taking breaks only to eat and catch *I Love Lucy* on TV. Every weekday Wyman walked five miles or more, determined to meet every voter in her district. Her main publicity piece, a card listing her priorities, emphasized boosting the city with new cultural institutions and baseball. When she received a donation of several thousand bars of soap, these were given away with some sentiment about cleaning up local government.

On election night, Wyman's campaign team listened for the results on the radio and heard the announcer say something under his breath. As Wyman would recall, it was "Stop handing me these reports that say Miss Wiener is winning. They can't be right."

The reports from the precincts were correct. Miss Wiener did win, becoming the youngest person ever elected to the council. The next year she was part of a majority on the council who approved a resolution urging every city, county, and state agency to cooperate in every way possible in order to bring a major-league team to the city. Every club in the country received a copy of the documents. The one sent to Brooklyn landed on Walter O'Malley's desk.

BETWEEN THE LOS ANGELES City Council's correspondence, Bill Veeck's two thick reports, and press accounts about the buzz over baseball in the West, Walter O'Malley was fully aware of the opportunity available in California. But in addition to these documents, which every owner in the league possessed, O'Malley also had constant contacts—letters, telegrams, phone calls—from Vincent X. Flaherty, *Los Angeles Examiner* columnist, baseball fanatic, and ceaseless promoter.

In one letter after another Flaherty tried to persuade O'Malley to either move the team to Los Angeles or sell it to someone who would. Although O'Malley often ignored him, Flaherty kept pitching with a combination of flattery, promises, and warnings that "someday you'll realize" what a "wonderful opportunity" awaits. At one point in the summer of 1954, O'Malley finally responded with a long letter explaining the Dodgers' situation in great detail and outlining his views on a business that seemed poised for big changes.

The way O'Malley saw it, the recent purchase of the St. Louis Cardinals by the beer giant Anheuser-Busch heralded a new era of corporate investment in the old game. A number of big companies—including another brewery, a distillery, and an auto manufacturer—were trying to buy teams, said O'Malley, and Wall Street "lads" were "working their slide rules overtime" to figure out deals that combined pay television systems and ball clubs in one entity. (Here O'Malley was remarkably prescient but decades premature.) Everyone, it seemed, saw great potential in a sport with momentarily depressed revenues but great long-term growth potential.

As owners of one of the strongest teams, O'Malley and his minor partners had already turned down a $6.5 million offer from a serious and well-qualified bidder. The decision was based on both the team's potential and an estimated $10 million value for the franchise, its players, and real estate holdings scattered from Montreal to Vero Beach.

But after describing "a sellers' market" and explaining why there was "no reason why the Dodgers should be given away at this time," O'Malley then made sure Flaherty understood why an investor might be enticed to pay top dollar. "In my opinion a businessman would be crazy to buy a low second division club in either league as it takes too much money and too much time to develop such a club into a contender." Cities should consider the same issues, he warned, as "a community that takes an inferior team runs the risk of seeing it not supported after the honeymoon is over."

In both the opening and the closing of this letter, O'Malley authorized Flaherty to share it with officials and businesspeople but denied him permission to make it public. He wanted certain people to be aware of his position and the conclusions the letter pressed on any reader were unmistakable. The Dodgers were not immediately available for sale or transfer. *But if they were,* the price would be at least $10 million and the city that claimed the team would be lucky to avoid the trap of enticing a big-league club with whatever incentives it might demand only to find itself with an unpopular loser. In short, he was the prettiest girl in the class, announcing: I'm expensive and probably unavailable, but don't let that stop you.

BY COYLY FLIRTING WITH Los Angeles, O'Malley tried to give himself an option to exploit if he couldn't solve his problems in Brooklyn. His frustration was evident in his relationship with his ally Schroth, who at one point had to remind O'Malley that he was on his side. Schroth had his own big problems, caused mainly by the changes in Brooklyn. The flight of the middle class had left his *Brooklyn Daily Eagle* with fewer readers and, consequently, fewer advertisers. When union contracts expired in the winter of 1954–55, Schroth couldn't meet worker demands for pay rates comparable to wages paid by papers across the river in Manhattan.

Once the biggest afternoon paper in the country, the *Eagle* could claim Walt Whitman as a former editor and 114 years of continuous publication. When it was closed by a strike on January 29, 1955, Schroth tried to sell it to anyone who might revive it, including Fortune Pope, the publisher of the Italian-language paper *Il Progresso,* whose brother Generoso owned the *National Enquirer.* When Pope backed out of a tentative agreement, the paper died. It was the last of eight dailies in the borough, and its demise silenced Brooklyn's voice and gave observers an occasion to question the community's leaders.

Appearing at the Pratt Institute, Brooklyn's college of art, design, and architecture, Robert Moses would mourn the *Eagle* and declare that the borough was a "strange" place that lacked adequate leaders and depended on a baseball team for its sense of well-being:

> If only a fraction of the genuine enthusiasm which the Dodgers arouse could be channeled into the building of a new Brooklyn, what a town it would be! When the Dodgers are on top it's the morning's morning in Flatbush and all Brooklyn believes that God's in His heaven and all's right with the world. When the Dodgers are down, there is no joy in Gowanus, no balm in Gravesend and the shades are drawn on the old Canarsie farm. What a people! Happy or blue, their disposition depends on the standing of a team.

It would be difficult to tell whether Moses was amused or exasperated by Brooklyn, but in his address to the Pratt class of 1955 he showed that he understood what the team meant to the borough. As he spoke, the Dodgers were in the middle of one of the best five-year runs in the history of the game. According to historian/statistician Bill James, only two previous National League teams—the Cubs of 1906–10 and the Cardinals of 1942–46—accomplished more than the Dodgers of 1952–56. In this period they averaged ninety-seven wins per year and finished the regular season in first place every year except 1954, when they were second. During all this time the lineup—as diverse as Brooklyn in its racial and ethnic composition—was changed little, which meant that many fans formed deep attachments to their favorites.

In this era, the Dodgers seemed to cast a spell of goodwill over Brooklyn. Some observers would credit the well-mixed team with inspiring the relative peace that reigned in a borough where demographic change could make many residents wary. Interethnic rivalries and suspicions had always existed in Brooklyn, but tensions could have been higher in the 1950s as whites moved out, and in many cases they were replaced by less affluent Hispanic immigrants and African-Americans. (Many of these were looking for shelter after being evicted by Moses-led slum-clearance projects.) The newcomers didn't support the baseball team quite so avidly, but in Robinson, Campanella, Newcombe, and Edmundo "Sandy" Amorós—the Cuban who became the regular left fielder in

1955—some felt they had a more personal stake in the team. As a borough of underdogs, in the shadow of Manhattan, Brooklyn could also relate to the team's World Series frustration and rivalry with the Yankees.

As the team with the highest average age—almost thirty—the Dodgers veterans approached the 1955 season knowing that it could be their last chance to win a World Series together. Although he didn't speak of it widely, Jackie Robinson believed that it would be his last in baseball. He explained this in a letter he wrote by hand on stationery from the Hotel Congress in Chicago and sent to the owner of the Brooklyn Dodgers. Addressed to "Dear My O'Malley," the letter began with thanks for a $500 donation O'Malley made to a school for poor black children, which was one of Robinson's favorite charities. It noted his pride in "the job we all have done" in the cause of equality and added: "What you did increases my feeling for the organization and my respect for you, which I admit has waned somewhat in the last few years."

Robinson was obviously self-conscious and worried, in writing, that he might be misunderstood. In his choice of words and point of view, he struggled to make himself clear and to be fair. He reported that he was aware that O'Malley had judged him negatively, offered his honestly voiced feelings, but also insisted that the owner really didn't know him "or what I have tried to do." Similarly, Robinson took responsibility for his own "mistakes" but then added that "as long as my efforts are honest and sincere I do not feel badly about them." Still, he didn't want to leave things the way they were, and added his hope that he and O'Malley would get "a chance to get to know each other" in the coming year.

Strained as it was, Robinson's letter suggested a relationship that, while sometimes rough, mattered to him and O'Malley. With his check, worth $4,000 in 2009, the Dodgers owner had made a gesture in Robinson's direction. With his letter, baseball's racial pioneer tried to share his feelings and plans. No copy of O'Malley's response, if he sent one, was held in the file where the Congress Hotel letter was kept. Over the long term Robinson would continue to hint at problems in his relationship with O'Malley. In the short run he held the option of changing his mind about retirement, and he reported to spring training with a feisty demeanor.

Early in the camp session Robinson complained to the press about Walter

Alston. After the two argued out their differences—a development O'Malley welcomed as a "healthy sign"—Robinson accepted a somewhat reduced role. In retrospect it would seem that both men were struggling to cope with the aging star's physical decline. Alston was trying to use him without wearing him out. Robinson was denying the effects of time, even though he was losing some of his quickness at the plate and in the field. The same was true for Pee Wee Reese, who was thirty-five, and for Carl Furillo and Roy Campanella, who were both thirty-three. However, as the season progressed these old-timers performed well. Campanella bounced back from the injury that had hampered him the previous year to add more than a hundred points to his batting average. Furillo hit better, too, with seven more home runs than he had had in '54.

With ten straight victories without a defeat, the Dodgers set a modern major-league record for season-starting success. Staying true to the playful character Walter O'Malley preferred, the team posed for a commemorative photo in front of a blackboard on which someone had scrawled "The Dodgers Dood It, 10 Straight!"

The streak was accomplished with surprisingly effective pitching. Seven different pitchers notched victories during the streak, foreshadowing a season when the staff's earned run average would rise from fourth in 1954 to first in the league. Although the team was well balanced, it was not always in harmony. In early May, Don Newcombe complained about not pitching, refused to throw for batting practice, and was suspended for a day. After he returned he pitched brilliantly, facing the minimum twenty-seven batters in a complete-game one-hitter. The victory came at the end of another long winning streak—this one was eleven games—that saw the team improve its record to a stunning twenty-two wins and two losses. (Those two losses were by one run each.)

Newcombe would play a central role through the entire season, at one point winning twenty and losing just five as the Dodgers ran away from the rest of the league. Their lead grew with each passing week, and fans came to expect easy victories when they went to the park. In July the team put on a Pee Wee Reese Night to mark the shortstop's fifteenth anniversary in the game. He was celebrated with speeches and gifts and then the lights were dimmed as he received a birthday cake ablaze with candles. When he blew them out, the lights came on and he was serenaded with a few songs of the South, in honor of his Kentucky home.

As the crowd cheered for Reese, the more observant noticed that a

Confederate flag had been added to the decorations by someone on the grounds crew. (Carl Erskine noticed and was troubled enough to think to himself, "I thought Jim Crow was dead.") A protest came from Roy Wilkins of the National Association for the Advancement of Colored People, who wrote to O'Malley to say, "We don't know who thought of this idea, but it is not calculated to win friends and influence people among the thousands of devoted Dodger fans who happen not to be white."

The letters that subsequently passed between Wilkins and O'Malley show two men of their time trying to grapple with an issue that few confronted directly or successfully. Both the NAACP and the Dodgers stood for racial progress. The Dodgers were beloved by many African-Americans who recognized that the team pioneered integration. Reese had gone against the southern stereotype and welcomed blacks to the team. But O'Malley struggled to understand Wilkins's point. At first he compared the event to use of the English flag at events attended by Irish Catholics and insisted no offense was intended. "The Civil War is over," he wrote, "and I doubt that the wound is still festering."

It was the honest perspective of a businessman who traveled first class, interacted mainly with the nation's elite, and would not know the everyday experience of ordinary black Americans. Wilkins took O'Malley's comments in this spirit but did not back down. "In the areas in which millions of Negroes move," wrote Wilkins, "the Civil War and manifestations of its aftermath are always present." He asked that the Dodgers avoid any act that would "comfort" bigots for whom the Confederate flag remained a symbol of white superiority.

"I have your fine letter of July 28th," was O'Malley's answer, "and I completely understand your feelings."

In another time, the flag incident would have prompted not a few letters but mass protests and then a defensive response leading to a public controversy. But Wilkins clearly appreciated what the Dodgers had done to advance racial understanding and was not inclined to escalate the argument. O'Malley, for his part, made sure Wilkins knew he had been heard and understood. The Confederate flag would not appear again at Ebbets Field. Wilkins spared O'Malley—and his team—the pain and embarrassment of a public dispute.

By early September the Dodgers were already planning for postseason play. O'Malley welcomed a writer from the *New York Post* to watch a game with

Milwaukee from the special owner's box that was built to hang under the upper deck, right behind home plate.

In one of the few records made of O'Malley at a game, the gifted features writer George Trow portrayed him shouting "Damnation!" after a disappointing play and cheering James "Junior" Gilliam with a hoarse cry of "Come on, Junyah!"

O'Malley had something to say about much of what he saw on the field. When a fan threw an empty beer can at an umpire, he remarked about how "they never throw full ones"; and when a Braves batter hit the ball to the top of the screen in right field, he knew immediately that it was a legitimate home run. The phone in the box rang and he picked it up to hear another team official complain that the ball had sneaked through a hole in the chain link and should have been ruled a double. "No," answered O'Malley. "I saw it go over."

In between his colorful description of an eagle-eyed owner, Trow allowed O'Malley to update New Yorkers on stadium issues. Once again he said the lack of good parking was killing attendance and he needed a new ballpark with plenty of spaces for cars. In midsummer he had set a deadline of 1958 for this change, and he stuck with this deadline when he spoke to Trow. He also defended his recent decision to play some games in a minor-league park in Jersey City, New Jersey, in 1956.

When the Jersey plan was announced, it seemed to wake up people in New York. Editorial writers at the *New York Times* urged the city and Mayor Robert Wagner to help the Dodgers even if it meant providing land. Wagner immediately summoned O'Malley, Robert Moses, and John Cashmore to a meeting on the veranda of his residence, Gracie Mansion.

For an hour O'Malley outlined his vision of a slum-redevelopment project that would include a new railroad station, the stadium, parking, and other possible features. At one point he even laid a huge map of Brooklyn out on the veranda floor and got on his knees to point out certain landmarks. The Dodgers were ready with $6 million for their share, he said, if only the government helped make the land available. O'Malley announced that Ebbets Field was for sale to any group that would give him a two-year lease, after which he expected to play in a different ballpark. He also reminded Wagner that Giants owner Horace Stoneham was also unhappy with his ballpark and parking and that the city risked losing two teams at once.

With every turn in his argument, O'Malley did his best to emphasize that the situation was dire for New York baseball fans. "It is serious, Mr. Mayor, very serious," said the Dodgers owner. Just then a strong breeze whipped across the veranda and made the awnings flap wildly. O'Malley made a stab at levity, calling it "Hurricane Dodger." The mayor joked, "That must be Horace Stoneham," reminding everyone of Stoneham's penchant for making long, loud speeches. (Bill Veeck said Stoneham had a "whiskey baritone.")

"Oh no," replied O'Malley, "there's not *that* much wind."

Despite the jokes, the undercurrent at the meeting was not pleasant. Appearing stiff and stern in a tan tropical suit, Robert Moses tilted his head back and looked down his nose as O'Malley spoke. In his response he suggested that the Dodgers were inflexible about the proposed site.

"What you're saying," said Moses, "is that unless a way is found to make a home for the Dodgers in this location you will pick up your marbles and take them away."

"Oh no," answered O'Malley. "I don't want to even consider ever having the Dodgers leave New York. You, Mr. Moses, never got anything without fighting for it. Well, I'm fighting for this. If I go down I want the record to show I went down swinging."

When Moses came back with objections to the use of slum-clearance funds, O'Malley noted that other cities, like Milwaukee and Baltimore, had found ways to build stadiums that were then rented to ball clubs. He wasn't asking for that much. He was offering to put up all the money and build a stadium himself if only he could have help obtaining the property. "We have to start trying to find out how it can be done," he begged, "not why it can't be done."

As to whether it was Flatbush and Atlantic or nowhere, O'Malley spoke with the knowledge gained from seven years of working on this problem. Searches in Brooklyn and nearby sections of Queens had failed to turn up a comparable site. "This is not a threat," answered O'Malley. "But we're down to what we believe is our last chance."

O'Malley's timing was perfect. The Dodgers were winning so many games, they seemed like the best baseball team on earth. At the same time, Willie Mays was thrilling Giants fans with an assault on Babe Ruth's single-season home run record. (He would finish nine short of Ruth's sixty.) City officials, who didn't want to be known for losing two baseball teams, responded positively.

"We had a very good conference this morning here," said Mayor Wagner, who shared a settee with O'Malley, who smiled benignly as newsreel cameras whirred. Wagner feigned ignorance of the Dodgers' long-term stadium problem, claiming "this is the first time" he had heard about it in detail. But now that he was aware of the issue, he added, "The City of New York wants to do everything it can to help preserve for Brooklyn its ball club."

Wagner and the city council soon agreed to fund a formal study of the Fort Greene site for a new stadium. (Thanks to a recent Supreme Court ruling, in a case titled *Berman v. Parker*, city officials could legally obtain land to sell to O'Malley.) Fan focus shifted from the front page of the papers back to the sports pages, and the Dodgers drove toward a pennant win.

It happened in Milwaukee on September 8, the earliest clinch date in history. Brooklyn's starting pitcher that day, Roger Craig, was one of several first-year starters who arrived in mid-season and won a combined fifteen games. (Another of these was a Brooklyn-born nineteen-year-old named Sanford "Sandy" Koufax.) Craig was disappointed that he had been pulled out of the game in the fourth inning, but he had staked the team to a lead that was more than enough for the victory.

Craig and the other rookies may well have been surprised by the subdued mood in the Dodgers' clubhouse after they clinched. A television crew on hand to film the celebration had to prod players into showing more than the calm smiles they wore coming off the field. The players were not worked up because their lead was so huge going into September, the pennant victory came as a matter of routine. They also burned with the desire for baseball's real prize, which had eluded them for so long. Owner O'Malley voiced what was on many minds when he said that he looked forward to a series, which he hoped would include Brooklyn's tormentors from the Bronx. He said, "We have to beat the Yankees once, some time or other, and this ought to be the time."

You've gotta have heart!
All you really need is heart!
When the odds are sayin' you'll never win,
  that's when the grin should start!

The musical *Damn Yankees* opened at the Forty-Sixth Street Theatre on May 5, 1955, the day when Walter Alston suspended Don Newcombe for insubordination. When Newcombe returned and pitched his near no-hit shutout, both he and the play were the talk of the city. (*Damn Yankees* would run for more than one thousand performances.) By the end of September, when the World Series began, the play's signature song, "Heart," was Kay O'Malley's favorite. The lyrics seemed to speak to the Dodgers' experience and her attitude about life. Yes, the team had lost many times to the Yankees. But as a woman who had overcome more serious challenges due to her disability, Kay had come to believe in the value of "heart."

Just as "Heart" inspired the hapless ballplayers on the stage, the 1955 series stirred Brooklyn's hopes, drawing a crowd that encircled Ebbets Field before the ticket windows opened for sales. In four hours every seat was purchased for the team's three home games, and thousands of standing-room passes had been sold for $4.20 apiece. The borough had let the team down in previous series, but this time the Dodgers would get sellout crowds for every game.

They were the better team, but games turned on unpredictable events, and so the hope that Dodgers fans allowed into their hearts was joined by fear. Brooklyn's followers had become connoisseurs of disappointment, and they worried about getting another plateful. Seventy-year-old Myrtle Power, a fan who lived on Long Island, was so superstitious about the World Series that she gave up her chance to win the grand prize on the TV quiz show called *The $64,000 Question.* Having reached the next-to-last step by answering questions about baseball, she declared that she had won the equivalent of a league pennant but wouldn't go for the championship because she didn't want to beat the Dodgers "to the draw." She took her $32,000 and went home to follow the series on TV.

Don Newcombe, one of the few pitchers who loved Ebbets Field—a hitter's park where "you couldn't fool around"—started game one at Yankee Stadium. Three homers gave the Bombers five runs and finished him in the sixth inning. The Dodgers responded with home runs by Furillo and Snider, and in the eighth inning Robinson, running on thirty-six-year-old legs, stole home. The effort was not quite enough, as the Yankees and pitcher Whitey Ford won 6–5. Although the Dodgers insisted they weren't discouraged, they had to be worried when they lost the second game. In that contest the Yankees ran up four runs in the fourth inning and cruised to a 4–2 win.

Cruising was the Yankee way, especially at their ballpark, where the ghost of

Babe Ruth and the exploits of Mantle, Ford, and the rest awed most visiting players. At Ebbets, where left-hander Johnny Podres took the mound to stop the Yankees, awe was never a factor. Everything was familiar. The ballpark echoed with the bellowing of Hilda Chester and the off-key melodies of the Sym-phony. And all the people who cheered for Podres wanted to see the Yankees crushed. They got their wish.

This time it was the Yankee pitcher, Bob Turley, who got sent to the clubhouse early. In the first inning Campanella tagged him for a two-run homer. In the second Turley loaded the bases and Robinson, on third, tormented him by repeatedly faking a steal. Turley threw ball four. Robinson walked home and the Yankee pitcher was done. By the end the Dodgers had won 8–3, their biggest victory margin ever in a World Series game, and Podres celebrated his twenty-third birthday with a complete game.

Carl Erskine started game four for Brooklyn against Don Larsen but was replaced first by rookie Don Bessent and then the team's most reliable reliever, Clem Labine. Once again the Dodgers slammed eight runs across the plate—a three-run shot by Duke Snider was decisive—and won 8–5.

With the series tied, the Dodgers stormed into the fifth game. Snider hit two more out, setting a league record of nine World Series home runs in his career. Rookie pitcher Roger Craig combined with reliever Labine to give the Brooklyn team a 5–3 win. The crowd at Ebbets, the largest ever to see a series game, was never louder or more delirious. But you didn't have to be there to feel the joy. At Bellevue Hospital in Manhattan, hundreds of disabled patients in the rehabilitation department began cheering when they heard about the Brooklyn win. No one heard a word of sympathy for the Yankees.

Yankees fans would remind their siblings in Brooklyn that their team's star, Mickey Mantle, had begun the series with an injured leg, which kept him out of four games. Mantle's troubles did hurt the Yanks, but they had other advantages that outweighed this loss. Most important was the psychological benefit of World Series experience. Five championships in the previous six years had taught them how to win under postseason pressure. In contrast, no one on the Dodgers had ever been part of winning a World Series. Worse, too many had experienced defeat in a way that left them worried and fearful. As he reflected on the challenge, Pee Wee Reese confessed he was plagued by memories of losing postseason battles. In his fifteen years with the Dodgers he had been part of two pennant playoff losses and six World Series losses at the hands of the all-powerful Yankees. He feared this would be his last chance ever to reach his goal and that history was against his team.

The type of anxiety confessed by Reese may have played a role in the sixth game. In the first inning Jim "Junior" Gilliam committed two fielding mistakes and Dodger pitcher Karl Spooner—starting instead of sore-armed Newcombe—couldn't throw strikes. The Yankees scored all their runs in the first inning and then sailed behind Whitey Ford's complete-game pitching to win 5–1. The Yankees had come back and forced an all-or-nothing seventh game.

In the Yankees' locker room the talk drifted toward money. As a rule, the big profit for owners came only after a series passed the four-game mark. This year the bosses were doing very well—the gate so far was almost $2 million—and the players agreed that they should assert themselves in winter contract talks. Overnight, local bookies made the Yankees 7–5 favorites.

On the Dodgers' side, manager Walter Alston was not troubled by the odds or memories of defeat. He had only been with the Brooklyn club for two years. This was his first championship fight and he had faith in his team.

The pitcher Alston chose to face the Yankees in the final game was similarly unburdened. Johnny Podres had seen just one previous Brooklyn-Yankees series. He had lost the one game he started in the 1953 classic, but he was a twenty-one-year-old rookie then. In the current series he had proved himself by winning game three with a confident display of both power and accuracy. In the first inning he had thrown just nine pitches to get the Yankees out. In the eighth he had needed just six.

Podres had matured into a much better pitcher, and as he faced the final game he announced, "We'll beat 'em tomorrow and wrap it up." But his appetite for gambling, drink, and women worried Dodgers management. Late on the night before game seven, Walter O'Malley went to Podres's hotel to check on him. In the lobby he pressed the call button for the elevator and stepped back to wait for it. A moment later Podres sneaked up from behind and tapped him on the shoulder.

"You're up pretty late, boss," said Podres. He then reminded the owner that the coming game was a big one, noted that he was headed for bed in hope of a good night's sleep, and recommended that O'Malley do the same.

ALTHOUGH THE YANKEES HAD admirers all across the country, America's sentimental favorites were represented by Brooklyn. In part the Dodgers were loved as challengers, a David to the Yankee Goliath. But they were also embraced because they seemed more human and accessible. Yes, the Yankees played in the Bronx, but they really represented Manhattan and all its intimidating power and sophistication. The Dodgers stood for everyone else. This was true even in Cuba, where fans gathered around TVs and radios to cheer native son Sandy Amorós, the Dodgers outfielder. Interest in the series was so high in Cuba that a TV station paid for an airplane loaded with equipment to circle south of Miami to pick up the broadcast signal and relay it to the island.

For a week the loyal fans who followed the team at the ballparks and from afar had expended enormous emotional energy on the team. In bars and living rooms and cars parked where the radio reception was clear, they wrung their hands and cursed and cheered. Many conducted superstitious rituals or carried good-luck charms and believed, to one degree or another, that they helped. The Dodgers' batboy did his part by using a ribbon to tie a horseshoe on the rack that held the team's bats. After the team got its first win in the series, Walter O'Malley wore the same shoes, suit, and tie to every game.

O'Malley went to the final game with his wife, Kay, and his daughter, Terry. Their guests were Mrs. Douglas MacArthur and Brooklyn borough president John Cashmore. They occupied box seats so close to the field that they could see the look in Johnny Podres's eyes. The young pitcher showed no anxiety as he took the ball in the first inning. Behind him were the Dodgers regulars, except for Jackie Robinson, who was unable to play because of an injured Achilles tendon. Podres pitched well, but was helped in the early going when a Yankee at third base was hit by a batted ball and called out. The freakish play helped kill a rally and keep the Yanks off the scoreboard.

More than fifty years later Podres would remember exactly how he felt that day, if not every pitch he threw. "I wasn't one of those guys who went into Yankee Stadium and got the shakes," he would say. "I wasn't nervous or in awe. Once I got on the mound I just saw what was in front of me and pitched the way I normally would."

It wasn't quite like pitching for the Witherbee town team, but the way

Podres remembered it, he didn't feel the weight of history and barely noticed the huge crowd in the stadium. He was so confident that at several points in the game he paused to find his father's face in the stands and offer him a reassuring nod.

With Yankee pitcher Tommy Byrne matching Podres pitch for pitch, the Dodgers couldn't score a run until the fourth. After they got another run in the top of the sixth, Alston jiggered the fielders, moving Gilliam from left field to second base, where he replaced Don Zimmer, and putting Amorós in the spot that Junior left open.

When he made these changes the manager decided the game. In their very next at-bat the Yankees got men on first and second with no outs and Yogi Berra at the plate. Expecting him to pull the ball to right, the outfield shifted in that direction. Berra then reached for an outside pitch and hit it down the left-field line. Having moved to the right, Amorós needed all of his speed to catch up with the ball. But unlike Gilliam, whose glove was on his left hand, Amorós fielded with his right. Using this to his advantage, he stretched and caught the ball on the fly. With Reese shouting to him, he made a perfect throw to shortstop, which led to a double play at first. In Cuba, Amorós fans tuned to radios and televisions went wild.

After Amorós's great play, Podres did some of his best pitching, holding the Yankees scoreless all the way to the finish. This success was the product of a deliberate strategy. Podres began the game throwing lots of slow changeups, but once the Yankees started expecting them and shadows began to make the ball harder to track, he switched to fastballs. With the final out, players ran from the dugout onto the field and mobbed Podres on the mound. The enormous crowd, though filled with Yankees fans, roared its appreciation.

In the stands, Walter O'Malley kissed everyone who shared his field-level box, including Borough President Cashmore. His daughter Terry burst into tears. A Yankee Stadium usher, mistaking her tears for joy for disappointment, patted her on the back and said, "Don't take it so bad, girlie. I'm a Yankee fan, too, but down deep I'm glad those Brooklyn bums finally won."

In Manhattan, trading ground to a halt on Wall Street and millions of bits of paper in all colors were thrown out of upper-floor windows. The telephone system in New York was so overwhelmed by callers eager to share their glee that it stopped working in some districts.

In Brooklyn, cheering crowds formed spontaneously in the street, women and children threw open windows and clanged pots and pans, firecrackers exploded on the pavement, and young men who had decorated their cars with banners and signs formed honking motorcades that paraded on Flatbush Avenue. On some corners homemade effigies labeled "Yankees" hung from lampposts and revelers took turns whacking them with bats. Brooklyn had never seen a happier day.

In the Bronx, some Dodgers fans poured out of Yankee Stadium and commandeered taverns, streets, and even the lawn of the county courthouse for their celebrations. Others made it onto the field, where they followed their heroes to the guarded entrance to the locker room. Inside, the players got a chance to shout, hug, and spray each other with beer. In one corner Don Newcombe, so fastidious that he once threatened violence if a pennant celebration left beer on his clothes, allowed Duke Snider to fill his hat with Schaefer and then press it down on his head.

In another corner of the locker room, pitcher Podres, so cool and competent in front of sixty-two thousand fans, struggled to compose himself in front of a handful of reporters. "Wow! Wow! Wow!" he shouted to no one and everyone.

"Hey, Pee Wee! What did I tell you? I said they wouldn't get a thing off me, didn't I?

"Wow! Wow! Wow! Hey, Duke, are you going to stay out all night like me? Let's have ourselves a time.

"Wow! What a catch Sandy made. I thought Yogi's ball was dropping in there, then he stuck out his glove the last minute and grabbed it. Wow!"

The moment belonged to the players and the fans and Walter O'Malley, who had finally brought to Brooklyn what no one—including Branch Rickey and Charles Ebbets—had been able to deliver. While most of the veterans on the team were developed under the Rickey regime, the manager and two stars of the game—Sandy Amorós and Johnny Podres—were groomed and elevated by the O'Malley crew. They were also responsible for the new Dodgers pitchers who together won more than thirty games during the season. In the clubhouse O'Malley offered his congratulations and gratitude but he did not linger. He intended to play host to the best party Brooklyn had ever seen, and needed to make sure all was ready.

The celebration at the Hotel Bossert drew so many players, friends, and luminaries that a second ballroom was opened to accommodate them all. Johnny Podres, whose appetite for booze and fun was more powerful than his left arm, would consider it the best night of his life. Champagne flowed so freely that all anyone had to do was hold up an empty glass to have it filled. So many happy fans made their own party in the street outside that a player only had to stand in the window to fill the neighborhood with cheers.

Nine

LAST-DITCH STAND

With the first world championship in team history, and the city offering $100,000 to study putting a stadium where he wanted it, Walter O'Malley was confident in his future in Brooklyn. Even before the series, he was so optimistic that he refused to meet with boosters from Los Angeles who came to New York on what were becoming annual baseball-hunting expeditions. Mayor Norris Poulson and City Councilwoman Rosalind Wyman had each sought an audience. (In her letter Wyman warned that she was contacting the Giants too.) O'Malley turned them away in a somewhat testy letter. In this note he wrote that a telegram sent to him by the Los Angeles City Council had reached the press before he ever saw it. "I assumed it was part of a publicity stunt," he told Wyman as he explained he was preoccupied with the pennant race and wouldn't be able to see her.

Coming out of the World Series, every sign pointed to continued success. O'Malley's baseball team was strong. Walter Alston was set to return as manager, and even the young broadcaster Vin Scully was proving to be a star. Before the series the *New York Times* judged him to be Barber's equal and urged that he be assigned to handle the games on TV. Afterward the paper's critic Jack Gould declared Scully superior to his partner on the World Series broadcasts, Yankee regular Mel Allen. Gould was among the first to note Scully's restrained style—he was no "homer"—calling it a refreshing break from Allen's "matinee of the cliché."

With all this success, however, fan support for O'Malley's Dodgers increased only slightly during the championship season, as the average per-game attendance rose by just 169 souls. Meanwhile second-place Milwaukee, which wasn't in contention, sold almost twice as many tickets. Five also-rans in the American League, including the bumbling Athletics in little Kansas City, surpassed the Dodgers by one hundred thousand or more. Still, the Brooklyns were above average for the National League and O'Malley would continue his drive for a new stadium in the hope that it might lure more fans from the borough and beyond.

The dome concept sketched in Collier's in 1952 still fascinated O'Malley, and he conducted his own research on the problems associated with building one. He also received lots of unsolicited advice, including a pitch from Norman Bel Geddes, who wrote to suggest a roof hung on cables attached to towers, like the deck of a suspension bridge. Any roof big enough to span a baseball field would have to be made of a light but strong material, and O'Malley turned to major glass, plastics, and aluminum companies for suggestions. By the middle of 1955 he favored something translucent that would admit sunlight for daytime events. Whatever the material, a roof would allow him to rent the stadium for any of the hundreds of dates when the Dodgers didn't need it and guarantee that weather wouldn't interfere.

In this dream stage, when it cost O'Malley nothing to indulge his imagination, he was inspired by Buckminster Fuller's concept for lightweight geodesic domes, built of aluminum tubes and plastic, which he had demonstrated at New York's Museum of Modern Art in the summer of 1952. An architect, writer, and self-made futurist, Fuller was well established as a playful promoter of humanist and even utopian ideals expressed through fantastic inventions like a flying car and villages that could float on the ocean. Like O'Malley, he was a self-invented man who dreamed big and enjoyed dealing with the press. The little house he installed at the museum attracted great media attention. A construction trade journal estimated that just one thousand tons of material would be needed to create a Fuller dome spanning eight hundred feet. (At less than a quarter the size, the dome of St. Peter's Basilica in Rome weighs ten times as much.)

Never shy, O'Malley wrote to Fuller about his stadium and received an enthusiastic reply. Fuller had already worked on the problem of a domed stadium for a minor-league club in Denver and estimated that a ballpark could be enclosed at a cost of roughly $1 million. Fuller also urged O'Malley to consider other innovations. He had worked on designs for a futuristic stadium interior that allowed patrons to park their cars next to "seating boxes" that would be mechanically rotated for automatic cleaning once an event was over.

The $1 million price tag for a dome fit O'Malley's budget, and Fuller permitted him to conduct an impromptu experiment to test the design concept. On a hot August day the Dodgers owner and some friends drove to Huntington, Long Island, where Fuller had built a small dome for the Air Force. The men picked up whatever rocks they could find on the ground and hurled them at the little plastic roof to simulate baseballs powered by major-league bats. The dome withstood every stone.

Though not commissioned formally, Fuller set his students at Princeton to work on a design for a Dodgers stadium, and just before Thanksgiving 1955 the two men drove together from New York to see what they had produced. With reporters and photographers on hand, O'Malley and Fuller listened to several presentations. One suggested a futuristic stadium with a reinforced domed roof strong enough to handle a little tramway to carry sightseers right across its peak. Another, which included a scale model, called for a thin plastic roof that would be thirty stories high and more than seven hundred feet in diameter.

The Dodgers estimated that an enclosed stadium like the ones proposed by Fuller's students would bring more than two hundred thousand fans per year to games they would otherwise skip because the weather seemed too cold, too hot, or too wet. The arena could also host other huge events, and as the first domed stadium in the world it would draw tourists and additional development to the borough. These factors moved Robert Moses to support the concept, if not construction at the site O'Malley wanted. "He apparently is so enthused about it," noted O'Malley, "that we might be able to convince him that he thought of it first."

In the crosscurrents of New York politics, the enthusiasms of Robert Moses mattered more than almost anything. The big challenge, of course, was in determining which way they were running. As much as O'Malley's detractors would complain that he was inscrutable and scheming, compared with Moses he was a political amateur. At the start of 1956, Moses told an aide that he had already decided against helping O'Malley build in Brooklyn. However, he added, "It is necessary to show that our opposition is based on something other than prejudice." For this reason he would spend another eighteen months toying with O'Malley and Dodgers fans, alternately giving them hope and then dampening it. His approach to Fuller's dome was a case in point. When he was with O'Malley he expressed great enthusiasm, but when it suited his purpose he would dismiss Fuller as a "wild professor of architecture."

Unfortunately for O'Malley, Moses remained consistent in his refusal to use Title I to help the Dodgers because they were a private entity. (This despite *Berman v. Parker*, which permitted the practice, and the fact that he allowed businesses to benefit from a huge slum-clearance project on Manhattan's Upper West Side.) He reiterated this position in early January 1956, when the *New York Herald Tribune* published a report on Fort Greene and noted that the same spot seemed to be reserved for both stadium and housing. He wrote to agree that the neighborhood was a mess and "the Long Island Rail Road Station is a disgrace." But he warned against speculation about a new stadium. "Why stir up the animals?" he asked pointedly. "Something constructive will no doubt be worked out, with or without the Dodgers."

Less than a month later Moses seemed to change direction, as he joined the mayor, Borough President Cashmore, and state lawmakers to propose creation of a state agency—the Brooklyn Sports Center Authority—that would be empowered to condemn land, sell bonds, and—unlike programs conducted under Title I—build a stadium. The ballpark would be just a part of a $30 million redevelopment project involving about five hundred acres of land, and O'Malley would have to invest in the bonds it would issue. When he promised to come up with $4 million for that purpose, Moses challenged him: "Well, Walter," he said, "I think you will have to *demonstrate* your ability to come up with four million dollars."

Although it seemed like a workable idea, the authority would have to be approved by city officials, state legislators, and the governor of New York. Even then opponents would likely challenge its legitimacy in court. Outright opposition came immediately from the New York Civic League, whose attorney Harris J. Klein opposed the use of public funds and power to benefit a private enterprise like the Dodgers. At the same time members of the city council who represented districts in the borough of Queens wondered why they should support special treatment for Brooklyn.

O'Malley was not entirely comfortable with getting the Dodgers tied into a massive redevelopment scheme that might require him to build on public land. He should have worried, too, about the long period of time that would be required to evict and relocate people—many of whom might resist—from such a huge area. A skeptic might wonder if, in proposing such an enormous and potentially unwieldy venture, Moses might be intending for it to fail.

Publicly, O'Malley insisted that he wanted to stay in Brooklyn, and he discouraged speculation about the chance that he might move the team. His critics would one day insist that he wasn't serious about staying, but his private letters reveal that he was sincere. When Vincent X. Flaherty sent an architect's drawing of a stadium in Los Angeles, O'Malley confessed it made his mouth water but insisted he wasn't ready to move and that he wanted to keep the team in its hometown.

"It is my sincere belief that the Dodgers belong in Brooklyn," he wrote. "If the Dodgers are forced to move it will not be because I have failed to do everything in my power to bring our problem to the proper attention of the authorities and the fans."

Day by day O'Malley scrambled to find support for a new stadium. He spoke about it at every fund-raiser, political dinner, and civic meeting he could attend. He lobbied politicians, bankers, reporters, and business leaders. He sent a box of autographed baseballs to the governor (who handed them out as gifts) and arranged to have a stadium model done by one of Fuller's students displayed at the Williamsburg Savings Bank for people to inspect.

All this effort became fodder for parody at the annual baseball writers' dinner, where Roscoe McGowan of the *Times* sang, "Oh, give me a home with a translucent dome," and Duke Snider appeared with a custom-made cap that had two bills: over one was stitched the familiar "B" for "Brooklyn"; when he flipped it around he showed the other side decorated with "JC" for "Jersey City." The hat reminded everyone that O'Malley was so tired of Ebbets, he was willing to flirt with New Jersey. It prompted *Times* columnist Arthur Daley to warn that "The O'Malley ain't foolin'" about vacating Ebbets Field at the end of 1957. If the Brooklyn team left, he added, the Giants might depart as well.

Other newspaper writers recognized the possibility that the Dodgers might leave, and fans had begun to shudder at the thought of losing not one but two teams. But as much as he tried, O'Malley didn't seem to be able to motivate public officials to act with any urgency. He feared that too many people thought the Brooklyn Sports Center Authority was going to give public money to the Dodgers—this was not part of the plan—and that the city might miss a precious opportunity to save part of a borough that was sliding toward decline.

"Frankly, I view this as a last-ditch stand not just for the Dodgers but for a worthwhile rehabilitation of perhaps the most important section of Brooklyn," he told prominent attorney Tracy Voorhees, who had recently returned from a job at the Eisenhower White House.

Soon O'Malley would see that backing for the Sports Center Authority wasn't as solid as it seemed. The very first time anyone got a chance to vote on the idea in the city council, it had to be withdrawn to save it from defeat. This misstep occurred when roughly half of the council members—Democrats and Republican alike—refused to support sending the proposal to Albany. The council eventually came around to allow the mayor to forward the plan to Albany, where it was approved, but their reluctance showed that baseball's future in Brooklyn was far from secure.

Mayor Wagner added to the uncertainty by delaying the appointment of the three-member board that would run the authority. In May he promised to name them within ten days, but then several prominent men turned him down. The *Journal American* reported that they had been "scared off by the coolness of City Construction Coordinator Robert Moses."

When the mayor finally announced his picks for the authority board, O'Malley was pleased to see his close friend Charles Mylod of the Myomacs would be the chairman. Mylod, who worked for the big developer Robert Goelet, had broad experience in real estate and was involved in civic affairs in Brooklyn, but he was not a powerful political figure. The two others appointed were businessmen Chester Allen and Robert Blum. Neither was especially influential, but Blum was close to Robert Moses. For his part, Moses was already trying to set the authority's agenda, timetable, and priorities. He argued against a dome and proposed dumping Praeger in favor of other engineers and planners.

Moses wasn't the only one who moved behind the scenes. In a letter he suggested be kept secret, O'Malley offered Mylod his advice, including suggestions for staff members who might be hired once the board got funding and warnings about a group that was going to be appointed to advise the authority. (Moses wanted three "hard-boiled experts" named.) Here O'Malley showed his political instinct, noting that a small advisory board like the one Moses wanted could be nimble enough to cause trouble, but a larger one could be "unwieldy" and ineffective, leaving Mylod to proceed unfettered.

The general outline of the plan that Mylod would pursue called for a stadium to be built first. Next, the authority would relocate the Fort Greene market, and then it would build the new railroad terminal. Last would come new housing for a 110-block area radiating out from the stadium and railroad hub. Of course, in order to move from hope to concrete, Mylod, Allen, and Blum needed money for an office, staff, and more studies, and the city was in no hurry to give it to them. In the meantime, consultants hired to survey the project issued a report that found it would take property worth nearly $110 million off the tax rolls, depriving the city of at least $5 million in annual revenue.

As THE POLITICAL PROCESS ground slowly and mysteriously toward an uncertain resolution of the stadium issue, the Dodgers who took the field did everything they could to hold the city's interest. Their 1956 campaign, recalled in detail by Michael Shapiro in *The Last Good Season*, began with a parade of Brooklyn's best—including Boy Scouts, Miss Flatbush, and five bakers from the famous Ebinger's—that ended at Ebbets Field, where a World Series flag was raised for the first time.

The team was essentially the same one that had grabbed the championship in 1955, minus Johnny Podres, who had been drafted into the military. But they were each a year older. Jackie Robinson's numbers—home runs, batting average, etc.—were in decline since he had turned thirty-seven, but he nevertheless abandoned his plan for retirement, which he had shared with O'Malley in January 1955. Instead he accepted a small pay cut in order to return for one more season. Pee Wee Reese, soon to be thirty-eight, had been a weaker hitter in 1955; and tough as he was, catcher Roy Campanella was now thirty-five, which was an advanced age for anyone assigned to the grueling job behind home plate.

Strong but easygoing, Campanella had been the league's Most Valuable Player in 1955 when his batting average was .318 and he hit thirty-two home runs. He was the heart of the team and had been recognized with the highest salary ever paid a Dodger, $42,000. But he would struggle in 1956, losing ninety-nine points off of his batting average and hitting just twenty homers.

While the Dodgers hitters slumped as a group, the team's pitchers would excel once again. The workhorse on the mound was Don Newcombe, who would win twenty-seven and lose just seven on his way to winning the first Cy Young Award in history. But Newcombe's best year ever wasn't enough to make up for the absence of Podres. That feat was accomplished by none other than the dreaded Dodger-killer Salvatore Anthony Maglie, the man most fans would have considered least likely to ever don a Brooklyn uniform.

From 1950 to 1954, Maglie had been an anchor for the rival Giants and dominated the Dodgers with twenty-two wins against six losses. But it was the way that Maglie won—with dangerous brush-back pitches and occasional direct hits on Dodgers batters—that bothered the Brooklyn team. Nicknamed The Barber because he gave close shaves, he hated the Dodgers and made a special effort to intimidate the team's stars with fastballs that buzzed over and behind their heads. "They'd get so damn angry that they'd try to kill me with home runs—be the big heroes—and they'd break their bats swinging at bad balls," he would recall.

In 1955, as Maglie passed the age of thirty-eight and suffered from a sore back, the Giants sold his contract to Cleveland in the American League. (The day before the sale, the Braves had pounded Maglie for four runs in the first inning of a game that he left without getting a single man out.) In Cleveland Maglie had more trouble, and by the middle of May the Indians' general manager, Hank Greenberg, called Buzzie Bavasi.

Greenberg hoped to recover some of the $25,000 he had paid to get Maglie, but mainly he wanted to be rid of his salary, which was almost $27,000, and open a spot on his roster. Knowing the bad blood that ran between Maglie and so many Dodgers, Bavasi checked first with manager Alston and captain Pee Wee Reese. Both had been impressed by Maglie's pitching in a Cleveland-Brooklyn exhibition game played in Jersey City two weeks earlier. They thought The Barber still had it and they wanted him.

The negotiation that brought Maglie east would go down in baseball lore. As Bavasi would tell it, he haggled with Greenberg until the price of Maglie's contract sank from $10,000 to $100. As a face-saving gesture for Greenberg, Bavasi agreed to announce that Brooklyn paid $10,000. But in fact, for $100 Bavasi and the Dodgers would get thirteen wins against five losses and a morale boost at a moment when the team was playing just a little better than .500 ball.

As Maglie became a Dodger, the personality that was so evil in a Giants uniform became a fiery inspiration. He was the kind of pitcher who could start an argument with an umpire—and get himself thrown out of the game—even as he was cruising through the sixth inning with a big lead and a one-hitter in the works. This happened on a late-August night when The Barber thought he had been robbed of a strike. When their starter was ejected by the umpire, the Brooklyns were forced to use a pitcher slated to start the next day, which disrupted the pitching rotation for a week.

Maglie's outburst was unnecessary, but at least it occurred in the course of events that were normal for baseball. At other strange moments in the season the team was plagued by the unusual disruptions and distractions that recalled the silly days of the old Bums. For example, instead of getting the warm welcome they expected in Jersey City, where they played seven games to bring attention to their stadium problems, they were booed and heckled mercilessly by fans who had long before pledged allegiance to the Giants and Yankees. Jackie Robinson came in for extra abuse after his remarks about the jeering fans were reported in the press. (While the Dodgers were generally rejected by the people of Jersey City, the experiment was a financial success, as the team sold about twice as many tickets as it did for comparable dates in Brooklyn and kept all the revenue from four thousand parking spaces.)

In Cincinnati, Duke Snider got into a scuffle with a fan who called him gutless. The next day someone threw baseballs at the Crosley Field scoreboard until he managed to break a big square clock that kept time above the score line. Six weeks later Gil Hodges apparently lost his glove between innings in a game against the Giants at Ebbets Field. An initial request for help from fans, issued over the public address system, produced no results, but when the announcer said anyone returning the glove "will receive a brand-new one . . . no questions asked," the missing mitt was returned by a man who appeared at a railing near the team's dugout.

The theft of Hodges's glove involved just one man, who may have been a Giants rooter, but it drew attention to the overall mood at Ebbets Field. Although the team had just won its first World Series, ticket buyers knew that the future of the team was in doubt, and in shifting games to Jersey City the Dodgers had signaled that time was running out. An incident that occurred early in the season suggested that tensions were rising. Unfortunately for the Dodgers, it involved the famous evangelist of positive thinking, Reverend Norman Vincent Peale.

Peale brought his children, wife, and stepmother to Ebbets in early June. Throughout the game, Peale reported, kids ran wild in the grandstand while ushers seemed unable to control them. At some point a hail of fruit, cardboard boxes, baseballs, and even canned goods rained down from the upper deck. A can hit Peale's white-haired stepmother, opening a gash in her head. Although she received medical help and bravely returned to her seat, Peale found the events at Ebbets appalling and recalled them with great drama in a newspaper column. The day after it was published, O'Malley received a note from a woman who called herself an "ardent Dodger fan" who said she was "scared to death" of the crowd at Ebbets. That note was followed by a letter from a Brooklyn lawyer who said he knew of many who had stopped going to Ebbets Field because of "rowdyism."

A split scalp and a frightened lady cannot prove that the mood at Ebbets in 1956 was much different from other years. But if people in Brooklyn felt uneasy and anxious, they had a right. Time was passing, and while Robert Moses pushed ahead with other projects, including a massive bridge to Staten Island that would devastate the lovely Brooklyn neighborhood of Bay Ridge, little energy was being expended to keep their team in the borough. O'Malley had set a 1957 deadline and he was holding to it. June 1956 saw the sale of the team's property in Montreal, which brought cash for future moves. Ebbets Field was also for sale, and whoever bought it was sure to tear it down and use the land for some more profitable purpose.

The sense of uncertainty that hung over the team's corporate future seemed to cast a shadow over its performance. After a brief appearance in first place in April, the aging Dodgers struggled to reach the top of the standings. Fortunately for them, no other team rose to dominate the league. As September arrived, the Dodgers were still in position to challenge the Cincinnati Redlegs and the Milwaukee Braves, who had traded the lead through the summer. The competition was so keen that at one point National League president Warren Giles mapped out a plan for a double-elimination tournament that would be held if the race ended in a three-way tie.

Although they failed to overtake them, Brooklyn had managed to stay close to the leaders all through the summer. On the next to the last day of the regular season, a doubleheader sweep of the Pirates finally guaranteed the Dodgers at least a share of the pennant. In the last game Newcombe beat the Pirates to win his twenty-seventh and send the Dodgers back to the World Series. Hundreds of fans hopped over the railings at the edge of the field to join the players, who were celebrating with hugs and backslapping.

The Dodger Sym-phony band followed the team into the locker room, where—unlike the previous year in Milwaukee—the team didn't need any prodding to show its glee. Amid sprays of champagne and beer Newcombe, stripped down to a pair of pink shorts, danced with a Sym-phony musician; and Pee Wee Reese, completely soaked with beer, declared that through its struggles the team had proven its character. It was the toughest pennant victory he had ever experienced because, he explained, "we're older."

THE DODGERS WERE OLD. Their stadium was old. And old, too, was the hope they carried into the 1956 World Series. For as long as men had played games, aging athletes had prayed for one more chance at glory and both the guile and the strength to seize it from younger, faster, more powerful opponents.

The Yankees were led by a twenty-four-year-old Mickey Mantle. During the season Mantle had hit fifty-two homers and batted in 130 runs. But he was not the only source of power in the lineup. Truly bombers, the Yankees led all of baseball in runs scored and were second in team home runs. Their pitchers, with a combined earned run average of 3.63, were roughly equal to the Dodgers staff.

According to the bookies, the numbers made the American Leaguers the favorites to win, even though the Dodgers had sentimentality on their side. President Eisenhower, campaigning for reelection, attended the first game, which was played at Ebbets Field. He arrived in a bubble-top limousine that took him onto the field while a military band played "Hail to the Chief." After throwing out the first pitch and receiving a Dodgers tie clasp, he took a seat in Walter O'Malley's box. (A Secret Service agent, equipped with a glove, was posted nearby to protect him from foul balls.)

With O'Malley at his side offering a steady stream of conversation, the president rooted for the Dodgers. He stood to cheer Jackie Robinson's second-inning home run and rose again when Gil Hodges smacked a three-run shot in the third. The Hodges blast provided the margin of victory in a game the Dodgers won 6–3. The winning pitcher was Maglie, who was the second-oldest player on either team. At thirty-nine, he used a crafty mix of curves and fastballs and stayed on the mound for the complete-game victory. His best moment came in the ninth inning, when Mantle came to bat with Enos Slaughter on first. In the owner's box, Eisenhower turned to O'Malley and said, "I've seen him hit a home run and I've seen him strike out. Now if he should hit into a double play I've seen him do everything." As if on command, Maglie threw the same type of pitch that Mantle had hit out of the park in the first inning. This time the curveball went where he intended, and the Yankee slugger hit it to second baseman Jim Gilliam for a double play.

A rainout pushed game two back a day, which meant that presidential candidate Adlai Stevenson, who had planned a visit to Yankee Stadium, went to Ebbets Field instead. He too sat in O'Malley's box, which served as a safe haven for dignitaries throughout the series. Their care was the owner's responsibility, and O'Malley, ever gracious, played the role with great enthusiasm. He also dealt with a steady stream of out-of-town visitors. Included this time was his constant correspondent, the Los Angeles newspaperman Vincent X. Flaherty.

Sent by the *Examiner* to cover the games, Flaherty sat with O'Malley to make another pitch for the fair city of Los Angeles. He told him that Washington Senators owner Calvin Griffith, who was unhappy with his antique ballpark, might grab the opportunity if O'Malley delayed. It would have been "unfair not to tell O'Malley what was going on," Flaherty recalled months later. But even with this information, the Dodgers owner rejected Flaherty's offer of a meeting with Los Angeles mayor Poulson, who was once again in New York seeking a team for his city. He turned him down with a brief note: "Not interested," he wrote, "as our Brooklyn Stadium matter is progressing satisfactorily."

Poulson was left to watch the games from the stands like everyone else. In game two he saw Don Newcombe give up six runs, including a grand slam to Yogi Berra, in just two innings. Newcombe was replaced and was in such a state of turmoil that he changed clothes and left the stadium.

Outside the stadium Newcombe walked toward a parking lot where the attendant, in true Brooklyn style, decided to heckle him. "What's the matter, Newk?" said Michael Brown. "A little competition too much? Do you fold up?"

What happened next would remain in dispute, but Brown later claimed that Newcombe punched him in the stomach. A police officer who witnessed the incident raced over to intervene. When both men declined to press charges, he let them go. (Later Brown would consult a lawyer and decide to swear out a complaint with the police. The judge in the case, who was once Mayor John J. "Red Mike" Hylan's secretary, dismissed the charges.)

If he had hung around the stadium, Newcombe would have seen his teammates bash the Yankee starter Don Larsen for six runs in the bottom of the second and then score another seven off half a dozen relief pitchers. A standing-room-only crowd of more than thirty-six thousand roared through the afternoon. When it was over, their team had won 13–8 and led the series by two games to none.

At little Ebbets Field the Yankees had never looked comfortable. In their home stadium they were a different team. In both games three and four they had the Dodgers finished by the seventh inning. And even the old warrior Maglie couldn't beat them in game five because Don Larsen turned in the only perfect performance ever recorded by a pitcher in a World Series. In the course of nine innings he threw a mere ninety-seven pitches, including seventy-one strikes. No Dodger managed a hit or a walk, and the Yankees scored two runs—on a Mantle homer—and were flawless in the field.

When the series returned to Brooklyn for the last two games, the Dodgers won the first, a tense ten-inning battle that Robinson ended with a single that made the score 1–0. This victory set up an all-or-nothing seventh game that Brooklyn would trust to Newcombe's strong right arm. The Dodgers' ace had enjoyed one of the best seasons ever recorded by a big-league pitcher. No Dodger pitcher since Dazzy Vance in 1924 had won as many games in a season. Considering his ability alone, he could be expected to beat the pitcher the Yanks were sending to the mound, a tall, skinny twenty-two-year-old named Johnny Kucks.

Tall and muscular, Don Newcombe looked strong enough to carry a team on his shoulders, and in twenty-seven regular-season victories he had proven he could. But as he faced the seventh game of the World Series, the expectations of his teammates and all of Brooklyn felt extremely heavy. For years his critics, including Charlie Dressen, had promoted the idea that Newcombe suffered from some terrible flaw that held him back at key moments. This talk often came with racist flourishes and was repeated by men on opposing teams and heckling fans. It was also completely erroneous.

Newcombe had won many key victories in his career, and in the games when he supposedly earned his reputation as a "choker"—in 1949, 1950, and 1951—he pitched twenty-seven innings and gave up a total of three runs. In these three losses it was the team's weak hitting that mattered, not Newcombe's temperament. But still the taunts continued. His critics seemed to enjoy tearing at his pride because he was a physically imposing person. But Newcombe was a sensitive man who felt tortured by the constant criticism. Unbeknownst to the press and the public, his postgame run-in with Michael Brown was not a unique event. After a game in late July he had a shouting match with fans who wanted autographs. A father who witnessed the event wrote to complain that the encounter with Newcombe had escalated from ordinary to profane in an instant. It was one more sign that the man was under too much pressure.

When game seven of the 1956 series began, Newcombe knew that some fans were just expecting him to fail. He tried to pitch as he would normally. After giving up a single to Hank Bauer, he threw six strikes in a row to get out Billy Martin and Mickey Mantle. Next he faced Yankees cleanup man Yogi Berra, who was on his way to setting an all-time record for driving in runs during a World Series. Berra hit a home run to left field, giving his team a quick lead. He repeated the feat in the third, only this time Martin was the man on base, and in the fourth Newk was done. The Dodgers would lose by a score of 9–0.

In the postmortems, critics would again find fault with Newcombe but make little of the fact that the Dodgers hitters, old and tired, were the worst ever in a seven-game series. Their batting average was .195, and in the last three games of the series they scored just a single run and got just seven hits. But while the Dodgers lost as a team, Newcombe took it hardest. He disappeared after the game and did not surface until the next day. After learning that his lawyer had won a postponement on the Michael Brown assault case (the charges would eventually be dismissed), Newcombe managed to get to the airport where the Dodgers were booked for a flight to Los Angeles. From there they would go on to Hawaii and then an exhibition tour of Japan.

BASEBALL TOURS HAD BEEN part of the American-Japanese relationship since before World War II. Meiji University sent a team to the U.S. in 1924 and several teams of American stars had barnstormed over there before the war. In 1955 the Yankees resumed the tradition under the sponsorship of several Japanese newspapers. Playing to vast and adoring crowds, they won sixteen games without a defeat. The Dodgers' tour of 1956, begun less than twenty-four hours after their defeat in the series, was also supposed to promote goodwill, but it got off to a rocky start. Don Newcombe drank his way across the Pacific and pitched terribly as Brooklyn lost two of the first three games in Japan. No visiting American team had ever played so poorly, and one Japanese manager complained that "we no longer have anything to learn from the Dodgers."

The Dodgers were tired and in some cases irritable. A young team executive, Dick Walsh, would recall that several players had been reluctant to make the trip, and when they got to Japan they seemed to be bothered by the littlest things, like the sandwiches served before games. Walsh, who had served in Japan with the military and spoke a little Japanese, helped them adapt to their surroundings while O'Malley got them to adjust their play. He accomplished this with a stern lecture on their duty to team and country. They responded by winning thirteen of the next sixteen games.

It was rare for O'Malley to address the team as a group. He was more likely to approach players as individuals, and when he did, he never told them how to play ball. Instead he dealt with them as performers who needed to be counseled or motivated. With this in mind, he took responsibility for delivering to Newcombe a letter sent to the team in Tokyo by President Eisenhower. With the envelope in hand he found his pitcher in the barbershop of the Imperial Hotel. Newcombe resisted taking the letter, but O'Malley insisted that he read it.

"Hard luck is something that no one in the world can explain," began the president. He wrote that he had rooted for Newcombe and reminded him of the twenty-seven victories "that were so important in bringing Brooklyn into the World Series." The note, which Newcombe would keep for the rest of his life, helped him get his bearings. Although a sore elbow meant he wouldn't pitch again during the trip, he stayed with the tour and got to bat several times as a pinch hitter. Before Thanksgiving, Newcombe would head home to claim the Most Valuable Player Award and learn that the Cincinnati Redlegs thought enough of him to offer $300,000 for his contract. Dick Walsh, having served as Walter O'Malley's key man, returned to Brooklyn with a much better sense of the man who was his boss.

"With Walter O'Malley things had to run smoothly. He didn't want any 'goddamn problems,'" Walsh recalled, but when problems arose, "he was a very good listener, and very empathetic." O'Malley was, according to Walsh, amiable but "Machiavellian" in the sense that he sought advantages where he could and revealed as little as possible. He had witnessed O'Malley's style up close when the team plane made a one-night stop in Los Angeles on the way to Japan. In the morning O'Malley went to a meeting at the coffee shop of the Statler Hotel, on the corner of Wilshire and Figueroa. The team was scheduled to depart Los Angeles at twelve thirty, and as the time approached, Walsh went to the coffee shop to check on O'Malley.

"Kenny Hahn [a Los Angeles County supervisor] was very, very aggressively selling the prospect of the Dodgers moving to Los Angeles," Walsh later said. O'Malley kept listening as Hahn suggested a stadium could be built in a district called Chavez Ravine, which had been all but emptied for a big public housing project—twenty-one thirteen-story buildings—that was then cancelled by a referendum vote.

As he waited anxiously for his boss to wrap up the meeting, Walsh got the impression that O'Malley, "who was born and bred in the East," wasn't enthusiastic about a move. At the end of the meeting, Hahn met with reporters and told them the Dodgers owner considered Los Angeles his second choice. He said that the Brooklyn Sports Center Authority was making progress and "that O'Malley thinks there is no likelihood of it not going through."

Nothing that Walsh heard or saw during the trip to Japan made him believe that O'Malley had misrepresented his intentions with Hahn or with fans, the press, and public officials back in New York. He was a New Yorker and would have preferred to stay in Brooklyn. But he was also worried about competing with clubs like Milwaukee and others that might in the future draw two million fans a year. "He felt like his pockets were not as deep as some of the others," said

Walsh. "He also insisted on being competitive. He might accept if we finished third, but we always had to be in the race."

O'Malley's formula required more money than he thought he could generate at Ebbets Field. If he was Machiavellian, as Walsh observed, it showed in his understanding of politics. He had pushed as hard as he could to get the city and state to create the Sports Center Authority, and he had warned his fans about their stake in events by shifting the team to New Jersey for some games. Finally, to demonstrate his seriousness, he sold his property in Montreal and openly offered Ebbets Field for sale.

With these moves completed, O'Malley enjoyed the World Series and departed for Japan. While there he watched games, toured with players' families, and consulted with officials in Tokyo on their construction of a new seventy-thousand-seat stadium that would be built and opened in less than two years. When the team returned home, O'Malley flew off in the opposite direction to vacation with Kay, their daughter Terry, and son Peter.

During his long absence, O'Malley's men back in Brooklyn completed negotiations for the sale of Ebbets Field. The buyer, Marvin Kratter, was a fixture in New York real estate and closely associated with Mayor Wagner. He had recently opened his own investment firm with national ambitions. In less than fourteen months he had been involved in the purchase of over $125 million worth of properties, including a full block along Wilshire Boulevard in Beverly Hills, California. He paid $3 million for Ebbets, which O'Malley added to the fund he was amassing to buy Sports Authority bonds and build a new stadium. Kratter would let the Dodgers lease the old place for a few years.

Besides converting an asset to hard cash, which gave O'Malley flexibility, the sale of Ebbets Field added the key element that had always been missing from the political equation: time pressure. Kratter was not going to refurbish, rebuild, or expand Ebbets; he was going to tear it down. This reality gave those who held power in New York a firm choice: either they supported the Sports Center Authority or they would lose the Dodgers. As he traveled with his family, taking himself out of the deliberations, O'Malley believed they would help him build a stadium in Brooklyn and keep the Dodgers where he thought they belonged.

Ten

O'MALLEY'S CHOICE

W alter O'Malley knew that in politics, timing and appearances mattered almost as much as the substance of an argument. He would retreat when he felt he had pushed hard enough and should let others play their roles. O'Malley had pulled back this way in February 1956, telling a banker friend "I should get out of town" until the Sports Center Authority was approved. He had done it again in the fall, accompanying his team to Japan and then completing a round-the-world journey with his family. This time, however, he returned to discover all momentum lost.

On December 6, 1956, O'Malley went to his office on Montague Street and found that the mail had brought a package from Japan. Inside was a complete set of plans for the stadium about to be built in Tokyo. (It would open in eighteen months.) He set them aside, thought about his own decade-long effort to replace Ebbets Field, and wrote to the city's chief lawyer, corporation counsel Peter Campbell Brown:

> On my return I was sorry to find that little or no substantial progress has been made of the redevelopment of the area . . . I understand Mylod and Blum have been on the verge of resigning. If there is anything I can do without muddying the waters and adding to the confusion, let me know.

O'Malley was upset because, six months after it was created, the Sports Center Authority still had no staff and no operating funds. If he felt the hand of Robert Moses at work, he would be correct. Moses was urging Mayor Wagner and other city officials to take away the authority's responsibility for the overall redevelopment of the Flatbush and Atlantic area and hand it to a new, separate committee. The diminished authority would not need "a bit of staff," he advised. Nor would it need the $278,000 that chairman Charles Mylod had requested to pay for engineers, surveys, and other expenses. Instead he suggested just $25,000 for a consultant. Under these conditions the Sports Center Authority would likely fail, a fate Moses considered hardly serious since the city could then move ahead with his previous plan for Title I housing on the same property.

Moses moved quietly, and months would pass before the public would learn that the Sports Center Authority was foundering. But O'Malley—who counted Mylod among his closest friends—knew, and he began to make moves to secure the option of transferring the team to Los Angeles. (Decades later Buzzie Bavasi would recall that at around this time O'Malley polled his executives on the idea of moving to Los Angeles. As he remembered it, "We were all opposed, except for Walter.") In the second week of December, O'Malley met with Chicago Cubs owner P. K. Wrigley. They discussed exchanging minor-league franchises: the Dodgers' team in Fort Worth for Wrigley's Los Angeles Angels.

Nothing was settled between Wrigley and O'Malley and no hint of their discussion leaked into the press. In the meantime Dodger fans got to focus on a momentary outrage that seemed even less likely than Sal Maglie's shift to the Dodgers. On December 13 the team announced that Jackie Robinson would be traded to the rival Giants. In exchange the club would get a moderately talented pitcher named Dick Littlefield and something between $30,000 and $50,000.

The deal was authored by Bavasi, who knew Robinson was thinking about retirement. Without consulting O'Malley, he had worked it out so that the team would get some value for Robinson's contract and Jackie could remain in New York, which Bavasi knew he preferred. Giants owner Horace Stoneham agreed to the arrangement because he needed a good player who could attract fans. In 1956, Stoneham's team had performed miserably on the field and at the gate.

They finished twenty-six games out of first place and drew fewer than 8,200 per game.

When the trade was announced, sentimental Brooklynites flooded the Dodgers' office with complaints. They didn't want to see Robinson go and they cringed at the thought of him in a Giants uniform. At home in Connecticut, Robinson told reporters that he would need time to decide whether he'd rather retire than play for a new team. He had tried to delay the announcement of the trade, because at the time it was being negotiated he had secretly decided to stop playing and accepted a job outside the game, as director of personnel for the Chock full o'Nuts restaurant chain. He also had agreed to announce his retirement exclusively in *Look* magazine, which would pay him $50,000 over the next two years as a consultant.

Constrained by his commitment to *Look*, which was published every two weeks and needed time to produce the report, Robinson had to hold his secret until after New Year's Day. But somehow the news got out before the magazine hit newsstands, and the scoop was ruined. Yet another uproar ensued as Bavasi criticized Robinson for letting the Giants and Dodgers announce the trade in the first place. "That's typical of Jackie," he said. "Now he'll write a letter of apology." In the moment, Robinson reacted sharply, saying he thought he was a good judge of people and had once trusted Bavasi "but maybe I made a mistake."

Robinson was similarly annoyed with Walter O'Malley. The team owner wrote him a note saying his retirement was "a sad day for us as well." But as Robinson later wrote, he didn't accept "the nice things" O'Malley expressed. This down note contrasted sharply with the positive evaluation Robinson gave O'Malley two years before. He had written approvingly of O'Malley in *Look* magazine, noting that while other organizations promised white prospects they wouldn't have to play with blacks, "Mr. O'Malley told me that the club wouldn't hesitate to put nine Negroes on the field if they were the best nine players."

So it went with Robinson and O'Malley. Admiration would mix with complaint and a lasting peace would remain elusive. However, they would continue to communicate in the years to come. Even though they moved in different worlds, they shared so many memories and so many interests that, as O'Malley predicted in his good-bye note, their paths would cross again.

WHILE THE NEW YORK press chased the newly retired Robinson, Walter O'Malley left town on a trip with his daughter Terry. He headed for the West Coast with two destinations in mind. First he would go to San Diego and the Convair aircraft factory to meet the famous flying ace Eddie Rickenbacker, who had risen to the top of Eastern Airlines. Eastern had arranged to buy twenty new twin-engine Convairs. Rickenbacker was checking on their progress. O'Malley found the old pilot and persuaded him to add one more plane to the Eastern order, at the airline's volume discount, and resell it at cost—a little more than $730,000—to the Dodgers. Unlike the old Dodgers DC-3, which seated twenty-two, the Convair 440 could carry more than forty, which meant an entire baseball team plus coaches, a manager, and executives.

After settling the airplane purchase, O'Malley went to Los Angeles. There he was met by the eager booster-newspaperman Vincent X. Flaherty, who served as volunteer chauffeur, tour guide, and interpreter. Fifty years later Terry O'Malley would recall Flaherty as a charming, energetic man who seemed to know everything and everyone. "He was a persistent character," she would say, "and I loved sitting in the backseat listening to the two of them rapping about things."

Flaherty arranged for a tour of Chavez Ravine, and O'Malley was impressed. On January 8, he wrote to minority owner James Mulvey, at Sam Goldwyn's offices in Los Angeles, asking him to go check the property, which was northwest of the city center and close to four different freeways and two wide boulevards. He described it as "about four hundred acres of sandy hills" and noted that it was the only spot for a stadium served by so many highways.

With a new airplane on order and a favorite stadium site identified, O'Malley's brief expedition to California brought him closer to moving the team there. Flaherty would eventually report that the Dodgers boss also used this trip to finalize the terms of his deal with Wrigley to trade the Fort Worth club for the Los Angeles Angels. And according to Norris Poulson, the Dodgers boss spent time with an advertising executive named Wick Crider, who was an expert on the local radio and TV market. With these moves O'Malley strengthened his options as he faced a year of decision. If the city of New York failed to find a way for him to stay, *he* was going to be the one to plant baseball in the West.

FOR YEARS O'MALLEY HAD said he couldn't remain at Ebbets Field, and the prospect of the Dodgers leaving Brooklyn had been widely discussed. In February 1956, John Lardner had asked "Would it still be Brooklyn?" if the team decamped. Writing in the *New York Times Magazine*, he noted that some locals didn't consider the team a civic asset worth saving. But he argued that the Dodgers stood for the spirit of the community and "we will do well to give them the home they need. In lean years and rich they will honor it, and us."

The choices were clear, and yet the city and Moses stalled. When O'Malley returned from California he told City Councilman Joseph Sharkey that the Brooklyn stadium was "dying a slow death" and warned that if he had to make a decision to leave, it would be irrevocable. Nevertheless, O'Malley continued to work with Mylod's group. In January he raised the amount he promised to invest in authority bonds from $4 million to $5 million and promised to find investors to buy up the rest of the issue. He also agreed to pay $500,000 per season—more than any major-league team was paying at the time—if he became a renter in a government-owned stadium.

As he made these promises, O'Malley also set a firm deadline. He told the Sports Center Authority's engineering consultant, Jack Madigan, that he would have to see "definitive positive progress by July 1 if the Brooklyn franchise is to remain in Brooklyn." Madigan, who was well connected to Moses, came back a week later with an extraordinary request. Would the ball club pay as much as $1.5 million *more* to cover the cost of issuing bonds for the stadium and other parts of the redevelopment scheme?

Having sold most of the team's hard assets to raise cash for the bond issue (or a move), O'Malley would have been hard-pressed to come up with another $1.5 million. But even if he could, the signals sent by Moses, Madigan, and Wagner—who didn't respond when O'Malley called to discuss the latest request—were clear. The Sports Center Authority was not likely to produce any real result. The stadium, in O'Malley's words, was receiving "the kiss of death."

What did O'Malley do?

He hired a clown. And not just any clown: he hired the perpetually sad-faced Weary Willy, played by the famous Emmett Kelly.

Baseball clowns, all former players, were common at the time but no team had ever drafted one from the circus. With Weary Willy, the Dodgers got one of the country's most recognizable clowns—millions had seen him perform for Ringling Bros. and Barnum & Bailey—and one who looked very much like the famous Brooklyn Bum drawn by cartoonist Willard Mullin. The idea was to "ease tension at Ebbets Field," said O'Malley, who had always favored Mullin's Bum. But there was one big difference between Emmett Kelly's creation and the cartoon: Kelly's character *never* smiled. While other clowns wore blazing colors and did frantic pratfalls, Willie appeared in a ragged black coat and often moved in slow motion. He was a kind of anti-clown who symbolized something very poignant and familiar to people in Brooklyn: a failing but never-ending struggle for dignity against great odds. Kelly was serious about his character and felt not funny but alienated whenever he performed. "I'm a misfit, a reject," he explained. He made people laugh out of discomfort and sympathy.

Weary Willy made his Dodgers debut at sunny Holman Stadium in Vero Beach during spring training. His performance, which included planting seeds at home plate and a turn at bat wielding a broom, drew only laughs. But as the season would progress at Ebbets Field, his mournful act could be seen as fore-shadowing real sadness to come.

AT THE 1957 SPRING TRAINING camp, players, coaches, executives, guests, and writers found the usual atmosphere. Hundreds of major and minor leaguers worked through drills and exercises. Teams trooped in from other Florida towns to play exhibition games. The O'Malley presided over his poker games and planned his annual St. Patrick's Day bash. Reports on the team's condition noted the progress of the creaky old-timers and the promise of youngsters such as pitchers Sandy Koufax and Don Drysdale and catcher John Roseboro.

As they followed the team's preparations for the season, noting sore elbows and rusty swings, the press corps also covered the drama around the team's future home. The first big development was the announcement of the O'Malley-Wrigley exchange of minor-league clubs. With the Angels franchise

O'Malley also got a little stadium, called Wrigley Field, which with improvements might accommodate a major-league team while a bigger park was being built.

The news prompted New York mayor Wagner to send O'Malley a telegram in which he recognized the team's stadium problem and promised "all possible efforts to arrive at a satisfactory solution." The *New York Times* ran a brief profile of O'Malley titled "A Sound Poker Player." In the article he confirmed that he was preparing for a move to the coast while planning also to stay in Brooklyn. This strategy would cause critics to describe him as coy and even manipulative. In fact he was being candid. He wanted to stay in Brooklyn but had set a deadline for the resolution of the stadium issue and had opened the door to offers from Los Angeles.

As a businessman, O'Malley was trying to guarantee a future for his corporation. As a sportsman, he was hoping to use this financial security to finance the pursuit of championships. On a personal level, he was seeking both a victory in his struggle with New York's power structure and some appreciation for the efforts that had transformed the Dodgers from bums into champions. Reporter Dick Young of the *Daily News*, who knew O'Malley well enough to merit the occasional private meeting, would see it this way. In a long article for *Sport* magazine, he lamented the possible loss of a team that helped to define Brooklyn and offered the theory that The O'Malley had developed "a king complex" and might leave, in part, because he felt unappreciated.

While other reporters followed O'Malley's moves from the outside, one played the role of secret confidant and adviser. Between visits to the Vero Beach ball fields and the Dodgertown bar, Vincent X. Flaherty wrote a five-page, single-spaced report filled with the history of the Los Angeles campaign for a team and suggestions for making the move west. Much of what he put down was a record of his own efforts, which made it seem as if he were central to the drama. Among the adventures he recounted were:

- dumping thousands of pro-baseball letters on the mayor's desk
- tramping around Chavez Ravine with Charlie Dressen
- checking out the Los Angeles Coliseum with Leo Durocher and Casey Stengel
- teaching Mayor Poulson how to talk about baseball.

After describing these events Flaherty confided that O'Malley occupied a very powerful position. Until recently, he said, Calvin Griffith had been determined to move the Senators to Los Angeles. Dressen, the Senators manager, had come to look at Chavez Ravine on Griffith's behalf. But the Washington owner had backed off, leaving the field open for the Dodgers. "You can call your shots," he wrote, "and Los Angeles will give you damn near anything." If O'Malley wanted, Howard Hughes would use one of his nonprofit foundations to build a stadium, said Flaherty. If that didn't seem right, then "the county has a couple of hundred million dollars" in its retirement fund that could be tapped should special financing be required.

The way Flaherty described the issue, the politicians in Los Angeles were so eager to deliver major-league baseball to their city that they would trample each other in order to claim the credit for it. Days after he gave this letter to O'Malley, the mayor of Los Angeles led a platoon of eager pols—including County Supervisor Kenneth Hahn—from Los Angeles to Miami. There they boarded the Dodgers' plane, which O'Malley in his showy style had sent to carry them on the last leg of their journey to Vero Beach. They were headed to Dodgertown camp on a mission Poulson called "Operation O'Malley."

A gangly-looking fellow with a big-toothed smile who wore thick black-frame glasses, Norris Poulson loved the ceremonial aspects of politics: ribbon cuttings, receptions, bill signings. (When the press wanted a picture when the California dairy queen visited, Poulson had happily milked a cow on the lawn at City Hall.) Flaherty considered him "a self-glorified boob," and yet he had risen steadily from state assembly to the U.S. Congress and finally the mayor's office.

Poulson won control of city hall with the backing of the *Los Angeles Times* and other business interests. He was a staunch opponent of public housing, which he associated with socialism, and once in office he led the city to abandon a 3,300-unit project planned for Chavez Ravine. This reversal left the ravine area, which had been almost emptied of residents, in a state of limbo.

In his pursuit of baseball, Poulson had joined Hahn and the young city councilwoman Rosalind Wyman. As first O'Malley and then Horace Stoneham made noise about their problems in New York; the Los Angeles group focused on the Dodgers. Eventually they made a deal with officials in San Francisco.

They could go after the Giants while Los Angeles courted O'Malley. As Poulson prepared to leave for Miami, San Francisco mayor George Christopher sent him a telegram wishing him well. "We consider this practically a joint venture," he wrote, "and know that if you are successful San Francisco also will eventually receive major league baseball."

At Vero Beach a happy Poulson and company waved brightly colored "Los Angeles" pennants and posed for photographs with O'Malley and slugger Duke Snider. They disappeared with O'Malley and emerged at five o'clock to brief reporters. The team owner said that nothing had been decided and that for the moment the Dodgers still belonged to Brooklyn. He said he believed the city of New York was making a sincere effort and hinted that his July deadline could be moved. But eventually he would have to see "excavation, steel construction, the pouring of concrete." Poulson said with his usual optimism, "Mr. O'Malley has a problem. We believe we can solve it, and quick."

Although their statements to the press seemed as if they summed up a day's work, the Californians and O'Malley were not finished. They retired, in private, to Bud Holman's Blue Cypress Ranch, the same place where young Buzzie Bavasi cemented the deal for Dodgertown. There in the rustic isolation—the ranch didn't even have a phone—the two sides continued to discuss what might have to be done to bring the Dodgers to Los Angeles.

In a few years Los Angeles Times columnist Jim Murray would report that during the Vero Beach visit, O'Malley gave Poulson a list of requirements that would have to be met before the Dodgers would move. At the top was land for a ballpark at Chavez Ravine with access roads built with public funds. Murray said the list changed hands when the men were alone in O'Malley's car. It may have also been discussed at the ranch. However, the exact locale was not as important as Poulson's response, which, according to Murray, was an enthusiastic "Yes!"

Given Poulson's style, Murray's description sounds right. It would be confirmed many years later with the O'Malley family's release of a letter that Walter wrote just a few days after the Los Angeles contingent departed. "The Los Angeles matter," he told his friend Frank Schroth, "is much further than the newspaper accounts indicate." In the same note he fretted about the New York Transit Authority, which had delayed renewing its agreement with O'Malley's Subways Advertising Company, which held the franchise for placing placards in subway cars. He figured it was "retribution" for all the publicity about a Dodgers move.

ON ST. PATRICK'S DAY 1957, Vice President Richard Nixon, in the midst of a three-week diplomatic tour of Africa and Europe, visited Pope Pius XII at the Vatican. He then stopped at the North American Pontifical College, where seminarians from the United States were trained. He gave a brief speech and then shocked a young priest from Brooklyn with the news that the Dodgers were headed for Los Angeles.

At the center of the small universe that was the California Republican Party, Nixon was well informed by friends at every layer of government. He would likely know that Norris Poulson had started telling people, "We've got the Dodgers." The Los Angeles mayor had also appointed two representatives to a committee of city and county officials that was working out all the problems that would have to be solved to put a stadium in Chavez Ravine and connect the site with both existing and future freeways.

In his private dispatches, Vincent X. Flaherty told Walter O'Malley that Poulson had gone "slightly berserk" and was showing anyone who wanted to see them plans for a Chavez Ravine stadium. Flaherty reported on the mayor's activities as if he were a spy behind enemy lines. Thanks to him, O'Malley knew that Yankees owner Del Webb was talking about putting the Kansas City Athletics in Los Angeles as early as 1958. Although the source of his influence over the Athletics was obscure, Webb was partnered in other business with the team's principal owner, Arnold Johnson. In early 1957, wrote Flaherty, Webb met often with Poulson and others to discuss shifting them to Los Angeles.

For a man with no power to make decisions and no apparent financial stake in the outcome, Flaherty poured a remarkable amount of effort into the Dodgers' cause. He said he had sounded out the board that ran the Los Angeles Coliseum and believed a majority would let the Dodgers play there. He urged O'Malley to sneak back out to California and stay at the Flaherty home to avoid publicity. "You can have one of my cars for as long as you like," he wrote, but he also volunteered to serve as a tour guide and social analyst. As if to prove his expertise, he offered his thumbnail description—as much a caricature as a serious review—of the region's demographic and geographic realities:

The money trade comes from West Los Angeles—Beverly Hills, Bel-Air, Brentwood, Westwood, Santa Monica . . . I say this because the people of West Los Angeles are the season-box trade . . . If I wanted to sell more bleacher seats than boxes I'd plant it [a stadium] in the middle of Los Angeles so all of the Mexicans and cullud [*sic*] folks could takeover. If I wanted a waiting list of those hoping to buy boxes on a season ticket basis I'd have to plant a ballpark in West Los Angeles . . .

In the course of his correspondence, Flaherty managed to drop enough big names from politics, business, and entertainment to make himself seem like he was the best-connected man in Los Angeles. He wrote of drinking all night with boxer Rocky Marciano, socializing with movie star Irene Dunne, and playing matchmaker for Brooklyn-born Edythe Marrener, who was known in Hollywood as the actress Susan Hayward. Flaherty made sure O'Malley knew that all of these connections—and more—could be put to use on the Dodgers' behalf. "I'm your boy," he said more than once.

O'Malley didn't answer every note from Flaherty and didn't show much interest in the celebrities he mentioned. But thanks to his letters, O'Malley knew what was being said by powerful people in Los Angeles. He knew that Poulson was talking to his baseball rival Del Webb. He even learned first, from Flaherty, that officials in Los Angeles had discussed buying the Angels' minor-league stadium—little Wrigley Field—if that would help make the move possible. Remarkably, this idea and many others floated by Flaherty would become part of the final bid Los Angeles would make for the team.

ON MARCH 27, New York mayor Robert Wagner went to the airport in Idlewild, Queens, to board a plane for a Florida vacation. Before he departed he confidently predicted that the Dodgers would never leave town. It was a wise bit of politics for a mayor facing an election in seven months, and naturally the mayor didn't admit that he was not in control of the process. Like other mayors before him, Wagner almost always ceded power to Robert Moses, who would allow elected officials a certain leeway to court voters but use threats to get his way. As the czar of housing, construction, and development, Moses would control the fate of the Dodgers stadium idea.

City council chairman Abe Stark was appealing for votes when he suggested for a moment that a stadium be built on the Parade Grounds at Prospect Park, a place as civically sacred and untouchable as Central Park. Similarly, John Cashmore was playing politics when he called O'Malley with the idea of conducting yet another study and requesting federal money to do it. The Dodgers owner discouraged him for fear the press would see it as a boondoggle and because it would only mean more delay.

With Los Angeles promising him everything he could want, and New York's leaders talking but producing nothing, O'Malley seemed to have little choice. In a letter to a fan in Pennsylvania he described Brooklyn as a borough in decline. The community had recently lost "3 of its biggest department stores, a chocolate company, a razor company and many other businesses." At the same time, people who moved to the suburbs, like O'Malley's correspondent, rarely returned to see a game. "We just cannot continue to have winning teams in Brooklyn without having a winning gate supported by fans."

On the last day of March, O'Malley said he had given up on the notion of "ever getting the politicians and saboteurs together" and declared that his efforts would be focused on moving the team. But even as he said this, in a private letter to his friend Schroth, he wondered whether Robert Moses might consider putting a stadium in Brooklyn's less treasured, and more convenient, Fort Greene Park.

"Now you see the inconsistency of the Irish mind," he confessed. "In one paragraph I am sailing into a distant port and in the last one I am trying to keep my anchor in Brooklyn."

O'Malley's ambivalence would be interpreted by his critics as proof that he was insincere. After all, *he* was the one who insisted on a new ballpark and parking lots. *He* had set the clock ticking when he sold Ebbets Field and declared that he must have concrete action by midsummer. But only the most cynical analyst would say that he had no attachment to Brooklyn. He knew what the team meant to millions of people, and even Robert Moses admitted The O'Malley's hope for a Brooklyn solution was sincere.

In contrast, Horace Stoneham had already concluded he was through with New York. Stoneham had first told O'Malley of his worries about the Polo Grounds and crime in nearby neighborhoods in 1954 when they met with Mayor Wagner to lodge complaints about a city tax on tickets. By the spring of

1957 he was ready to leave town. Stoneham confessed his plans to O'Malley during a three-hour private talk at a league meeting in Clearwater, Florida. The Giants were going to Minneapolis, he said, and he wanted O'Malley to know that he would compensate the Dodgers' St. Paul farm team, because he would be invading its territory.

Minneapolis appealed to Stoneham because he already owned the minor-league franchise there and the city's new municipal stadium, served by large parking areas, could be readily expanded. He had even consulted with a steel company about supplying materials to get the place ready for 1958. O'Malley didn't try to persuade Stoneham to stay in New York, but he did suggest he consider San Francisco instead of Minneapolis. If he moved there and the Dodgers went to Los Angeles, they could create an instant West Coast rivalry and offer visiting teams games in two cities, which would make travel more efficient.

Stoneham had not made much noise about moving the Giants. After issuing a few public complaints about the Polo Grounds and noting that he needed a new stadium, too, he had quietly pursued his options out of the glare of publicity. In taking the opposite approach, O'Malley had spent a great deal of time and money to reach roughly the same position that Stoneham occupied. In the spring of 1957 he may have even envied his crosstown rival. At least he didn't have to deal with Robert Moses.

O'Malley was in baseball commissioner Ford Frick's office when he was called to the telephone to speak to Moses, who invited him to come to his house on Long Island. O'Malley complied, driving that afternoon to Babylon, where Moses occupied a rambling old home near a stream called Carlis Creek.

At sixty-eight, Moses was still an imposing figure. When he spoke directly, he spoke with complete authority, and here he spoke directly. He told O'Malley that he had no chance at a stadium in the part of Flatbush he preferred. They talked about the Parade Grounds and Fort Greene Park and dismissed them both. It seemed, said Moses, that the Dodgers might not be able to build anywhere in Brooklyn. O'Malley would need no more definitive verdict. If Moses said that Brooklyn was out, it was out. In response he told Moses that outside of the team's home borough, New York City enjoyed no sentimental advantage over any other place.

There in Babylon, Moses and O'Malley both knew that, barring some near miracle, the borough of Brooklyn was going to lose its beloved team. They also knew that there were few places anywhere in the entire city where they could find enough land for a modern stadium and space for cars. O'Malley had done his own thorough study and could think of only one long-shot option: Flushing Meadows Park in Queens.

Site of the 1939 World's Fair, Flushing Meadows was 50 percent larger than Central Park, and Moses had long imagined it would become a vast green oasis to serve the entire region. For more than twenty years he had nursed plans for the park's development, and a publicly owned stadium could fit the vision. The men agreed to look the place over together in four days. O'Malley brought his friend Schroth and his engineer Emil Praeger. Robert Moses was accompanied by George Spargo. As they tromped around together, Moses said he liked the idea of placing a dome on the stadium, which meant no more rainouts. And since the land was essentially vacant, the stadium could be built without the slow and wrenching process of property condemnations, evictions, and demolition.

The main drawback at Flushing Meadows was its relative isolation. Little mass transit was available, and since the Long Island Expressway was still a concept and not a highway, drivers would have to reach the stadium via the Grand Central Parkway, which was often overcrowded. O'Malley also had to consider that at Flushing he would be a renter, not an owner, and the lease agreement would be pricey. Moses wanted the Dodgers to cover $10 million in construction costs and all annual maintenance. This could cost O'Malley $1 million or more annually.

It was not the deal O'Malley wanted, but he tried to be receptive. He believed that Moses might still help the Dodgers and feared that Mayor Wagner was actually blocking the stadium. In an account written on the day of the tour, O'Malley noted that Moses hadn't discussed the site with Mayor Wagner or Borough President Cashmore and preferred to keep their tour secret.

The secret got out almost immediately, and the reaction could have been predicted. Brooklyn Borough President Cashmore opposed it and said he would help solicit signatures for a petition urging the city to keep the team in Brooklyn. Brooklyn fans were outraged and soon O'Malley would back away from the idea too. Politics would require that city officials who faced elections in November still talk about doing something for the Dodgers. In the summer to come, they would be seen scurrying to meetings and making pronouncements. But it would be mostly drama for the sake of fans and the electorate.

No one understood the situation in New York better than O'Malley, and he promptly took off for Los Angeles. He arrived at Los Angeles International Airport wearing a pin that said "Keep the Dodgers in Brooklyn." Waiting on the tarmac to greet him, County Supervisor Kenneth Hahn playfully tried to pluck it off his lapel. For the next four days O'Malley would dash around Los Angeles meeting with government officials and business leaders. The public highlight was a fifty-minute ride in a tiny sheriff's department helicopter. Strapped inside the chopper's open-sided Plexiglas bubble, O'Malley gripped the side of his seat as the pilot swooped over Chavez Ravine and the surrounding roadways.

From high in the sky, O'Malley would have been able to make out the peculiar pattern of growth in the city. In Los Angeles, commercial districts grew along main thoroughfares like Wilshire Boulevard. New houses were clustered in vast new developments as builders continually pushed the boundaries of greater Los Angeles outward. (Growing in this way, the population of neighboring Orange County would rise from 200,000 in 1950 to 750,000 in 1960.) The builders also pushed up both sides of the Santa Monica mountain range, which separated the San Fernando Valley and the Los Angeles Basin. The homes they balanced on the slopes allowed for growth even in older communities.

Even in 1957 the boulevards and highways that connected all the pieces of greater Los Angeles were filled with cars. Mass transit, in the form of buses and a rapidly disappearing system of Red Car trolleys, served only a tiny portion of the population. Everyone else drove, and this necessitated acres and acres of parking lots around businesses, factories, and shopping centers. From above, at a time when the cars had not yet overwhelmed the road system, the view of all these vehicles whizzing along freeways and finding their way to their destinations would have left anyone who was airborne with the impression of a place that bustled and moved with the energy of an ant colony. It was also the image of what many people in the postwar era expected the America of the future, in all its sunny, technological, and economic glory, to look like. This vision— something like Tomorrowland at the recently opened Disneyland—included efficient freeways and the swirling, modernist architecture found in the Capitol Records Building, the Beverly Hilton Hotel, and countless futuristic-looking coffee shops, gas stations, bank branches, and motels.

Waiting for O'Malley as the helicopter landed were Hahn, local undersheriff Peter Pitchess, and Del Webb, the Yankees owner. Webb had many reasons to be interested in O'Malley's adventure in Los Angeles. He was, in general, a proponent of expanding baseball to the West Coast and he had pushed the idea of putting the Kansas City Athletics in Los Angeles. But he was also a construction magnate who was interested in the millions of dollars that would be spent wherever the Dodgers built a stadium.

In general, O'Malley got such a warm welcome that it seemed as if the only real problem he would encounter in Los Angeles lay in the competition over who would help him more. Mayor Poulson even arranged for O'Malley to meet the mayor of San Francisco, George Christopher, to discuss the idea of moving the Giants to his city and preserving the Giants-Dodgers rivalry. In the midst of this talk, which took place at the Beverly Hills Hotel, O'Malley telephoned Stoneham in New York and urged him to consider the idea.

During his stay in Los Angeles, O'Malley met resistance only once, in a brief exchange with some members of the board of supervisors. They pressed him for a final commitment and worried that O'Malley was still weighing Los Angeles against New York. In fact Los Angeles had just about won the competition. O'Malley set Emil Praeger to work designing a baseball field that would fit into the dimensions of the Los Angeles Coliseum. And in a burst of candor he said that if the club left Brooklyn it would be for "Los Angeles or some place like that, before it'll be Queens." But O'Malley was not going to declare the matter settled, because the league had yet to grant him permission to move and his team was still playing games at Ebbets Field. As Vincent X. Flaherty would explain to County Supervisor Warren Dorn, "Mr. O'Malley's Brooklyn Dodgers have a full season to play in Brooklyn. If he makes any strong utterance about transferring his franchise, there is a strong chance Brooklyn fans will boycott his games."

A BOYCOTT OF SORTS may have already begun. On opening day, just 11,203 people had come to watch the reigning National League champions defeat the Pittsburgh Pirates. By the start of June the Dodgers had sold twenty-two thousand fewer tickets than they had during the same period in 1956. This apathy was caused in part by the many signs that the team was preparing to leave. It also had something to do with lower expectations about their performance.

The Dodgers team that started the 1957 season was not as strong as previous lineups and they were picked by the nation's sportswriters to finish second to the Milwaukee Braves. The Giants' prospects were considered even less promising, and they saw even fewer fans when they played their season opener at the Polo Grounds. But what else could the players and owners expect? Every day seemed to bring news confirming that the two teams were slowly slipping away, and none of the leaders who might prevent this loss seemed up to the task.

To make matters worse for those who hoped to keep the teams in New York, Californians appeared on a regular basis to woo O'Malley and Stoneham with promises of sunshine and stadiums. According to the National League, no team could announce it was moving prior to October 1, when the regular season would end. (At that point they would have a three-week period to propose a shift.) Walter O'Malley would adopt this date as his deadline and hold to it. But nothing prevented him, or Stoneham, from negotiating with out-of-town officials who came calling.

In mid-May, San Francisco's mayor made a very public visit to New York and posed with the two owners at the Lexington Hotel. While everyone agreed that the rules of baseball barred them from announcing a club transfer until October 1, George Christopher jotted down the terms of a lease agreement that would govern the Giants' use of a new municipal stadium in San Francisco. He also agreed to send Stoneham a formal "letter of intent" as soon as he returned home. After the meeting Christopher announced that his city was ready with millions of dollars to build the new ballpark A few days later, after a New York City councilman complained about baseball pirates from the west, Christopher laughed and said, "If I can steal the Giants away from New York I will do it."

Christopher found allies among the National League owners, who agreed at a May meeting in Chicago to let the Giants and Dodgers move. Final approval would have to wait until October, but according to a wire service report, the jump west had received unanimous support and the owners had reviewed the arrangements, including proposed agreements for TV broadcasts. With two teams heading west instead of one, visiting clubs could economize on travel. They would also create an instant rivalry that would give every fan in California a stake in the National League.

In the face of this challenge, the Sports Center Authority dithered over surveys of sites that Robert Moses had already declared unfit. In a spasm of silliness, city council president Abe Stark proposed that the city become stockholders in the teams. Mayor Robert Wagner called everyone to another meeting. This time, however, Walter O'Malley said no. The citizens of Los Angeles had just killed a $39 million bond issue that would have funded a stadium in Chavez Ravine. Norris Poulson was in town and O'Malley would meet with him instead. While they were together, Poulson suggested that his city might accept the little minor-league ballpark used by the Angels, which O'Malley had just acquired, as even payment for hundreds of acres in Chavez Ravine. Instead of leasing the property, O'Malley would own it.

The big struggle over the Dodgers and Giants was just about finished and New York's mayor knew it. Wagner told the press, "If the owners were set on leaving, we'll just have to pick up our marbles and go home." His petulance showed he was hoping to deflect blame and prepare the city for the loss of two baseball teams. Other politicians would use the baseball crisis to practice political posturing. In the U.S. Congress, Brooklyn representative John J. Rooney stood up to denounce the Dodgers and owner O'Malley. "I say let them move to Los Angeles, if the alternative is to succumb to an arrogant demand to spend taxpayer money to build a stadium for them in Brooklyn."

Rooney was a bit off on the facts. No proposal called for public money to build a ballpark. O'Malley reminded him of this detail in a private letter he sent to his Washington office. "If you were not an old pal," he wrote, "I would really be quite upset with you." He allowed that Rooney had a right to grandstand for "the home folks" but criticized him for being ill informed. O'Malley also telephoned California congressman Patrick J. Hillings and asked him to tell Rooney "all would be forgiven" once he got his complaints out in the letter.

More members of Congress quickly jumped on the issue as the House antitrust subcommittee held another series of hearings on sports monopolies. The cast of characters had changed little since the fruitless investigation conducted earlier in the decade. Brooklyn Democrat Emanuel Celler was still chairman and Patrick J. Hillings was still leading Republican member. (Earlier in the year

Congressman Hillings had attacked the "horsehide cartel" that kept baseball out of his state.) Ballplayers again provided a star quality to the proceedings. Future Hall of Fame pitcher Bob Feller called team owners "arrogant" men who used players as "pawns" and should be brought under antitrust regulations.

Walter O'Malley was summoned on the last Wednesday in June, when Washington was warm and muggy. He took a chair at the witness table after lunch and began his testimony with an exchange with Celler that would give his future critics reason to doubt his sincerity. The transcript of his first exchange with Celler shows the following:

> THE CHAIRMAN: Now Mr. O'Malley, I have to ask you that burning question. Can you tell the committee at this time whether or not the Dodgers will play in Los Angeles next year?
>
> MR. O'MALLEY: I'm sorry, I cannot answer that question.
>
> THE CHAIRMAN: Why?
>
> MR. O'MALLEY: I do not know the answer.
>
> THE CHAIRMAN: Why do you not know?
>
> MR. O'MALLEY: I do not know the answer for two reasons. One, I do not know what the result of Mayor Wagner's study in New York City will bring. Two, I do not know whether or not Los Angeles will be ready for major league baseball next spring.
>
> THE CHAIRMAN: What preparations have you made for moving to Los Angeles?
>
> MR. O'MALLEY: None whatsoever.

There may be some legalistic definition of the word "preparations" that would make this answer accurate. But as people generally understand the word, O'Malley had definitely made preparations. He had purchased the Angels and their stadium and requested Emil Praeger to lay out a diamond in the Coliseum. There was no sin committed in these acts and they didn't amount to a full commitment to put the Dodgers in Los Angeles. But for some reason O'Malley just wasn't comfortable acknowledging them.

For a man who was so skilled in business relationships and negotiations, O'Malley gave a surprisingly bad performance as a public witness, and without the friendly crowd his father played to at City Hall back in 1921, he didn't have the benefit of a chorus. At several points he followed simple questions with long, convoluted answers that didn't provide the information the committee sought. At other moments he engaged in unnecessary verbal duels. Just like his father, he offered a flurry of detailed observations on everything from the price of meat in the public markets to the value of certain airplanes.

Some of O'Malley's talk showed a bit of wit. He got a laugh when, in the middle of a discussion of the Sports Center Authority, he said, "We had that magic which is so important in politics, we had two Democrats and one Republican, we had a Catholic, a Protestant, and a Jew, and it looked like everything was fine." At another moment, when pressed to confess that he was in baseball to make money, he admitted playfully, "I have never said that baseball was not a business. I think it is a sort of silly business, but it is a business anyway."

In general, however, O'Malley's jousting with the committee made it look like he was being coy when he didn't have to be. As the long hearing transcript reveals, O'Malley explained in great detail why he needed assistance finding a site in Brooklyn. He told how local officials had failed to provide it and then revealed why he was considering Los Angeles. Most important, he reminded the members of the committee that when they last brought baseball officials to Washington, one of their main complaints was the game's neglect of the West.

"Of course, five years ago you gave a great deal of encouragement to move out to Los Angeles," said O'Malley, "but now you are reversing yourselves."

He was right. Major-league baseball was under pressure to move west. Brooklyn fans may well have expected this to be accomplished through expansion, with new teams being created. But Los Angeles and San Francisco were valuable territories. It made sense that owners who were already inside the game but frustrated with their current conditions would recognize the gains to be made. Why would O'Malley and Stoneham let newcomers seize such enormous opportunities?

WALTER O'MALLEY LOST BROOKLYN fans at the Celler hearing. News of this divide came from the calm and literary Red Smith of the *Herald Tribune*. On the day O'Malley testified, Smith attended a press conference where George V. McLaughlin, O'Malley's onetime mentor, called on the city to fund a team that would replace the Giants and Dodgers if they departed. The club could occupy the site in Flushing, Queens, he said, and keep New York in the National League.

Columnist Smith, who presented McLaughlin as a public-spirited "man-about-Brooklyn," wrote that New Yorkers were growing impatient with the dickering over the Dodgers. Bypassing Moses, the mayor, and other officials, Smith laid the blame on the team's owner. The Dodgers had made more money than any other in recent years, he said. Of course, like any businessman, O'Malley had the right to move. But Smith suggested he "go to Los Angeles leaving the Dodgers behind."

Through the summer, New Yorkers were challenged to accept that two great teams, long entwined in the emotional life of the city, were about to depart. Robert Moses moved to deflect blame and heap responsibility on O'Malley with a long article in *Sports Illustrated* titled "Robert Moses on the Battle of Brooklyn." Few other people in the world could have commandeered more than half a dozen pages of the nation's leading sports magazine. But on July 22, there was Moses making his case and staring out at readers from a photo that made him look like a trout wearing a bow tie.

At length Moses repeated the false claim that O'Malley wanted a government-built park and the equally fictional claim that he wanted it reserved for the exclusive use of a baseball team. After describing a process in which, he said, "O'Malley and his chums have kept us dizzy and confused," he concluded that no stadium would be built in the Brooklyn site under consideration. "It won't happen," he declared, and he then argued for his long-planned stadium in Queens. He acknowledged those in Brooklyn who might grieve the loss of the team but added, "It could hardly be classed as a tragedy." Certainly Moses himself, who described baseball fans as "oafs . . . hecklers and bottle throwers," would not mourn.

After Moses condemned the Brooklyn stadium idea, it surprised no one that the final engineering reports on the borough's sites affirmed his judgment. According to these studies, the cost of acquiring land, clearing it, and building a park would exceed $20 million. Other improvements in the area would cost even more. These prices seemed to make the project a poor investment, according to the analysts, who said investors would be unlikely to buy the bonds offered to pay for it.

Although no elected official ever acted and no vote was taken, with the reports and declarations of the engineers, Robert Moses killed the proposal to build a stadium in Brooklyn. But the next man to act was not O'Malley but Horace Stoneham, who didn't seem much concerned about the league rule about delaying franchise moves until October 1. On August 19 he accepted an offer from Mayor Christopher of San Francisco. It included a thirty-year lease on a new $8 million municipal stadium and every penny earned from concession sales. Rent would be 5 percent of the clubs' receipts at the stadium, minus taxes and payments made to the league and visiting teams. No rent would be charged for postseason play or all-star games.

Besides a new stadium on favorable terms, Stoneham got a relatively affluent and growing local market with three million residents. San Francisco officials estimated that the Giants would bring as much as $40 million worth of economic activity to the region, not to mention the effect on local pride. Other baseball team owners praised Stoneham for moving to the coast, and in Los Angeles, County Supervisor Kenneth Hahn said the Dodgers would announce their move west in a month or two.

At the Dodgers office, executives made plans for transferring their franchise to Los Angeles. A confidential interoffice memo dated August 12 spelled out fifteen major issues and tasks that would have to be considered, ranging from staff relocation to publicity spending in Southern California. The plan, which envisioned games played at the Los Angeles Coliseum, noted millions of dollars in expenses and short-term losses in revenues. At the bottom of the last page O'Malley inked in the number 16 and wrote, "How about $10 million cost for the type stadium we want?"

Publicly, team officials left open the possibility that the right arrangement would keep them from leaving Brooklyn, and in response a desperate scramble ensued. The city's counsel, Peter Campbell Brown, challenged Robert Moses with a legal argument in favor of using government power to put together a site for a private stadium. At the same time Nelson Rockefeller came forward with a few million dollars to contribute to the cause. The convoluted plan called for the city to spend $8 million on the site and then sell it to Rockefeller for $2 million. He would then give the team a free lease of the land for twenty years or let the Dodgers buy it from him.

Mayor Wagner got baseball fans excited by summoning O'Malley and Rockefeller to discuss the idea, but he gave them only false hope. According to the Byzantine rules that governed development in the city, such an end run around Robert Moses would require support from a body called the Board of Estimate. So few members of the board supported the idea, they didn't even have to take an actual vote to kill it. Moses himself forecast Rockefeller's defeat. In a letter he sent to the mayor's secretary, he wrote, "Nelson has been badly advised" and the city had "nothing to gain" from his proposal. "This Dodger business," he concluded, "reminds me of the jitterbug jive."

MAYOR WAGNER CAPTURED HEADLINES with his last-minute efforts, and the publicity—combined with opposition by the Board of Estimate—would be useful as he campaigned for reelection in November. While he sought political cover, fans who sensed the end of both the New York Giants and the Brooklyn Dodgers grieved in their own ways. Some gave up going to games. Others made sure to get to the ballpark for old times' sake. In a season when attendance at the Polo Grounds averaged less than 8,500, more than 57,000 went to see the last three-game series between the Giants and the Dodgers.

The final game played in New York by the two clubs was won by the Giants, who would leave New York with a record of 656 wins against 606 losses in baseball's most fevered intracity rivalry. Two weeks later the Giants then ended their dismal season (sixty-five wins and eighty-five losses) at home before about eleven thousand people. Old-time players hailing from as far back as the 1890s attended the game and were introduced to great applause. The widow of John J. McGraw, who managed the team through three decades, received a big bouquet of roses. Amid the nostalgia the Giants lost to the Pirates 9–1.

After almost all the fans had departed, many carrying souvenir pieces of turf, three horn players occupied the visitors' bullpen and fired up the Giants' fight song. They were joined by a dozen or so fans who added their voices to the performance. Normally a rousing call for cheers and excitement at Coogan's Bluff, the song in this context was a dirge. This was especially true when they got to the last lines:

Come watch those Polo Grounders
Do their stuff.

As the song echoed around the empty stadium, stragglers in the grandstand, including an old woman who wiped tears from her eyes, complained about the tune, insisting it was too happy to be played at a wake. But as he listened to them complain, a lone Brooklyn fan who had come to gloat asked, "What are you moaning about? You're lucky the Brooklyn Sym-phony didn't attend the wake. They would have haunted the Giants all the way to San Francisco."

Despite a tradition of making a ruckus, the Sym-phony wasn't even noted in newspaper accounts of the last game at Ebbets Field. Played on a cool Tuesday night after the team had been eliminated from the pennant race, the game attracted just 6,702 people. The small turnout—and complete absence of ceremony—might be blamed on confusion, since Walter O'Malley had said he would delay his decision on the team's future until early October. No former Brooklyn greats or wives of famous managers attended. The sad-faced clown Emmett Kelly pretended to wipe tears with his sleeve, and once the Pirates had been defeated 2–1, organist Gladys Goodding affirmed their assumptions by playing "Auld Lang Syne."

THE CLOWN AND the organist believed the Dodgers were leaving, but the deal between O'Malley and the city of Los Angeles was not set. Mayor Poulson and the young city council member Rosalind Wyman, who had emerged as a leader of the baseball cause, had met some opposition. A few members of the council resisted setting aside money for roads into the Chavez Ravine ballpark site. Others thought the ravine property, roughly three hundred acres of steep hills and gullies, was worth more than Wrigley Field, which the city would get in trade. These concerns had to be overcome before the city could even begin to negotiate.

Unlike Robert Moses, the mayor and other key officials in Los Angeles believed they could help develop a stadium site with public funds. Of course, the circumstances were different. In New York, the city would have had to clear a densely developed urban neighborhood. In Los Angeles most of Chavez Ravine was already public property, and while a few residents still lived there in defiance of eviction notices, no great relocation effort was required because the place had been emptied for the public housing project that never materialized.

Los Angeles officials also believed they were competing with other cities for an asset with real value. Harold "Chad" McClellan, who was appointed to deal with O'Malley, argued that Los Angeles was getting the team at a bargain price. Milwaukee, Kansas City, and San Francisco offered their clubs city-built stadiums. All O'Malley wanted was to swap Wrigley Field for the ravine. If the city built some roads, he would build the stadium. Naturally he would then own it and benefit from its revenues, but if he paid for it, why shouldn't he profit?

All these points were made during a long council meeting in September, during which the plan got preliminary approval. In early October they met for most of a day to hash out the final offer. In the course of the debate the council added a public recreation area to the site, and O'Malley conceded rights to any oil that might lie beneath the property. With TV news cameras rolling, one section of spectators cheered for the proposal as if they were at a ballgame. In another section, opponents matched them with cries of "Giveaway!" Pro-baseball citizens presented a fifty-foot-long petition covered with signatures. A lawyer named Julius Rubin said he had filed a lawsuit against the deal.

Finally, on the night of October 7, the mayor and Wyman labored to get the two-thirds majority required for the council's final approval. Several votes depended on a guarantee that O'Malley was going to accept the terms. When they retreated to a private office to call him, Poulson suddenly got nervous and pushed the phone into Wyman's hands. She picked it up and introduced herself. (During more than a year of campaigning to bring the Dodgers west, she had never actually met the owner.) She then pressed him for a commitment.

"I am going to the floor," she said. "I would like to say you are coming."

As Wyman later recalled, even at this late date O'Malley refused to limit his own options:

He said, "Mrs. Wyman, I am grateful for everything you have done, I am grateful for everything the mayor has done, but I have to tell you if I could get my deal in New York, I'd rather stay in New York."

I said, "My God, I can't go to the council."

I felt relieved for a minute when he said, "I think everything is right for me there in L.A." But then he went back again and said, "I think baseball is an unknown out there."

For someone who had never before dealt with The O'Malley, it was a confusing conversation. She wanted reassurance. He gave it to her—and took it away in the next breath. It was possible he was still angling for the best deal or revealing his own true ambivalence. Critics would say that evasion was merely part of his style. However, in previous talks with city officials, O'Malley had talked about being "burned" by public officials in New York. He was worried about it happening again.

Whatever lay behind O'Malley's ambivalence, Roz Wyman experienced his wavering as a bit of political torture and realized that if she reported everything he had said, she might lose the vote. As she hung up the phone she decided that her only option was to pray that no one asked her if he had made a firm commitment. Like O'Malley, she hedged. No one asked the direct question she feared, and when the roll was called, she won.

Two days later, at four in the afternoon, Dodger publicity man Arthur "Red" Patterson walked into a pressroom set up at the Waldorf-Astoria Hotel in New York for reporters covering the Yankees-Milwaukee World Series. He handed out a single-sheet press release that tersely declared the end of major-league baseball in Brooklyn.

So much had been said and written in advance of this formality that it didn't generate a big press outcry. Also, thanks to the Soviet Union's surprising launch of Sputnik on October 4, a much bigger issue occupied the media's attention. The satellite was serious business. It made people worry about geopolitics and nuclear war. Though an emblem of civic pride, the Dodgers were also a business and the owner had every right to pack up and move. The editorial writer for the *New York Times* recognized these facts and—after expressing gratitude for zany Bums, Jackie Robinson, and thrilling games—wished the team "a grand slam success for the future."

Others, especially kids who imagined they were Newcombe and Snider as they played stickball in the streets, were upset. Not quite ten years old, Brian Mylod had been closer to the struggle over the Dodgers' future than any kid in Brooklyn. His father was head of the Sports Center Authority. His godfather was Walter O'Malley. He had hoped with all his heart that they would succeed in keeping the team in the borough. When they failed, he felt devastated.

In part because of his personal connections, Brian Mylod would recover, accept the loss, and even marvel at Walter O'Malley's ambition and risk taking. But for others, sadness would harden into resentment. It was one thing for Lou Perini to transfer a broken franchise to Milwaukee and a fresh start. But the Dodgers were both financially sound and competitive on the field. No one had ever moved such a successful franchise. Branch Rickey criticized the decision on these grounds and later called it "a crime against a community of three million people."

The tragic view of the Dodgers' move would be encouraged and preserved by a culture of grievance built on stories, accusations, emotions, and black humor. The founding father of this art form was Dick Young of the *Daily News*. A talented pioneer of more assertive sports reporting, Young also knew how to play to the hometown crowd. Two weeks before the decision was final, he began what would become a long-running attack by writing that baseball was just a passing interest for O'Malley, who was really concerned about real estate. The day after the move was announced, Young's report, which ran on the news pages, began, "Walter O'Malley, the most momentous manipulator baseball has ever seen, yesterday officially moved the Brooklyn Dodger franchise to Los Angeles."

A few days later the Milwaukee Braves of Hank Aaron and Eddie Mathews won the World Series in a decisive fashion, becoming the first non–New York champions in a decade. Freed of what *Time* magazine called "a civil inferiority complex," the beer capital of the country staged a celebration that was bigger than the bash that accompanied the end of Prohibition. Major-league players who watched the Braves claim their victory could only envy them for an experience that capped a season that Aaron called "the best year of baseball that any city ever had." Major-league owners, O'Malley included, might find themselves jealous of the all-time attendance and cash-receipts record set by the seven-game contest. Perini, it seemed, had made the right choice.

Eleven

THE BATTLE OF CHAVEZ RAVINE

On the morning of October 23, 1957, the twin-prop Dodger Convair hummed down the main runway at New York's LaGuardia Airport and lifted off the ground. Observers in the control tower and travelers who happened to gaze out terminal windows would have seen that a sign painter had written "Los Angeles" above the Convair's portals, where markings had previously announced to the world that the plane carried the "Brooklyn" Dodgers.

Rising toward and then piercing the low-hanging clouds, the plane carried Walter O'Malley and about thirty others—executives, broadcasters, secretaries—who were moving west with the team. O'Malley left behind his lifelong home and more than sixty years of Brooklyn baseball history. He took with him a few regrets and enormous hope.

The regrets included his failed attempt to build a stadium in Brooklyn. He loved the borough and the city of New York, and neither his wife, Kay, nor his daughter, Terry, wanted to leave friends, family, and the only home they had known. Most of his employees felt the same way. He also regretted how he had handled his communications with the press and public. "Our public relations have been very bad and probably I am the one to blame," he had confessed earlier in the month. The hope that balanced these regrets revolved around his dream of building and owning a great stadium that would be home to a team capable of competing at the highest level every year.

A perennial contender could be maintained only with high attendance and the cash flow to pay for big stars and player development in the minor leagues. The Braves had proven this point. After leaving Boston with the third-worst record in all of baseball, they had built a winning team by selling an average of more than two million tickets per year for five years running. The effort had just been rewarded, as the Braves defeated the Yankees in the most recent World Series. The championship was their first since 1914.

If O'Malley wanted to be the best, he had to match if not beat the Braves, who were powered by double the ticket sales he had made in Brooklyn. Moving to Los Angeles was one of his ideas for reaching this goal. Another involved pay TV. After years of exploring subscription television, O'Malley had concluded that televised games cost teams more in lost ticket sales than they made up in fees paid by broadcasters and advertisers. He was working closely with the pay TV pioneers at Skiatron, who promised to solve this problem.

Promoted by a former advertising man named Matty Fox, Skiatron planned to sell set-top boxes that customers could use to descramble special TV signals and watch ball games, movies, and other programs. The charge, say $1 per game, would make the easy chair in a fan's living room into the equivalent of a revenue-producing seat at the ballpark. O'Malley, who met often with Fox and was excited about Skiatron, estimated that pay TV could generate $4 million or more per season in Los Angeles. With this in mind, he and Horace Stoneham had worked on a pilot contract with Fox that could lead to games on pay television up and down the West Coast. O'Malley would also lend Fox and Skiatron more than $120,000 in the hope that the firm would win permission to operate in Los Angeles and start generating cash flow.

In imagining the possibilities in California, O'Malley was not so different from the millions of Americans who had moved to the state since the end of World War II. This wave of relocation was, by itself, an engine of opportunity, creating demand for goods and services and jobs in the businesses that grew to meet these needs. Baseball wasn't an essential product, but O'Malley was certain of the demand and would have the state's biggest market all to himself. Even so, his plan was remarkably ambitious. With roughly $4 million in cash, he would try to create a winning team and construct the first private major-league stadium since Yankee Stadium was built in 1923. His success would depend on the city's appetite for baseball, the vagaries of the game itself, and a political process that no one could control.

And unlike other California seekers, O'Malley would pursue his quest in public. It was part of the bargain team owners struck as they pursued a business that was generally associated with community spirit and identity but also dependent on the cooperation of various levels of government. Teams got "deals" involving land or municipal stadiums because political leaders believed their presence stimulated economic activity and gave a city status that somehow translated into growth and development. Because of the relationship created by these attachments and arrangements, many people felt as though they owned the hometown team.

In Los Angeles this feeling of ownership was so strong that on October 23 local radio and TV stations reported on the progress of the Dodgers plane in the same way that they followed Santa's sleigh on Christmas Eve. Those who tuned in knew that the Convair had landed for fuel at Oklahoma City. They were told when it passed over Prescott, Arizona. Thousands headed for Los Angeles International Airport when they heard the plane would touch down at 5:55 p.m., just moments after sunset.

Dusk was also the perfect time for viewing the large booster rocket orbiting with Sputnik, the Soviet satellite, as it streaked along the horizon, because it caught the sun's reflection from the other side of the earth. Some of those who waited for the Dodgers plane would spot the sparkle. Everyone heard the cheers as the distinctive Dodgers aircraft, decorated with a big image of a red-stitched baseball under the pilot's window, swooped down onto the runway and then rolled to a stop. Police let the official welcoming party, led by Councilwoman Roz Wyman and County Supervisor Kenneth Hahn, onto the tarmac. They were followed by the crowd of well-wishers, a squad of sixty "Bruins Belles" from the University of California Los Angeles, and even small trucks bearing TV cameras and bright lights. Behind them massed the Inglewood Boys Band.

Inside the plane, the crew waited for the propellers to stop whirling and then released a folded set of steps that swung down to the ground. The O'Malley, a large man weary from a long flight, appeared in the doorway wearing a fedora, blazer, and neatly knotted tie. With the band playing as he stepped into the television lights, a roar came from the crowd. The Belles tossed flower petals.

He waved and smiled broadly as he descended to be greeted by Wyman and Hahn, who wore blue caps emblazoned with the letters "L" and "A". More of these hats were distributed to the passengers waiting onboard, and most wore them as they followed O'Malley into the bedlam.

A microphone and loudspeaker had been set up beside the airplane, and after Roz Wyman shouted "Welcome to Los Angeles!" she stepped aside so O'Malley could utter a few words. Amid the cheers he said, "I just hope, for all of you, an early world championship team." Then, with the TV cameras still rolling, a couple of men muscled through the crowd to reach the knot around the dignitaries. One carried a sign that read, "We want the Bums but not the bum deal." The other held a paper out for O'Malley to take and said in a voice loud enough for the news crews to hear: "Greetings from the City of Los Angeles. We're glad to have you here. Here's a summons from the people of Chavez Ravine."

O'Malley wasn't bothered by the process server. "You did your job," he told him. O'Malley then tucked the paper away and moved on to the downtown hotel where the team would establish an office and he would take up temporary residence. The coming days would bring a full schedule of meetings and a "Welcome, Dodgers" luncheon attended by more than a thousand of the city's business and political leaders.

Every table at the Pacific Ballroom of the Statler Hotel was decorated with Dodgers pennants and piled high with peanuts, Cracker Jack, and soda pop. Mayor Poulson wandered the hall wearing a sash reading, "Lord Mayor of Baseball," and as the police band played "California, Here I Come," Walter O'Malley led a lineup of team officials and players—Campanella, Snider, and others—to the head table. When the honored guests reached their chairs and a retired local umpire cried "Play ball!" they collected sponge-rubber baseballs that had been set on the table and threw them into the crowd.

The banquet gave the city a chance to celebrate its victory over New York and elevation to baseball's major leagues. It also provided a social setting where vendors, buildings, bankers, and others could meet team executives who might offer them business. Branch Rickey was part of this crowd, and he later ushered a banker named Howard Rust into a private session with O'Malley, who spent the better part of a week receiving visitors at an office in a downtown hotel.

Between the social events, political maneuvering, and a stream of supplicants, O'Malley at work resembled John McCooey and other powerful men of old-time New York. Of course, he sat atop a private corporation rather than a political organization. But baseball teams were almost civic entities. The stadiums they occupied were landmarks and, as hosts of major events, became hallowed places in the public mind. New ones generally required some government cooperation, and this always gave the people a sense of ownership. For these reasons the men who owned teams and pushed for new ballparks tended to look, sound, and move like politicians. Among them The O'Malley, who could balance hundreds of relationships in the pursuit of innumerable goals, was the best. His cigar-waving, favor-granting style would be familiar to anyone who had ever walked into Tammany Hall. O'Malley's success was all the more remarkable given the limits on his power. He controlled no votes or party jobs or precinct apparatus. His only leverage was in his power to give a city baseball or take it away. And having made his choice, he was vulnerable.

LESS THAN A MONTH after O'Malley was welcomed like a hero, an armored truck pulled up to Los Angeles City Hall. As reporters and photographers gathered on the sidewalk, the driver and a guard armed with both a shotgun and a pistol got out and retrieved some boxes from the truck's locked compartment. Together they crossed the sidewalk, climbed the steps to an arched portico, and then marched inside to find the city clerk's office. There they delivered a referendum petition with the signatures of more than fifty thousand citizens who wanted to reconsider the deal that brought the Dodgers to Los Angeles.

The petition had been circulated by a group called the Citizens Committee to Save Chavez Ravine for the People. The name suggested it was a grassroots organization formed to benefit the handful of households still living in the ravine. In fact it was a well-funded political group that had hired a professional contractor to collect signatures. (According to some reports, the collectors actually told some of those who signed that the petition actually favored the city's arrangement with the team.)

Support for the committee came from local theater owners and television executives who feared competing with Dodgers, especially if games were broadcast on pay TV and fans could watch at home for a small fee. It was led by J. A. Smith, one of two Los Angeles brothers who owned the Pacific Coast League team in San Diego. If the Dodgers deal went forward, Smith stood to lose fans who would choose the big league over his Padres. Naturally, Smith never mentioned his personal stake in the issue. Instead he complained that "nitwit politicians" had given O'Malley too many acres at Chavez Ravine and charged that city officials hadn't considered the value of possible oil deposits beneath the sandy surface of the land.

Smith didn't mention that no survey had ever found oil on the property or that O'Malley had already given the city rights to anything of value—oil, gold, silver, etc.—that might ever be discovered there. O'Malley had also accepted several reductions in the size of the ravine tract. Originally, Mayor Poulson had talked about 650 acres. The ultimate agreement called for the team to receive a site half that size where, considering slopes and gullies, only about a hundred level acres could be put to use. Of these, O'Malley would have to give up forty for a city recreation area. What would remain would be adequate for a fifty-two-thousand-seat ballpark and, this being the car capital of the world, parking for seventeen thousand cars.

But even if the arrangement was more equitable than opponents claimed, the opposition did have the public relations advantage of claiming to speak for a village of poor Mexican-Americans descended from the first settlers to occupy land granted to them in 1781 by King Carlos III of Spain. In this tale the Dodgers were displacing a vibrant community of hundreds of people who had managed without the aid of city services to build a warm, nurturing home. Of course, anyone who visited would discover that Chavez Ravine was almost uninhabited. The city had bought nearly every home for its cancelled housing project. In 1957 only about twenty families actually remained in the ravine. But how many voters would make the effort to find the place and navigate its dirt roads and paths to see for themselves?

With the Citizens Committee to Save Chavez Ravine for the People, O'Malley faced the same kind of almost mythic populist challenge he had met in Brooklyn, where the press acted as if he had crushed every heart in the borough. The difference was that his opponents in Los Angeles had the power of the referendum, which was approved for a vote in June 3. Called "Proposition B," it would require people to vote yes to approve the land swap.

Instead of a paradise filled with opportunity, O'Malley's Los Angeles had turned out to be a place where process servers greet you at the airport and business competitors ask the voters to ruin your plans. While all this went on, O'Malley also ran into problems with the Coliseum commission. Disputes arose over the rent and how a baseball field would be set up inside the giant oval-shaped arena.

Through all these early challenges, O'Malley received insider advice from Vincent X. Flaherty. In his long letters Flaherty informed O'Malley on personalities and policies and assured him that even "those who don't like me, respect me, because I have a lot of bodies buried on my chart." Flaherty called Jim Smith, the head of the commission that ran the Coliseum, "an all-American ass" but praised Roz Wyman for her baseball efforts, which included pitching for the Dodgers on local TV news broadcasts. Flaherty also passed along season-ticket requests from Bob Hope and other Hollywood figures.

O'Malley's anxieties were revealed in his responses to Flaherty, which show a man who felt besieged. He worried over members of the council who seemed to be having second thoughts and broadcasters aiming to defeat the Dodgers because of pay TV. "I honestly believe the publishers and writers will do a terrific job on the referendum," he told Flaherty, "but the local radio and TV boys will probably murder us. Enough for now," he concluded. "I might feel better tomorrow."

Always a booster, Flaherty did his best to encourage O'Malley, telling him that he should expect to sell three million tickets a year in his new hometown. He said "the Chavez group is a well-organized minority" that could be "knocked for a loop" if The O'Malley could harness the pro-baseball sentiment in the city. The Pasadena Rose Bowl could be an attractive alternative for the Coliseum, he added, even if it was a bit far from the center of the city. "If you can get a good deal over there, by golly take it."

If O'Malley held any hope for a good deal at the Rose Bowl, it was soon dashed. On the day that he toured the Pasadena stadium with National League president Warren Giles, a local lawyer announced he would organize a referendum to block the Dodgers there because the city parks board was legally barred from letting any profit-making group use the stadium. With this option clouded and their home opener just three months away, the Dodgers faced the prospect of camping at Wrigley Field, which could seat just twenty-two thousand.

It was the least attractive option and could deprive O'Malley of the revenue he needed to profit in his new home. Throughout baseball, his friends and competitors agreed that if he had it to do over again, the Dodgers boss would not have left Brooklyn. One National League owner feared that the move to the West had been made in haste. Larry MacPhail said O'Malley's decision to go to Los Angeles was shaping up to be a colossal mistake and that the Dodgers would never occupy the Coliseum, the Rose Bowl, or Chavez Ravine. But they all agreed that the Dodgers owner was too proud and stubborn to ever return.

As he made one last run at the Coliseum commission, O'Malley offered $600,000 for a two-year agreement but held firm on his demand that the field be laid out with home plate at the west end of the stadium. The college and pro football teams who used the Coliseum objected to this scheme because they thought it would cause the most damage to their field. But after considering the cash and weighing the public relations cost of turning the Dodgers away, the commission gave O'Malley access to the big stadium. He didn't get all he wanted, as the commission maintained its ban on beer sales, but the vote "ended my longest losing streak," said a beaming O'Malley. It also began one of the quirkiest episodes in the history of major-league play.

SOON AFTER THEY WON the commission vote, the Dodgers began to construct a playing field that would fit into the Coliseum. Typical baseball stadiums of the era were shaped like diamonds or blunted triangles. Home plate would be wedged into a corner and foul lines ran straight along the base paths out to bleacher seats located about 325 to 400 feet from home. Maximum distance to deepest center field was rarely more than 410 feet. A short section of the outfield, like the 310-foot left field at Fenway Park in Boston, could be made less dangerous for pitchers with a tall fence or wall. Balls that failed to clear these barriers could be played by fielders.

Challenged to put a diamond-shaped field in a long oval, the Dodgers had to allow for one very short section of outfield. Given a hometown lineup with several good right-hand hitters, they made the short side left field, and then bought a forty-foot-high steel-mesh fence to protect spectators. Even with this barrier, a right-handed batter could get a home run with a pop-up that would be an easy out in every other major-league ballpark. The far corner of right field was also short—300 feet—but the fence that began there was angled out to make right-center field so vast that it would be extremely difficult to hit a home run in that direction. Besides mapping out the dimensions, the Dodgers had to construct a pitcher's mound on a platform that could be lifted off the field for football games and then reinstalled.

For fans, the Coliseum would offer about forty thousand seats with reasonable views of the diamond and another fifty-two thousand that were so far from the playing field that it would be hard to follow the action without binoculars. In a city accustomed to major-league baseball, no owner would expect to fill many of these bad seats. But in Los Angeles, where the game was new and people seemed to have a special appetite for spectacle, O'Malley could reasonably expect crowds of sixty thousand and more.

The crowds would get to watch a Dodgers lineup that included old stars such as Pee Wee Reese, who was almost forty, and Carl Furillo and Gil Hodges, who were in their midthirties. Familiar names from the sports pages and TV broadcasts, their presence would reassure true fans that they were getting the real Dodgers. But the team would be without its inspirational heart, the perennial all-star and three-time league's Most Valuable Player, Roy Campanella.

At the end of January, the Dodger catcher was paralyzed in a car accident. The crash happened at around 3:30 a.m. on a stretch of road less than two miles from Campanella's home on the north shore of Long Island. News reports said only that the car, which he was driving alone, skidded on a wet road, turned onto its side, and slid into a telephone pole. A doctor who lived nearby heard the crash and rushed outside while his wife called the police. He found Campanella trapped in the car and gave him a sedative to keep him calm while rescue workers pried open a door to get him out. Campanella arrived at a local hospital conscious but unable to move. Surgeons operated on broken vertebrae in his neck. Despite the severity of the injury, they offered hope that he might recover well enough to walk.

A spirited performer who was liked by almost everyone in the game, Campanella was not the type of player who could be readily replaced. He described himself as "still a kid" and so devoted to baseball that he couldn't imagine retiring. "They'll have to cut my uniform off my back," he said. In the weeks after his injury Campanella would mention getting back in the game, but this was never a realistic prospect. He would not leave the hospital for months, and the team planned to honor him by retiring his number.

Campanella's recovery was followed closely in the press, and his absence depressed the mood at spring training. Ironically enough, the man most affected may have been the one who had hoped to take Campanella's job. Twenty-four-year-old John Roseboro had been called up from the Montreal Royals in the middle of the 1957 season, in part so he could be tutored by Campanella. At spring training he was expected to compete with Campanella for the starting position and team officials believed the contest would be good for both men. Instead, like all the other Dodgers, Roseboro would face the season without the advice and steady presence of a veteran catcher who had helped focus the team for a decade.

As the regular season approached, players wondered about what awaited them in their new hometown. Those with families worried about finding houses in places where they could enroll their children in good schools. Rambunctious bachelors like Johnny Podres looked forward to being celebrities in a city where they could meet movie stars and would-be stars in nightclubs and restaurants. O'Malley and Buzzie Bavasi, who had been given the new title of general manager, brought Charlie Dressen back to the team as a coach. (Despite their previous contract battle, O'Malley considered Dressen "one of my best baseball friends.") They hoped his outgoing personality would balance the quiet style of manager Walter Alston.

When they left Vero Beach, the team headed westward instead of north and played exhibition games in Texas, Nevada, and Arizona. In Tucson they had an old "Bums" kind of moment. The team had decided to let coaches use a base runner's name to signal a steal. Outfielder Gino Cimoli was on third base when a photographer snapped his photo and called out, "Who was that?" Coach Charlie Dressen answered, "Cimoli," and his dutiful player took off for home, where he was promptly tagged out.

The Dodgers arrived in California ahead of the Giants, landing at the airport in San Francisco, where Mayor Christopher greeted them and said, "I just hope we don't beat you too badly." The Giants were officially welcomed later with a parade witnessed by more than one hundred thousand people. The players rode in cars accompanied by various marching units, including the Chinese Girls Glockenspiel Band.

The same Widow McGraw who witnessed the last Giants game at the Polo Grounds attended their first in San Francisco, along with the roughly twenty-four thousand who packed minor-league Seals Stadium. Before the game Mrs.

McGraw reported that she had recovered from the shock of the Giants' move to San Francisco and approved of Horace Stoneham's decision. The home team won 8–0 on a day that was sunny and warm. The playful headline in the next day's *San Francisco Chronicle* cried "We Murder the Bums."

Back in New York, where radio station WINS had aired a re-creation of the Giants-Dodgers opener via teletype reports, the editors of the *New York Times* played the West's major-league debut on the front page. Under a headline that noted games "Everywhere But Here," side-by-side photos showed the big crowd at Seals Stadium and a lone maintenance man cleaning empty seats at the Polo Grounds. Around the region, *Times* writer Murray Schumach found bitterness (mostly in Brooklyn) and resignation. In the reactions of three representative Dodgers fans, he documented the themes that would dominate the analysis of the team's departure for decades to come:

A man on the street in Brooklyn said, "Why did the Dodgers leave? I'll tell you. Because they were greedy. They made money here but they wanted more."

A Long Island homeowner, recently arrived from Brooklyn, confessed, "Since we've moved out here we care more about crabgrass and weed killers."

A cabdriver parked near quiet Ebbets Field concluded, "It's a damn shame. It wouldn't happen if La Guardia was alive."

These three witnesses got it right. Although Walter O'Malley would call it ambition rather than greed, his lifelong hunger for more of everything had propelled the process that brought the Dodgers to the West. Nevertheless, even the most anti-O'Malley fan would have to allow that fans had abandoned the team as they moved to the suburbs and city leaders bore great responsibility for the loss of not just one team but two at the same time. Roz Wyman, the young city councilwoman who had courted O'Malley, would never get over the magnitude of this mistake. Los Angeles and San Francisco didn't steal their new ball clubs, she would say: New York let them go.

Of course, New York was the last thing on Wyman's mind as she anticipated the Dodgers' first game in Los Angeles. The buildup to the home opener had gone on for weeks as the rich, powerful, and famous jostled for the best tickets. Roz Wyman, who had just given birth to her first child, had to win an argument with her obstetrician before he agreed she was well enough to attend. Seven-year-old Jimmy Hahn, who would grow up to become mayor of Los Angeles, joined his county supervisor father in the parade of cars, including a fleet of

Edsels, that brought the team from downtown to the Coliseum. (Jimmy, dressed in a little Dodgers uniform, sat in the backseat of one car, wedged between shortstop Don Zimmer and outfielder Norm Larker.)

While confetti rained on the Dodgers in downtown Los Angeles, the Giants dressed in their locker room at the Coliseum and trooped onto the field for batting practice. Some laughed out loud when they saw the layout. Right-handers imagined popping flies over the left-field fence, while left-handers wondered how they could ever get a home run in a place where a shot to right-center field would have to travel at least 445 feet to go out. "They weren't thinking of [left-handed] Duke Snider when they built this ballpark," noted Willie Mays. "He ain't gonna reach that fence." When he got his turn, Mays hit six over the left-field screen.

Pitchers were not so amused. San Francisco's Johnny Antonelli took one look and declared the ballpark "a farce," and Dodger Ed Roebuck said it was the "Grand Canyon with seats." When he first saw the Coliseum arranged for base-ball, Red Smith, the dean of American sportswriters, said the field was designed along "scandalous and stultifying proportions." He called it "the O'Malley Fun House" and questioned whether the events conducted there could be rightly called major-league baseball games.

The only good thing that Smith could say about the Coliseum was that it held a huge number of spectators, and on opening day 78,672 showed up. Carl Erskine, who pitched for the home team, was impressed by the size of the crowd but a bit puzzled by the relative quiet. "They didn't make half as much noise as thirty thousand in Ebbets Field," he would recall.

All through spring training Erskine had felt as though he were embarking on just another season, but in San Francisco he had been hit by the reality of the team's move. Sentimental by nature, he would miss Brooklyn and worry about the distractions in Los Angeles. "I was on the mound in the third inning and noticed that half our guys were looking at the movie stars in the stands."

Erskine managed to lead the Dodgers to a 6–5 win, but he gave up two home runs to the short-left field. The Giants came back to take the next two games and win the home-away series four games to two. Eleven home runs were hit over the left-field fence in the first three games at the Coliseum, seven by the visitors. When Erskine got his second start in the Coliseum, a Cubs pinch hitter blooped a very good pitch—on the handle of the bat—over the left-field fence to win the game. Erskine, feeling cheated, glared at the screen and fought the impulse to throw the ball over it to prove "how cheap that home run was."

Cheap hits contributed to an uneasiness that infected the entire pitching staff and continued through the season. Tops in the league for earned run average for 1957, the pitching staff was last in 1958. The hitters were no better as the long-mighty Dodgers plunged to seventh place and finished twenty-one games behind the pennant-winning Braves.

The experience was most frustrating for Duke Snider, who suffered a self-inflicted injury during an early Dodgers home stand when, during practice, he tried to throw a baseball out of the cavernous Coliseum. Responding to a $200 dare from shortstop Don Zimmer, he dislocated his elbow on his third try. The sore arm caused him to miss one game, for which he was fined $200 by Buzzie Bavasi.

As the season wore on, the strange ballpark stymied Snider as a batter and he went from hitting forty home runs the previous year to just fifteen. Dodgers pitchers also suffered, but the odd ballpark wasn't to blame for all of their troubles. Don Newcombe hated the Coliseum and considered it "a ridiculous place to pitch," but he was also undone by the varied nightlife available in Los Angeles. Recently divorced, he became a regular at the most popular clubs and dated several glamorous women, including the singer and movie star Dorothy Dandridge. He lost six games and won none before the team traded him to Cincinnati.

Other Dodgers had trouble adjusting to Los Angeles simply because it was so different from Brooklyn. They found the freeways puzzling and their families felt out of place. "There was complete chaos on the ball club," recalled pitcher Don Drysdale. More than once, players wondered why the team ever left Brooklyn, and Drysdale—who was born and raised in California—agreed with those who wished the move had never been made. Scattered in neighborhoods all over the Los Angeles area, "we lost that community closeness," he would write in his autobiography.

To no one's surprise, certain people in Brooklyn took great pleasure in the Dodgers' struggles, which they were able to witness on television, thanks to a new station that had arranged to broadcast games every time the team played in St. Louis or Pittsburgh. An enterprising *New York Times* reporter named Gay Talese, who would one day be regarded as a pioneer of the New Journalism, tracked down a handful of Brooklynites in mourning and gave them a chance to speak. Lou Soriano of the Sym-phony reveled in the team's last-place standing, while Hilda Chester scoffed at the idea of taking a bus to see them play in Philadelphia, the nearest National League town. Michael Brown, who had once called Don Newcombe a choker and then found himself in a scuffle, said he couldn't be happier.

Sour grapes could be expected from fans who felt abandoned, but Jackie Robinson's criticism of O'Malley was especially bitter. Dismissing the contributions of newcomers like Sal Maglie and Sandy Amorós, he told New York reporters that the Dodgers' 1956 World Series should be credited to Branch Rickey and that Walter O'Malley alone should be blamed for the team's troubles in Los Angeles. Robinson made this assessment as he criticized the National Urban League's decision to honor O'Malley and the team for its contribution to racial progress. "That's preposterous," he said upon learning of the award. O'Malley, who had supported Robinson's signing and the addition of many other black players in the Dodgers system, did not respond.

THE PAPERS IN New York published frequent reports on the Dodgers' struggles, and some of the coverage played to those who relished the idea of the old team and Walter O'Malley stumbling. In Los Angeles the two sides in the battle over Chavez Ravine revved up a fierce campaign. J. A. Smith, the minor-league team owner who poured money into stopping the Chavez Ravine land swap, did his best to frame his fight as a stand against a sly outsider who was taking advantage of a city drunk on the spirits of baseball.

As Smith noted, O'Malley was getting a much bigger and vastly more valuable property in the ravine, which was close to downtown Los Angeles, than he was giving up at old Wrigley Field, which was in a run-down neighborhood. He also claimed that the Dodgers owner had inflated his potential investment in a new stadium. The initial estimate of $10 million was growing, in some reports, as high as $15 million, but Smith insisted the job would be done for about a quarter of that amount. Denying he acted "for selfish reasons," Smith presented himself as a champion of the taxpayer and gave ten-to-one odds to anyone who would wager that the voters would approve the O'Malley deal.

A more pointed argument came from a group that called itself the Committee for Public Morality, which distributed a pamphlet that revived long-standing suspicions about local politics. According to the committee, a "totalitarian clique" was trying to "kick aside the Constitution." The clique included the same suspects—politicians, businesspeople, newspaper publishers—identified a few years earlier in a book called *Billion Dollar Blackjack* written by a former president of the Los Angeles City Council named William Bonelli. According to Bonelli, this powerful group used money and influence to dominate local politics for their own benefit. In the case of Chavez Ravine they had killed the public housing program and preferred private development. He predicted that Mayor Poulson would do their bidding.

In theory California's referendum system offered ordinary voters a counterweight to the power elite, but in many conflicts it was hard to tell where the interests of the typical citizen might rest. Powerful individuals and institutions could and did use their money and manpower to put items before the voters and then campaign for their approval. In the case of the Dodgers, most of the business community lined up behind O'Malley, and hundreds devoted both time and money to seeing the proposition pass. Business boosters could see the value of developing Chavez Ravine and bringing crowds of people to the downtown area for games.

The other side of the issue was also backed by wealthy individuals who stood to gain if they prevailed. J. A. Smith and his allies found a spokesman in city council member John C. Holland, who denounced the land trade at every city council meeting. (These sessions also offered opportunities for any citizen with the impulse to be heard. At one, a veteran character actress named Glen Walters stood up and shouted about O'Malley "stealing my oil" until she was dragged out of the room by police.)

More than others, Holland made the fight personal. He described O'Malley, whose portly appearance gave him the look of an old ward heeler, as a "political boss" who "tried to assume veto powers over public transactions." The inference was clear: California was getting slickered by a New York operator. Holland was joined by City Councilman Karl Rundberg, who claimed that public roads promised for the stadium would raise the value of the Chavez Ravine land, most of which was purchased for less than $1.3 million, to $18 million. When he was challenged by Rosalind Wyman, he rose to his feet and shouted, "I'm sick and tired of your needling every time I discuss the Dodger deal."

Wyman had become O'Malley's lead supporter on the council and in the community. The big crowds at the Coliseum had made her more convinced than ever that the benefits of keeping the team merited the bargain the city had struck. In the weeks leading up to the June 3 election, she got deeply involved in the campaign, which called on people to vote yes on Proposition B, for "baseball." As part of the effort, the Dodgers handed out lots of free passes for ball games and Wyman's mother infiltrated opposition meetings to bring back insider information. Others promoted the ballpark as a futuristic development, like the recently opened Disneyland, that would add one more wholesome attraction to a region that represented a modern way of life characterized by neat suburbs and commuter-packed freeways. Editorial writers and columnists at all the major papers favored the Dodgers. The most aggressive was Vincent X. Flaherty of the *Examiner*, who defended the Chavez Ravine deal in column after column and wrote that opponents sought to make Los Angeles "the biggest backward city in the world."

The backing of the press helped O'Malley maintain an optimistic front, but the prospect of a defeat weighed on his mind. When a writer from *Sports Illustrated* came to follow him around for a few days, he talked mainly about baseball's potential in California. He thought the "sports-starved" state could eventually support four major-league teams and fans would travel a hundred miles to see them play "if it's made convenient and pleasant for them." But in a less-guarded moment he allowed himself to wonder "why people are turning against me." He quickly changed his tone, however, adding, "Baseball is a democratic game. I can't say I'm not disappointed, but I've got to take it now. Let's hope and expect the referendum vote will be overwhelmingly in our favor, so there'll be no question of Los Angeles keeping its agreement."

O'Malley didn't make a concerted public appeal until the very end of the debate when many of the city's showmen (and a few women) put on a television pitch for the passage of Proposition B. Dick Walsh, a Dodgers executive at the time, would recall that the team paid for the TV time, making it an advertisement and not the kind of political program that would require the station to give the other side equal time.

As the "Dodgerthon" went on the air, the Associated Press was reporting that the majority intended to vote against the Chavez Ravine deal. Then Jerry

Lewis, Debbie Reynolds, and Dean Martin started talking. They were joined by George Burns and Jack Benny, who told jokes to spice up their pleas, and Ronald Reagan, who opted to play it straight.

"Chavez Ravine has been sitting there in the heart of Los Angeles for years and nothing was done with it," said Reagan, who had yet to jump from acting to politics. "Now that a baseball team is to have it, it's worth a lot of money, we are told. Sure, Walter O'Malley got a good deal when he was offered Chavez Ravine as a site for his ballpark. Any deal, to be good, must be fair to both sides."

Over the course of nearly five hours broadcast over channel KTTV, the Hollywood stars were supplemented by Jackie Robinson and Casey Stengel, who supported the cause via videotape. Altogether, pro baseball was promoted as a community asset and an all-American antidote to juvenile delinquency. More than 1.8 million people saw some part of the extravaganza, and more than seven thousand of them got so excited they went to the airport to welcome the team as it returned that night from a road trip. Cameras set up there showed cheering fans waving pennants and placards that read, "Vote for baseball."

On election day, when the voters got their ballots, they saw a summary of the agreement that would turn Chavez Ravine into a baseball mecca. It explained that the Dodgers would receive land worth up to $6 million and roads and grading that would cost the city and county as much as $4.7 million. In exchange the team would donate Wrigley Field to the city and build a forty-acre recreation area at the ravine, which they would maintain at a cost of $60,000 per year.

The turnout for the election was very high, as more than 62 percent of the registered voters showed up at the polls. With the Dodgers scheduled for a night game against Cincinnati, O'Malley went to the Coliseum to await the tally. On the field his young pitcher Sandy Koufax, not yet the dominant star he would become, walked four in a row before he had to be replaced in a losing cause. In the press box O'Malley obliged news photographers who asked him to pose with a hot dog and the tape from a news ticker machine.

The reporters and team executives hardly paid attention to the game as the Dodgers' chief publicity man, Red Patterson, held a telephone to his ear and periodically barked out early vote counts. His source was not the best. The first count was 17,559 in favor of the Chavez Ravine deal and 16,648 against. This was followed in five minutes by another count that also found the measure passing, but the margin was 5,681 to 5,178. The game would end with a Dodgers loss before any conclusive result came from city hall.

By the end of the night Proposition B was approved by a margin of roughly 25,000 out of 675,000 votes cast. The voting pattern, which showed that many districts voted against the position held by their city council representatives, suggested a very independent electorate. Most surprising was the huge yes vote in the very district where the ravine was located. Represented by an opponent of the land swap, Edward Roybal, the area was home to a relatively poor and mostly black and Hispanic population. Given the demographics, one might expect them to resent the notion of families being displaced. However, the people of the district knew the ravine and its history better than others, and apparently preferred to have baseball there. The main opposition came from the mainly middle-class and white districts of the San Fernando Valley, but it was not strong enough to overcome overwhelming approval for the proposition in places like South Central and Downtown.

Immediately after the election, O'Malley talked about clearing land in the coming months. But before anyone could stick a shovel in the earth, a California court ruled in favor of taxpayers who had sued the city council in hopes of invalidating the Chavez Ravine agreement. The judge said that the city council had exceeded its authority and violated rules requiring that development of Chavez property serve a public purpose. The city's attorney immediately asked the California Supreme Court to overturn the ruling. The court accepted the case, but no work would be done on the site as it deliberated.

All of the struggle, ending in a continued stalemate, led one City Hall worker to tell *Look* magazine, "It is the courtship of a lunatic ball club and a lunatic city. Naturally the wedding ceremony has to be one for the lunatic book."

WHILE VARIOUS SIDES MADE their legal moves, the Dodgers continued to play baseball—poorly. The team's hitters popped lots of home runs over the short-left-field fence, but their opponents hit even more. Dodgers pitchers, who had to cope with the strange ballpark during half the games on the schedule, never got used to it, and their collective earned run average was the worst in the league. They did, however, capture a couple of records. Sandy Koufax threw the most wild pitches and Don Drysdale hit more batters than anyone else in the league.

In general the Dodgers seemed distracted and preoccupied. As they plummeted toward a seventh-place finish and their worst record in fifteen years, fans joked about the possibility of bringing a big-league team to their city. But even as they teased and sometimes booed, people still came to the ballpark. Through the long summer, when the temperature in the Coliseum often reached one hundred degrees, they broiled in the bright sun and cheered as the losses mounted. Ultimately 1,807,426 paid to see a game, the most ever recorded in the history of the franchise. In all of baseball, only Milwaukee drew more fans—the margin was about 125,000—but *they* finished in first place. As a nearly-last-place team, the Dodgers' drawing power was remarkable. They far surpassed the world champion Yankees, who, despite having New York all to themselves, actually sold seventy-five thousand fewer tickets than they had the previous year.

The Dodgers' success was based in part on novelty, but it was also built on the voice of broadcaster Vin Scully, whom O'Malley brought to Los Angeles from Brooklyn. O'Malley had been encouraged to hire a local announcer, but he had confidence in Scully. Before the season began, the two men discussed the tone of the broadcasts and O'Malley wondered, "Don't you think you ought to root for the team?"

"I was trained to go down the middle," answered Scully.

"I appreciate that," answered O'Malley. "That's what the people like here, so you stick with it."

From opening day Scully served as a reliable guide to the game's nuances, characters, and history. He taught millions who listened in cars, homes, and workplaces to appreciate good play and strategy. Dogged in his pregame research, he always had a tidbit to tell about a player coming up to bat and an anecdote about the relief pitcher warming up in the bullpen.

Because most Dodgers away games were played in later time zones, Scully had a huge audience of commuters who tuned in on the drive home from work to catch the first innings of night games played in the Midwest or East. Drivers became so enraptured that when they got to their homes they remained in their cars until the end of an inning. Others raced inside to switch on radios that played through the dinner hour. All across Southern California, the genial Scully became a virtual guest in dining rooms and kitchens.

Scully had his greatest effect on fans in the stadium who brought transistor radios—a rather recent invention—and listened as he narrated the game they were watching. While most knew the stars on the field, Scully helped them to know every player and to grasp the flow of the game. The sound from thousands of tiny speakers could be heard by players on the field, and feedback "gave the engineers fits," he would later recall. And all the eyewitnesses put extra pressure on Scully to be accurate. He quickly grew comfortable with the relationship and sometimes played with the crowd. Once he organized them to shout "Happy Birthday" to an umpire at the end of an inning.

The bond Scully created with Los Angeles fans helped them to make the Dodgers their own, even though they arrived with a deep history. The connection also helped the broadcaster through a tough year that included the Chavez Ravine controversy and the first losing season in his Dodgers broadcasting career. "We had a choice to come out with fresh new faces or the old familiar team that people had heard about," said Scully. "We came out with that recognizable team, but a lot of them turned out to be over the hill. Still, the people supported us. And I never saw Mr. O'Malley really discouraged. Instead I could see his mind working all the time, working on the solutions to the problems."

THE DODGERS ENDED the 1958 season with a loss at the hands of the Cubs. The only player who left the Coliseum with any feeling of accomplishment was Snider. After the game he had gone back onto the field with Don Zimmer to settle the wager they had made in April. This time Snider hurled a ball over the rim of the stadium. Zimmer gave him the $200. With Bavasi forgiving the fine levied for his absence in April, Snider felt as if he had made a nice end-of-season bonus.

While the players retreated for the off-season, Walter O'Malley took a break to celebrate his daughter Terry's marriage to a young investment executive named Roland Seidler. The wedding marked the start of a long and very happy marriage, and the reception introduced the newcomers from the East to yet another peculiar part of life in Los Angeles: wildfires. During the party, which was held outdoors at a hotel in Pasadena, ashes from a nearby fire danced in the wind like snowflakes.

When O'Malley returned to work, the management group led by Buzzie Bavasi focused on reviving the team that would take the field at the Coliseum for a second season. O'Malley and Bavasi discussed replacing manager Walter Alston, but then decided "to let him have a bad year," as Bavasi said, and still keep the job of manager. Bavasi made one significant trade, sending Gino Cimoli to St. Louis for an outfielder from St. Louis named Wallace "Wally" Moon, who, though a bit older, seemed a much better hitter.

Winter brought good news from the California Supreme Court, which upheld the Chavez Ravine agreement, rejecting claims from citizens who argued that the arrangement was one-sided and violated restrictions on the transfer of public land to private interests. The plaintiffs in the case planned appeals and promised to go all the way to the United States Supreme Court if necessary. In the meantime, however, the state decision would allow some of the work related to the stadium to proceed.

As they went to spring training for the 1959 season, the Dodgers could feel a bit more secure about their future home. At Vero Beach the team, especially its younger pitchers, showed signs of improvement. They got a big shot of inspiration when Roy Campanella arrived to work as a coach. Campanella, who had remained on the team payroll, had some use of his arms and hands but even with extensive physical therapy would never walk again. Though strapped into a wheelchair, Campanella was able to critique hitters and coach the young catcher John Roseboro.

When the Dodgers flew west to start the regular season, Campanella followed. After a good start that put them in second place, the team took a break from the normal schedule to play an exhibition game against the New York Yankees in honor of Campanella. The largest crowd ever to attend a baseball game—93,103—turned out to pay tribute to a man who had never played in a Los Angeles uniform. He was introduced to great cheers before the game and honored, at the end of the fifth inning, when the lights were dimmed and tens of thousands in the stands held up lighted matches and cigarette lighters.

Those who witnessed the Campanella tribute would recall it as one of the most stirring sights they ever saw. James "Jimmy" Hahn, the future mayor, stood by his father on the field and was awestruck as he watched the flames flicker,

row by row, up to the rim of the Coliseum. He was also impressed as his politician father, ever mindful of news photographers, eased an attendant aside so he
could push Campanella's wheelchair onto the field. After the game Campanella
would receive a share of the proceeds, and his relationship with the club and
friendship with O'Malley would continue for the rest of his life.

ON THE MORNING AFTER Los Angeles poured its heart out for Roy Campanella, a caravan of patrol cars, moving vans, utility trucks, and construction
equipment arrived at Chavez Ravine and stopped at one of the few little houses
still occupied by a family. Television news crews quickly followed and filmed
continuously as sheriff's deputies knocked on the door and workmen closed
water mains, shut off gas supplies, and shut down the electrical service.

One by one, the deputies escorted people from this home and one other.
Some went quietly, but others were literally carried out screaming and thrash-
ing. Deputies kept them away as possessions were hauled out and into the mov-
ers' vans. When this work was done, the operator of a waiting bulldozer revved
its engine and drove it, blade first, into the first home. In a short time both
houses were reduced to rubble and splintered wood.

Led by sixty-seven-year-old Manuel Arechiga, the evicted residents refused
to leave. Instead they pitched tents and announced they would stay the night.
Supporters arrived and by evening forty people gathered around campfires.
Their city councilman, Edward Roybal, visited to offer his outrage over an act
he deemed "very cruel," and Mr. Arechiga complained that he had been offered
$10,500 for a house worth $17,000.

Television reports of the eviction stirred outrage in the city, and within days
the Arechigas and their supporters packed into the city council chamber to
confront those who had ordered the deputies to act. They told such a sad and
compelling story that members of the council offered money from their own
pockets—$250—for the family to use to rent a temporary home. But sympa-
thies soon shifted as local papers reported that the tale of hardship was not
entirely accurate. Instead of being poor squatters, the Arechigas were owners of
eleven additional properties scattered around Los Angeles. After hundreds of
families accepted payments and left in the early 1950s, they had lived rent- and
tax-free at Chavez Ravine for more than five years.

The immediate public concern over the evictions receded as the press filled in the background of the conflict. Those who knew recent history understood that the city had begun to dismantle the traditional community in Chavez Ravine long before the Dodgers even considered coming to the West. This action, the first step in the housing program that was subsequently cancelled, was a tragedy for those who loved the community. It was also typical of redevelopment efforts around the country in which officials ignored positive elements of poor communities and, seeing only substandard housing, traumatized residents as they replaced vibrant neighborhoods with sterile housing blocks.

In Chavez Ravine, the housing never materialized and over time a legend developed. O'Malley and the Dodgers became villains, along with city officials, and the displaced community was recalled as an ethnic paradise of lush gardens and frequent fiestas. Many who followed the team believed that this conflated version of events led Mexican-Americans to resent the Dodgers and stay away from games. The true effect of the conflict would be difficult to measure, but the team did try to appeal to the Latin American community with Spanish-language broadcasts of Dodgers games. But for years announcer Jaime Jarrin, hired by O'Malley in 1959, would encounter anti-Dodgers sentiment, even among his own friends.

"It became this truth, even though the facts were different," recalled Jarrin many years later. "Some people just decided that what happened in Chavez Ravine was all because of the stadium and wouldn't listen to any other point of view."

THE BATTLE OF Chavez Ravine left some in Los Angeles angry and resentful, but people who voted for Proposition B paid to watch the team at the Coliseum and, tuned in to hear Vin Scully's play-by-play, quickly forgot the conflict and focused on the team on the field. What they saw was a younger, more effective group of hitters and a pitching corps that was greatly improved. New outfielder Wally Moon, relying on advice he got from Stan Musial—he recommended a well-timed wrist flick—popped a bunch of home runs over the left-field screen. Dodgers pitchers finally adapted to the strange layout at the Coliseum by keeping the ball away from right-handers and forcing lefties to hit it into the huge expanse of right-center field.

Playing with new energy and confidence, the Dodgers reached August having won thirteen more games than they lost. Drysdale led the league in strikeouts. The next day the team moved past Milwaukee and into second place. Just ahead, in first, were the newly relocated San Francisco Giants. All of California went baseball mad and the crowds at both the Coliseum and Seals Stadium grew bigger. On August 8, more than ninety thousand people came to see the Dodgers beat Milwaukee. That night's attendance would have set a record for a regular-season game if not for the fact that more than twenty thousand got in free and thus couldn't be counted. On August 31, in a sign of things to come, Sandy Koufax struck out eighteen batters in one game, setting a new league record.

With San Francisco matching them win for win, the Dodgers-Giants rivalry burned as fiercely as it had in New York. Both teams jostled with the Braves for the pennant and the Dodgers passed the two million mark in attendance on September 16. The next day five thousand people showed up to watch a groundbreaking ceremony for what O'Malley called "the greatest stadium in baseball," the stadium at Chavez Ravine.

The support Los Angeles showed for the team matched the Dodgers' unexpectedly good play. A similar scenario played out in San Francisco as fans in both cities began to hope they would see a World Series. To add to the excitement, crews at Candlestick Point began working round the clock so they could finish the Giants' new ballpark in time for postseason games.

In an echo of years gone by, the Giants and Dodgers played each other in a critical series as the season neared its end. The Dodgers won all three games, ending their rivals' hopes for a first-place finish and setting up a race with the Braves. In their last game of the regular season, the Dodgers beat the Cubs at Chicago's Wrigley Field and secured a first-place tie with Milwaukee. Fans in Los Angeles, listening to Vin Scully call the game, rejoiced to hear their team had risen from next to last in 1958 to a share of first in 1959.

The tie required the team to stay in the Midwest and travel by train from Chicago to Milwaukee for the first game in a best-of-three playoff. This event should have affirmed the wisdom of the National League's move into profitable new territories, which the Braves had led as pioneers. But a strange thing happened at County Stadium in Milwaukee. When the teams took the field, more than half the seats were empty. Here Milwaukee's boys were fighting for a shot at the World Series and only 18,297 people bothered to show up. Arthur Daley of the *New York Times* wondered if success—two pennants and a world championship—had spoiled local fans. Whatever the cause of their apathy, the team responded with a desultory performance, losing 3–2 in a game that wasn't nearly as exciting as the close score might have suggested.

The second game of the playoff series was held in Los Angeles, where the crowd at the Coliseum was twice as big as the one in Milwaukee. Because of the time zone difference, the TV broadcast of an afternoon game reached fans in the East as they finished the workday. Millions watched as the Dodgers scored three runs in the bottom of the ninth to gain a tie and force extra innings. The ABC network preempted programs called *Sugarfoot* and *Wyatt Earp* to show the game as it stretched into the bottom of the twelfth. Viewers were rewarded with more drama than any TV show could ever provide.

Holding true to the Hollywood formula, which requires a crushing setback just before the hero prevails, the Dodgers loaded the bases in the bottom of the eleventh but couldn't squeeze a single run out of their rally. In the next inning aged Carl Furillo, no longer a starter, hit a single with two outs and sent Gil Hodges home with the winning run. In just their second season the Los Angeles Dodgers had gone from next to last in the National League to the World Series.

Even before the series began, the Dodgers of 1959 had given Los Angeles and major-league baseball a pennant-run story better than most. The onetime Bums from Brooklyn had gone west and found great success with a mix of old and young players. As the championship round arrived, they were blessed with a fitting opponent. The Chicago White Sox hadn't won a pennant since they were disgraced by the World Series betting scandal in 1919. With their success, Chicago had gone so crazy for the team that when it clinched the pennant, 750,000 turned out to hail them in a parade.

Chicago hosted the first game and, with the standing-room folks included, more than forty-eight thousand jammed Comiskey Park to watch the home team slug their way to an 11–0 win. It was an uncharacteristic performance for both teams, but especially the Sox. They had hit lightly all season long and depended on walks and steals to win in a hustling style they called "go-go" baseball.

Many fans in Los Angeles followed the games on TV. Others listened to

Scully on the radios that blared the play-by-play in banks, libraries, movie studios, and even a funeral home. At the airport control tower, where radios were
banned, anxious staff sent teletypes begging for updates. The whole region felt
some relief when the Dodgers took the second game 5–4. Soon after play ended,
the teams, the families, and league officials were airlifted to Los Angeles on
seven airplanes chartered from United Airlines. (The only man missing was
Buzzie Bavasi, who fell ill during the game and was hospitalized for exhaustion.) White Sox fans filled every scheduled flight heading west from Midway
Airport, with many happy to make connections through San Francisco and
other cities. Those who went without holding tickets would be hard-pressed to
find them. Early birds had scooped up every one—roughly 276,000—available
for the three games.

Advance sales guaranteed that the Dodgers would break the single-game
World Series attendance record of 86,288 set when the Braves visited the Cleveland Indians in the 1948 series. It also meant that players would have to struggle
to see the pitched ball against a background of fans, many of whom would wear
light-colored clothes. (During most games the seats in the distance behind the
pitcher were empty, creating a grayish backdrop.) This problem affected umpires, who sometimes lost sight of the ball after it left a pitcher's hand, and
outfielders who couldn't track pop-ups. Joe DiMaggio said it was so severe that
he wouldn't even attend the games at the Coliseum because he couldn't follow
the ball.

Thanks to the Coliseum board's ban on beer sales in the stands and a scoreless contest on the field, the 92,394 who did attend the first game at the great
bowl sat rather quietly through six innings. They finally erupted as the Dodgers
loaded the bases and scored two on another Furillo single. Catcher John Roseboro gunned down three "go-go" runners attempting to steal, and the Dodgers
won by a score of 3–1. More then twenty-four million people, a record for any
program, watched the game on TV.

In the next game a 5–4 win gave Los Angeles the hope that they could capture
the championship at their home field. However, the White Sox scrambled to win
1–0 and send the series back to Illinois. Dodgers fans, many of whom sat so far
from the action they had to use binoculars, nevertheless cheered for both squads.
Educated by Vin Scully's radio lessons, they were showing an appreciation for
the game that would distinguish Dodgers crowds for decades to come.

The visiting team and many out-of-town reporters were happy to flee the Coliseum, where the sun baked the field to nearly a hundred degrees and the strange configurations of the diamond made purists cringe. (Writers said left fielders were forced to play a game they called "Screeno," when hits bounced off the fence.) But even at Comiskey Park, where conditions were cool and comfortable, the White Sox couldn't quiet the Dodgers hitters. They scored six runs in the fourth inning—and sewed up the championship—by winning 9–3. With the final out, horns blared on every freeway in Los Angeles,

A championship affirmed Walter O'Malley's leadership. With Alston managing and many key players products of the new regime, no one could call the team a Branch Rickey creation. It was Walter O'Malley's team and it had just set records for World Series attendance (420,784), revenues ($2.6 million), and payments to players ($892,365).

The series also confirmed the wisdom of opening the West Coast to baseball and cemented the team's relationship with greater Los Angeles. As the record-setting crowds at the Coliseum showed, the region loved the Dodgers and the team unified people in Southern California in the same way that it had unified Brooklyn.

At first glance the comparison may seem strange. Brooklyn was an old, compact, traditional urban place. Los Angeles was new, sprawling, and quirky. But just like Brooklyn, it comprised many distinct communities and was deprived of a true downtown center that created a firm sense of place. Superficial as it may seem, the Dodgers became a kind of social glue that bound all these communities together with a sense of pride. Anyone who doubted this fact only had to glance at the crowd of thousands who converged on the airport to greet the team as it returned from Chicago. Included were television stars, high schoolers, laborers, and people from various ethnic backgrounds. Among the many signs was one hoisted by a group from the Mexican community that read "Bravo Pancho O'Malley."

IN JUST THEIR SECOND season in Los Angeles, Walter O'Malley's Dodgers had broken New York's eleven-year grip on the World Series and brought the first championship to California. And they were, without doubt, O'Malley's Dodgers. Only one player from the Rickey era, Gil Hodges, played in every game of the series, and all four of the Dodgers' wins were notched by post-Rickey pitchers.

O'Malley had just about everything he needed, except for a final ruling on the land he needed to build a permanent home. He was still waiting for the United States Supreme Court to rule on citizen lawsuits protesting the Chavez Ravine deal. As the defendant, the city and its lawyers, argued the case, O'Malley was left on the sideline. However, he was so confident in the outcome that he didn't pursue alternative plans or grumble in public about construction delays. He simply waited, certain the court would rule in his favor.

Ten days after the world champions returned to Los Angeles from Chicago, the United States Supreme Court finally rejected all the challenges and affirmed the Chavez Ravine land agreement. The news from Washington cleared the last real barriers between O'Malley and construction of his stadium. In light of this success, his approach to a little zoning squabble was a bit excessive.

The conflict occurred when local officials balked at approving O'Malley's plans for the ravine because the set of drawings his staff gave the city showed restaurants, souvenir stands, and other businesses outside the stadium. His opponents rose against using the land for these shops. In the discussion that ensued, O'Malley again threatened that the team might leave if he didn't get his way. When the city council was assured that the stadium development wouldn't include the extra businesses—the plans showing them may have been submitted in error—they approved the plans. O'Malley got what he wanted, but in the process he gave his critics ammunition.

"Until the wily Walter reached the Pacific Coast, the Angelenos didn't know what a curve ball looked like," wrote Arthur Daley in the *New York Times*, which continued to cover the Dodgers with special interest. "But they sure know now. O'Malley has thrown so many curveballs that they instinctively back away from the plate as soon as he goes into his wind-up."

In time O'Malley would confess that he had been "high-handed at times" when dealing with politicians in Los Angeles. "I have a temper," he said, "and when irritated I can tell people off." But he also would claim that he had been confused by the local political culture and that his honest mistakes contributed to a negative image. "I had been informed that a western politician was a hearty, candid fellow whose handshake was his bond," he told an interviewer. "I learned otherwise—about some of those with whom I have dealt—and my reaction is responsible for that word you used: image."

For O'Malley's doubters, the extras in his plans for the ravine revealed his own tendency to seek an advantage whenever possible. In fact, the mistrust that arose between O'Malley and some city officials revealed that politics is the same the world over. Elections in Los Angeles were nonpartisan and candidates tried to present themselves as the very antithesis of East Coast ward heelers. But in reality they could be as manipulative and power hungry as anyone in Tammany Hall.

O'Malley's adjustment to this style of politics was rough. He stumbled again when he give local sportswriters color TVs for Christmas in 1959, and the clucking gossip at City Hall grew loud enough to make it into the newspapers. City officials then felt compelled to report the gifts he had given them. Norris Poulson confessed to getting a bat autographed by players. Roz Wyman had received some perfume. This embarrassing episode would mark a change in O'Malley's approach. In the future he worked even more quietly behind the scenes and tried to change his style—including a shift to more casual clothes—to fit his new home.

Twelve

EL DORADO

On February 23, 1960, roughly two hundred curious Brooklynites trooped through the grand rotunda at old Ebbets Field and gathered in the forty-degree sunshine near home plate. Joined by Ralph Branca, Carl Erskine, and Roy Campanella, who sat in a wheelchair, they applauded when little boxes of dirt were handed to the retired players and listened to a band play "Auld Lang Syne." Then a crane positioned near third base lifted a wrecking ball—painted white with crudely drawn red stitches—over the visiting-team dugout. The operator let the ball loose and it crashed through the dugout roof with a hollow thud. Carl Erskine, feeling sick to his stomach, turned and walked away.

In the two years since the Dodgers departed for Los Angeles, Ebbets Field had hosted soccer teams from Italy, Spain, Sweden, and Great Britain. (More than twenty thousand came to see Edinburgh defeat Manchester in May of '58.) High school, college, and labor union teams had played amateur baseball in the old park, and the Negro American League brought Satchel Paige and Joe Black in for some exhibition games. These events had put a little life into the place but never changed its fate.

Anyone looking for resentment about the Dodgers would find it in the newspapers. Just before the wrecking ball swung, *New York Times* columnist Arthur Daley noted that it would complete the work that Walter O'Malley "cold-bloodedly started" and declared, with melancholy, that "only priceless memories" remained. Daley and Dick Young of the *Daily News*, who had already charged O'Malley with seeking the "the adulation and fawning" of "Coast sycophants," would periodically needle the Dodgers owner for years to come.

But as much as the New York press might demonize O'Malley, the people of the borough didn't show much anger toward him in the period immediately following the team's flight. As Roger Kahn reported at the time, "There were no pickets, no mass protests, no suicides. In fact, there was almost no reaction. . . . [W]ithout the Dodgers in Brooklyn it develops, you still have just about what you had before—a busy, crowded heterogeneous borough." Similarly, Brooklyn had barely reacted when the Dodgers won the 1959 World Series. So few were interested in the Dodgers games broadcast on local TV that the station's management decided to stop showing them. The divorce, it seemed, was final.

In Los Angeles, O'Malley had too many problems even to think about the old neighborhood. Referendums, lawsuits, and squatters had added another two years to his quest for a stadium. The delay had raised the estimated cost of construction from the $10 million estimated in 1957 to as much as $15 million in 1959. Big cost increases are typical for major construction projects. In San Francisco, where voters had approved a $5 million bond for Candlestick Park, the real price turned out to be three times as much. However, taxpayers would share the burden in San Francisco, while at Chavez Ravine, every penny of extra cost would be paid by O'Malley alone. This was the bargain he had struck as he sought to build and own his personal baseball palace, and he stood to gain enormously if he succeeded. But the risk was also great, and he operated under real pressure.

Assessing O'Malley's risk would be difficult. As a private entity, the Dodgers filed no public accounting reports. However, many of the team's key financial facts—attendance figures, ticket prices, Coliseum rent, player salaries—were reported in the newspapers, and anyone who was curious could make a stab at estimating O'Malley's financial position. Traditionally, baseball fans, players, and sportswriters have made a game out of guessing an owner's wealth, in part to imagine how the other half lived and in part to determine whether enough money was being spent to get the best players.

Before the 1960 season began, writer Jim Murray analyzed the Dodgers for *Sports Illustrated* and concluded that in California O'Malley had found the mythical New World city of El Dorado. Counting the windfall from postseason play, Murray guessed that O'Malley's team took in roughly $7 million in 1959, compared with $3.8 million for their last World Series season in Brooklyn. Expenses were also substantially higher, but he estimated that net income before taxes topped $3 million, which was more than any team had ever earned. O'Malley "saw gold in the West," wrote Murray, and he had "cornered a nice solid part of it."

Had Murray been privileged to see them, the Dodgers' books would have shown him a little less gold than he imagined. Due to some quirks in the lease, rent for the Coliseum would rise by $500,000 in the coming year. At the same time O'Malley would be required to spend almost as much to compensate minor-league clubs for the invasion of their territories. Finally, there was the expense of acquiring the few acres of Chavez Ravine land that didn't come in the deal with the city. Before O'Malley came along, these properties, combined, were appraised at less than $93,000. He would spend half a million dollars to get them.

As the money poured out, O'Malley obsessed over the stadium project, continually scanning reports on every aspect of design and construction and making decisions on every key element. He wanted the best quality at the best price and dug for the information that would help him get it. The purchase of seats—he needed more than fifty thousand of them—was a case in point. The American Seating Company began by asking for $16 apiece. When company officials met with O'Malley the price came down to $14.95. He then spoke to Horace Stoneham and learned that the city of San Francisco had paid $12.50 for regular seats and a dollar more for bigger ones to put in expensive boxes. Stoneham warned O'Malley that the contractor in San Francisco had promised to keep the price break secret, but O'Malley was able to use the information to save more than $100,000.

When he couldn't get answers himself, O'Malley jotted questions on slips of paper and passed them to Dick Walsh, the team executive he had made his lead man on the job. He also ordered countless modifications and additions to make the stadium fit his vision. Some of his pet concepts, like a dining room named after Room 40 in the Hotel Bossert, were sentimental. Others, like two-person "love seats" for fans, were copied from Disneyland. A few were self-indulgent. O'Malley gave himself a big glassed-in office above the third-base line and a private box for twenty-four.

The memos and scratch-pad jottings O'Malley left behind from this period reveal dozens of ideas that were considered and then rejected as impractical or outside building codes and city regulations. Among them were:

- a residence atop the stadium
- a compressed-air system to make Old Glory wave continuously on a tall flagpole
- a water tower shaped like a baseball that would be lighted in different shades during games, depending on whether the team was winning or losing
- twenty-five-cent trams to bring patrons from parking lots to the entrances.
- water and light shows made by fountains matched with colored spotlights
- a huge statue—a tripod of bats topped by a baseball—that could be seen from ten miles away.

These ideas and others reveal the same showman's instinct that had prompted O'Malley to hire a clown for Ebbets Field. However, many of them clashed with the basic design philosophy he had worked out with Emil Praeger, which called for a more graceful style. Built almost entirely out of smooth concrete, the stadium was to be nestled into the ravine in a way that would allow people to park their cars in adjacent lots, enter the building, and find their seats with the fewest possible steps. Once inside, they would find that each one of the fifty-two thousand seats had an unobstructed view of the field. Refreshment stands and restrooms—forty-eight in all—would be close at hand.

Besides these conveniences, O'Malley insisted that the ballpark be beautiful to look at. He wanted none of the cold darkness that could be found at traditional stadiums in the East and Midwest. Built for families who would arrive by car from every direction on the compass, Dodger Stadium—that's what it would be called—was to be bright, open, and as cheerful as Disneyland. And he wanted it built to last.

The concrete elements of the stadium were made with more cement, and thus were sturdier, than the state of California required for bridges and roadways. All of the twenty-five thousand concrete parts, some weighing as much as thirty-two tons, were cast on the site. They were then numbered and placed in orderly rows on the ground. While this work proceeded, earthmovers leveled a three-hundred-foot-high hill and used the earth to fill parts of the ravine.

In order to place the concrete sections together, Praeger and the main contractor, a local company called Vinnell Constructors, had to import a crane from Germany that, once assembled, would be the largest at work in North America. The monstrous machine was set inside the stadium, where it picked pieces of the structure off the ground, swung them around, and then hoisted them into place. It was dangerous work and the derrick collapsed twice during the project, causing extensive damage both times and halting work.

Delays cost money and financing the burden became a big challenge. A group of four local banks had agreed to lend O'Malley $8 million, but by the middle of 1960 he discovered they wanted to charge a higher interest rate than they first offered and add fees equal to 1 percent of the loan. "This increase over our budget would, of course, be financially fatal," he wrote in a letter to his wife and son. O'Malley also confided in his colleague, Buzzie Bavasi, who was such a close friend that he was named in O'Malley's will. Bavasi offered to arrange a loan from his wealthy mother. "Walter said he was grateful, but he never took me up on it," recalled Bavasi. "He found a different option."

The option that saved O'Malley materialized when he met with Reese Taylor, head of locally based Union Oil. Union Oil had $27 million in profits the previous year and was on track to make even more in 1960. Taylor, who had long been involved in the "Bring baseball to Los Angeles" drive, wanted to buy the rights to the team's radio broadcasts. He was prepared to pay $1 million per year for eight years.

O'Malley proposed instead a more substantial arrangement. He asked that Union Oil act as his prime construction financier, lending the Dodgers $8 million at a lower rate than the bankers had requested. (For the first two years O'Malley would make no payments and the interest rate would be zero.) In exchange, he'd let Taylor pay $1 million per year for the broadcast rights for ten years, not eight. As an added incentive, he would give Union Oil exclusive rights to advertising inside the stadium and a concession for a gas station to be built in the parking lot.

Between the grace period and all the cash that Union Oil would pay for radio rights, O'Malley saw this arrangement as a "self-liquidating" loan. No banker would ever accept such terms. But Reese Taylor, apparently smitten with the idea of Union Oil being connected with the Dodgers, saw an opportunity. After action by the oil company's board of directors, the money that would make O'Malley's dream stadium was deposited in a Dodgers account.

O'MALLEY'S BALLPARK WAS going to be different from the Coliseum in almost every way. It would have a perfectly symmetrical playing surface, with the right- and left-field corners both 330 feet from home plate, which was set in the west end of the park so the sun would have a minimal effect on batters or fielders. Seats would be available on six levels, and many of the spectators would be shielded from the sun by upper decks and a wavy roof at the very rim of the stadium. Most would also get a pretty view of either downtown Los Angeles or the distant San Gabriel Mountains.

The outline of this baseball paradise was easy to see once the shape of the stadium was carved out and Vinnell began to put the concrete pieces together. At sunset a visitor could stand above the field level, behind where home plate would be, and watch the sky behind the mountains turn pink, orange, and deep purple. Cool air filtered in from nearby canyons and chased away the heat of the day. The sight of the work in progress thrilled O'Malley, who wrote to his old friend Frank Schroth to describe watching "the dream come true."

For the ballplayers who still labored at the Coliseum, completion of the new park couldn't come too soon. Although some in the baseball business thought the 1959 championship heralded a new dynasty, the Dodgers weren't quite ready for an extended run. With one exception, the young players brought in to replace departed Brooklyn stalwarts couldn't measure up to their predecessors. The exception was shortstop Maury Wills, who revived the art of base running in the league by stealing fifty bases and getting thrown out just once. No National Leaguer had grabbed that many bases since 1923. Wills helped the Dodgers draw an all-time league record of 2,253,887, but the effort wasn't enough to make up for mediocre hitting that left the club in fourth place at season's end.

In 1961, their last year in the Coliseum, the Dodgers saw Sandy Koufax develop into a dominant pitcher and win eighteen games. Johnny Podres won the same number and the pitching staff as a group chalked up more strikeouts than any team in the major leagues. The Dodgers finished second. And even though the team drew the most fans of any in the league, total attendance fell by more than four hundred thousand. The decline said nothing about the region's appetite for baseball. As it happened, the American League put a team called the Angels in Los Angeles that year. Owned by a group that included the singing cowboy Gene Autry,* they attracted more than six hundred thousand to little Wrigley Field. So altogether, Angelenos actually bought more baseball tickets than ever.

On the day the 1961 season ended, Walter O'Malley was so certain his new ballpark would be ready for spring that he had home plate removed from the Coliseum. His son, Peter, who had recently earned a degree in business from University of Pennsylvania and was working with the club, helped a groundskeeper dig it up. A few days later the National League conducted its first expansion draft, allowing two new teams that would start play in 1962 to claim players from around the league. One team, the Houston Colt .45s, selected Dodger infielder Bob Aspromonte; the other, the New York Mets, took Roger Craig and Gil Hodges.

The Mets were the product of an effort to return the National League to New York. During the campaign, the city had seen Ebbets Field reduced to rubble. And Robert Moses had won permission to build his long-planned stadium in Flushing Meadows. Eager to write history himself, Moses made his dealings with Walter O'Malley the main theme of his speech at the groundbreaking ceremony for the municipal stadium. With allusions to Titus, Homer, and Rabelais, he claimed that more effort was made to keep O'Malley in New York "than to keep the French in Algiers." But the effort was to no avail, he said, and the Dodgers left: "Strong men wept and little children cried in the streets . . ." Without a trace of irony, the imperial Moses then declared the stadium project a "triumph of the democratic process" and predicted a glorious future for what was still a forlorn bit of land.

Constructed with none of the delays and controversies that plagued Dodger Stadium, the Moses-built ballpark—eventually named after Mets booster

---

* The great baseball entrepreneur Bill Veeck would claim that O'Malley played a key role in Autry's rise to the major leagues. In his autobiography Veeck wrote that O'Malley worked behind the scenes with Commissioner Ford Frick to keep stronger owners—including Hank Greenberg and C. Arnholt Smith—out of the market and force the Angels to play at little Wrigley. If Autry resented the arrangement, he never showed it. Instead he paid O'Malley to use the Angels' name and paid rent to use Dodger Stadium from 1962 through 1965, when they moved into Anaheim Stadium.

William Shea—would be a large circular structure as devoid of charm as a white cardboard hatbox. Many similarly utilitarian, government-sponsored stadiums opened in the 1960s. Built in Atlanta, Washington, Houston, and other cities, each was intended to host baseball, football, and other events. To suit these uses, architects and builders had to compromise the baseball fan by placing too many seats too far from the field.

In contrast to these awkward all-purpose municipal parks, Dodger Stadium was as perfectly suited to baseball as old Ebbets Field or Fenway Park, but its curves and colors—drawn from the earth and sky—gave it a modern California flair. Its beauty was obvious even as unusual winter rains—seventeen inches—turned the site to mud and slowed the construction crews who raced to finish. O'Malley reassured fans that the park would be ready. "I'm a stubborn man," he said. "We will hit the target date, no matter what the weather." He then brought in helicopters and a jet engine to dry the field and parking lots with blasts of air. Vegetable dye was applied to the washed-out grass to make it look lushly green.

On opening day, fans were guided to parking lots coded to match their tickets. Although the park was on the edge of downtown Los Angeles, the landscape of the ravine and the wide-open parking gave the setting a suburban mood. This feeling was reinforced as people walked toward a structure that was nestled down into the ravine in a way that made it seem not looming but welcoming. Instead of heading to a main gate, like the central rotunda at Ebbets Field, ticket holders walked straight to one of more than a dozen entrances that brought them immediately into the park, where they got a panoramic view of the sun-washed diamond.

Along with the game, fans would be treated to a level of service and comfort designed in every detail by the team's owner, who reminded his staff, "There is some show business in this . . ." In one memo after another, O'Malley had set standards for every aspect of the stadium's operation, right down to the price of coffee and the type of peanuts—Virginia Jumbo—supplied in a fifteen-cent bag. He required that the entire stadium, including every seat, be cleaned after every game, and he expected the restrooms, which could be appallingly rank in some old stadiums, be cleaner than any in the major leagues.

As opening day had approached in the spring of 1962, public curiosity about the baseball Taj Mahal that had been built in Chavez Ravine reached a peak.

Every ticket was sold well before game time, and all but a few of the cheap seats were occupied when Kay O'Malley threw out the first pitch. Johnny Podres, hero of the Dodgers' first championship, started the game and pitched well against the Reds, who had won the previous year's pennant. Cincinnati's Wally Post hit the first homer ever smacked in the stadium and the Reds won 6–3. The Dodgers got revenge the very next day as Jim Gilliam hit the first Dodger home run in Chavez Ravine and Koufax threw a four-hitter.

With their victory the team displayed the style—tough pitching, aggressive base running, and light but effective hitting—that would carry them through the entire schedule. However, the big star of the season would be the stadium. Fans would encounter a few problems, the most notable being a lack of drinking fountains (soon rectified) and terrible postgame traffic tie-ups, especially when an afternoon game ended at rush hour. But traffic was nothing new to Angelenos, and many adapted to the challenge by leaving before the game ended and listening to Vin Scully's description of the last inning or two on their car radios. While fans in other cities might look down on those who depart early, this practice was accepted as readily as the foot-long franks called Dodger dogs.

As he settled into his new stadium, which ultimately cost more than $20 million, Walter O'Malley had to deal with a long list of minor problems. Among those that were merely annoying was a faulty lock on the door of the bathroom adjacent to O'Malley's private box. "I spend more time opening toilet doors than I do watching the games," wrote O'Malley in a note sent to the Yale lock company. Other problems were expensive and difficult to fix. This was especially true of a wiring mix-up that made it impossible to turn off many of the lights. Between replacement bulbs and extra electric costs, this problem cost the team thousands of dollars per month as lamps burned through the night.

The O'Malley could afford plenty of lightbulbs because, beginning with the very first home stand, fans flocked to Dodgers home games in record numbers. In the first twenty-one dates the team drew more than seven hundred thousand people. As the Dodgers blazed through opponents, the pace never let up and they headed for an all-time major-league record of 2,755,184 tickets sold in a season. With the rival Giants performing just as well, games played against San Francisco became happenings. Movie actors and moguls clamored for choice seats, while ordinary fans hoped to sit near them. The luckiest were invited to the owner's box. Bob Hope, Jack Benny, and Jimmy Stewart signed the guest book in the first year.

With only one regular fielder left from the Rickey era (Duke Snider), the 1962 team was led by Maury Wills and Don Drysdale. Wills set an all-time record for steals—104 in one season—surpassing a mark set by Ty Cobb. Whenever he got on base, the stadium was filled with chanting—"Go, go go!"—and he did more than half the time. He was named the Most Valuable Player, while Drysdale, who simply overpowered batters to win twenty-five games, captured the Cy Young Award as best pitcher in all of major-league baseball.

In another season the Drysdale-Wills Dodgers might have run away with the pennant, but in 1962 the Giants played nearly as well. California's baseball frenzy grew so intense that *Sports Illustrated*, in an article titled "Boom Goes Baseball," declared that the sport had been rescued from decline and O'Malley should get the credit. As the season neared an end, people in Los Angeles and San Francisco had difficulty talking about anything other than the pennant race. James Reston, the dean of the nation's political writers, noticed this when he visited to cover a debate between gubernatorial candidates Richard Nixon and Pat Brown. He wrote, "When a political reporter asks around here who's going to win the answer is invariably 'the Dodgers.'"

A terrible end-of-season slump—they lost ten of thirteen games—landed the Dodgers in a best-of-three playoff with the Giants, who made up a four-game gap in eight days. Duke Snider, recalling Bobby Thomson's playoff home run in 1951, said, "We've owed the Giants something since 1951. Now we'll get a chance to pay them back."

Snider spoke as if the competitive fire that had burned in New York had been transferred west. He was right. The two teams still hated each other and the Giants were so desperate to win that they actually had groundskeepers soften up the infield dirt at Candlestick Park to slow Maury Wills. Before the first pitch, an umpire forced the stadium crew to compact the dirt with heavy rollers; but as it turned out, the Giants didn't need the advantage they had sought. Only a handful of Dodgers got on base as the Giants routed them 8–0.

The Dodgers broke a thirty-inning scoreless streak in the next game, which they won 8–7. The deciding game was also played at Dodger Stadium, where almost forty-seven thousand urged the Dodgers on. With Wills collecting four hits, the home team went into the ninth inning with a 4–2 lead. Then they gave the game away, allowing the Giants to score four runs on two hits and four walks. The collapse marked the team's first real heartbreak on the West Coast and thus turned Los Angeles fans into true baseball connoisseurs. In San Francisco, fully fifty thousand people went to the airport to meet their returning heroes. Scheduled flights had to be diverted when the crowd broke through police lines protecting the tarmac. Team officials ordered their charter to put down on a distant runway, where players were loaded into cars and whisked out of a little-used gate, escaping the crowd.

SAN FRANCISCO LOST a seven-game World Series to the Yankees, but their success proved, beyond any doubt, that Stoneham and O'Malley had brought the best of baseball to the West and invigorated the entire sport. In five years their two franchises had won three pennants and one world championship. Despite playing two years in little Seals Stadium, the Giants drew on average twice the number of fans they had attracted at the Polo Grounds in 1957. The increase for the Dodgers had been even more pronounced, as they became one of the richest clubs in all of organized sports. This occurred despite the collapse of Skiatron, which O'Malley once hoped would provide a new revenue stream. Instead the company, which failed to win city approval for its operations, went under, owing the Dodgers more than $123,000. Fox owed others more than $3 million.

As he thought about investing his cash, O'Malley the builder considered adding a movable partial cover to Dodger Stadium. (It would shield the infield and thousands of seats behind first base, home plate, and third base.) He described the concept in a letter to Buckminster Fuller, explaining that it might create a twenty-thousand-seat indoor space suitable for basketball or hockey. This idea never went further than O'Malley's imagination, but he did find other projects to pursue. He upgraded his team airplane, buying a four-engine Electra II that he named the *Kay O'* after his wife. The plane was a turboprop capable of crossing the country nonstop and was outfitted with bunks, worktables, and seats for sixty-six people. O'Malley made another big investment at

Dodgertown, which he had placed under his son Peter's direction. There he bought the land he previously leased and replaced the little pitch-and-putt golf course with a full-size one.

More land development, including a second golf course, would follow in Florida as all the risk O'Malley assumed in moving to Los Angeles and building his stadium produced a river of cash that he had to invest. This success was fueled by the astounding growth in the region's population and economy. By the middle of the 1960s greater Los Angeles had surpassed Chicago to become the second-biggest urban center in the country, with a population of 6.5 million. Though a late bloomer—barely eleven thousand lived there in 1880—the city had become a manufacturing powerhouse and, thanks to the movie and television industries, the center of culture for the masses. Nearby Orange County, also part of the Dodgers base, had grown just as rapidly, adding more than one million residents between the middle of the fifties and the middle of the sixties.

This growth was beginning to produce some unpleasant side effects—more highway congestion, increased smog, overcrowded schools—but Los Angeles still represented a bright future to newcomers who embraced everything the place had to offer, from the beaches to the mountains to the Dodgers, who continued to win. In Dodger Stadium's first five years, the team averaged 2.2 million fans per year. No other club came close.

With a solidly wealthy team and growing income, O'Malley rewarded himself with a big, chalet-style home on Lake Arrowhead, north of the city. (His wife, Kay, often drove him back and forth in a day, logging 180 miles.) He also organized adventures of the kind other people only saw in movies or dreamed about as cadets in military school. O'Malley and friends hunted for polar bears in the arctic, elephants in Africa, and tigers in India.

Typically these trips began with a banquet in a Manhattan restaurant such as the '21' Club. The party would then go to the airport, board the Dodgers plane, and hopscotch across the world. Refueling stops in Europe, the Middle East, or Asia became opportunities for banquets and tourism. Once they arrived at their final destination, the group would trek into the wild with servants, guides, and supplies.

Although a few conservationists were beginning to oppose big-game hunts, in the 1960s the species O'Malley hunted were not endangered and luxury safaris were still a tradition indulged in by wealthy sportsmen from around the world. A South African newspaper account of one O'Malley hunt called it "a silk-lined safari" and described a group traveling with Dodgers hats and a portable refrigerator. They were led by two of South Africa's greatest white hunters, Lionel Palmer and Harry Selby, and locals were agog over the cash they spread around. The money the "tycoons" spent on supplies, licenses, and staff produced "undreamed-of prosperity," noted the newspaper.

O'Malley was the kind of man who prized success and its symbols, and the hunts produced trophies—a lion, elephant tusks, a polar bear—that were displayed in his office in the special members-only Stadium Club ballpark restaurant. The safaris also yielded great stories of adventure and mishap. O'Malley loved to talk about the lion he shot in what became Botswana: "I got down from the truck to take the first shot and the lion went down. When I started back to the truck, puffed up like a pouter pigeon, they were all yelling at me. I figured it was a gag until I turned around. The lion was up and he was coming after me. I jumped to the truck, reloaded and fired. And I shot the radiator cap off the truck."

For Peter O'Malley, who was being groomed to take over the family business, these trips offered long stretches of time with his father away from ordinary concerns. "It might take a couple days' journey just to reach the camp," he recalled years later. "Once you were there you'd be out of touch with Western Union, no telephone. On the big safaris there would be a cook, trackers, gun bearers, and drivers. We might get up at four a.m. and do miles of walking."

As he aged, Walter O'Malley spent more time in blinds, waiting for game to approach, than he did with trackers. "Really, I do very little shooting; on the last trip practically none," he told an interviewer. "It's a good vacation for me. I enjoy seeing the animals in their natural habitat and I like to meet the people." O'Malley relished the chance to be with friends who didn't want to talk about business. And he enjoyed the opportunities for high-level tourism afforded to wealthy Americans who went abroad in these times. In Africa, O'Malley once bought a pair of cheetah cubs that he gave to the Los Angeles Zoo. In India a high-ranking government official invited him to his home, where he kept a three-hundred-pound pet tiger. "We were invited to play with him," wrote O'Malley in a letter to his wife. "I got flipped real good." On the same trip a stop in Iran led to dinner with members of the Shah's family and the purchase of tins of golden caviar that was consumed with evening drinks in the bush.

Safaris were peak indulgences that O'Malley enjoyed about half a dozen times. He found similar experiences of male bonding and bonhomie every summer at the famous (some would say infamous) Bohemian Grove in Northern California. Begun in the nineteenth century as a summer camp for the Bohemian Club of San Francisco, the Grove had become the site of a three-week summer bash for a few thousand of America's most powerful men. In the seclusion of a sequoia forest they put on shows, hosted lectures, and indulged in plenty of drink and high jinks. The capper for each session was a dramatic Cremation of Care ceremony with torches and a big fire.

The ceremony, like the camp's rustic luxury, impressed most first-timers, but the major draw for campers at the Grove came in the opportunity for meeting other powerful men in a casual setting. Among the friends O'Malley made there was Supreme Court Justice Earl Warren. Presumably Warren held to the code of the Grove, which forbade the discussion of serious matters and any mention of the camp's affairs outside the gates. For generations, members of the Grove had kept their doings private, but in the political atmosphere of the 1960s the gathering of so many powerful men aroused suspicion, and reporters and academics revealed many of their secrets, including membership lists and accounts of various events. In 1971, press concern about President Richard Nixon giving a private talk there caused him to cancel an appearance.

Having earned his way in, Walter O'Malley saw nothing wrong in belonging to an exclusive club. He still believed in the "democratic principles" he cited as a boy who had resisted leaving home for Culver Academy, and those principles included the right of association and the privileges that came with achievement. And if he joined a group—the Scouts, a club, or a league—he supported it fully.

Loyalty and commitment were O'Malley's most important values. With employees, his one-year-at-a-time contracts served to remind them that their loyalty and performance would be reviewed annually. The pressure of this policy was hard for some to take. But O'Malley would keep his end of the bargain, offering new contracts to his most committed executives year after year. This was how he maintained an organization that produced consistent winners on the field and the profits that allowed him the pleasures and privileges he enjoyed.

DURING THE DODGERS' FIRST decade in California, O'Malley's business team was led by the same small, trusted group including general manager Buzzie Bavasi, who was given almost complete authority over players, coaches, and managers. O'Malley intervened only in extreme circumstances. One notable case arose when he took the Dodgers on a second tour of Japan, in 1966. The tour was a major success, and O'Malley received the highest award the Japanese government could bestow on a foreigner. O'Malley would prize the award forever, but the tour was marred by the sudden departure of base-stealing star Maury Wills. Citing an injury, Wills left for home but was seen—by a vacationing Buzzie Bavasi—playing banjo in a nightclub in Hawaii. O'Malley, who had watched his team struggle on the field in Japan, demanded Bavasi get rid of him. Wills played the next year in Pittsburgh.

The Maury Wills case was a true exception. Bavasi would recall that in all his years with O'Malley it was the one time he was so adamant about a player. In a few other situations he expressed opinions but didn't make demands. This was even true when it came to salary decisions. Operating within an overall budget, Bavasi handled all player contract negotiations, which—in those pre-union, free-agency days—remained a lopsided game. Every winter players came, one by one, to discuss their future. Bavasi genuinely enjoyed toying with them, using a variety of tricks and ruses to make them shrink from their demands or believe they actually won a few extra dollars.

Among Bavasi's favorite ploys was the fake contract. He would have his secretary type up a document that showed a very low salary for a top player. When a less talented man came in to talk about his deal, Bavasi would be conveniently called away and leave the document in plain view. He gave the fellow time to study the papers, then returned to offer him a slightly higher figure. Impressed that he might earn more than the star, the player almost always signed.

In the early 1960s, Bavasi used his wiles to keep the Dodgers' payroll below the league average. Some players trusted him so fully that they just accepted his first offer. One winter Johnny Podres sent a telegram accepting Bavasi's terms before his papers were even mailed out. But when it came to his own pay, Bavasi was less skilled. Born into wealth, he wasn't quite as assertive as some of his players, and for years he didn't even ask for additional pay. When Walter

O'Malley finally told him to set his own figure, Bavasi still demurred, certain the boss would notice and give him a generous boost. The boss didn't, and Bavasi stayed at the same rate.

Throughout the organization, executives and staff people followed the same general pattern, accepting average pay in exchange for greater security and higher levels of responsibility than they would find in other organizations. Under this system, turnover was almost nonexistent and firings were so rare that they became the subject of great speculation. This is why O'Malley's dismissal of ticket manager Harold Parrott, who had come west from Brooklyn, would be a matter of dispute for decades.

As guardian of the team's ultimate commodity, Parrott occupied a position filled with responsibility and the opportunity for mischief. The official price stamped on a ticket is the same whether the team is a contender or a cellar dweller. However, as any scalper knows, a ticket's true market value—the amount a fan is willing to pay—can vary wildly. For example, a ticket for a Giants-Dodgers game, with the pennant on the line, can be worth a hundred times what the club might be paid at the box-office window.

Traditionally teams used every method they could imagine, including discount sales to middlemen, to hedge against losses when demand was low. Of course, these middlemen also got to reap the benefits when the actual value of a seat at the game rose. When the Dodgers arrived in Los Angeles, a number of hotel managers, restaurateurs, and even an occasional car dealer came forward to play the ticket game. In all the wheeling and dealing, people who actually handled the tickets for the team had plenty of opportunities to enrich themselves.

According to Bavasi, Parrott came under suspicion because his lifestyle, which included a house in expensive Malibu, seemed more expensive than his salary should permit. An audit led O'Malley to fire him, even though Parrott disputed the findings. Parrott's backers, including his sons and Bavasi, would forever say the dismissal was unwarranted. "I think it was because he was a Rickey man," said Bavasi. "That made Parrott a dead duck."

In his memoir, Parrott would describe O'Malley as an imperious boss who was critical of his previous association with Branch Rickey. The ultimate truth of the Parrott case would be impossible to prove, but in general O'Malley was not impetuous. He kept other so-called Rickey men around for many years.

Those who stayed benefited from one of the first profit-sharing plans in sports, which made even some lower-level management workers well off by the time they retired.

The profit figures used to determine employee payments rose as Los Angeles won the 1963 pennant and beat the Yankees four straight in the World Series. The championship, which came in manager Alston's tenth year, was followed by another in 1965. Alston and Bavasi were so good at their jobs that O'Malley rarely had to intervene in the operation of the team. He even held off when Don Drysdale and Sandy Koufax, one of the best pitching duos ever seen in the majors, formed a two-man union and demanded that Bavasi pay them much more money.

Drysdale and Koufax had just powered the Dodgers—and Walter O'Malley's business—through a hugely successful season. More than 2.5 million people came to see the two star pitchers and the team win the pennant. The World Series had been one of the most compelling ever played, as Koufax won two games in four days. It also was the richest series played up until that time, with the Dodgers and Minnesota Twins selling almost $3 million worth of tickets.

With all the money flowing into the Dodgers organization, Koufax and Drysdale wanted a bigger cut. According to one estimate, based on a comparison of attendance for games they started and games they did not, the two pitchers brought an extra $600,000 in revenue to the club. (If postseason revenue had been added, the figure would be even higher.) They considered this record and compared their previous contract experiences and concluded that they were being paid less than they deserved. At the suggestion of Drysdale's wife, Ginger, they decided to negotiate their 1966 contracts together. They asked Bavasi for a three-year deal paying them each $500,000.

"He [Koufax] had made O'Malley millions," recalled Bavasi decades later. "I knew why he and Donald expected more, but they started at a ridiculous figure." No player in baseball was paid as much as Koufax and Drysdale wanted, and, Bavasi reminded them, the Dodgers didn't offer multiyear contracts.

Walter O'Malley stood behind Bavasi, but as an old pro in the game of negotiations he appreciated what his pitchers were trying to do. "I admire the boys' strategy," he told *Sports Illustrated*. O'Malley saw "nothing wrong" in their union-style tactics and allowed that "a sophisticated union would be good for the players." But he didn't want to deal with the Hollywood agent, J. William

Hayes, whom the pitchers sent to represent them. "There are too many agents hanging around Hollywood looking for clients," O'Malley said. Owners around the league felt the same way and were pressuring O'Malley to make sure that agents stayed out of the game.

As Koufax and Drysdale sat out spring training in 1966, the national press publicized the holdout and fans in Los Angeles worried over the prospect of a season without their star pitchers. Koufax argued that he and Drysdale were trying to make the point that "ballplayers aren't slaves, that we have a right to negotiate." To show they were serious, the two players signed contracts to perform in a movie that was in production.

According to Bavasi, O'Malley finally gave him an extra $40,000 to settle the problem. He flew from Florida to Los Angeles and negotiated with the players, not their agent. He broke the budget by $10,000 but got them signed. In the season that followed, Drysdale suffered a decline but Koufax had one of the best years a pitcher ever had, winning twenty-seven games and leading the team to another World Series. This time the Dodgers lost in four straight. Koufax, at the top of his game, then suddenly retired to save his arm, which was so damaged that doctors advised him to quit.

Sandy Koufax would take his place in history as one of the best pitchers ever to play, and his quiet character would make him one of the most admired sports figures of the century. But his effect on baseball as a business wouldn't get the attention it deserved. The holdout he conducted with Drysdale marked the first successful effort by players to organize on their own behalf. In agreeing to treat them as a unit and then giving them significantly more money, Bavasi and O'Malley also showed some flexibility at a moment when managers and owners in both leagues were stiffening against a broad effort to form a players' union.

In the spring of 1966, while Koufax and Drysdale had made their very public stand, a new and soon-to-be-powerful figure had quietly visited every major-league team. For more than a decade Marvin Miller had helped lead the United Steelworkers of America, one of the strongest unions in the world. He had moved into baseball at the request of players who made him their first salaried, professional organizer. The timing was no accident. Since 1950, owners had received huge increases in revenues from broadcasting fees and higher ticket prices. At the same time mean salaries for players had changed little when adjusted for inflation. Many players harbored deep suspicions about the basic fairness of their negotiations with owners, and while owners kept the data secret, these feelings were well founded. Salaries as a share of team revenue had declined by about 50 percent since the 1930s. The owners were not sharing the wealth.

Slightly built with graying hair and a thin mustache, Miller had been born in Brooklyn in 1917 and spent many boyhood afternoons at Ebbets Field. During the Great Depression he watched his father struggle as a coat salesman and never forgot seeing him dye his hair in a desperate attempt to appeal to women customers. ("It shocked the pants off me," he would recall.) Union values were in his blood—his mother and father were both active in organized labor—and he believed such values could be applied in almost every workplace. He thought that players had denied themselves the benefits of a union because they had bought into the idea that the game wasn't a business like any other and that the owners weren't making much money.

Miller arrived on the scene right after baseball's owners had named a retired general named William "Spike" Eckert commissioner. A quick study, he recognized that Eckert had little background in the game or the baseball business. He also determined that in the exclusive club of team owners, Walter O'Malley was first among equals and the most powerful executive in the major leagues. (Branch Rickey had died in December 1965 at age eighty-three.) Since he worked in baseball full-time, when most owners did not, the others looked to O'Malley for advice, and at their meetings his voice carried the most weight. "He was smarter than all of them," Miller recalled, "and always the best prepared."

At their first meeting, O'Malley impressed Miller by noting they had a mutual friend in David McDonald, past president of the steelworkers union. In retirement McDonald had settled in California, attended some Dodgers games, and been befriended by the owner. More than fifty years later Miller would reconstruct the scene from memory, beginning with what O'Malley said he had learned from the former union leader.

"He told me that you don't think 'profit' is a dirty word. Why is that?"

"It's very simple, Mr. O'Malley. There's a tremendous difference between negotiating a contract with a company that's well in the red and one that's well in the black."

O'Malley beamed at Miller and said, "A lot of people hope you are not successful, but I hope you are. If you reach a point where there's something I can help you with, call me." Miller tested this promise when the commissioner's lawyer Bowie Kuhn (who would one day be commissioner himself) stonewalled the players' request for a payroll deduction to cover their union dues. He called the Dodgers owner, who asked for a little time to look into the problem. He then telephoned Miller and said, "I think you'll have no problem now." Within a week the payroll system was in place.

Following a path set by Miller, the players quickly won new pension and health care benefits; and the league minimum salary, which had risen just $1,000 in twenty years, was increased from $6,000 to $10,000. Among all the owners, Miller found O'Malley, a member of baseball's executive council, to be the most open-minded and realistic when it came to accepting this change and others promoted by the players' organization.

The attitude O'Malley showed while working with Miller was the product of his long years dealing with union workers at Ebbets Field. It was also influenced by the fact that O'Malley's grandfather had organized postal clerks at the turn of the century. O'Malley respected the players' efforts to improve their situation collectively. He quickly adapted to the union's presence, and when the first-ever strike vote was taken in 1972, he was concerned about the four players who stood against their teammates and opposed the walkout. "Even though they voted to strike, he wanted them to be unanimous," said Miller. "He wanted unity on his team and he didn't want anyone to act like they were tools of management."

"O'MALLEY UNDERSTOOD THE WAY power works," said Marvin Miller. He noted that the old owner had studied the game's legal problems since the 1940s, and knew its antitrust exemption was subject to the whims of Washington. He was also a politically sensitive capitalist who understood the game depended on public support. In the mid- to late 1960s, the public was hardly inclined to favor high-handed bosses. In California especially, the sixties counterculture was in full bloom and it was hardly the time to stand in the way of anyone seeking to assert their rights. Baseball could not be seen as an absolute oligarchy and retain its hold on the American heart.

Throughout the decade, changing public attitudes and traumatic events had challenged baseball as a quasi-public institution. As a symbol of integration, the Dodgers seemed to get a pass during the race riots of 1965, when movie theaters and museums closed and other events were cancelled. While gun dealers reported a run on weapons in both black and white neighborhoods, the games went on as usual and without incident at Dodger Stadium.

For Angelenos of all races, the Dodgers remained a source of common interest and pride, and fans flocked to the stadium in ever greater numbers. No community in baseball was more allied with its team than Los Angeles, and O'Malley's success was highlighted by the demise of the team that had started the realignment of baseball, the Milwaukee Braves. After a decade of profits made possible in part by a taxpayer stadium subsidy, Lou Perini claimed a loss in 1962 and promptly sold the team for a record $6.2 million. For a while the new owners obscured their intentions, but locals soon found out they planned to move their team to Atlanta, where they could rent a government-built stadium at a giveaway price and draw ticket buyers and TV viewers from a six-state area. The team moved in 1966. In 1967 the onetime Philadelphia Athletics would follow suit, forsaking Kansas City for Oakland, California.

With these moves into new territories, baseball continued to participate in the explosive growth in all big-league sports. Following the examples set by Los Angeles and others, cities across the country had competed furiously to seduce existing teams to move or to win new franchises. During the 1960s, hockey, baseball, football, and basketball grew more than thirty new franchises. From Buffalo (football) to Seattle (baseball), cities mounted expensive campaigns to attract teams to subsidized stadiums and arenas.

Among the National League owners, O'Malley was the most supportive of an orderly but steady expansion program that included a new team for San Diego, the Padres, that would drain fans from the Dodgers. When the Padres joined the league in 1969, they debuted with O'Malley's former top executive Buzzie Bavasi in charge.

The two men had grown apart during the decade, a fact confirmed by O'Malley's decision to remove Bavasi from his will. Years later Bavasi would say that his own ambition was part of the problem. He wanted to own stock in a team and O'Malley wouldn't offer him any. His frustration made him consider O'Malley more critically, and he began to find fault with his old friend. He thought he had been pushed aside as O'Malley formed new relationships with the Hollywood types—Cary Grant, Frank Sinatra, Milton Berle—who visited the stadium. Bavasi also began to dwell on the idea that he was underpaid and underappreciated. When the San Diego organization said he would get a stake in the team if he became general manager, he jumped at the chance.

O'Malley replaced Bavasi with Fresco Thompson, who, with minor-league director Bill Schweppe, was one of a triumvirate who had served at the top ranks since the Brooklyn days. At sixty-six, Thompson had worked in baseball for his entire adult life. He was known for his sense of humor and wealth of baseball stories. As general manager of the Dodgers he reached the highest level short of ownership. However, the appointment was more an act of kindness and tribute than a realistic promotion. On the day he was promoted, Thompson was already suffering from serious pancreatic and kidney disease, and he died in November of 1968.

With his two top executives gone, O'Malley considered the team's future— and his own. He had just turned sixty-five, an age when men of his time generally retired. His health was good but not great. Over the years he had undergone surgery to remove growths from his colon, and all the beefsteak banquets, lunches at '21,' and dinners at the best restaurants in Los Angeles had added significantly to his weight. O'Malley consumed life with the same gusto that he brought to cooking and food, but he also knew that his own mother had died at age fifty-seven and his father, Edwin, had lived only to sixty-nine.

Unlike Edwin, who had retreated after his big battle in the public arena, Walter O'Malley had stayed in the game and won. He also had an heir who had trained in business school and then worked in the Dodgers organization. After running Dodgertown and the minor-league club in Spokane, Peter O'Malley had overseen the stadium operation in Los Angeles and become the club's executive vice president and chief troubleshooter. (When asked about his son's duties, O'Malley had said they included "mending the fences I break down.") Peter was only thirty years old, but Walter had run several businesses and opened a big law practice by the time he was the same age. His heir seemed ready, and with no real fanfare Walter announced he would retire in the coming year and hand him day-to-day control of the team.

Peter O'Malley shared his father's competitive drive, and in his first ten years as team president the Dodgers would capture three pennants. He was also extremely loyal. Walter Alston continued as manager until he retired in 1976 after eighteen years. He was replaced by Tommy Lasorda, who held the job even longer, giving it up only after a heart attack. Similarly, Peter O'Malley employed just two general managers, Al Campanis and Fred Claire. Both would log more than thirty years in the organization.

But while he shared his father's preference for experienced executives, Peter O'Malley operated with very little of Walter's old-fashioned political style and a great deal of his mother's quiet sincerity. He kept Walter Alston as manager of the team and reached out to Don Newcombe, who had been in a long struggle with alcoholism. The young O'Malley got Newcombe's World Series ring out of hock and gave him an office job. In 1972 he reached out to Jackie and Rachel Robinson.

As Robinson's biographer Arnold Rampersad would note, "the one unhealed wound" in the great star's relationship with baseball was his estrangement from the Dodgers. At his induction into the National Baseball Hall of Fame in 1962, Robinson had felt saddened by this state of affairs and two days later addressed it in a letter to Walter O'Malley. In it he confessed that at Cooperstown he had reflected on his days at Ebbets Field and "kept wondering how our relationship had deteriorated." He said the trouble probably began when Branch Rickey departed and O'Malley took over. And he admitted to being stubborn and said that his wife, Rachel, had often urged him to talk over his problems with O'Malley directly. "Of course there is a possibility that we are at an impasse, and nothing can be done," he added. "I feel, however, I must make this attempt to let you know I sincerely regret we have not tried to find the cause for this breach." The letter ended with Robinson noting that he would be in Los Angeles on the coming Friday. He said that he would call, and if O'Malley had fifteen minutes free, Robinson would come for a visit.

The problem Robinson sought to resolve did begin when Walter O'Malley assumed control of the Dodgers from Branch Rickey. But if Jackie felt this as an affront, O'Malley had plenty of reasons to feel offended too. Robinson had blamed him publicly for the team's struggles in 1958, and O'Malley had come out poorly in a 1960 book that Robinson had worked on with journalist Carl Rowan.

Despite all that had occurred, O'Malley had often responded generously to calls for help from Robinson's mother, who lived in Pasadena. (In a letter to his friend Frank Schroth dated February 9, 1962, O'Malley said that Mrs. Robinson had visited on "the day Jackie was elected to the Hall of Fame" and asked for "financial assistance.") O'Malley also gave Jackie's brother Mack a job at Dodger Stadium.

When Robinson wrote to suggest the meeting, O'Malley sent a telegram saying he wouldn't be in town but added, "Delighted to see you any time." In the weeks that followed the two men exchanged a few more notes. The last, written by O'Malley on August 20, 1962, said, "Why not get out of your mind that we have any differences?"

Warmer notes followed over the years, and before he died Robinson's mentor, Branch Rickey, also reached out to O'Malley, telling him, "I think you have done a great job on the field, as well as off." But while Rickey and O'Malley seemed to be able to get past their discomfort, the Dodgers owner had not reached the same level of understanding with Robinson. When an old-timers' game was scheduled for 1972, O'Malley's son Peter asked Don Newcombe to help persuade Robinson to come see his number retired.

"I called him on the phone," recalled Newcombe, who said that at first Robinson said, "Hell no, I'm not coming. Fuck the Dodgers."

Robinson's anger showed that even after the efforts he and O'Malley had made at reconciliation, he still harbored anger and resentment. Writer Roger Kahn, whom Robinson trusted enough to ask him to handle his mail as his eyesight failed, had heard his friend's grievances many times. Although Buzzie Bavasi took full responsibility, Kahn knew that Robinson suspected that O'Malley was responsible for trading him to the Giants. He also felt slighted because the Dodgers, and then other teams, never offered him a job as an executive or team manager. "Jackie was furious" about those things, reported Kahn.

However, he was not so furious that he could turn down a trip to Dodger Stadium if Newcombe made the invitation a matter of their friendship. As Newcombe would recall it, "I said, 'Robbie, will you come for me?' And he said, 'You're goddamned right I will.'"

Despite poor health, including near blindness, Robinson attended the game on June 4, 1972, and spent a long time talking with Peter O'Malley. Walter O'Malley attended the event, too, and what transpired did ease Robinson's mind. He told reporters that he and Peter had talked about race relations in baseball, particularly the need for black managers, and he had come away "very much impressed." He also said that he had not been bothered when he was traded from the Dodgers to the Giants and that he had been caught in the contest between Rickey and O'Malley. "The problem," he added, "was never between Jackie Robinson and Walter O'Malley."

Juxtaposed with Kahn's account of Robinson's feelings about O'Malley, the old infielder's generous comments at Dodger Stadium proved that, like everyone else, his moods were changeable and sometimes depended on the moment, his audience, and new information. Kahn, who was aware of times when Robinson struggled financially and would have appreciated a job offer from O'Malley, would recall most keenly the statements that showed "he despised Walter." But the totality of the evidence, including their letters, statements, and other gestures, show a more nuanced relationship. At the worst moments Robinson did express real hostility, but at other times he expressed regret and a desire for a more positive relationship.

Throughout the summer that followed Robinson's last appearance with the Dodgers, he was cheered at events around the country and in October threw out the first pitch at a World Series game. He died a few weeks later. Peter O'Malley attended the funeral.

IN BRINGING JACKIE ROBINSON back to his team, Peter O'Malley honored the club's history, which included the Brooklyn years. Like his sister, Terry, Peter was sentimental about the borough and uncomfortable with the way some people, especially in the press, periodically poked at the scar left when the team moved. Whenever an important bit of the Dodgers' past was recalled, whether it was Robinson's debut at Ebbets Field or the home run hit by Bobby Thomson, there was a good chance that a sportswriter would take a whack at Walter O'Malley, likening him to Cassius or Benedict Arnold.

The most important source of anti-O'Malley rhetoric was Dick Young, the columnist for the *Daily News*. Once the team started playing in Los Angeles, he mocked O'Malley as a great "philanthropist" sitting on his "fat proposition." He described the Chavez Ravine deal as a land grab motivated by greed. By the 1970s he would use O'Malley as the standard for avarice wherever it arose, adding his name to a cruel column about Mets pitcher Tom Seaver, in which he concluded, "Both are very greedy."

Young wasn't alone in the attack on O'Malley. Other writers, including *New York Times* columnist Arthur Daley, called him a villain and habitually mentioned Machiavelli when writing O'Malley's name. Eventually, Red Barber would attack O'Malley as "about the most devious man I ever met."

Curiously, no one said anything similar about Horace Stoneham, who had never put much effort into staying in New York. The difference between mostly blue-collar Brooklyn and upscale Manhattan might partly explain why Stoneham got away with it. Stoneham also possessed a persona—seemingly guileless, gullible, and harmless—that masked his true ambition. In contrast, O'Malley looked and acted like a crafty poker player and he seemed like he could take a punch.

O'Malley was tough, but the constant criticism, coming from men who had joined him for hours at the poker table in Vero Beach, affected him. In 1968, when a writer visited his office, he closed the drapes on the window overlooking the stadium, explaining, "If I didn't, I'd imagine I could hear some fan saying, 'Get a load of old Fatso sitting up there counting his money.'"

O'Malley and his family had to know that some people were influenced by critical eastern writers. But while it was relatively easy to brush off the insults of a few highly opinionated fans, they felt a little worse about the idea that the team's move west had caused never-ending heartache for Brooklynites overall.

Was it true? Was Brooklyn suffering? In 1963, after the Dodgers vanquished the Yankees in the World Series, the *New York Times* editorial writers declared "Joy in Flatbush" and "at last the wounds are healed." In 1969, when the Mets won the World Series four games to one, Brooklyn honored them with a rally at Borough Hall. The victory made the Brooklyn Dodgers seem like ancient history and should have marked the end of any and all hostilities for Walter O'Malley. After all, a huge number of old Brooklyn Dodger fans had left for Long Island and New Jersey and rarely even went back to the old borough. They had been replaced by immigrants who never knew Ebbets Field or trolleys or the *Daily Eagle.*

But then in 1972 Roger Kahn published one of the most affecting and romantic baseball books ever written. *The Boys of Summer* turned the Brooklyn Dodgers into living symbols of all that was good about America before the challenge of the sixties counterculture, the shock of political assassinations, and wrenching defeat in the Vietnam War. "It was a Book of the Month Club pick and Harper & Row published it very well," recalled Kahn. "It sold 250,000 copies very quickly and just kept going."

Thirty years later Kahn could sit in his secluded home in upstate New York and marvel at the *Boys of Summer* phenomenon. "They had a party at Tavern on the Green in Central Park and brought in Erskine and Snider. Philip Roth was there and people really began to talk about the book. Players went on television with me and I wound up doing four different tours."

As he reflected on the excitement around the book, Kahn, at age eighty, realized he had enjoyed a rare experience. "The publisher gave me lots of cash, maybe a thousand dollars, just for walking-around money. Everything they did was first-class. Nobody gets that anymore. Today they send you coach, if they send you at all."

Kahn's book traveled first-class all the way to the top of best-seller lists. Besides the publicity effort and book club selection, the book rose on its merit as a good read infused with the author's love for the team. But Kahn wouldn't argue against the idea that it also benefited from something in the national mood. After years of social turmoil, political assassinations, and trauma in Vietnam, many Americans were ready to live, if only for a few hours, in the pages of a book that presented the past in a warm and idealized way.

Time magazine noted the nostalgic national mood as it assessed the book's success soon after it was issued. The magazine described it as part of a wave of nostalgic works of popular culture, including movies like *The Last Picture Show* and the musical *Grease*, that arose in 1971 and continued to swell. The phenomenon, in which the mass media shaped and delivered memories for millions of people to share, was widely observed and studied even as it occurred. In a 1979 study called *Yearning for Yesterday*, sociologist Fred Davis described how artists had reconstructed the past to make it special and redeeming. He noted both the positive and negative effects of this process and concluded it might help the country regain its balance after a turbulent time.

While academics analyzed the nostalgia craze, the products it produced changed the way people thought about the past. *Grease* made leather jackets and delinquency cute. *The Boys of Summer* made Carl Erskine, Clem Labine, and other players into paragons of goodness while making Walter O'Malley a cheerless, money-obsessed old man. From the moment the book was published, this version of the story gained power and grew, especially among people in the East who were alive when the Dodgers still played in Brooklyn.

In fact, Kahn's view of O'Malley was more nuanced. Decades after the publication of *The Boys of Summer,* he said that he was of "two minds" about O'Malley's move west. He still believed that with some additional parking facilities the Dodgers could have stayed at Ebbets Field. The stadium would have become a cherished baseball shrine comparable to Fenway Park or Wrigley Field, he said, and the team would have been loved as dearly as the Cubs and Red Sox. However, he also recognized that "someone had to bring baseball to California" and that O'Malley had done the job well. He also believed that the animus expressed by O'Malley's harshest critic, Dick Young, was more personal than professional. Young was upset "because he lost his beat" when the team moved west, explained Kahn.

In O'Malley the man, Kahn saw a certain grand style—evidenced by the Dodgers plane, the stadium, and the Vero Beach training complex—that he admired. As the owner of a minor-league team in Utica, New York, Kahn had himself learned to be "manipulative" with players and the press, just as O'Malley had been. But as much as he understood Walter O'Malley, sentiment kept Kahn from agreeing that O'Malley deserved the game's highest honors. If given a vote, Kahn said, "I couldn't put him in the Hall of Fame."

FACED WITH A SENTIMENT powered by a type of mass psychology, Walter O'Malley and his family could only try to understand the resentment that came in the occasional letter or newspaper column. They focused more on their success in Los Angeles and in the baseball business. In 1971, Mayor Sam Yorty and more than a thousand civic leaders honored O'Malley and three others who had brought landmark development to the city in the past decade. O'Malley's Dodger Stadium was the only private facility honored. (The others were the County Museum of Art, the Music Center, and the Convention Center.) In accepting his award, an engraved silver platter, O'Malley said, "It's a nice feeling for this little old taxpayer to be here."

In his semiretirement, O'Malley would continue to appear at public events, but he was finished with the daily business of running the Dodgers. However, he wasn't finished with baseball. As the team's owner and chairman of the board, the senior O'Malley would continue to serve as a member of the owners' executive council and retain his position as the most influential executive in either league.

As a group, the owners operated almost like the College of Cardinals in Rome, deliberating and debating until they reached a consensus. Officially they were equal in power. However, experience, knowledge, and personality put O'Malley on a slightly higher level. Even as he approached age seventy, he was still the best at making a case for his point of view and constructing a majority to endorse it.

O'Malley also set the tone for the way baseball managed its public affairs. His leadership in this area was practiced quietly, but reporters covering the league sometimes got a glimpse of O'Malley in action. This happened once at a league meeting in Chicago when the chairman of the Mets' owners group, M. Donald Grant, left a private conference and was immediately surrounded by reporters. Grant started to answer their questions. Then he heard a voice from inside the room: "Donald, the agreement was not to speak to the reporters until after our final meeting." It was The O'Malley. Grant promptly apologized to the reporters and stopped talking.

Throughout the 1970s, people at the top of baseball commented on O'Malley's influence with a combination of respect, gratitude, and wariness. As longtime baseball executive Bill Giles would recall, only a young George Steinbrenner of the Yankees seemed inclined to oppose O'Malley. "The two of them needled each other mercilessly," recalled Giles. But in fact Steinbrenner studied the Dodgers operation intently and regarded O'Malley as "the recognized master." The recognition Steinbrenner noted came from outside baseball too. As one football team owner said at the time, "Compared to Walter, we're just running pushcarts."

The aura of power would remain as O'Malley steadily pared back his involvement with his own team, letting Peter take over, and focused on the future of baseball. He played a mostly conciliatory role in the game's adjustment to the players' union and free agency. In 1972 he noted the damage done to the game's reputation and revenues and pushed for a quick end to a players' strike. In 1976 he got his fellow owners and then-commissioner Bowie Kuhn to end a labor lockout and return to negotiations. His argument? Baseball couldn't afford to alienate the fans.

O'Malley's detractors, who could still be heard in Brooklyn and beyond, would see some irony in his devotion to the game's image. This was the same O'Malley who had cited the cold, hard facts of business as he pulled the team from its ancestral home and headed west. As much as anyone, he had challenged the romantic attachment many fans felt for the game. And yet he also loved baseball as something bigger than a business. With his team and his ballpark he believed he had struck exactly the right balance between tradition and modern appeal and that this style of ownership could keep the sport healthy.

Eager to maintain relationships, Walter O'Malley kept up correspondence with hundreds of old friends. Like most men who reach old age, he often reflected on his life and enjoyed reminiscing. In a note sent to an old friend in Michigan, he expressed his gratitude for copies of a recent article about Robert Moses and tried to describe his relationship with the great power broker:

> As to friendship, Bob and I knew each other over a long span of years and we were very close. Bob became an enemy when he sabotaged our plans to build a stadium in Brooklyn. He became a benefactor when his opposition became so violent that we left Brooklyn and happily became established in California.
>
> ... He would have made it big had he been chief of the White House staff under Dick Nixon. I am sure we would have had a dictatorship or a monarchy.

In other musings O'Malley addressed in private controversies that he avoided confronting in public. For example, in a long letter to Horace Stoneham he pieced together his recollections of their earliest talks about relocating. It all started, O'Malley believed, when the owners of New York's three ball clubs met with Mayor Wagner to discuss a tax on baseball tickets. Later, O'Malley recalled, the two men had talked about the Dodgers-Giants rivalry and began considering ways to replicate it in the future.

Besides giving him a chance to consider the past, semiretirement gave O'Malley time to respond to requests for advice and favors. Ballplayers came to him with business problems and in many cases he helped them sort them out. Bob Aspromonte's acquisition of a valuable beer franchise in Texas was one case in point. "He made me feel like I could do it, and it made all the difference in my life," recalled Aspromonte. Others came to O'Malley with grievances or requests he couldn't accommodate. Vincent X. Flaherty, who took to calling himself "The Forgotten Dodger Man," wrote rambling notes to remind O'Malley of all he did in the past.

"I alone am responsible for major league baseball AND pro football on the West Coast," wrote Flaherty as he complained about credit lavished on others. When he wrote of his struggles to find work, O'Malley asked members of the Dodgers staff to help him but apparently nothing worked out. In 1974, Flaherty told of how he had listened to radio broadcasts of the Dodgers-Athletics World Series because his television was broken. It was his last letter.

Whenever he could, O'Malley opened his door to those who wanted to learn from him, especially owners and baseball executives who were interested in his way of doing things. For a supposedly wily backroom operator, he was remarkably frank. When C. Raymond Grebey became baseball's labor negotiator, O'Malley gave him a thorough assessment of every owner and club in both leagues. As Grebey later told writer John Helyar, "He was one hundred percent right one hundred percent of the time."

Grebey met O'Malley in 1978. The Dodgers owner had turned seventy-five that year, and age slowed him in ways that competition never could. In Los Angeles, O'Malley was a well-recognized public figure and he could count friends in Hollywood, sports, finance, and other industries. But they had seen less and less of him during the 1970s. The ones who knew O'Malley well understood that he had cut back his social life, as well as his time at the office, in order to care for his wife, Kay, who suffered the first of several strokes at Dodgertown in the spring of 1972. (When it happened she was flown to the Mayo Clinic in Minnesota, where she received care for several weeks before going home to Los Angeles.)

"They were very private and devoted to each other," recalled their daughter, Terry Seidler. "I won't ever forget the way he took care of her, the way he put his arm around her as they watched the games together on TV."

When she was able, Kay still accompanied Walter to games and she returned to spring training in Vero Beach, where he piloted a golf cart around the premises, practiced poker, and still presided over the annual St. Patrick's Day bash. His last Dodgertown days came in 1979 as he struggled with cancer. He stayed close to his quarters that year, but when Marvin Miller arrived to talk with players, Peter O'Malley gave him a message. "He said his father wanted to see me," recalled Miller. "I thought that given his illness it might not be appropriate, but Peter said, 'No, he asked to see you.'"

Miller found the once formidable O'Malley shockingly thin but gamely cheerful. "He had difficulty talking, but a nurse brought him some medication and a drink and he regained his voice. Once he was able to talk, he kept saying how happy he was to see us, how happy he was that we could visit. I found myself thinking, 'This was a guy who could have been anything in the world. He was someone who had everything it took to be a success and the drive to do it.'"

Like many, Marvin Miller talked about O'Malley as if he were a force of nature. By age seventy-five, O'Malley had made a permanent mark on baseball and, with Dodger Stadium, built a landmark that helped to define and unify Los Angeles. His son, Peter, who with his wife, Annette, had three children, was firmly in control of the family business. His daughter, Terry, was happily married to Rollie Seidler and mother of nine (eventually ten) children, whom he called "The Pirates" after a cartoon strip called *Terry and the Pirates.*

In his last season, the force that was Walter O'Malley returned to the focus that had captured it more than fifty years before: his wife, Kay. While she dealt with the effects of several strokes and he grew more debilitated by cancer, they listened to Vin Scully call the Dodgers games and comforted each other. In early July, Walter returned to the Mayo Clinic. He was hospitalized in Rochester when Kay died on July 12. She was recalled in the *Los Angeles Times* as a recipient of the paper's Woman of the Year Award in 1971 in honor of her civic work. But the quotes attributed to her reflected a life focused on family, friends, church, baseball, and the man she first knew as a boy who called himself Retlaw. "I have lived a full life," she said near the end. "That's due to my husband, of course."

In his last major interview with a reporter, The O'Malley said, "I've had a marvelously interesting life. I don't know what there was that I missed." He had pursued life with a passion and will to succeed that propelled him through enough battles and adventures to satisfy several men. The same will had kept him going despite the cancer that riddled his body, until Kay died. He finally let go of life a month later. Terry, his daughter, liked to think that in his last moment he heard Kay whispering the lyrics to "Always" in his ear.

For Walter O'Malley the world was an old-fashioned beefsteak banquet where the man at your elbow was a fine fellow and there was never any shame in asking for more. Whether it was a brawl on the university campus, a pennant race, or a political fight, he threw himself into the moment with fearless confidence and manly gusto. Who else would dare move the Brooklyn Dodgers or organize an African safari?

Rivals could complain that The O'Malley sometimes bent the rules, but they would have a difficult time proving he committed any serious sins. He did plot and scheme and practice politics, but no more ruthlessly than his opponents. Branch Rickey, for example, managed to make himself look like a saint and a victim as he forced O'Malley to pay a premium for his stock. Robert Moses outmaneuvered O'Malley so skillfully that the truth about the stadium struggle wouldn't emerge until long after they were both dead.

For as long as he lived, O'Malley withheld certain details of his contests with Rickey and Moses, including information that might have made him a more sympathetic figure. Considering the way he treated others after a battle—welcoming Rickey in Los Angeles, offering Charlie Dressen a return to the team—it seems O'Malley fought hard but sought friendship after hostilities ceased. He looked forward and left the hand-wringing and recriminations to others.

Of course, it's easier to shrug off the past when you win the fight, and most of the time O'Malley came out the winner. His successes, and the fact that he achieved them without false modesty, were resented in some quarters. At the time of O'Malley's death, Red Smith of the *New York Times* recalled a victory party where his companion complained that the Dodgers owner was "a little too much the grand seigneur for my taste." In the same column Smith wrote that O'Malley was the first to say "out loud" that baseball was a business. "In Brooklyn, there was something approaching heartbreak" when the Dodgers left, he added. "From that day on some of the fun of baseball was lost."

In acknowledging that major-league baseball was at bottom a business, O'Malley did tell a truth that others denied. His decision would eventually be added to a host of events that nostalgic people would blame for a certain loss of innocence. In this view a blissful era was replaced by conflict, disillusionment, and turmoil that culminated in the crises of the late 1960s and early 1970s.

However, the same events could be seen as part of an awakening when people finally told the truth about many aspects of American life, including business, politics, and a divided society. The 1950s may have been a gauzy idyll for white American males with adequate incomes, but the myths denied great inequalities and obscured the real workings of power. Walter O'Malley did bring the economic reality of baseball to the fore, but in his open pursuit of profit and championships he treated others as mature adults who could handle the truth. Baseball has always been a business with the potential for great profits and the power to affect the mood and attitudes of local communities and the nation as a whole.

Under O'Malley a strong, stable Dodgers franchise continued the racial progress begun by Branch Rickey. He sparked unequaled growth in his industry and created wealth that was eventually distributed far more equitably to players, managers, and coaches of all races and backgrounds. Walter O'Malley's truth, while painful for Brooklyn, made the game thrive in ways that benefited millions of fans while he lived, and millions more after he died.

Those who hated O'Malley could only be correct from a perspective frozen in Brooklyn in October 1957, but there were many who shared this icy point of view. Dick Young of the *New York Daily News* was so resentful that he couldn't give O'Malley a break even in death. As he read obituaries that praised him, wrote Young, "I got sicker and sicker." Beginning in 1981, when his name was first mentioned for the honor, voters who agreed with Young blocked O'Malley's admission to the Hall of Fame every time he was considered.

During the same time period baseball lovers in Los Angeles backed

O'Malley's admission to the hall. While famously describing the man as "part oaf, part elf," Jim Murray of the *Los Angeles Times* wrote of O'Malley, "He did more for baseball than any commissioner who ever ran it." Others, most notably the writers Michael Shapiro and Neil Sullivan, suggested reconsideration of the Dodgers' departure from Brooklyn with Robert Moses in the villain's role.

No one did more harm to Brooklyn than Moses. He split Bay Ridge in two to build the Verrazano-Narrows Bridge, neglected public transit, hobbled the waterfront district, and built highways to the suburbs that hastened the departure of the middle class. Along Brooklyn's shoreline he replaced villagelike communities with high-rises. In Cobble Hill and Red Hook he put entire neighborhoods under the shadow of a six-lane elevated highway. In Fort Greene, where O'Malley had hoped to build his stadium, Fred Trump never developed the property that Moses had reserved for him. A year after O'Malley left, city officials were so shocked by conditions in the district's tenements that they cut short their visit because they feared getting sick. While other cities across America used new ballparks to stimulate local economies, much of Brooklyn declined as more than 150 manufacturers departed and little development occurred. The borough started to bounce back in the 1980s, and in 2004 a developer proposed an indoor sports arena for the site O'Malley had been denied. The Atlantic Yards project didn't progress any faster than O'Malley's domed stadium. As of 2009 the place where O'Malley would have built remained untouched.

Just as time healed Brooklyn, it eventually broke the spell that kept O'Malley out of the Hall of Fame. As he was admitted in 2008 the baseball world officially adopted a less parochial view of the man. Contrary to Red Smith's argument, the hall voters recognized that O'Malley had actually spread the fun around. He brought a major-league game to a huge city, state, and region that had been deprived for too long. He also pioneered a way of doing business that helped baseball survive ever-fiercer competition from other sports. (This was most evident in Los Angeles, where, in the age of pro football, the Dodgers dominate the scene and the nearest National Football League club is in San Diego.)

And although his harshest critics would never admit it, in his pursuit of profit and personal success, O'Malley actually helped to preserve some of the romance of baseball. Under O'Malley, the Dodgers became as deeply rooted in

Los Angeles as the Cubs were in Chicago and the Yankees were in New York. Winning teams, low ticket prices, and a bias-free approach to signing players helped build support from fans of every type.

The stadium, which O'Malley had tried to give Brooklyn and ultimately built in Chavez Ravine, was a significant factor in the team's stability. Other clubs sought government subsidies in the form of public stadiums and could be wooed from their homes by cities offering better deals. The Dodgers had the perfect place to play and the perfect lease arrangement of zero dollars per year. The team's home city was a great winner in this dynamic too. While economic studies showed that other communities lost money on their municipal stadiums, Los Angeles got a premier team for the cost of a onetime land swap and a few million dollars' worth of roads.

The city's affection for the team grew in the years that O'Malley's son Peter was in charge. In the 1980s, *Forbes* magazine called the younger O'Malley "the most valuable executive in either league." The Dodgers won two more championships—in 1981 and 1988—and drew six million fans more than the next-most-popular team. The organization was nearly as dominant in the 1990s, as The O'Malley's son added to a career record of nineteen first- or second-place finishes in twenty-seven seasons. He made the team a more international organization by promoting foreign-born players such as Fernando Valenzuela, Hideo Nomo, and Chan Ho Park. In 1987 he built the first top-level major-league training center in the Dominican Republic. "Prior to that," he would recall, "you could visit a ball club's camp and see a goat, literally, on the front steps of the players' quarters." The players trained at Campo Las Palmas include Pedro Martinez, Raul Mondesi, and Pedro Astacio.

Peter O'Malley accomplished these goals in an age when baseball became a much bigger business with more teams and higher stakes. Walter O'Malley had thrived in a time when a man could make bold moves in a cloud of cigar smoke. After he was gone, agents, union rules, and shifting social mores demanded different things from owners. Women reporters worked in the press box. A ballplayers' strike killed the 1994 season. Hardly anyone smoked cigars anymore. If Peter O'Malley was less flashy and more circumspect than his father, it was because he had to be.

By the mid-1990s nearly every family that was in baseball when the Dodgers moved to Los Angeles had sold out and withdrawn from the same. As then-

commissioner Bud Selig noted, the business was too expensive for family own-
ers who didn't have substantial outside interests. "You need a broader base than
an individual family [fortune] to carry you through the storms," he explained.
Looking at a future in which more than a dozen heirs might share ownership,
Peter and his sister Terry decided to sell. The price, $325 million, was paid by
Rupert Murdoch's News Corporation.

Fox had expected to derive great benefits from owning both the team
and television outlets that delivered games to viewers, but the corporation
never got the hang of it. After failing to make the playoffs six years in a row,
Murdoch sold to a Boston real estate developer named Frank McCourt. He
promised to "restore the glory days."

The Dodgers fared a little better under McCourt, but two first-round playoff defeats in five years hardly constituted glory. Nevertheless, the Dodgers were
such a part of Los Angeles that people still filled the stadium. In 2007, as they
muddled to a next-to-last finish in their division, only the Yankees drew more
fans. Before the year was out, Walter O'Malley was finally elected to the Baseball
Hall of Fame. Five decades after the Dodgers Convair left LaGuardia Airport
carrying the team and major-league baseball westward, The O'Malley was recognized for his foresight, resilience, strength, and nerve.

In early 2008, the city of Los Angeles began a year of celebrations marking
the fiftieth anniversary of the team's arrival. To kick things off, more than
115,000 jammed the Coliseum, the Dodgers' first home in Los Angeles, for an
exhibition game against the Red Sox. The Dodgers set yet another record, drawing the biggest baseball crowd ever to see a baseball game.

More than a few of the older fans at the Coliseum wore Brooklyn jerseys
and caps to the fiftieth-anniversary game. As they joined in the cheers for Roz
Wyman, who was honored for her role in bringing the team west, it was difficult
to imagine they still resented The O'Malley. Only the most hardened sons of
Flatbush would deny the man's contribution to the game and to a deserving
city. Only the most hardheaded would refuse to forgive him for making the
most out of the Dodgers.

Acknowledgments

Forever Blue benefited from the recollections and personal papers of people who knew Walter O'Malley. It is also descended from the previous reporting and writing of dozens of journalists and authors. Whatever insight may be found here is informed by these sources.

Peter O'Malley and his sister, Terry Seidler, opened to me, without reservation, a family archive that holds tens of thousands of items. There, with the continuous and enthusiastic help of Robert Schweppe and Brent Shyer, I discovered documents ranging from a card sent by young Walter to his mother to a long letter, written by hand, from Jackie Robinson to O'Malley the team owner. No box or file was placed out of bounds and I am indebted to them for the raw data the archives contained and the thrill of opening a folder and watching a Christy Mathewson baseball card flutter out and down to the floor.

Among the writers and broadcasters who went before me and generously offered advice, wisdom, and aid, I can thank Roger Kahn, Vin Scully, Dave Anderson, Mel Durslag, Lee Lowenfish, Richard Sandomir, Rudy Marzano, Jeff Katz, Stu Nahan, and Jaime Jarrin.

Former—and therefore forever—Dodgers who graciously answered questions they have heard many times before included Ralph Branca, Carl Erskine, Maury Wills, Duke Snider, Don Newcombe, Ron Fairly, Bob Aspromonte, and Tommy Lasorda, who welcomed me as a *paisan* and finished our lunch with a song for everyone present in Room 40.

Two great figures from the Dodgers past, Johnny Podres and Buzzie Bavasi, gave me hours of their time in what turned out to be the final months of their lives. Johnny met me at a gas station in a car with "MVP" on its license plate and led me to his home for a three-hour chat. Buzzie, who wore a tie every time we met, gave me Cokes and candy bars and paid me the best compliment I could imagine: "You would have made a good baseball man." Rachel Robinson indulged my questions, even the more personal ones.

Others who worked for the Dodgers, or in the service of the team and the game of baseball, generously offered their anecdotes and insights. Rosalind Wyman, still one of the most influential women in California politics, made time in her hectic schedule to recall how the Dodgers came west. H. R. "Bump" Holman painted a vivid picture of Vero Beach and Dodgers in flight. Tom Villante explained the relationship between broadcasters and baseball teams, and executives Bill Giles, Dick Walsh, and Fred Claire helped me to understand baseball as a business. Bill DeLury described the everyday workings of a team operation. Similar insights on the inner workings of the game were offered by Richard Moss and Marvin Miller, labor advocates who did as much to change the game as The O'Malley.

Archival assistance for my research was provided by Jeff Barton of the Brooklyn Historical Society and Thomas Lannon of the Manuscripts and Archives Division of the New York Public Library. I received further help from the staff at the Charles E. Young Research Library of the University of California Los Angeles.

Those living who knew a younger Walter O'Malley on a social basis are few, and I benefited from their patience and memories. Members of the Mylod family, especially Katherine Mylod—an original Myomac—did their best to recall days long past. So, too, did Rex Sita, Lou Mento, and Danny Wilson, of the Dodger Sym-phony Band.

As always, I depended on my own team, including David McCormick, Brian Lipson, Laura Perciasepe, and my extraordinary editor and publisher, Geoffrey Kloske, who pushes at the right moments and indulges my neuroses. David Chesanow, Marie Finamore, Peter Grennan, and John Morrone copyedited and proofread my book with great patience and skill. More essential support came from the three women who are the center of my life: Toni, Amy, and Elizabeth. They may not grasp my fascination with baseball and days gone by, but their love, intelligence, and support sustain me every day.

Selected Sources

═══════════════

This bibliography lists only primary sources for key events. All private letters noted are held by the O'Malley family archive unless otherwise indicated. Data on population trends are from the United States Census. Scores, statistics, and events from historic games reported in *Forever Blue* have been drawn from contemporary newspaper accounts, baseball-reference.com, baseball-almanac.com, and several encyclopedic volumes, including:

Bill James, *The New Bill James Historical Baseball Abstract* (New York: Free Press, 2001)

Burton Solomon, *The Baseball Timeline* (New York: Avon Books, 1997)

William F. McNeil, *The Dodgers Encyclopedia* (sportspublishingLLC.com, 2003)

INTRODUCTION

Roscoe McGowan, "Dodgers Defeat Pirates in Ebbets Field Finale," *New York Times*, Sept. 25, 1957, p. 33.

Emmett Kelly's recollections of the last game at Ebbets Field from "A Clown's Eye View of Baseball," *New York Times*, July 4, 1965, p. S3.

Jack Newfield's evaluation of O'Malley appears in Peter Golenbock, *Bums* (Chicago: Contemporary Books, 2000), p. 492. It is routinely quoted when O'Malley is mentioned in the press.

Hamill's "never forgive, never forget" comment appeared in Pete Hamill, "Baseball Hall of Fame Opens Doors for Former Dodger Owner Walter O'Malley," *New York Daily News*, Dec. 4, 2007. Other comments about O'Malley can be found at PeteHamill.com.

CHAPTER 1

For Edwin O'Malley's appearance before the state investigating committee, see "O'Malley in Rage Quits as Witness; Case up to Swann," *New York Times*, Sept. 1, 1921, p. 1.

For a sense of corruption in New York City government, see: Milton McKaye, *The Tin Box Parade: A Handbook for Larceny* (New York: McBride and Company, 1934); William B. Northrup and John B. Northrup, *The Insolence of Office* (New York: G. P. Putnam's Sons, 1932); Charles E. Still, *Styles in Crimes* (New York: Lippincott Company, 1938); and Oliver E. Allen, *The Tiger: The Rise and Fall of Tammany Hall* (New York: Addison-Wesley, 1993).

For Plunkitt's "opportunities," see William L. Riordan, *Plunkitt of Tammany Hall* (Whitefish, Montana: Kessinger, 2007), p. 3.

For "talking Irish" and a serious analysis of Irish-American culture, language, and social attitudes, see Monica McGoldrick et al., *Ethnicity and Family Therapy* (New York: Guilford Press, 1982), pp. 310–39.

The letters sent to Culver to support Walter O'Malley's application and exchanges between father and son are held by the O'Malley family archive.

Walter confessed to his stubborn streak in "Pete Martin Calls on Walter O'Malley," *Philadelphia Sunday Bulletin Magazine*, May 2, 1965, p. 4.

Culver background from interview with academy historian Robert B. D. Hartman and from his book *Pass in Review* (Culver, Indiana: Culver Educational Foundation, 1993).

For hazing, see Charles Peters, *Five Days in Philadelphia: The Amazing "We Want Willkie!" Convention of 1940* (New York: Public Affairs, 2005), p. 26.

For change in American life after World War I, see Frederick Lewis Allen's *Only Yesterday*, first published in 1931, reprinted in 1986 (New York: Bonanza Books, 1986). See in particular pp. 61–64, 104, 230–31.

For the baseball scandal, see Eliot Asinof's book *Eight Men Out: The Black Sox and the 1919 World Series* (New York: Henry Holt, 1963).

The stories of O'Malley's days at Penn are based in part on "Pete Martin Calls on Walter O'Malley," *Philadelphia Sunday Bulletin Magazine*, May 2, 1965, p. 4; and Andrew K. Becker and Michelle A. Woodson, *Rites of Passage: Student Traditions and Class Fights*, from online archives of the University of Pennsylvania.

Flour fight recalled in a Walter O'Malley letter held by the family archive. See also "Sophomores in Flour Fight," *Daily Pennsylvanian*, Oct. 19, 1922, p. 1.

Letter from young Walter O'Malley to Katherine "Kay" O'Malley from O'Malley family archive. Her sports interest is noted in Austin Scott, "Kay O'Malley, 72, Wife of Dodgers Owner, Dies," *Los Angeles Times*, July 14, 1979, Part II, p. 1.

CHAPTER 2

The Walker story is told in detail in Herbert Mitgang, *Once Upon a Time in New York* (New York: Free Press, 2000).

The story of economic growth in the 1920s is told, in capsule form, in Kevin Phillips's *Wealth and Democracy* (New York: Broadway Books, 2002), pp. 59–66.

For an overview of changes in design, see David Raizman, *History of Modern Design* (London: Laurence King Publishing, 2004).

For the rise of radio and other changes in the 1920s, see Frederick Lewis Allen's *Only Yesterday* (New York: Bonanza Books, 1986). See in particular pp. 105, 161–67, 190–91, 270–73.

Edwin O'Malley's real estate work noted in Mrs. Edwin J. O'Malley's obituary in the *New York Times*, June 4, 1940, p. 24.

Walter O'Malley's salary is noted in the L. G. Fenton, Engineer in Charge, letter "To Whom It May Concern," March 1, 1933, held by O'Malley family archive.

Thomas F. Riley letter to support O'Malley's application to the bar, March 2, 1933, held by O'Malley family archive.

For Walter O'Malley's recollections, see Roger Kahn, "Exported to Brooklyn," *New York Herald Tribune*, April 11, 1954; and "Walter in Wonderland," *Time* magazine cover article, April 28, 1958.

Albert Conway notes his relationship with O'Malley in a March 1, 1943, letter held by the O'Malley family archive.

The Myomacs were recalled by Katherine Mylod, a member of the group, in an interview with author.

Information on John McCooey from "Herbert J. McCooey, Lawyer, Dies at 35," *New York Times*,

Nov. 1, 1936. See also Jerome Krase and Charles LaCerra, *Ethnicity and Machine Politics* (Lanham, Maryland: University Press of America, 1991), pp. 28–51. Quotes from WalterOmalley. com.

Information on O'Malley's business contacts, social outings, and clients are included in his personal journals, which are held by the O'Malley family archive. O'Malley discussed his reorganization work in Charles Maher, "Friends, Enemies Respect Dodger Owner," *Boulder Camera*, undated clipping in University of Pennsylvania Archive, O'Malley file.

For McLaughlin, see "McLaughlin Quits Police, "*New York Times*, March 20, 1927, p. 1. McLaughlin is also described in author interview with Emil "Buzzie" Bavasi and by Robert Moses in Robert Caro's *The Power Broker* (New York: Vintage Books, 1975), p. 137. For Moses's criticisms of McCooey and others, see *The Power Broker*, p. 357.

For banquets, see Paul Lukas, "Gluttonous Rite Survives Without Silverware," *New York Times*, Jan. 30, 2008, p. F1.

For the complete story of Ebbets Field, see Bob McKee, *The Greatest Ballpark Ever* (New Brunswick, N.J.: Rivergate Books, 2006).

For the transformation of baseball and the myth of opportunity, see Steven A. Reiss, "Professional Baseball and Social Mobility," *Journal of Interdisciplinary History* 1 (Autumn 1980), pp. 235–50.

The shooting is recalled in David W. McCullough, *Brooklyn and How It Got That Way* (New York: Dial Press, 1983), p. 111. See also Peter Golenbock, *Bums* (Chicago: Contemporary Books, 2000), pp. 290–91.

Stephen McKeever is described in Harold Parrott, *The Lords of Baseball* (New York: Praeger, 1976), p. 86.

A summary of the Ebbets-McKeever feud, as well as the role of Barnewall and the trust company, is in a lengthy memorandum sent by Walter O'Malley to Branch Rickey on Sept. 20, 1950, and held by the O'Malley family archive.

Larry MacPhail is portrayed throughout Harold Parrott's *The Lords of Baseball*. See the introduction by Red Smith and passages about MacPhail on pp. 111-21. See also Lee Lowenfish, *Branch Rickey* (Lincoln, Nebraska: University of Nebraska Press, 2007) and Ralph Berge's MacPhail profile published online by the Society for American Baseball Research, http://www.bioproj.sabr.org/bioproj.cfm?a=v&v=l&bid=1070&pid=8621.

Durocher's background from Gerald Eskenazi, *The Lip* (New York: William Morrow, 1993). His treatment of Babe Ruth is described in Peter Golenbock, *Bums*, pp. 15-22.

Barber's hiring and vaudeville dream noted in Peter Golenbock, *Bums*, p. 179.

Life in Brooklyn and its neighborhoods is depicted in *The Neighborhoods of Brooklyn* (New Haven: Yale University Press, 1998). See also Anita Brenner, "A Borough, a City, Another World— Brooklyn," *New York Times*, Jan. 22, 1939, p. 99.

O'Malley letter to General Gignilliat, Dec. 29, 1937, held by the O'Malley family archive.

Details of O'Malley's life in Brooklyn from interviews with his children, Peter O'Malley and Theresa O'Malley Seidler.

Gignilliat letter held by the O'Malley family archive.

CHAPTER 3

Ring information from *Sports Illustrated*, April 29, 1985.

The beaning and MacPhail's response appear in Harold Parrott, *The Lords of Baseball* (New York: Praeger, 1976), pp. 114–15.

Reiser's story is told in Lee Lowenfish, *Branch Rickey* (Lincoln, Nebraska: University of Nebraska Press, Lincoln, 2007), pp. 282–83 and 310–11. See also Walter Lanier ("Red") Barber, "Prescription for a Ball Player," *New York Times*, Sept. 13, 1942, p. SM13.

Medwick's batting style is noted in Walter "Red" Barber, 1947: When All Hell Broke Loose in Baseball (New York: Doubleday, 1982), pp. 198–99. See also Leo Durocher, The Dodgers and Me (Chicago: Ziff-Davis, 1948), pp. 56–57.

Mrs. Edwin J. O'Malley's obituary appeared in the New York Times, June 4, 1940, p. 24.

Life in the O'Malley home is described by Peter O'Malley and Theresa O'Malley Seidler in interviews. Other recollections from Katherine Mylod Mainzer.

The problem of theft in the cash-handling system is noted in Roger Kahn's Good Enough to Dream (Lincoln, Nebraska: Bison Books, 2000), p. 56.

Durocher's wrangling with MacPhail is reported in Leo Durocher, The Dodgers and Me (Chicago: Ziff-Davis, 1948), pp. 97–106.

MacPhail in the shower recalled by John Helyar, Lords of the Realm (New York: Villard, 1994), p. 43.

MacPhail's comments are from minutes of the Brooklyn Dodgers board of directors meeting, held by O'Malley family archive.

For the Hugh Casey–Ernest Hemingway fight, see Stan Isaacs, "The Cuban Baseball Days of Ernest Hemingway," www.thecolumnists.com. Also see Red Barber, "Ernest Hemingway and the Tough Dodgers," New York Times, Nov. 14, 1976, p. 190.

Jay Topkis, "Monopoly in Professional Sports," Yale Law Journal 58, no. 5 (April 1949), pp. 691–712.

Clete D. Mitchell, "The Rise of America's Two Pastimes: Baseball and Law," Michigan Law Review 97, no. 6 (May 1999), pp. 2042–61.

Anthony C. Krautmann and Margaret Oppenheimer, "Free Agency and the Allocation of Labor in Major League Baseball," Managerial and Decision Economics 15 (1994), pp. 459–69.

Reserve clause reviewed in Marvin Miller, A Whole Different Ballgame (New York: Birch Lane, 1991), pp. 41–42. For Cronin quote, see pp. 80–81.

"Ripen into money" quote reported in Lee Lowenfish, Branch Rickey (Lincoln, Nebraska: University of Nebraska Press, 2007), p. 122.

Rickey's salary and bonuses noted in John Helyar, Lords of the Realm, p. 45.

For quip about Rickey being "a trifle too good," see Lee Lowenfish, Branch Rickey, p. 85.

"Ferocious gentlemen" is uttered by Rickey in "Rickey Defends Dodger Players," New York Times, June 14, 1945, p. 22.

Walter Lanier ("Red") Barber, "Prescription for a Ball Player," New York Times, Sept. 13, 1942, p. SM13.

The wild side of the Dodger clubhouse is revealed in Red Barber, 1947: When All Hell Broke Loose in Baseball, pp. 28–29; and in Leo Durocher, Nice Guys Finish Last (New York: Simon & Schuster, 1975), pp. 237–39.

O'Malley's letters to Herbert Smith (March 4, 1943), Colonel Martin H. Hay (March 4, 1943), and Captain E. S. Pratt (March 8, 1943) held by the O'Malley family archive.

Babe Dahlgren's story is told in full by his grandson Matt Dahlgren in Rumor in Town (Ashland, Ohio: Woodlyn Lane, 2007).

For Rickey's meeting with the Dodger board at the New York Athletic Club, see Arthur Mann, Branch Rickey: American in Action (Boston: Houghton Mifflin, 1957), pp. 212–13.

The O'Malley mission to scout Silvio Garcia is reported in Roger Kahn, The Boys of Summer (New York: Harper & Row, 1972), p. 426.

Andrew Hanssen, "The Cost of Discrimination: A Study of Major League Baseball," Southern Economic Journal 64, no. 3 (1998), pp. 603–27.

CHAPTER 4

For wartime baseball, see Thomas Gilbert, Baseball at War (New York: Franklin Watts, 1997). See also Bill Gilbert, They Also Served: Baseball and the Homefront, 1941–1945 (New York: Crown

Publishers, 1992); and Richard Goldstein, *Spartan Seasons: How Baseball Survived the Second World War* (New York: Macmillan, 1990).

Rickey's financial condition noted in Arthur Mann, *Branch Rickey: American in Action* (Boston: Houghton Mifflin, 1957), p. 230.

John L. Smith's relationship with O'Malley from Herman Obermeyer. "Dem Bums Get New Boss Herman," *Long Island Press*, Nov. 19, 1950, p. Q 21.

Smith's appraisal of Rickey is from J. G. T. Spink, "Meet Mr. Penicillin," *Sporting News* (St. Louis), June 26, 1946, p. 1.

Rickey's demand to buy stock in the Browns noted in Lee Lowenfish, *Branch Rickey* (Lincoln, Nebraska: University of Nebraska Press, 2007), p. 64.

Conversation between O'Malley and Rickey from private memorandum sent by O'Malley to Rickey, Sept. 20, 1950, held by the O'Malley family archive.

"Rickey Purchases Share in Dodgers," *New York Times*, Nov. 2, 1944, p. 24.

John Smith's stake in the team was revealed in Roscoe McGowan, "Dodgers Chief Says Job Is to Play Ball," *New York Times*, Jan. 26, 1945, p. 18.

Details on Dodgers executive moves from board of directors' minutes.

For Chandler's attitude, see "Stand Reaffirmed by Sen. Chandler: 'Can't and Don't Intend to Be Lenient,'" *New York Times*, May 7, 1945, p. 13; and Peter Golenbock, *Bums* (Chicago: Contemporary Books, 2000), pp. 135–36.

Comment on spring training group from Leo Durocher, *The Dodgers and Me* (Chicago: Ziff-Davis, 1948), pp. 206–7.

"Durocher Is Arrested on Charge of Beating Veteran at Ebbets Field; Durocher Accused of Beating a Fan, Detectives Arrest Pair," *New York Times*, June 11, 1945, p. 1.

Investigator's report held by the O'Malley family archive.

For Durocher payout, see Lee Lowenfish, *Branch Rickey*, p. 347.

For Chandler's quote and more detail on the Christian case and Durocher, see Gerald Eskenazi, *The Lip* (New York: William Morrow, 1993), pp. 182–5.

Details on the sale of Ebbets stock from "Ebbets Hearing June 30th," *New York Times*, June 8, 1945, p. 14.

"Ebbets Estate Settled," *New York Times*, Dec. 14, 1949, p. 37.

Private memorandum dated Sept. 20, 1950, Walter O'Malley to Branch Rickey, held by the O'Malley family archive.

Memorandum of Agreement, Sept. 21, 1945, between John L. Smith, Walter F. O'Malley, and Branch Rickey held by the O'Malley family archive.

For Mulvey and Samuel Goldwyn, see "Hollywood Renegades Archive" at http://www.cobbles.com/simpp_archive.

Anthony Chen, *The Passage of State Fair Employment Legislation, 1945–1964*, Institution for Research on Labor and Employment Working Paper Series (Berkeley, California: University of California–Berkeley, 2001).

Robinson's military experience and playing for the Monarchs, as well as Rickey's early interest and O'Malley's support, noted throughout Arnold Rampersad, *Jackie Robinson: A Biography* (New York: Ballantine, 1997).

"U.S. Negro League Is Launched with Brown Dodgers in Brooklyn," *New York Times*, May 8, 1945, p. 22. See also Lee Lowenfish, *Branch Rickey*, pp. 386–87.

Robinson's experience is told in great detail by Arnold Rampersad in *Jackie Robinson*.

Bavasi quote from interview with the author.

Major League Steering Committee report of Aug. 27, 1946.

MacPhail claimed authorship of the report during testimony before a congressional committee. See "MacPhail Urges Four More Major Leagues Be Formed," *New York Times*, Oct. 25, 1951, p. 38.

Fifteen-to-one vote recounted in Red Barber, *1947: When All Hell Broke Loose in Baseball* (New York: Doubleday, 1982), p. 80.

Dodgers' plan for a 1948 run from board minutes.

Baseball's postwar style noted in Bill James, *The New Bill James Historical Baseball Abstract* (New York: Free Press, 2001), pp. 197–8.

Cars and O'Malley resentment noted in Rudy Marzano, *The Brooklyn Dodgers in the 1940s* (Jefferson, N.C.: McFarland, 2005), pp. 123–4.

For the relationship between O'Malley and Rickey, see Lowenfish, p. 401, and Harold Parrott, *The Lords of Baseball* (New York: Praeger, 1976), pp. 15–16.

Data on Dodgers spending, revenue, and financial concerns from minutes of the board of directors.

For Rickey's gawking, see Harold Parrott, *The Lords of Baseball*, pp. 21–22.

For Landis quote, see David Pietrusza, *Judge and Jury: The Life and Times of Kenesaw Mountain Landis* (South Bend, Indiana: Diamond Communications, 1998), p. 361.

O'Malley describes his meeting with the lawyer for the Pasquels and offers his opinions in a May 14, 1946, memo to Branch Rickey held by the O'Malley family archive.

CHAPTER 5

Robinson's debut from Arnold Rampersad, *Jackie Robinson: A Biography* (New York: Ballantine, 1997), p. 169; and Jackie Robinson, *I Never Had It Made* (New York: G. P. Putnam, 1972), p. 70.

Arthur Daley, "Opening Day at Ebbets Field," *New York Times*, April 16, 1947, p. 32.

For MacPhail's opposition to Robinson and antipathy toward the Dodgers, see Red Barber, *1947: When All Hell Broke Loose in Baseball*, p. 80.

Pegler's attack is described in Red Barber, *1947: When All Hell Broke Loose in Baseball*, pp. 96–97, as well as in Lee Lowenfish, *Branch Rickey*, pp. 408–9.

For a profile of Pegler, see Diane McWhorter, "Dangeous Minds," *Slate*, March 4, 2004, at http://www.slate.com/id/2096673/.

"Love thief" and other details of Durocher's 1947 controversies are noted in Harold Parrott, *The Lords of Baseball* (New York: Praeger, 1976), pp. 180–4.

O'Malley letter to Durocher, Jan. 24, 1947, from the O'Malley family archive.

For information on owners, see "Dan Topping Dead at 61; Yankee Owner for 22 Years," *New York Times*, May 20, 1974, p. 34. See also Bill Veeck and Edward Linn, "Walter O'Malley: Boss of Baseball," *Look*, July 3, 1962, pp. 80–93.

The story of Happy Chandler's handling of Durocher, MacPhail, the Yankees, and the Dodgers is told in Durocher's *Nice Guys Finish Last* (New York: Simon & Schuster, 1978), pp. 250–60; in Arthur Mann, *Branch Rickey: American in Action* (Boston: Houghton Mifflin, 1957), pp. 248–52; in Lee Lowenfish, *Branch Rickey*, pp. 404–25; and in Red Barber, *1947: When All Hell Broke Loose in Baseball*, pp. 115–23.

Rickey memo of July 5, 1947, held by the O'Malley family archive. See also MacPhail, "Seeing Chandler Today," *New York Times*, Sept. 11, 1947, p. 34.

Reiser's injury is noted in a June 5, 1947, letter from Walter O'Malley to Fred Walker held by the O'Malley archive.

For the Yankees' racial policies, see Roger Kahn, *The Era, 1947–1957* (New York: Ticknor & Fields, 1993), pp. 45 and 189–90. See also Howard Bryant, *Shutout: The Story of Race and Baseball in Boston* (Boston: Routledge, 2002), pp. 50–51.

James Walker and Robert Ballamy, "Baseball on Television," *Nine* (spring 2003), p. 17.

"Film Leaders Map Communist Policy; Secrecy Marks Session Here as Committee Prepares Report on Employment," *New York Times*, Nov. 25, 1947, p. 33. See also Larry Englund and Steven Caplair, *The Inquisition in Hollywood* (Champaign, Illinois: University of Illinois, 1980), pp. 330–40.

For the Rickey and Gardella lawsuit, see Marvin Miller, *A Whole Different Ballgame* (New York: Birch Lane, 1991), p. 179.

For attendance figures and Robinson, see Joseph Dorinson and Joram Warmund, *Jackie Robinson: Race, Sports and the American Dream* (Armonk, N.Y.: M. E. Sharpe, 1998), pp. 175–90.

For the shift from urban to suburban, see Elaine Tyler May, *Homeward Bound: American Families in the Cold War Era* (New York: Basic Books, 1988), pp. 24–28; and Jane Jacobs, *The Death and Life of Great American Cities* (New York: Vintage, 1992), pp. 195–98.

Durocher's departure is chronicled in Roger Kahn, *The Era, 1947–1957*, pp. 149–56.

For Smith's unhappiness, see Joseph Dorinson and Joram Warmund, *Jackie Robinson: Race, Sports and the American Dream*, pp. 182–5.

Rickey's salary has been variously reported in the $40,000 to $50,000 range. Over five years his bonuses totaled $730,000. For this figure, see "Celler Releases Dodgers Figures," *New York Times*, Nov. 8, 1951, p. 39. The Dodger payroll was about $313,000 in 1946 and $430,000 in 1950, according to "Findings of Subcommittee Show Salary Increases Paid in Baseball," *New York Times*, May 21, 1952, p. 32.

Dodger football losses from Arthur Young and Company audit held by the O'Malley family archive.

Conditions at Vero are discussed in an Oct. 5, 1960, letter from O'Malley to Vincent X. Flaherty held by the O'Malley family archive.

For Meany see Roger Kahn, *The Era, 1947–1957*, pp. 143–4. For coziness, see pp. 164–5.

For Rickey's anticommunism, see Murray Polner, *Branch Rickey* (New York: Signet, 1982), pp. 214–5.

Robinson's testimony and white reaction is covered in Arnold Rampersad, *Jackie Robinson: A Biography*, pp. 211–6.

The Truman story is in Roger Kahn, *The Era, 1947–1957*, pp. 225.

Ring story recalled in, among other sources, John Helyar, *Lords of the Realm* (New York: Villard, 1994), p. 47.

O'Malley's plan for the football team was recorded in handwritten notes made to document the late-night meeting held to discuss the future of the franchise. These notes and a memorandum outlining the concerns Rickey discussed with league officials in Chicago are held in the O'Malley archives.

O'Malley's involvement in Rickey's real estate and the fertilizer lawsuit is recorded in a series of letters from attorney Richard Carvel to Walter O'Malley held in the O'Malley family archive.

For a fine consideration of the Cleveland Browns and the AAFC, see Dave Anderson, "Long Forgotten Perfection by the Lake," *New York Times*, Jan. 27, 2008, p. S4.

The scapegoat role is mentioned in a memo from O'Malley to Rickey dated Sept. 19, 1947, held by the O'Malley family archive.

O'Malley letter regarding fishing dated Aug. 30, 1948.

The rivalry with Rickey is noted in many places, including Roger Kahn, *The Era, 1947–1957*, p. 298; see also Murray Polner, *Branch Rickey*, pp. 215–6.

Dodgers radio is described in Jules Tygiel, *Past Time: Baseball as History* (New York: Oxford University Press, 2001), pp. 152–3.

The trip Rickey and O'Malley took to Philadelphia is recorded in a private memo O'Malley sent to Rickey dated Sept. 20, 1950, held by the O'Malley family archive.

Rickey's offer to the Kennedy family is noted in a Feb. 9, 1962, letter from Walter O'Malley to Frank Schroth.

Rickey confirmed his financial problems in Dan Daniel, "Rickey Gives Inside on Brook Dismissal," *Sporting News* (St. Louis), Dec. 29, 1950, p. 1.

Rickey's expenses are divulged in a memo written by Arthur Mann to Max Kase of the *New York Journal-American* dated Oct. 25, 1957, held by the O'Malley family archive.

For the biographer's evaluation of Rickey, see Lee Lowenfish, *Branch Rickey*, p. 488.

Lowenfish also covers aspects of the sale of Rickey's stock in *Branch Rickey*, pp. 484–8.

For the stock sale and Rickey's effort to sell, see also Murray Polner, *Branch Rickey*, pp. 217–22.

CHAPTER 6

The description of the office is based on recollections from many interview subjects and an article by Red Smith titled "On Dark and Bloody Ground" that was published in late November 1953 in the *New York Herald Tribune*. Undated article held by the O'Malley family archive.

For quote on race and ballplayers, see http://www.walteromalley.com/thisday_10_30.php.

O'Malley's comment on race is noted in a column titled "The Old Scout: Dodgers Still Seek Negroes" published in the *New York Sun*, Oct. 30, 1951.

Joe Williams, "O'Malley Defends Bums as Name for Dodgers." Williams wrote for the *New York World Telegram*. Article is from either 1952 or 1953 (the exact date is not noted) and is held by the O'Malley family archive.

Radio Electronics Television Manufacturers Association annual report, 1953.

For an assessment of lifestyle changes, see Elaine Tyler May, *Homeward Bound: American Families in the Cold War Era* (New York: Basic Books, 1988), pp. 97–90.

For a recollection of the rough crowd at Ebbets Field, see Neil J. Sullivan, *The Dodgers Move West* (New York: Oxford University Press, 1987), pp. 11–12.

Joe King, "Dodgers to Build Along Yankee Style," *Sporting News* (St. Louis), Nov. 1, 1950, p. 3.

For the Yankee model, see Lance A. Berger with Dorothy R. Berger, *Management Wisdom from the New York Yankees Dynasty* (New York: Wiley, 2005).

Bavasi's history and recollections are from an interview with the author.

O'Malley's regret from Joe King, "Down O'Malley's Alley," *Sporting News* (St. Louis), May 7, 1952, p. 13.

Chandler's handling of the TV contract from John Helyar, *Lords of the Realm* (New York: Villard, 1994), pp. 76–77.

For Hollywood stars, see Richard Beverage, *The Hollywood Stars* (Mount Pleasant, S.C.: Arcadia Publishing, 2005), pp. 41–43.

Vincent X. Flaherty, "Pitch-by-Pitch Tale of the Battle for a Major League Franchise," *Sporting News*, Oct. 30, 1957.

For The McManus, see William Riordan, *Plunkitt of Tammany Hall* (Whitefish, Montana: Kessinger, 2007), pp. 23–25.

For Dressen controversy, see Dave Anderson, "May Not Sign Dressen Until Season's End," undated 1953 clipping from *Brooklyn Eagle* held by the O'Malley family archive; and Ruth Dressen, "Should a Wife Interfere?" in *American Weekly*, Dec. 6, 1953, pp. 4–6.

Columnist Bob Cooke accused Bavasi of working to oust Dressen in his column, "Another Viewpoint," published in *New York Herald Tribune* in Oct. 1953.

O'Malley recalled his post-negotiation meeting with Dressen and speculated about Ruth Dressen's intentions in an Oct. 29, 1953, letter to writer Gene Cuneo held by the O'Malley family archive.

Bavasi describes his meeting with Reese and Alston's hiring in Buzzie Bavasi, *Off the Record* (Chicago: Contemporary Books, 1987), pp. 53–54.

For O'Malley's respect for Rickey and "stands by his word," see Red Barber, *The Broadcasters* (New York: Dial, 1970), p. 172.

Scully's experience and attitudes taken from interview with the author.

DC-3 story from author's interview with H. R. "Bump" Holman, copilot of the DC-3, and Bud Holman's son.

Population trends from Elliot Willensky, *When Brooklyn Was the World* (New York: Harmony Books, 1986), p. 229; and Harold Connolly, *A Ghetto Grows in Brooklyn* (New York: New York University, 1977), pp. 14, 75, and 141. For Brooklyn Navy Yard history, see http://www.columbia.edu/~jrs9/BNY-LH.html.

Walter O'Malley tells the story of Mrs. Walton in Gerald Holland, "A Visit with the Artful Dodger," *Saturday Evening Post*, July 1986, p. 24.

Edwin's troubles are outlined in Constance Heath's letter to Walter O'Malley dated May 1953.

For Bingham at Normandie, see Joseph Baloski, *Beyond the Beachhead* (Mechanicsburg, Pennsylvania: Stackpole Books, 1999), p. 132.

For a portrait of Stoneham, see Bill Veeck and Ed Linn, "For He's a Jolly Good Fellow," *Sports Illustrated*, May 31, 1965. See also Thomas Rogers, "Horace Stoneham, 86, Owner Who Moved Giants to the West Coast," *New York Times*, Jan. 9, 1990, p. D23.

For Robinson on Mays, see Harvey Rosenfeld, *The Great Chase* (Jefferson, N.C.: McFarland, 1992), p. 63.

Robert Moses is revealed in Robert Caro's *The Power Broker* (New York: Vintage, 1975). See in particular pp. 716–34 as well as Chapter 34, "The Mayors."

For the end of the season and Reese's quote, see Harvey Rosenfeld, *The Great Chase*, Chapter 5.

For the door-kicking incident, see Arnold Rampersad, *Jackie Robinson: A Biography* (New York: Ballantine, 1997), p. 239.

O'Malley's moment of doubt is noted in a clipping held by the O'Malley family archive. It is undated and the newspaper is not noted. It is titled "O'Malley Almost Ready to Concede."

For the ultimate account of the Thomson home-run game, see Joshua Prager, *The Echoing Green* (New York: Pantheon, 2006).

"Sink, sink, sink," from Harvey Rosenfeld, *The Great Chase*, p. 236. Estimate of O'Malley's losses from same text, and pp. 227–237 and 253. See also "Dodgers Out $25,000," *New York Times*, Oct. 6, 1951, p. 25.

CHAPTER 7

Luther A. Huston, "Frick Says Formation of Third Major League on Coast Is Up to Owners There," *New York Times*, Aug. 1, 1951, p. 27.

Luther Huston, "Baseball Before Congress," *New York Times*, Aug. 5, 1951, p. 120.

"Fathead" quote from Joe King, "Down O'Malley's Alley," *Sporting News* (St. Louis), May 7, 1952, p. 13.

"Dodger Chief Says Farms Lose Money," *New York Times*, Nov. 7, 1951, p. 42.

"Celler Releases Dodgers Figures," *New York Times*, Nov. 8, 1951, p. 39.

"Findings of Subcommitee Show Salary Increases Paid in Baseball," *New York Times*, May 21, 1952, p. 32.

The Palica story is told in Harvey Rosenfeld, *The Great Chase* (Jefferson, N.C.: McFarland, 1992), pp. 28–31.

Bavasi's criticism of Palica is from Carl E. Prince, *Brooklyn's Dodgers* (New York: Oxford University Press, 1996), pp. 70–71.

O'Malley's meetings with the Palicas from his datebooks.

The details of the relationships between O'Malley and the Robinsons are drawn from interviews with Rachel Robinson and Jackie's autobiography, *I Never Had It Made* (New York: Ecco Press, 1995), pp. 92–105.

For Robinson's improved relationship with O'Malley, see Arnold Rampersad, *Jackie Robinson* (New York: Ballantine, 1997), pp. 264–6.

For a capsule review of the season, see John Rossi, *A Whole New Ballgame* (Jefferson, N.C.: McFarland, 1999), especially pp. 94–104.

Brian Goff et al., "Racial Integration as an Innovation: Empirical Evidence from Sports Leagues," *American Economic Review* 92 (March 2002), pp. 16–26.

For picking contest, see Clarence Hersey, "Fond Memories of Millionaires," TCPalm.com.

O'Malley notes the publicity value of a fishing hole in an Oct. 16, 1952, letter to L. M. Merriman.

Roscoe McGowan, "O'Malley Not Izaak Walton, but Compleat Mangler as an Angler," *Sporting News* (St. Louis), March 18, 1953, p. 17.

Bill Roeder, "Bums on the Prowl for Screwballs," *New York World Telegram*, Feb. 23, 1953.

Profit-and-loss data from Jim Thorn, ed., *The Glory Days: New York Baseball 1947–1957* (New York: HarperCollins, 2007), pp. 127–30.

O'Malley reports lobbying Spargo in a Dec. 2, 1952, letter to Emil Praeger held by the O'Malley family archive.

Spargo's status in New York is described in Robert Caro, *The Power Broker*, pp. 719, 747, and 766.

Planks are discussed in an April 29, 1952, O'Malley letter to Holman held by the O'Malley family archive.

O'Malley answers critics in an April 24, 1952, letter to Merrill P. Barber, president of the Indian River Citrus Bank.

For Holman Stadium and Perini, see www.WalterOmalley.com/Vero Beach.

"Milwaukee Plans 7-Day Celebration; Week of Welcome for Braves Starting April 8 Includes Rally and Parade," *New York Times*, March 20, 1953, p. 30.

"Lou Perini, Owner Who Took Braves to Milwaukee, Is Dead," *New York Times*, April 17, 1972, p. 36.

Gilbert Mill Stein, "More Brooklyn Than Brooklyn," *New York Times Sunday Magazine*, July 5, 1953, p. 10.

For Robinson's accusations and retraction on salary issues, see Arnold Rampersad, *Jackie Robinson*, pp. 264–6.

John Drebinger, "Robinson Accepts Dodger Pact; Yanks Sign Three Rookies and Giants Four," *New York Times*, Jan. 29, 1954, p. 25.

O'Malley letter to Moses dated June 18, 1953, held by the O'Malley family archive.

O'Malley letter to George McLaughlin dated June 18, 1953, held by the O'Malley family archive.

Moses letter to O'Malley dated June 22, 1953, held by the O'Malley family archive.

O'Malley's meeting with Moses at the Coal Hole and subsequent turmoil over a stadium site are described in Michael Shapiro, *The Last Good Season* (New York: Broadway Books, 2004), pp. 36–43.

Moses letter to Walter O'Malley dated Oct. 20, 1953, held by the O'Malley family archive.

For the full story of Moses and urban redevelopment, see Joel Schwartz, *The New York Approach: Robert Moses, Urban Liberals and the Redevelopment of the Inner City* (Columbus: Ohio State University Press, 1993).

Alexander Von Hoffman, "A Study in Contradictions: The Origins and Legacy of the Housing Act of 1949," *Housing Policy Debate* 11, no. 2, Fannie Mae Foundation, Washington (2000), pp. 299–326.

For Murchison, see "Biography Research Center" at galegroup.com and *Time* magazine cover story on Murchison, May 24, 1954.

For the Flaherty brothers, see Bill Hickman biography of Pat Flaherty in "The Baseball Biography Project" at sabr.org.

Handwritten note from Flaherty to O'Malley on stationery of St. John's Hospital, Santa Monica, dated Aug. 27, 1953.

Veeck described the negotiations in detail in Bill Veeck, *Veeck as in Wreck* (Chicago: University of Chicago Press, 2001), pp. 299–307.

"Cubs Obtain Veeck as Coast Advisor," *New York Times*, Oct. 18, 1953, p. 37.

"Cash Bid Decisive Factor in Authorization of Athletics' Shift to Kansas City; Los Angeles Move Barred by League; Johnson's Kansas City Offer Approved Despite Sentiment for Jump to West Coast," *New York Times*, Oct. 14, 1954, p. 39.

CHAPTER 8

Bernard Kalb, "Lunch in Central Park—Not June 15, but Feb. 15, and 68," *New York Times*, Feb. 16, 1954, p. 1.

The letter to Cashmore from the meat council is noted in Michael Shapiro, *The Last Good Season* (New York: Broadway Books, 2004), p. 42.

"Held in Torso Murder; Housepainter Accused in Death of Woman in Brooklyn," *New York Times*, Jan. 10, 1951, p. 22.

O'Malley describes his tour in a Feb. 17, 1954, letter to Frank Schroth of the *Brooklyn Daily Eagle*.

"Vast Housing Plan Set for Brooklyn; Slums Will Be Cleared Near Manhattan Bridge—Two Projects to Be Erected," *New York Times*, Dec. 11, 1952, p. 39.

"Group Backs Plan to Rebuild Slums," *New York Times*, Feb. 6, 1954.

Moses letter to O'Malley dated Oct. 20, 1953, held by the O'Malley family archive.

Moses letter to O'Malley dated Nov. 2, 1953, held by the O'Malley family archive.

Spargo's brush-off letter dated April 7, 1954, held by the O'Malley family archive.

For a sense of Spargo's role, see Robert Caro, *The Power Broker* (New York: Vintage Books, 1975), pp. 719, 747, and 766.

Moses "spasm" letter is addressed to Frank Schroth and dated June 24, 1954.

O'Malley letter to Moses dated Aug. 17, 1954, held by the O'Malley family archive.

"Skiatron Opens Offices," *New York Times*, Sept. 28, 1949, p. 48.

Alston's relationship with Robinson is revealed in Arnold Rampersad, *Jackie Robinson* (New York: Ballantine, 1997), pp. 264–9, and in author interview with Duke Snider. Alston's challenge to Robinson is recalled in Jack Mann, "The Name of the Man Is Alston," *Sports Illustrated*, Oct. 10, 1966.

"Study on to Find New Dodger Park; Cashmore Starts $100,000 Survey on Rehabilitation of 500-Acre Brooklyn Area Report, to Be Ready in Six Months, Also Will Cover New L.I.R.R. Station," *New York Times*, Nov. 2, 1955, p. 37.

Roscoe McGowan, "Robinson Singing Set-to-Quit Blues; Has Only a Year of Baseball Left, Dodger Says—Would Settle Now for TV Pact," *New York Times*, March 5, 1954, p. 23.

Roscoe McGowan, "Alston Retained as Dodger Manager Next Season Under One-Year Contract," *New York Times*, Nov. 24, 1954, p. 27.

Milwaukee story is *Sports Illustrated* cover story on Aug. 19, 1954.

O'Malley's view of a future with franchises all over is spelled out in a July 9, 1954, letter he wrote to Charles E. Nash, president of the Fort Worth Chamber of Commerce, held by the O'Malley family archive.

"Planning a Sound Foundation for Major League Baseball in Los Angeles, Dec. 1, 1953," held by the O'Malley family archive.

"Facts on the Coming Expansion of Major League Baseball to the Pacific Coast, Nov. 19, 1954," held by the O'Malley family archive.

For the Nixon-Douglas campaign see Greg Mitchell, *Tricky Dick and the Pink Lady: Richard Nixon vs. Helen Gahagan Douglas—Sexual Politics and the Red Scare, 1950* (New York: Random House, 1998).

Anne Norman, "Roz Wyman Has Simple Method to Win Votes: She Rings District Doorbells and Gets to People," *Los Angeles Times*, April 7, 1957.

O'Malley lays out his standing in a letter to Flaherty dated Aug. 17, 1954, held by the O'Malley family archive.

Schroth reiterates his support in a Dec. 28, 1954, letter to O'Malley, held by the O'Malley family archive.

For a brief history of *Brooklyn Daily Eagle*, see http://onepeople.org/archives/000211.html.

Remarks of Robert Moses at commencement of Pratt Institute, June 3, 1955.

For a consideration of ethnic/racial issues in 1950s Brooklyn, see Carl E. Prince, *Brooklyn's Dodgers* (New York: Oxford University Press, 1996), pp. 102–18.

George Trow, "This Man Doesn't Miss a Thing," *New York Post*, Sept. 4, 1955, p. 2M.

Wagner's meeting with O'Malley recorded in Telenews newsreel held by UCLA Film and Television Archive, Aug. 19, 1955: "New York City—Mayor to Aid in Keeping Dodgers in Brooklyn."

Documents noting O'Malley's efforts in Brooklyn and Queens include, among others, a memorandum he wrote dated August 14, 1955, and a June 1, 1954, report by Emil Praeger. Both are in the O'Malley family archive.

Anecdote about Podres at the elevator told in Jimmy Burns, "Spotlighting Sports," *Miami Herald*, Feb. 29, 1956, p. C1.

CHAPTER 9

Rosalind Wyman letter to O'Malley dated Sept. 1, 1955, held by the O'Malley family archive.

O'Malley letter to Rosalind Wyman dated Sept. 7, 1955, held by the O'Malley family archive.

Flaherty letter to O'Malley dated Sept. 18, 1955, held by the O'Malley family archive.

J. P. Shanley, "Autumn Madness," *New York Times*, Sept. 1, 1955, p. 13.

"Baseball Attendance Increases Because of Transfer of Athletics," *New York Times*, Sept. 26, 1955, p. 27.

Letter from Norman Bel Geddes to O'Malley dated Sept. 30, 1955, held by the O'Malley family archive.

For a fine profile of Buckminster Fuller, see Elizabeth Kolbert, "Dymaxion Man," *New Yorker*, June 9, 2008, p. 64.

O'Malley's report on Moses's attitude is from a memorandum he wrote April 15, 1956.

Moses letter to city editor, *New York Herald Tribune*, dated Jan. 13, 1956.

Moses's early comments on the outcome of the stadium battle reported in DailyKos.com, Jan. 25, 2007.

Moses derides the dome in a memorandum on the Sports Center Authority dated July 25, 1956.

Moses's comments on O'Malley's investment noted in *Official Verbatim Transcript of Hearings Before Special Subcommitteee of the House of Representatives in Connection with Its Study of the Anti-trust Laws, June 26, 1957*, Bureau of National Affairs, Washington, D.C.

O'Malley notes his "last ditch stand" in a letter to Tracy Voorhees, Feb. 10, 1956.

Moses memorandum on Sports Center Authority dated July 25, 1956, held by the O'Malley family archive.

O'Malley letter to Mylod dated July 31, 1956.

Roscoe McGowan, "Robinson Accepts Dodgers' Terms; Yankees Sign Mantle; Brooks Star's Pay Is Cut to $33,000; Robinson Agrees to Drop of $4,500—Mantle Gets Rise to $30,000," *New York Times*, Jan. 25, 1956, p. 37.

"Campanella Signs for $42,000, Top Player Pay in Dodger Annals," *New York Times*, Jan. 26, 1956, p. 36.

For Maglie's style and attitude toward the Dodgers, see Sal Maglie and Robert H. Boyle, "The Great Giant-Dodger Days," *Sports Illustrated*, April 22, 1968.

For Dodger windfall, see Irving Ruud, "Brooklyn Dodger Heyday in Jersey Field Recalled," *New York Times*, Feb. 20, 1972, p. 102.

"Snider and Fan Clash," *New York Times*, July 18, 1956, p. 30.

"Maglie Scoffs at Redlegs, Claims Dodger Broke Scoreboard Clock," *New York Times*, July 20, 1956, p. 11.

Letter to O'Malley from Ann Dinistari dated June 4, 1956, held by the O'Malley family archive.

Letter to O'Malley from attorney Robert Feckles dated June 7, 1956, held by the O'Malley family archive.

Reese "older" comment noted in Michael Shapiro, *The Last Good Season* (New York: Broadway Books, 2004), p. 293.

Flaherty notes his meeting with O'Malley at the series in Vincent X. Flaherty, "Pitch-by-Pitch Tale of the Battle for a Major League Franchise," *Sporting News* (St. Louis), Oct. 30, 1957, p. 14.

O'Malley's note turning down Poulson is held by the O'Malley family archive.

"Fan Is Reported Hit by Newcombe," *New York Times*, Oct. 6, 1956, p. 25.

For Judge Fagan and his ruling, see "Matthew Fagan Judge Dies at 66," *New York Times*, July 3, 1966, p. 35.

For criticism of Newcombe and its overtones, see Carl E. Prince, *Brooklyn's Dodgers* (New York: Oxford University Press, 1996), pp. 68–74.

Newcombe's conflict with fans reported in July 27, 1956, letter from John McFeeley to Walter O'Malley, held by the O'Malley family archive.

A fine account of the game and the entire series appears in Michael Shapiro, *The Last Good Season*, pp. 293–307.

Eisenhower letter to Newcombe dated Oct. 12, 1956. Copy supplied to author by Newcombe.

Dick Walsh's recollections from interview with the author.

CHAPTER 10

O'Malley described his retreat strategy in a letter to John W. Hooper, president, Lincoln Savings Bank, dated Feb. 20, 1956, held by the O'Malley family archive.

O'Malley letter to Peter Campbell Brown dated Dec. 6, 1956, held by the O'Malley family archive.

Moses laid out his ideas for stripping the Sports Center Authority of many of its responsibilities and limiting its funding in a Dec. 7, 1956, letter to Mayor Robert Wagner.

In a letter to Frank Schroth dated Dec. 27, 1956, O'Malley says that the Sports Center Authority might be a matter to discuss "in the past tense."

Joseph M. Sheehan, "Giants Get Robinson for Pitcher and Cash; Dodgers Trade Robinson," *New York Times*, Dec. 14, 1956, p. 1.

The cash paid to the Dodgers was, according to Bavasi, $50,000. However, news accounts and various other sources report figures as low as $30,000.

Arnold Rampersad, *Jackie Robinson* (New York: Ballantine, 1997), pp. 303–5.

Jackie Robinson, *I Never Had It Made* (New York: Putnam, 1972), pp. 131–4.

James F. Lynch, "Jackie Robinson Quits Baseball," *New York Times*, Jan. 6, 1957, p. S1.

O'Malley note sent to Robinson dated December 14, 1956. Robinson reported on his conversation with O'Malley in Jackie Robinson, "A Kentucky Colonel Kept Me in Baseball," *Look*, Feb. 8, 1955, p. 82.

Arrangements for the franchise trade and recollections of the January trip from an interview with Terry Seidler and from Vincent X. Flaherty, "Pitch-by-Pitch Tale of the Battle for a Major League Franchise," *Sporting News* (St. Louis), Oct. 30, 1957, p. 14. See also Norris Poulson's unpublished memoir, *Genealogy and Life Story of Erna and Norris Poulson*, held by the library of the University of California–Los Angeles.

O'Malley letter to Sharkey dated Jan. 17, 1957, held by the O'Malley family archive.

Meetings with Madigan, Wagner's neglect, and "kiss of death" evaluation are contained in internal Dodger memoranda written by O'Malley on Jan. 29 and Feb. 6, 1957.

Dick Young, "To Hell with the Los Angeles Dodgers," *Sport*, Aug. 1957, p. 14.

The details of Norris Poulson's career and politics are contained in his unpublished memoir, *Genealogy and Life Story of Erna and Norris Poulson*, held by the library of the University of California–Los Angeles.

"LA Mayor, O'Malley to Meet Today," *Los Angeles Times*, March 6, 1957, p. 1.

The Los Angeles–San Francisco agreement noted by Rosalind Wyman in "Baseball Comes West," *Western Family Magazine*, April 1958, p. 20.

Christopher's telegram to Poulson held by the O'Malley family archive. See also Jim Murray, "Norrie's Nest?" in *Los Angeles Times*, April 9, 1962, "Sports," p. 1.

O'Malley letter to Frank Schroth dated March 11, 1957.

Flaherty information taken from a series of letters from Vincent X. Flaherty to Walter O'Malley written in March, April, and May of 1957, held by the O'Malley family archive.

News of the city/county committee and Christopher's plotting with Poulson from Gladwyn Hill,

"How to Finance Dodger Project Preoccupies Los Angeles Group," *New York Times*, March 22, 1957, p. 20, held by the O'Malley family archive.

"Mayor Confident Dodgers Won't Go; Predicts City Action to Keep Team in Brooklyn Despite Threats to Move West," *New York Times*, March 27, 1957, p. 33.

For a sense of how Moses controlled mayors, including Wagner, see Robert Caro, *The Power Broker* (New York: Vintage Books, 1975), pp. 799–806.

O'Malley wrote about Brooklyn's troubles in a March 13, 1957, letter to C. V. Ednies of Brookhaven, Pennsylvania.

Walter O'Malley letters to Frank Schroth dated March 26 and 31, 1957, held by the O'Malley family archive.

O'Malley described the 1954 meeting, in which Stoneham complained about the Polo Grounds, in a letter to Horace Stoneham dated Jan. 27, 1971. The date of this meeting is confirmed in "Tax Relief Hinted Over Ticket Issue," *New York Times*, June 30, 1954, p. 29.

The 1957 encounter, when Stoneham revealed his decision to go to Minneapolis, is in an O'Malley file memorandum dated March 23, 1957.

O'Malley's meeting with Moses in Babylon is recorded in his memo dated April 11, 1957.

For Moses's plans for Flushing Meadows, see Robert Caro, *The Power Broker*, pp. 182–7.

The Flushing field trip is detailed in an O'Malley memorandum dated April 15, 1958. This memo is supported by an undated fact sheet titled Municipal Stadium Flushing Meadows Park. The $1 million rent-maintenance estimate depends, in part, on an April 22, 1957, letter from Moses to New York deputy mayor John J. Theobald. This letter explains how a $10 million stadium at another locale would be amortized and maintained.

The 1958 adventure in California is well described at walteromalley.com

The meeting with Mayor Christopher and Poulson is in Poulson's unpublished memoir, *Genealogy and Life Story of Erna and Norris Poulson*, held by the library of the University of California Los Angeles, pp. 202–3.

For a sense of Los Angeles in the period, including "up and out" construction patterns, see Christopher Rand, *Los Angeles: The Ultimate City* (New York: Oxford University Press, 1967), pp. 8–12.

Praeger's early work on the Coliseum layout is noted in a letter sent to him by O'Malley dated May 17, 1957.

O'Malley's comment about "Los Angeles or someplace like that" is from www.walteromalley.com.

Flaherty explained O'Malley's reticence to supervisor Dorn in a letter dated May 2, 1957.

Christopher noted that he would send "letter of intent" in a May 15, 1957, letter sent to Walter O'Malley.

O'Malley's no and Poulson's visit noted in the statement made by Representative John J. Rooney of Brooklyn in the *Congressional Record* of June 3, 1956.

O'Malley responded to Rooney in a letter dated June 4, 1957.

Poulson's meeting with O'Malley and its contents are described in a contemporary timeline held by the O'Malley family archive. The Chavez–Wrigley Field exchange was first noted in a memo written by city attorney Roger Arnebergh dated May 3, 1957.

Official Verbatim Transcript of Hearings Before Special Subcommittee of the House of Representatives in Connection with Its Study of the Anti-trust Laws, Wed., June 26, 1957, Bureau of National Affairs, Washington, D.C.

For an analysis of Moses and his attitude toward O'Malley, see Peter Ellsworth, "The Brooklyn Dodgers Move to Los Angeles," *Nine* 14, no. 1, pp. 19–40.

Stoneham's forthrightness and profits are noted in "New York and the Giants," *New York Herald Tribune*, July 19, 1957, p. 10.

Interclub memo from Dick Walsh to Walter O'Malley dated Aug. 12, 1957.

Moses's "jitterbug jive" letter dated Sept. 20, 1957.

"Stoneham Booed, Mrs. Mac Cries as Jints Shutter PG," *Daily News*, Sept. 30, 1957, p. 54.

Howard M. Tuckner, "Two Trumpets and a Trombone Sound Dirge in Empty Ballpark," *New York Times*, Sept. 30, 1957, p. 48.

Roscoe McGowan, "Dodgers Defeat Pirates in Ebbets Field Finale," *New York Times*, Sept. 25, 1957, p. 33.

Chris Kieran, "Take Them Away, LA! Flock Cops Finale, 2–0," *Daily News*, Sept. 25, 1957, p. 50.

Anne Norman, "Roz Wyman Has Simple Method to Win Votes: She Rings District Doorbells and Gets to People," *Los Angeles Times*, April 7, 1957.

"Opposition Arises to Chavez Ravine," *Los Angeles Times*, June 13, 1957, p. C2.

Wyman's recollections from interview with the author.

O'Malley's complaint about being "burned" is recalled in a memo by Harold "Chad" McClellan titled "The Truth About the Dodgers," dated Aug. 9, 1963.

Brian Mylod's experience from interview with the author.

Rickey's position on the move is from Lee Lowenfish, *Branch Rickey* (Lincoln, Nebraska: University of Nebraska Press, 2008), p. 540.

Dick Young, "Young Ideas," *Daily News*, Sept. 25, 1957, p. 69.

Dick Young, "It's All Over Fellows, The Dodgers Move West," *Daily News*, Oct. 9, 1957, p. 3.

Glen Gendzel, "Competitive Boosterism: How Milwaukee Lost the Braves," *Business History Review* 69, no. 4 (Winter 1995) pp. 530–66.

CHAPTER 11

O'Malley's regrets were voiced in Michael Gavan, "Never Relished Idea of Moving, O'Malley Says," *New York Journal American*, Oct. 7, 1957.

Skiatron and other elements in the Dodger move are discussed in Robert Shaplen, "O'Malley and the Angels," *Sports Illustrated*, March 24, 1959, p. 62.

O'Malley's investment is noted in an August 18, 1960, letter written to him by the law firm of Olvaney, Eisner and Donnelly.

McClellan noted the great financial risk in O'Malley's move in his document "The Truth About the Dodgers," dated Aug. 9, 1963.

Author interviews with Bud Holman and Roz Wyman. See also Rube Samuelson, "LA Flips Lid in Greeting to Its Dodgers," *Sporting News*, Oct. 30, 1957, p. 16.

O'Malley's arrival was filmed by Telenews and the footage is available at the University of California–Los Angeles film archive.

Don Normark, *Chavez Ravine, 1949: A Los Angeles Story* (San Francisco: Chronicle, 1999).

For the number of families in the ravine, see Thomas S. Hines, "Housing, Baseball and Creeping Socialism: The Battle of Chavez Ravine, Los Angeles," *Journal of Urban History* 8, no. 2 (Feb. 1982), pp. 123–43.

For a review of the referendum process, see the website of the initiative and referendum, Institute of the University of Southern California, http://www.iandrinstitute.org/California.htm.

O'Malley's exclamation about "no boss" is from Neil J. Sullivan, *The Dodgers Move West* (New York: Oxford University Press, 1987), p. 138.

"Dodgers May Return Here, Says O'Malley," *New York Journal American*, Dec. 6, 1957; "Dodgers' Future Is Not All Roses; Taxpayers Group Moves to Block Use of Pasadena Bowl by Ball Club," *New York Times*, Jan. 8, 1958, p. 93.

Owners' doubts from Arthur Daley, "In Little Old New York," *New York Times*, Jan. 31, 1957, p. 17. See also Neil J. Sullivan, *The Dodgers Move West*, pp. 140–1.

Flaherty letters to O'Malley dated Nov. 11, 1957, Oct. 17, 1957, and Sept. 24, 1957. Also undated letters from later in the same year, held in the O'Malley family archive.

O'Malley's schedule, including meeting with Rickey and bankers, from his date books.

DeLury's experience from interview with the author.

Roy R. Silver, "Campanella Paralyzed in Crash; Broken Neck Is Expected to Heal; Dodger Catcher Pinned Half Hour in Overturned Car—In Surgery 4 Hours," *New York Times*, Jan. 29, 1958, p. 1.

Spring training jaunt to Havana from Don Drysdale with Bob Verdi, *Once a Bum, Always a Dodger* (New York: St. Martin's, 1990), pp. 177–8.

Player sentiment from author's interviews with Johnny Podres, Don Newcombe, and Duke Snider. O'Malley's fondness for Dressen is noted in a May 12, 1966, letter he wrote to Johnny Podres.

"Cimoli Out; He Acted Instead of Reflecting," *New York Times*, April 13, 1958, p. S2.

Erskine recalled his frustration in Steve Springer, "Former Dodgers Reflect on Coliseum," *Los Angeles Times* online edition, March 25, 2007.

For missing Brooklyn, see Don Drysdale with Bob Verdi, *Once a Bum, Always a Dodger*, pp. 69–70.

Gay Talese, "Brooklyn Is Trying Hard to Forget Dodgers and Baseball; Bitterness Yields to Apathy but Cure Will Take Time," *New York Times*, May 18, 1958, p. S3.

"Robby Blasts O'Malley for L.A. Deterioration," *New York Daily News*, May 9, 1958, from the O'Malley family archive (no page number listed).

J. A. Smith summed up his position in an article by Phil Collier, "Smith Sees 'No' on Chavez Issue," *San Diego Union*, June 1, 1958, first sports page.

Flyer signed by Robert Angier, chairman, Committee for Public Morality.

William Bonelli, *Billion Dollar Blackjack* (Beverly Hills, California: Civic Research Press, 1954).

Eric Avila, *Popular Culture in the Age of White Flight* (Berkeley, California: University of California, 2004), pp. 145–86.

Accounts of the council proceedings from a collection of clippings from the *Los Angeles Times* and *Examiner* newspapers held by the O'Malley family archive. Headlines include "Harsh Words Erupt in Council's Debate Over Dodgers Chavez Deal," "Battle Rages in Council," "Row Halts Chavez Discussion," and "Councilmen Walk Out on Holland's Latest Blast," *Los Angeles Examiner*, May 28, 1958, p. 6.

For Dodgers-Disneyland connection, see Eric Avila, *Popular Culture in the Age of White Flight*, pp. 145–86.

Dodgerthon from walteromalley.com. See also "Dodger Vote Supporters on TV Four Houses," *New York Journal American*, June 2, 1958, no page noted. Clipping from Center for American History, University of Texas at Austin.

For a review of the election, see Tom Cohan, "The West Produces Baseball's Strangest Story," *Look*, August 1958, p. 50.

Vin Scully's experiences are recounted in an interview with the author.

Snider's injury and later success in throwing a ball out of the stadium from Steve Springer, "Former Dodgers Reflect on Coliseum," *Los Angeles Times* online edition, March 25, 2007.

Press box scene described in Hank Hollingsworth, "Sports Merry-Go-Round," *Long Beach Press Telegram*, June 4, 1958, p. C1.

Analysis of results from *Los Angeles Newsletter*, July 5, 1958.

"Judge Outlaws Dodgers' Pact," *Los Angeles Mirror News*, July 15, 1958, p. 1.

"Dodgers' Chavez Ravine Contract Held Invalid," *Washington Post*, July 15, 1958, p. A15.

"Court Dismisses Ravine Appeals; High Tribunal Rejects Bids to Prevent Dodgers from Acquiring Land for Park," *New York Times*, Oct. 20, 1959, p. 51.

"Alston Reported Out in 10 Days Unless the Dodgers Start to Win," *New York Times*, July 29, 1958, p. 26.

Campanella night recalled by James Hahn and his relationship with O'Malley from the author's interview with Joni Campanella Roan.

Pamphlet, *Chavez Ravine: A Day That Will Live in Infamy*, held by the O'Malley family archive.

"Protesters Camp at Chavez Ravine," *New York Times*, May 10, 1959, p. 86.

"Evictions Revive Dodgers Dispute," *New York Times*, May 17, 1959, p. 64.

Supreme Court decision issued October term 1959, *Louis Kirshbaum v. The City of Los Angeles, Los Angeles Dodgers Inc., and The Housing Authority of the City of Los Angeles.*

Arthur Daley, "Sports of The Times: Sounding a Lupine Alarm," *New York Times*, Nov. 11, 1959, p. 47.

O'Malley commented on western politics in Bob Oates, "It's Goat Hill, Not Chavez Ravine— O'Malley," *Los Angeles Times*, Feb. 18, 1969, first sports page.

"Council Airs O'Malley Yule Gifts," *Los Angeles Examiner*, Dec. 31, 1959.

CHAPTER 12

Gay Talese, "Ebbets Field Goes on the Scrap Pile; Iron Ball Begins Demolishing Dodger Home and Raises Clouds of Nostalgia; Watchers Recall Daffy Days," *New York Times*, Feb. 24, 1960, p. 39.

Arthur Daley, "Warmed-Over Memories," *New York Times*, Jan. 6, 1960, p. 40.

Kahn's report on the borough's reaction to the Dodgers' departure is made in Roger Kahn, "Something's Changing About Baseball," *New York Times Magazine*, April 5, 1959, p. SM49.

Gay Talese, "Brooklyn Displays Little Enthusiasm After Dodgers Win," *New York Times*, Oct. 9, 1959, p. 34.

The San Francisco stadium story is told throughout George Dorsey, *Christopher of San Francisco* (New York: Macmillan, 1962).

The financial standing of the Dodgers is outlined in James Murray, "The $3,300,000 Smile," *Sports Illustrated*, Feb. 29, 1960, p. 54.

"Dream come true" from Sept. 21, 1960, letter from Walter O'Malley to Frank Schroth.

Team payments to the minor leagues noted in Dick Walsh memo to Walter O'Malley dated Dec. 19, 1960.

Details of construction from interviews with Richard Walsh, two-hour recorded interview of construction supervisor Jack Yount (held by the O'Malley family archive), and resources at walteromalley.com.

Stadium seating information in Walter O'Malley letter to Emil Praeger dated June 29, 1960.

O'Malley spelled out his financial concerns in a letter to his wife, Kay, and son Peter dated June 15, 1960.

Robert Moses, *Remarks at the Groundbreaking of the Flushing Meadow Park Municipal Stadium*, published by New York World's Fair 1964–1965 Corporation, 1961.

For a review of stadiums built or under construction in the 1960s, see "The New Look Stadiums," *American Engineer*, Sept. 1965, p. 33.

O'Malley runs through details of stadium operations in a memo to Richard Walsh dated April 13, 1961.

Show-business quote from Nov. 7, 1961, O'Malley letter to Emil Praeger.

Bathroom door problem noted in June 30, 1962, letter from O'Malley to James Young.

Electrical issues described in May 1, 1962, O'Malley letter to Emil Praeger.

Skiatron loss noted in August 18, 1960, letter from law firm of Ovaney, Eisner and Donnelley to Walter O'Malley. See also "Skiatron Is Said to Lack Funds for Development of Pay TV," *New York Times*, April 30, 1960, p. 32.

Partial dome discussed in O'Malley letter to Buckminster Fuller dated Dec. 12, 1963.

Airplane purchase and Dodgertown development from walteromalley.com.

For the growth of Los Angeles and the evolution of its image, see David Reid, *Sex, Death and God in L.A.* (New York: Random House, 1992), pp. xiv–xxv.

Carol Birkby, "Each Day Is Peanuts to the Hunters," is an undated clipping from an unnamed South African newspaper held by the O'Malley family archive.

Safari stories from interview with Peter O'Malley and Walter O'Malley's letters and cards sent to his wife during these expeditions. The quote from Walter O'Malley is from an unidentified clipping held by the O'Malley family archive.

Charles Mohr, "African Experts Back Curb on Animal Skin Trade," *New York Times*, Nov. 14, 1970, p. 10.

Jack Mann, "The King of the Jungle," *Sports Illustrated*, April 18, 1966, p. 115.

For Bohemian Grove, see John van der Zee, *The Greatest Men's Party on Earth: Inside Bohemian Grove* (New York: Harcourt Brace Jovanovich, 1974), and G. William Domhofer, *The Bohemian Grove and Other Retreats: A Study in Ruling-Class Cohesiveness* (New York: Harper & Row, 1974).

O'Malley's relationship at the Grove with Earl Warren noted in a letter dated April 16, 1971, which he received from Charles R. Carroll.

O'Malley's interest in the Watergate hearings is noted in a letter he sent to Mike Roy and Dennis Bracken dated July 25, 1973.

O'Malley's Japan tour and Maury Wills issue from walteromalley.com and from author interviews with Buzzie Bavasi, Peter O'Malley, and Maury Wills.

"Buzzie Bavasi Money Makes the Player Go," *Sports Illustrated*, May 22, 1967, p. 50.

The story of the Koufax-Drysdale contract issue based on author interview with Bavasi as well as Jack Man, "The $1,000,000 Holdout," *Sports Illustrated*, April 4, 1966, p. 26.

The $600,000 in revenue credited to Koufax and Drysdale is explained in Leonard Koppett, "New Math in Baseball," *New York Times*, April 6, 1966, p. 46.

Buzzie Bavasi, "The Great Hold Out," *Sports Illustrated*, May 15, 1967, p. 78.

See also Jane Leavey, *Sandy Koufax* (New York: HarperCollins, 2002), pp. 205–12.

For Koufax as a pitcher in historical context, see Bill James, *The New Bill James Historical Baseball Abstract* (New York: Free Press, 2001), pp. 852–3.

For the decline in players' salaries as a share of revenue and other issues in the business of baseball, see Michael J. Haupert, "The Economic History of Major League Baseball," at www.eh.net/encyclopedia/article/haupert.mlb.

For a review of players' salaries versus ticket prices and the value of baseball franchises, see Michael J. Haupert, "The Economic History of Baseball."

Peter Bart, "Los Angeles Whites Voice Racial Fears," *New York Times*, Aug. 17, 1965, p. 1.

George Vecsey, "O'Malley Plans to Retire in 1969," *New York Times*, Dec. 6, 1968, p. 63.

For quote about Peter O'Malley's role with the team, see Bob Oates, "It's Goat Hill, Not Chavez Ravine—O'Malley," *Los Angeles Times*, Feb. 18, 1969, first sports page.

Jackie Robinson letter to Walter O'Malley dated July 25, 1962.

Carl Rowan, *Wait Till Next Year: The Story of Jackie Robinson* (New York: Random House, 1960).

Rickey praises O'Malley in a letter he sent Sept. 25, 1963.

Newcombe recalled Jackie Robinson's attitude about visiting Dodger Stadium in an interview with the author. See also "Jackie Robinson Seeks and Finds Sensitivity," *Los Angeles Times*, June 5, 1972, p. 1.

Young described O'Malley as kingly, greedy, and grasping in many columns, including those published in the *Daily News* on March 11, 1958, May 17, 1958, June 3, 1958, May 13, 1960, and Sept. 14, 1960. The O'Malley-Seaver column appeared on June 15, 1977.

For Daley's treatment of O'Malley, see his "Sports of The Times" columns published Jan. 31, 1959, Nov. 11, 1959, Dec. 9, 1960, and Jan. 11, 1961.

For "devious," see Red Barber and Robert Creamer, *Rhubarb in the Catbird Seat* (Lincoln, Nebraska: Bison Books, 1997), p. 279.

O'Malley showed his sensitivity in Gerald Holland, "A Visit with the Artful Dodgers," *Saturday Evening Post*, July 1968, p. 24.

The *New York Times* declared "The Wounds Are Healed" in an editorial titled "Joy in Flatbush" published Oct. 4, 1963, p. 32. See also David Boroff, "Beach, Bohemia, Barracks—Brooklyn," *New York Times Magazine*, Sept. 29, 1963, p. 233.

Kahn's comments on his book are from an interview with the author.

Roger Kahn, *The Boys of Summer* (New York: Harper & Row, 1972).

The nostalgia trends, including *The Boys of Summer*, were noted in "True Grease," *Time*, May 29, 1972.

Fred Davis, *Yearning for Yesterday: A Sociology of Nostalgia* (New York: Free Press, 1979).

For O'Malley and the players' union, see Marvin Miller, *A Whole Different Ballgame* (New York: Birch Lane, 1991), pp. 219–22 and 264–8.

O'Malley assessed Moses in an Oct. 18, 1975, letter to Tom Downs of Lansing, Michigan.

O'Malley letter to Horace Stoneham dated Jan. 27, 1971.

George Steinbrenner letter to O'Malley dated Oct. 27, 1977.

Flaherty's various letters held by the O'Malley family archive.

John Helyar, *Lords of the Realm* (New York: Villard, 1994), pp. 178–83. For Grebey and O'Malley, see pp. 218–19.

Kay and Walter O'Malley's deaths recalled by Peter O'Malley, Terry O'Malley Seidler, Marvin Miller, and Mel Durslag.

Austin Scott, "Kay O'Malley, 72, Wife of Dodgers Owner, Dies," *Los Angeles Times*, July 14, 1979, p. 1.

Penelope McMillan, "L.A. Ravine Fertile Soil for O'Malley," *Los Angeles Times*, June 4, 1978, p. 1.

POSTSCRIPT

Red Smith, "The O'Malley Pro and Con," *New York Times*, Aug. 13, 1979.

Dick Young, "The Truth about the Late Walter O'Malley," *New York Daily News*, Aug. 13, 1979.

Jim Murray, "Which Way to Chavez Ravine?" in *Los Angeles Times Sunday Magazine*, June 27, 1993, p. 16.

Alex Storozynski, "Robert Moses Still Felt in Brooklyn," *New York Sun*, Jan. 20, 2006, available at 2nysun.com.

The net economic losses suffered by cities that subsidize teams with government-built stadiums are documented in Frank Jozsa and John J. Guthrie, *Relocating Teams and Expanding Leagues in Professional Sports* (Westport, Connecticut: Greenwood, 1999), pp. 20–24, 67–71, and 136–9.

Ira Henry Freeman, "Brooklyn Slums Shock Officials," *New York Times*, Nov. 19, 1958, p. 31.

Peter O'Malley's success is noted in John Merwin, "The Most Valuable Executive in Either League," *Forbes*, April 12, 1982, pp. 129–38.

Charles V. Bagli and Richard Sondomir, "Yo, Dodgers? No Way! Brooklyn Is Betting on the Nets for Revival," *New York Times*, June 16, 2004, p. A1.

Murray Chass, "O'Malley Says He Will Sell Dodgers," *New York Times*, Jan. 7, 1997, p. B9.

Richard Sandomir, "Fox Group Reaches Deal to Buy Dodgers; Fox Reaches Agreement with O'Malley for Dodgers," *New York Times*, Sept. 5, 1997, p. B7.

"Baseball Owners Approve Dodgers Sale," *New York Times*, Jan. 30, 2004, p. D2.

Index

About the Author

Michael D'Antonio is the author of many acclaimed books, including *Atomic Harvest, Tin Cup Dreams, Mosquito, The State Boys Rebellion,* and *Hershey.* His work has appeared in *Esquire,* the *New York Times Magazine,* the *Los Angeles Times Magazine, Discover,* and other publications. Among his awards is the Pulitzer prize, which he shared with a team of reporters for *Newsday.*